H.E. Chehabi is a professor of International Relations and History at the Frederick S. Pardee School of Global Studies, Boston University. He has also taught at Harvard University, UCLA, and the University of St. Andrews. He has authored, edited, or co-edited over ten books, most recently (with Grace Neville) *Erin and Iran: Cultural Encounters Between the Irish and the Iranians* (2015), and (with Farhad Khosrokhavar and Clément Therme) *Iran and the Challenges of the Twenty-First Century*.

Peyman Jafari is a lecturer at the History Department of the University of Amsterdam, and Fellow at the International Institute of Social History.

Maral Jefroudi is a historian working on modern Iran and Turkey. She is co-director of the International Institute of Research and Education in Amsterdam.

'This is a magnificent collection of articles on modern Iranian social and political history. Original and timely, it will be of great value to both the expert and the more general reader.'
—Stephanie Cronin, University of Oxford

IRAN IN THE MIDDLE EAST
Transnational Encounters and Social History

Edited by H.E. CHEHABI, PEYMAN JAFARI
AND MARAL JEFROUDI

New paperback edition published in 2018 by
I.B.Tauris & Co. Ltd
London • New York
www.ibtauris.com

First published in hardback in 2015 by I.B.Tauris & Co. Ltd

Copyright Editorial Selection © 2015 Houchang Chehabi, Peyman Jafari and Maral Jefroudi

Copyright Individual Chapters © 2015 Ali M. Ansari, Manoutchehr Eskandari-Qajar, Janet Afary, Mansour Bonakdarian, Serhan Afacan, Valentine M. Moghadam, Peyman Vahabzadeh, M.R. Ghanoonparvar, Kaveh Ehsani, Erik-Jan Zürcher

The right Houchang Chehabi, Peyman Jafari and Maral Jefroudi to be identified as the editors of this work has been asserted by the author in accordance with the Copyright, Designs and Patents Act 1988.

All rights reserved. Except for brief quotations in a review, this book, or any part thereof, may not be reproduced, stored in or introduced into a retrieval system, or transmitted, in any form or by any means, electronic, mechanical, photocopying, recording or otherwise, without the prior written permission of the publisher.

Every attempt has been made to gain permission for the use of the images in this book. Any omissions will be rectified in future editions.

References to websites were correct at the time of writing.

ISBN: 978 1 78831 094 9
eISBN: 978 0 85773 765 6
ePDF: 978 1 78673 980 3

A full CIP record for this book is available from the British Library
A full CIP record is available from the Library of Congress

Library of Congress Catalog Card Number: available

Typeset in Garamond Three by OKS Prepress Services, Chennai, India

For Touraj Atabaki
*In honour of his contributions to the study
of the history of Iran, Turkey and Central Asia*

CONTENTS

List of Illustrations ix
Acknowledgements xi

Introduction 1
Peyman Jafari

Part I: The Constitutional Revolution and Nationalism
1. Mohammad Ali Foroughi and the Construction of
   Civic Nationalism in early Twentieth-Century Iran 11
   Ali M. Ansari
2. Subversive Subalterns: The Bagh-e Shah Twenty-Two 27
   Manoutchehr Eskandari-Qajar
3. The Place of Shi'i Clerics in the First Iranian Constitution 49
   Janet Afary

Part II: Transnational Connections
4. Iranian Nationalism and Global Solidarity Networks
   1906–18: Internationalism, Transnationalism,
   Globalization, and Nationalist Cosmopolitanism 77
   Mansour Bonakdarian
5. 'The Paris of the Middle East': Iranians
   in Cosmopolitan Beirut 120
   H.E. Chehabi

Part III: Social History

6. Foreign Goods, Native Consumption: Popular Reactions to Foreign Economic Domination in Iran (1921–3) 137
   Serhan Afacan

7. Hidden From History? Women Workers in Modern Iran: A Theme Revisited 161
   Valentine M. Moghadam

8. A Generation's Myth: Armed Struggle and the Creation of Social Epic in 1970s Iran 183
   Peyman Vahabzadeh

9. Oil and Persian Fiction: Literary Depictions of Coping with Modernity and Change 199
   M.R. Ghanoonparvar

10. The Cultural Politics of Public Space in Tehran's Book Fair 213
    Kaveh Ehsani

Part IV: Historiographical Reflections

11. The Opening-up of the Past and the Possibilities of Global History for Iranian Historiography 235
    Maral Jefroudi

12. Village and Empire: Recent Trends in the Historiography of the Late Ottoman Empire and Modern Turkey 249
    Erik-Jan Zürcher

Contributors 262
Appendix: Life and Work of Touraj Atabaki 268
Bibliography of Touraj Atabaki 273
Index 280

LIST OF ILLUSTRATIONS

Figure 2.1. The Bagh-e Shah Twenty-Two in E.G. Browne's
The Persian Revolution. (Source: E.G. Brownes', *The Persian
Revolution 1905-1909*, pp. 210–11)   28

Figure 2.2. The Bagh-e Shah Twenty-Two, in Vahidnia's
Dar zir-e tigh. (Source: Seyfollah Vahidnia, *Dar zir-e tigh*,
Appendix, p. 6)   30

Figure 8.1. The posters of Iran's most wanted men,
members of the PFG, Spring 1971. (Source: Mahmud Naderi,
Cherikha-ye Fada'i-ye Khalq: az nakhostin konesh ta
Bahman-e 1357, jeld-e avval, vol 1).   190

Figure 10.1. Crowds at the old Book Fair in 2003.
(Credit: Kaveh Ehsani)   220

Figure 10.2. The Mosalla Complex in 2006 during the
Book Fair. (Credit: Kaveh Ehsani)   225

Figure 10.3. Prayer time at the Mosalla during the 2006
Book Fair. (Credit: Kaveh Ehsani)   227

Figure 10.4. Folk dancing at the Mosalla during the
2006 Book Fair. (Credit: Kaveh Ehsani) 227

Figure 10.5. Sacred space as shopping mall: the 2006
Book Fair at the Grand Mosalla. (Credit: Kaveh Ehsani) 228

ACKNOWLEDGEMENTS

Convincing scholars overwhelmed with teaching and writing engagements to contribute to an edited volume is always a daunting challenge. In this case, however, our invitation was met with great enthusiasm – for two reasons. The contributors, although working in different disciplines, were all convinced of the necessity to advance research on the modern history of Iran. But they were even more excited to hear that they would contribute not just to a volume, but to a *Festschrift* dedicated to Touraj Atabaki. It is not a coincidence that the contributors have been inspired by Atabaki's writings, and that they can all look back on pleasant experiences of working with him either as his PhD students or as his peers, colleagues, and collaborators in different books, research projects, conferences, and professional associations.

We are very grateful to Marcel van der Linden, who encouraged us to initiate this project. We also thank our colleagues at the International Institute of Social History and the Leiden University Institute of Area Studies, Leo Lucassen, Henk Wals and Maghiel van Crevel in particular, who supported us in any way possible. When we sought the advice of Houchang Chehabi, he kindly accepted our invitation to join us as a co-editor. Kaveh Ehsani's comments have been indispensible. Finally, the patience and advice of Azmina

Siddique, Allison Walker, and Iradj Bagherzade at I.B.Tauris made our adventure a great pleasure. We are thankful to them and others who inspired and assisted us in completing this volume.

Peyman Jafari
Maral Jefroudi

INTRODUCTION

Peyman Jafari

Modern Iranian historiography has been dominated by a number of prominent themes, most importantly nationalism, modernization, religion, autocracy, revolution and war, which have led to animated debates and controversies among historians. These debates have often been conducted within a limited theoretical framework informed by civilizational approaches (pre-Islamic versus Islamic), Orientalism and other forms of essentialism, while the expansion of the state encouraged a top-down view that privileged the role of elites and marginalized the subaltern.

In the past two decades or so, however, Iranian historiography has witnessed important changes. While the mentioned themes and approaches have not quite disappeared, a growing number of publications have drawn our attention to understudied topics and shed new light on the old ones by applying recent historiographical approaches and new archival sources. To begin with the last aspect, while access to archival material has suffered from political restrictions and lack of professional archiving in some areas since the Iranian Revolution, in others it has gradually increased due to a number of factors. One can think of the foreign sources that have become available, for instance those of the former Soviet Union and the US Central Intelligence Agency. Moreover, a number of institutions outside Iran, such as the International Institute of Social History (IISH) in Amsterdam, have acquired valuable collections. Finally, some institutions inside Iran have improved their acquisition activities and public facilities, for instance through digitalization and the use of new sources, most importantly oral history. These include the National Library and Archives Organisation of Iran, and Center of the Archives of the Iranian Parliament.

Following the historiographical developments of the past 20 years and the contributions of gender, subaltern and comparative studies to this field, historical studies of Iran are also increasingly incorporating the newly-generated perspectives. This trend, although weaker in the historiography of Iran than in that of many other countries, has created more interest for understudied subjects such as social and economic history; it has given more attention to culture and language, international connections, and regional varieties within the geographical boundaries of the nation states.

Touraj Atabaki is one of the scholars who has made a significant contribution to these historiographical advances, in terms of both archival acquisitions and research projects. As a tribute, this edited volume adds new dimensions to four areas of his historical studies: the history of the Constitutional Revolution, transnational connections in the making of Iranian history, the social history of Iran, and historiography. Atabaki's life has been shaped by the important events of the second half of the twentieth century, which have in turn made a lasting impact on his intellectual development (see Appendix). As he has in many ways influenced students and researchers of Iranian history, and indeed the empirical and theoretical orientations of this volume, it merits taking a brief look at his contributions in the areas of archival acquisition and historical study, before we discuss the structure and content of this volume.

During the past two decades, Atabaki has helped to collect a great number of valuable documents at the IISH. As the Soviet Union started to unravel in the late 1980s, he secured a number of important documents, and organized oral history projects to document everyday life experiences under Stalinism and the political upheavals in Central Asia in 1989–91. Very special was the acquisition of a microfiche collection including the archives of the State Political Directorate (GPU), the Soviet secret service on individuals in the Caucasus, Iran, and Turkey in 1999. In the same year, the IISH received the papers of the Iranian feminist Sadiqeh Dowlatabadi and the archives of the League of Iranian Writers in Exile. Other important acquisitions were made in Turkey, building on the materials collected earlier by Erik-Jan Zürcher. Most significantly, he has managed to collect a great part of the archives of Iran's Tudeh Party and a large number of journals, books, and pamphlets of other organizations of the Iranian Left. Quite characteristic of his efforts to creatively document the experiences of the subaltern is the project that he commissioned to collect pictures of Afghan migrant workers and refugees in Iran in the 1990s. He also initiated the collection of documents, photos, and films about the Green Movement that erupted in the aftermath of the June 2009 presidential election in Iran.

In 2005, the archives of the Centre for Iranian Documentation and Research moved from Paris to the IISH, and in 2014 Dr Siagzar Berelian donated a rich collection of archive and library materials. Atabaki has also helped to bring together, in conjunction with the International Qajar Studies Association, a collection of documents related to the Qajar dynasty. Finally, the IISH has also become a repository of documents on the social history of oil in Iran. As a result of all these efforts, the IISH has over the years accumulated a rich collection on the history of Iran, which has opened new paths for historical research.

Atabaki's contribution to historical research is no less impressive than his role in collecting unique archival materials. His numerous books and articles span a number of issues and themes, four of which have guided the writing and compilation of this volume. First, a considerable number of Atabaki's articles focus on the pivotal period in Iranian history that begins with the Constitutional Revolution of 1905–11 and ends with the assumption of power by Reza Shah Pahlavi. This was a period of unprecedented creativity and debate, in which some of the cleavages and fissures that would characterize Iranian society and politics in the second half of the twentieth century took shape.[1]

The first three chapters in this volume concern this period. In the first chapter, Ali Ansari looks at the intellectual and political life of Mohammad Ali Foroughi as one of the founders and articulators of modern Iranian identity and nationalism, and discusses the importance of his writings in shaping the *Weltanschauung* of the Iranian elite in the first three decades of the twentieth century. Using one of the most iconic photographs of the Constitutional Revolution of 1905–9, Manoutchehr Eskandari-Qajar reminds us in Chapter Two that revolutions are not abstract processes – they are ultimately made and unmade by individuals and their collective actions, and elaborates on the role, social background, and ideas of the 22 chained men in this photograph. In Chapter Three, Janet Afary analyses the role of two important social groups in the making of the Constitutional Revolution: the liberal and social democratic intelligentsia on the one hand, and the Shi'a clerics on the other hand.

Both groups, while internally diverse, were entangled in a conflict about the authority of the clerical establishment and religion in a modern society. Afary explains how this conflict played out and which compromises were achieved in the formulation of the Supplementary Constitutional Law, judicial regulations, civil liberties, and freedom of the press.

The second important feature of Atabaki's research and writings on Iran is their transgression of geographical boundaries, critique of methodological nationalism, and the highlighting of the flow of ideas, people and materials in time and space. In 'Disgruntled guests: Iranian Subaltern on the Margins of the Tsarist Empire', for instance, he analyses the push and pull factors that caused mass migration in nineteenth- and early twentieth-century Iran, the formation of the Iranian subaltern community in the Caucasus, the community's social structure (gender, ethnicity and age), the migrants' working and living conditions, and their political culture.[2] This transnational perspective can be found in his other writings as well.[3] In the past few years, Atabaki has also conducted extensive archival research on the vicissitudes of Iranian migrant workers and revolutionaries who ended up in the Soviet Union in the decades after the Russian Revolution.

Chapters Four and Five of this volume are written from this transnational perspective. In Chapter Four, Mansour Bonakdarian de-provincializes the historiography of Iranian nationalist struggles in the early twentieth century by locating them within the global anti-imperialist networks of that period, which included activists from Europe, Arab countries, Turkey, India, and China. This involves a discussion of how the Iranian nationalists ideologically both borrowed from and also contributed to nationalist thought and movements elsewhere through observation as well as direct and indirect interaction. In Chapter Five, H.E. Chehabi turns his attention to Beirut, which beginning in the 1880s attracted a growing number of Iranian residents. These Iranians went to the Ottoman city to receive a Western education, while remaining within the lands of Islam, and many of them rose to social prominence upon their return, some as educational pioneers, others as businessmen, still others as politicians. Highlighting this aspect is particularly important because Iran's connections with the Arab parts of the Ottoman Empire have received less attention than its connections with Istanbul, Izmir, and other Turkish parts of the Ottoman Empire.[4]

INTRODUCTION 5

The third aspect of Atabaki's contribution to Iranian historiography is the engagement of his writings with social history. Without ignoring the importance of political history, to which he has given considerable attention, Atabaki has maintained throughout his career a focus on social history in general and on labour history in particular, documenting the history of subaltern groups rather than elites. His approach falls into a category that Eric Hobsbawm referred to as 'history from below'; his writings on modernity provide a good example. In *Men of Order: Authoritarian Modernization under Atatürk and Reza Shah*, which he edited with Erik-Jan Zürcher, various contributors analyse the modernization process in Turkey and Iran from the perspective of the state and its elites, while in a complementary sequel volume edited by Atabaki, the societal actions and responses that shaped modernization from below are explored.[5]

Within social history, Atabaki has made a particular contribution to the history of labour in Iran, which remains largely marginal to Iranian historiography. He has promoted and facilitated the study of various aspects of labour history in Iran, while at the same time challenging the crude materialist and over-politicized approaches that still dominate it. In turn, he has highlighted the importance of cultural practices and the interactions between class, ethnic, and gender identities. His contribution in this field received acknowledgement in January 2010, when he was awarded a major grant by the Netherlands Organization for Scientific Research (NWO) for a grand project on the social history of labour in the Iranian oil industry.[6]

Various aspects of Iran's modern social history are explored in Chapters Six to Ten of this volume. In Chapter Six, Serhan Afacan discusses the emergence and development of excessive imports and chronic trade deficit in Iran during the late nineteenth century and early twentieth century. He focuses on grassroots dimensions of the ensuing reactions to the ever-increasing inflow of foreign ready-made products and argues that the anti-import debates should be seen as a façade, if a significant one, beneath which various class-based political and social tensions rested. Furthermore, by analysing such tensions through the petitions sent from the various strata of the Iranian society, such as merchants, tradesmen, craftsmen, and workers, his chapter also provides an example of state–society interaction in Iran.

In Chapter Seven, Valentine M. Moghadam examines the history and historiography of subaltern women's role in production and reproduction in Iran. She explores women's economic roles and their social positions in the context of the world-system, the mode of production, the state, and class location in different periods of capitalist development: the late Qajar period, the period of early modernization under Reza Shah, rapid industrialization under Mohammad Reza Shah Pahlavi, and the Islamic Republic.

In Chapter Eight, Peyman Vahabzadeh casts new light on one of the key oppositional forces against the last Shah of Iran, namely the People's Fada'i Guerrillas. Using Georges Sorel's theory of revolutionary violence, he argues that the Siahkal episode, in which the guerrillas attacked a police station, created a cultural myth (of dissent) that gave these guerrillas a greater social weight than their numbers.

In Chapter Nine, M.R. Ghanoonparvar discusses several works of fiction that deal with the encounter of the Iranian society with oil and the oil industry, and consequently with Europeans and Americans. He illustrates how these literary works reflect the cultural, political and socioeconomic conflicts that resulted from this encounter.

In Chapter Ten, Kaveh Ehsani looks at the transformation of Iran's annual International Book and Media Fair after 1988, and analyses its symbolic functions as a cultural event as well as a public space. He argues that as a public space, it reflects the paradoxes of the Iranian society that result from the state's unsuccessful attempts to control cultural practices.

The fourth dimension of Atabaki's writings is related to historiographical perspectives and debates. In his inaugural lecture in December 2002 at the University of Amsterdam, Atabaki criticized essentialist conceptions of the history of the Middle East and Central Asia, whether articulated within Orientalist, nationalist, or Islamist discourses.[7] He went on to edit *Iran in the 20th Century: Historiography and Political Culture*, in which a number of eminent historians explore the way the present has refashioned our reading of the past and how the Iranian historiography has interacted with the political culture of the country in the twentieth century.[8]

The final two chapters in the book speak to historiographical concerns. In Chapter Eleven, Maral Jefroudi evaluates the debates on the development of Iranian historiography and argues that these debates can be enriched by the introduction of new perspectives, particularly those provided by global history. In this volume's final chapter, Erik-Jan Zürcher reviews recent trends in the historiography of the Ottoman

Empire, noting that two stand out: studies that focus on the mechanisms of political bargaining, particularly between the imperial centre and local elites, and comparative macro-studies in which a conscious effort is made to generate a better understanding of developments in the Empire by comparing it to the other great continental empires of Europe, i.e., Russia and Austria-Hungary. Areas that deserve more attention, he concludes, are labour history, the period from the 1940s to the late 1950s, and scholarly biography.

Notes

1. See Bibliography.
2. Touraj Atabaki, 'Disgruntled Guests: Iranian Subaltern on the Margins of the Tsarist Empire', *International Review of Social History* xlviii/3 (December 2003), pp. 401–6.
3. See for instance Touraj Atabaki, 'The Comintern, the Soviet Union and Working Class Militancy in Interwar Iran', in Stephanie Cronin (ed.), *Iranian-Russian Encounters: Empire and Revolution since 1800* (London: Routledge, 2012), pp. 298–323; Touraj Atabki, 'Constitutionalists *Sans Frontières*: Iranian Constitutionalism and its Asian Connections', in H. E. Chehabi and Vanessa Martin (eds.), *Iran's Constitutional Revolution: Popular Politics, Cultural Transformations and Transnational Connections* (London: I.B.Tauris, 2010), pp. 341–56; Touraj Atabaki, *Iran and the First World War: Battle Ground of the Great Powers* (London: I.B.Tauris, 2006).
4. Touraj is also one of the few Iranian scholars who have not merely looked beyond geographical boundaries when writing about Iran's history, but who have also conducted serious research on the history of countries and regions in its vicinity. His mastery of Russian and Turkish, and familiarity with the archives of the Soviet Union has allowed him to write insightfully about the history of its former republics in the Caucasus and Central Asia. He has co-edited a volume on transnationalism and diaspora in Central Asia and the Caucasus, and another volume on various aspects of the post-Soviet era in Central Asia. He has also made an important contribution in advancing the historiography of Ottoman and Turkish labour history. In 2010 he co-edited a supplement of the *International Review of Social History* on this topic.
5. Touraj Atabaki and Erik-Jan Zürcher (eds.), *Men of Order. Authoritarian Modernization under Atatürk and Reza Shah* (London: I.B.Tauris, 2004); Touraj Atabaki (ed.), *The State and the Subaltern. Modernization, Society and the State in Turkey and Iran* (London: I.B.Tauris, 2007).
6. Under his supervision, a team of three researchers – Kaveh Ehsani, Maral Jefroudi, and Peyman Jafari – works on this project, which makes a unique contribution to the study of the oil industry by focusing on issues such as the

formation of the work force, the emergence and development of industrial towns, industrial relations, the daily lives of the workers, gender and ethnic relations, labour activism and organization, class consciousness, and the relationship between the workforce, the company, and the state. Some preliminary results of this research have already been presented in a special issue of the *International Labor and Working-Class History* edited by Touraj, and he is currently writing a monograph on the social history of labour in the Iranian oil industry in the period 1908–41.

7. Touraj Atabaki, *Beyond Essentialism: Who Writes Whose Past in the Middle East and Central Asia?* (Amsterdam: Aksant, 2003).
8. Touraj Atabaki (ed.), *Iran in the 20th Century: Historiography and Political Culture* (London: I.B.Tauris, 2009).

PART I

THE CONSTITUTIONAL REVOLUTION AND NATIONALISM

CHAPTER 1

MOHAMMAD ALI FOROUGHI AND THE CONSTRUCTION OF CIVIC NATIONALISM IN EARLY TWENTIETH-CENTURY IRAN

Ali M. Ansari

Mohammad Ali Foroughi, Zoka' al-Molk, was one of the leading intellectuals of the Constitutional era, enjoying a distinguished career in both politics and academia. Born in 1877 to a bureaucratic family, Foroughi reflected a tradition that combined public service with intellectual endeavour. He published an impressive corpus of material, ranging from his introduction to Western political thought through to his commentaries on Persian literature and his beloved *Shahnameh*, the social value of which he argued for passionately throughout his life. He was elected a member of the second Majles (parliament) in 1909 and became the Speaker of the Parliament for a short period in 1911. He occupied a series of ministerial posts including a succession of key appointments in the cabinet of Reza Khan, providing a now-famous coronation oration at the latter's formal assumption of the crown in 1926. He oversaw the establishment and development of the Farhangestan (the state cultural and language institute) and played a crucial role as prime minister during the abdication of Reza Shah and the subsequent enthronement of his 21-year-old son, Mohammad Reza Shah, in 1941. He died in 1942, with his country in the throes of yet another political crisis: occupied by Allied forces and with the ambitions of the Constitutional era incomplete and its achievements uncertain.

Despite Foroughi's pivotal role in the creation of modern Iran – and perhaps more accurately, the *idea* of Iran for the modern age – his legacy and achievements have been neglected by scholars and political activists alike.[1] In part this reflects a concentration on a political career overshadowed by far more important events such as the Constitutional Revolution itself – of which Foroughi was but one of a startling constellation of intellectual activists. Many of these were far more political and keener on self-publicity than Foroughi, the archetypal 'quiet' bureaucrat, ever desired to be. This quality undoubtedly endeared him to Reza Khan, always mindful of where the credit should be due, and Foroughi never achieved the fame that the triumvirate around Reza Shah – Firuz, Davar and Teymourtash – achieved. Nor, of course, did he share their fates, outlasting his master to faithfully ensure a peaceful transition to the untested and somewhat apprehensive heir.

It also reflects the reality that access to Foroughi's corpus of written material has often been difficult, at least until recent years when his works have been patiently collected, edited, and published through the invaluable efforts of dedicated individuals, most obviously the late Iraj Afshar.[2] Yet Foroughi was much more widely published than many of his contemporaries, for whom the practical obstructions to research would have been far more obvious. There have been, perhaps, more political reasons why Foroughi's legacy has not been properly assessed. Indeed, the ideological nature of subsequent historiography has tended to affect the way in which Foroughi has been presented and it is ironic that one of the real founders and articulators of modern Iranian identity and nationalism should have found himself relegated to the margins of events he did so much to shape because of the desire of some to exaggerate the impact of the ruler he served (a fate he might not have minded), and the much more damaging attempt of others to dismiss his patriotism as the facile product of foreign emulation. This 'emulation' has proved all the more damning to Foroughi's reputation because it has been associated with the British, and even worse (if that were possible) with his membership of the Freemasons.[3]

Yet Foroughi's association with Freemasonry was neither unique nor, certainly in the context of his time, emblematic of a hidden agenda that was antithetical to the national interests he sought to pursue. Quite the contrary, they represented for him membership within an international intellectual brotherhood — a Republic of Letters — that saw no contradiction between patriotism and internationalism.[4] Nor did he see any contradiction between the pursuit of civic and political ideals that might draw on European political philosophy and defence of the interests of his country against the policies of the very countries he admired.[5] Foroughi's position was a much more subtle, nuanced, yet profound engagement with the ideas of nationalism than his detractors would care to admit. Marrying the ideas of the (European) Enlightenment with his own bureaucratic inheritance, Foroughi sought to 'educate his masters' in the best traditions of the Persian mirrors for princes, except that in his case, his 'masters' were the people themselves.

In a lecture to students at the Faculty of Law in 1937 (which had become part of the new University of Tehran in 1934), Foroughi reflected on what had been achieved and what remained to be done.[6] His main aim, however, appears to have been to remind his young wards of the distance, in political, social, and intellectual terms, the country had come since the onset of the Constitutional Revolution and from just what a low base Iran's reforming and revolutionary elite had to start. It was a measure, in some ways, of the success of succeeding reforms that few, he suggested, could now perceive the paucity of the political environment that confronted Iran's bureaucratic-intellectual elite and the many paradoxes that faced them. The provision of education and the establishment of the rule of law were central to Foroughi's conception of the modern 'nation-state' supported and sustained by an educated and politically-aware citizenry. It was not sufficient to have a codified legal system; it had to be understood by a people who were engaged. This, it might be argued, was an ambitious task for the most modern and progressive of states, but for a country that had in the eyes of many stagnated for the better part of a century and failed to keep in touch with its own social changes, let alone developments in the wider world, this was an enormous problem. To establish a legal and educational platform for development, one needed the tools; and the reality was that Iran possessed neither the tools nor the budget to acquire them. In Foroughi's terms, Iran had none of the prerequisites in place; the government was bankrupt, it had no professional cadre of judges or lawyers with which to begin the construction of a functional judiciary, and most importantly it had no codified system of laws.[7]

Appreciating this context helps us understand the enthusiasm of the response, and while Foroughi was undoubtedly more measured in his public pronouncements on the malaise facing Iran (unlike Taqizadeh for example), his response drew on the same ideas that had informed many of his revolutionary contemporaries, including Taqizadeh. These ideas noted above drew on the European Enlightenment, and were practically expressed and applied through his membership, along with almost every other significant leader of the Constitutional Movement, in Freemasonry; specifically the 'Iran Awakening' lodge.[8] This association and affiliation has been seen as enough in the eyes of some to diminish, and discard onto the scrapheap of history, the ideas and achievements of men like Foroughi, whose adherence to the ideas of the Enlightenment make them deeply flawed, as if they are guilty by association of all the ills of European colonialism, the genesis of which some see in an Enlightenment that apparently launched Europe into a prolonged global exercise in liberal evangelism. Such an assessment, however, that tends to conflate different trends and historical periods – and has been much reinforced by the dominance of Marxist historiography within counter-Enlightenment narratives – both simplifies and generalizes a process of intellectual discovery that was much more cosmopolitan before it became 'European'. Indeed that which became known as the European Enlightenment saw its own intellectual roots in a humanist tradition that transcended national and local cultures while at the same time not necessarily seeking to denigrate those distinct cultures.[9]

If the Enlightenment movement had a target for criticism, this was contemporary organized religion, which was regarded as overly ritualistic, superstitious, and contrary to the intellectual growth of mankind.[10] Those who sought to challenge the orthodoxies of the day, be they religious or political, and being aware of the sensitivities towards such iconoclasm from those in authority, naturally sought intellectual stimulation and personal safety in a society that was hidden from general view. In the eighteenth century this resulted in the dramatic growth of Masonic lodges.[11] This international intellectual brotherhood was firmly Deist, if antithetical to the dominant religious orthodoxies of the day (which in Europe meant Christianity), and as such there was little difficulty in attracting adherents from the Muslim world who likewise had problems with the contemporary religious dogma.[12] No less a figure that Jamal al-Din al Afghani, the father of modern political Islam, was a

Freemason, going so far as to found his own lodge when the one he had been affiliated with proved less than enthusiastic about Afghani's determination to engage in politics.[13] In sum, membership of the Freemasons was not the preserve of an irreligious minority beholden to the West. On the contrary, recent research suggests that it was far more widespread among the progressive elites of the Middle East, providing an avenue for engagement with ideas that was far from an attempt to 'emulate' Europe. Indeed, if Afghani's response to the French philosopher Ernest Renan is an accurate reflection of his views, not only had he absorbed many of the ideas of the Enlightenment – especially with respect to philosophy and education – but he categorically rejected emerging European ideas on race that contradicted those tenets.[14]

Foroughi's ideas and motivations reflected this dual inheritance, drawing on the cosmopolitanism of the Enlightenment and marrying them to the humanism that was particular to a Persian bureaucratic-intellectual tradition. Both were Universalist in their aspirations. Foroughi was proud of his Iranian inheritance but neither conceited nor complacent, and his irritation at the condescension of Europeans – not least the British – who felt that the Iranians were incapable of governing themselves, was palpable in much of what he wrote. For him Iran represented a civilization, one that may have lost its way but a civilization nonetheless, that with a period of 'enlightenment' could once again contribute constructively to the progress of mankind. It would not be too much to argue that Foroughi, borrowing from Hegel, understood Iran as the civilization in which 'first arises that light which shines itself and illuminates what is around'.[15] It was itself a cosmopolitan force for enlightenment; always generous, almost to a fault.[16] But Iranians had now lost their way. In a memorable passage outlining the problems facing the country, Foroughi wrote,

> To summarize, my point is this that today the Iranian people neither worship God, nor love their country, nor seek freedom or honour, they do not pursue dignity, nor to they seek art, or search for knowledge, something needs to be done so that the people despair of charlatanism, racketeering (*howchi-gari*) and intrigue, and distance themselves [from such things]...[17]

To the question of what must be done, Foroughi stated in the best Whig tradition, 'We must educate the people'.[18]

This education had three distinct aspects. The first and perhaps the easiest to achieve, at least on a superficial level, was to restore a level of pride and dignity in Iranian culture and civilization. In this, as in other aspects of the programme he pursued, Foroughi sought to justify his actions by referring to the European experience. So the love of history and culture, language and literature were all encouraged on the basis that such pursuit of knowledge lay at the basis of European development and growth. Indeed the possession of history and the development of a historical consciousness were essential prerequisites for modernization not least, but by no means exclusively, because such knowledge gave peoples the confidence to face the future. Those in possession of a long history were by extension blessed among nations.[19] It should perhaps not be surprising that Foroughi was among the first to author histories of his country, with his history of Sasanian Iran published in 1898 and another more broadly on ancient Iran in 1902. Similarly, in an article on Iranian literature, Foroughi made it clear that the Iranians are in receipt of a blessing that they have yet to fully appreciate, adding for good measure that if one knew about Europe one would be aware that Europeans' rapid progress was initiated during the Renaissance, a period when they became reacquainted with their classical literature.[20] Iran was fortunate, argued Foroughi, that it possessed a rich reservoir of classical literature all its own, but it had yet to develop, as the Europeans had done, a rigorous syllabus founded upon the 'humanities'.[21]

It is perhaps worth noting, given Foroughi's subsequent reputation among his detractors and his role in the Farhangestan (the Language Academy that was subsequently established under Reza Shah to oversee the rules, regulations and development of Persian), that he was an enthusiastic supporter and promoter of the classical literature of the Islamic era, and that as early as 1915 Foroughi was arguing vehemently against the trend in some quarters to replace the Arabic script with the Latin one and purge the Persian language of Arabic words. For Foroughi, the replacement of the script would simply deprive Iranians of easy access to their history and literature, and would be enormously counterproductive, but he added for good measure that the inclusion of Arabic words often reflected the reality that equivalent idioms in Persian had not existed, or that the Persian words that had existed were neither as suitable or as aesthetically pleasing as their Arabic equivalent. This last statement will undoubtedly have come as something of a surprise to those who view Foroughi as an ardent ideological nationalist, but it very much reflects the position he took years later against zealots in the Farhangestan who regarded the Language Academy merely as a factory for inventing new words and for completely ridding Persian of its Arabic loanwords.[22] In an account reminiscent of Reza Shah's own frustrations,[23] some years later Foroughi recalled an incident in which a writer had been criticized for using the word *mellat* to mean 'nation'. When the writer challenged his critic to come up with a suitable alternative, the critic announced that he had discovered just such a word in Persian but proceeded to mumble as he clearly had trouble pronouncing his new word – *barproshan*. 'Now imagine,' argued Foroughi, 'how ridiculous and distant from the comprehension and mind of the people that when we want to say the Iranian nation (*mellat*) or the English nation we should say the Iranian *barproshan* or the English *barproshan*!'[24]

In his extended discourse on the value of the Language Academy, Foroughi made clear his frustration with the trivialization of the process of education that had been inaugurated. If one goal had been to restore dignity to the Iranians by reacquainting them with their culture and civilization, this had not necessarily been matched with the sort of understanding and appreciation that Foroughi had sought. Put simply, the breadth of the development had not necessarily been matched by concomitant depth, with the result that the sort of dynamic and sustaining citizenry he had in mind was proving more difficult to mould. Moreover, a superficial knowledge and pride in the past was proving less liberating inasmuch as it reinforced a tendency to become fixated in the past and resist, rather than embrace, the changes of the modern world. In order to achieve depth and understanding, one had to move away from the factual aspects of education and knowledge acquisition and move towards an appreciation of the essence.

Fortunately for Foroughi, Iran was similarly amply blessed with the means to compensate for the possible shortcomings by the possession of a 'national' mythology that was not only a repository of the nation's mythopoetic heritage, but in the form of the *Shahnameh* also provided a manual of ethical behaviour.[25] Foroughi was passionate about the *Shahnameh*, going to great lengths to promote it through lectures, abridgements, and selections of key passages for students. He professed quite simply to 'love it'.[26] This was not a text to be read but to be absorbed, and there were important lessons to be learnt from its narratives. These were myths, but not necessarily fantasies, and Foroughi took pains to point out that mythologies surround us and cloak histories both near and far, so it was not necessary to dismiss the narratives of the *Shahnameh* as 'mere myths', since they were, in his eyes, emblematic of greater truths.[27] Digesting these truths would not only instil pride but it would also give courage to Iranians and provide them with an ethical point of reference. It was perhaps with this particular point in mind that Foroughi drew allusions to the mythical and ancient kings of Iran during his oration on the occasion of Reza Shah's coronation. If all civilizations worthy of the name possessed histories and myths commensurate with their stature, then Iran possessed a worthy civilization, but with such an inheritance came responsibilities and it was the responsibility of all Iranians, not least the king, to live up to expectations.[28]

In delivering the Coronation Oration and urging the new monarch to absorb the responsibilities and weight of history, Foroughi was in many ways reverting to the traditional duties of the Persian bureaucratic elite. Indeed for all the ambitions of this period to educate the people and forge the nation, given the paucity of general education, the target of much of this educational programme remained the literate elite. The poetic nature of the *Shahnameh* of course facilitated recitation and memorization by the non-literate, and foreign observers frequently noted that the epic was perhaps the only history believed by most Iranians.[29] The truth remained, however, that a major objective of this period was not the education of the people but of the elites, insofar as good governance (indeed the existence of governance itself) was a prerequisite for much of the wider reform envisioned. In his reflection on the modernization of the law in Iran, Foroughi made the pointed remark that one of the obstacles to the development of a rationalized legal order subject to amendment through periodic legislation was the political elites themselves, who despite complaining about the state of affairs were more fearful of their loss of status and power. 'The elite,' argued Foroughi, 'abstain from assuming the responsibility for a variety of reasons: some out of negligence or lack of necessary knowledge, some due to carelessness, nonchalance and lack of ambition, and some because of their own personal motives and interests. Man always seeks his own personal interests, but, unfortunately, he does not always recognize them correctly.'[30]

The education of the elites became central to much of Foroughi's efforts, especially if political discontent and revolt were to translate into meaningful – institutional – change. Foroughi therefore authored what might best be termed a series of textbooks for the elites, providing them with a comparatively easy introduction to the ideas and philosophies that had underpinned the development of European civilization. This involved introductions to classical history, most obviously the histories of Greece and Rome, and most famously surveys of Western thought from Socrates through the nineteenth century, published in several volumes from 1931 to 1941, but whose origins lay in his study of Socratic thought published in 1918. Among other lesser-known if still influential studies was one on political economy entitled 'The Principle of the study of national wealth', first published in 1905, which is one of the first texts on economics and economic theory to be published in Persian.[31] Indeed, this earlier Constitutional period was among Foroughi's most productive and interesting, and following the formation of the first Majles he produced a summary paper (in current printed form it stretches to some 60 pages) on fundamental laws, or 'The Rules of Constitutionalism of States'.[32]

This is an intriguing document and the debt to French law and vocabulary is clear throughout the text, although the ideas reflect as much a British understanding of constitutionalism, insofar as it discusses the notion of a constitutional monarchy rather than a formal Republic based on the French model. But it is the didactic nature of the text that makes it most interesting, directed as it was towards the newly-enfranchised constitutional revolutionaries who clearly were in need of a rapid education in the manners and forms of constitutional government. Foroughi therefore starts at the beginning with a definition of terms, most obviously that of 'law' (*droit*),[33] before proceeding to distinguish between internal and external rights, external being the province of international law between states which is itself divided between the public and the private; the latter relating to the activities and rights of the citizens of one state in another. The internal or domestic law can relate to constitutional laws, which provide the overall frame of reference for the activities of the state so constituted, while the more detailed administrative laws serve to regulate procedures.

Foroughi then proceeds to discuss these two types of law, noting that while administrative laws can be discussed, amended, and indeed produced in the legislature, the constitutional laws can only be amended through the convening of a special constitutional body. The practical implications of this would seen in the discussions that would later take place over the deposition of the Qajars in 1925, with Taqizadeh famously objecting on the basis that this was a matter reserved for a special constitutional commission. On the nature of states, Foroughi distinguishes monarchies and republics, both of which (he suggests) can be legally and constitutionally limited or authoritarian and absolute. Foroughi helpfully points out that a constitutional system is one in which powers are limited and it is this political system that most thinkers now attest to.

Foroughi then goes on to outline the notion of a national monarchy, which is effectively his synonym for a constitutional monarchy, complete with a representative legislature.[34] The nomenclature is interesting in that supporters of Reza Shah argued that this was what fundamentally distinguished the new Pahlavi monarchy from that of the Qajars, and Reza Shah himself seems to have held this distinction in some significance, even if in practice matters were less clear. Nevertheless, what Foroughi, and by extension the Constitutionalists, appeared to be suggesting by these terms was that unlike absolute monarchies or despotism, sovereignty in a 'national' monarchy lay with the nation. It was the nation that held the authority and the rights and bestowed these upon the monarch. Such views echoed the mood at the time and were reflected in Article 8 of the Supplementary Fundamental Laws enacted in 1907.[35] This was an important distinction and one that went to the heart of the debate over authority and the sources of authority in the constitutional movement. There is no suggestion of any Divine Right in Foroughi's concept of a national monarchy.

He continues to elaborate on the form of legislature and proceeds to discuss the role of parliament, which is to hold governments to account, and not, he emphasizes, to run the government which is in the hands of ministers. These ministers are either appointed by the king (or in the case of a Republic, the president), or the king appoints the leader with the highest supporters in the parliament to select a cabinet. Here, Foroughi is effectively referencing the British constitutional system. Following a discourse on ministerial responsibility, Foroughi moves to the next chapter, which deals with the rights of the state. Here he relates the benefits of a bicameral parliament and also outlines the various types of suffrage that may be applied, noting that the best form is universal suffrage. He then adds that such a situation should only be applied when the peoples have achieved a measure of political progress (maturity), noting for good measure that many states in Europe retain a limited suffrage for just this reason.[36] There follows an extensive discourse on the rights and rules of parliament, what is permitted by way of its chambers, how laws may be enacted, and the rights of individual delegates, as well as the role of ministers and their rights and responsibilities with respect to parliament. One can only imagine what an invaluable handbook of procedure this must have been to new parliamentarians hitherto used to protest but not to the responsibilities of government.

The next chapter, which is perhaps the most interesting, deals with the rights of the nation, or people. The general rights of the people, notes Foroughi, can basically be divided into two themes: freedom and equality. 'Freedom means that an individual has the right to do anything they desire on the condition that it harm no-one else. Thus, one should not confuse freedom with stubbornness (*khod-sari*),[37] since freedom does not mean that an individual can do whatever they want, and an individual's rights have limits and those limits include the obligations an individual has towards other people. And lastly those obligations are required for the harmony of society.'[38] Foroughi adds that the law must not, however, be seen as restricting freedom but rather regarded as a means of facilitating it. This is another important distinction in which Foroughi seeks to inculcate the view that the law exists for the common weal, not for the purposes of the state to effectively oppress the people. Indeed, just to be clear, Foroughi then proceeds to list what individual rights consist of: the right to life, the right to property, the right to a home, the right to work, the right to belief, the right to thought, the right to gather and to form an association, the right to education, and the right to protest/petition. Each of these rights is subsequently discussed in some detail, stressing that each person has the right to hold whatever political or religious belief they choose and that the right to free thought is essential if individuals are to be true to themselves and avoid the pitfalls of ethical corruption *(fased al-akhlagh)* and lying.[39]

As for equality, Foroughi clarifies that it means equality before the law and not equality of status or achievement, which are clearly related to an individual's position in society and talents. Once again, Foroughi stresses that equality before the law has not always existed and that, on the contrary, it has been normal in the past for some classes to seek privileges over others, and that some classes have been exempt from particular laws. This is, however, no longer the case and equality can be understood in four distinct areas: before the law, before the courts, in employment, and in taxation. Although the first two seem more important that the latter two, the principle of general taxation applicable to all and equality in employment subject to merit are important statements of careers open to talents, and responsibility for all.

Mohammad Ali Foroughi, Zoka' al-Molk, was one of the leading intellectuals of modern Iran, passionately advocating and articulating a view on Iranian nationalism and identity. His detractors have sought to diminish and marginalize his contributions as an exercise in European emulation of the worst kind, pointing in particular to his affinity for Western (read British) constitutionalism and his participation in Freemasonry. Yet, as has been argued above, neither of these accusations bear scrutiny either in the context of the time, or indeed when one looks at the details of Foroughi's arguments and the breadth of his learning. No-one would suggest that Foroughi was a profound thinker intent on promoting a distinct philosophy; he was much more a conveyor of ideas than a creator of them, although reading through his contributions strong themes do stand out. The dominant themes are those of the Enlightenment: education, progress, and acquisition of the manners of civilization. That European civilization now championed these manners was, for Foroughi and others like him, a product – even an accident – of history. Europe had no prior claim to such civilizational attributes and all could, with the right education, achieve them. This was at heart a Whig philosophy drawn from an understanding of the Enlightenment that was cosmopolitan, progressive, and above all optimistic. It was also programmatic and zealous in its ambition to educate mankind towards a better future. Unlike some of his contemporaries, Foroughi was a quiet activist, far more eager to work in the background. It is possibly this that explains both his survival and his relative marginalization in the historical record. In this, perhaps, Foroughi drew the lessons of his own traditional bureaucratic heritage and in this respect he really was one who straddled two distinct, if remarkably overlapping, cultures.

Foroughi's strong affectation for the traditions of Iran is often explained as a simple and clear expression of his nationalism and there is little doubt that for all his promotion of an understanding of Western history and philosophy, his real enthusiasm was reserved for the history, legends, and literature of his native land. Critics might argue that this also reflected the inherent contradictions of early nationalist thought, at once Western-orientated yet locally focused. But this is to fundamentally misunderstand the 'Whiggish' philosophy that this chapter argues underpinned Foroughi's approach. Change could only be constructively administered when a political culture was firmly and confidently anchored to its traditions: continuity begat change with a social contract (to paraphrase Edmund Burke) that looked to the past as well as the future. A lack of confidence in oneself and in one's traditions obstructed a realistic diagnosis and hindered progress. Recounting his early experiences, Foroughi related that being short-sighted he had been encouraged to wear glasses lest his eyesight fail altogether. Walking down a dark alleyway he found himself nonetheless edging forward to prevent falling down when a young boy seeing him advised 'Sir, take off your glasses in order to see'.[40] Perhaps few anecdotes better illustrate Iran's continued struggle with 'modernity'.

Notes

1. One notable exception is the short study by Ali Asghar Haqdar, *Mohammad Ali Foroughi va sakhtarha-ye novin-e madani* (Mohammad Ali Foroughi and the construction of new civics) (Tehran: Kavir, 2005). For a list of Foroughi's publications (including 14 books), see pp. 165–8.
2. Most obviously in this regard has been the collection in two volumes of Foroughi's assorted papers, speeches, and lectures: Mohammad Ali Zaka' al-Molk, *Maqalat-e Foroughi*, vol. 1 (Tehran: Tus, 2005), and vol. 2 (Tehran: Tus, 2008). A more recent and immensely valuable collection of Foroughi's political writings is Iraj Afshar and Hormoz Homayunpour (eds.), *Siyasatnameh-ye Zoka' al-Molk, maqalehha, namehha, va sokhanraniha-ye siyasi-ye Mohammad Ali Foroughi* (The Book of Politics of Zoka ol Molk, the political articles, letters and speeches of Mohammad Ali Foroughi) (Tehran: Ketab-e Rowshan, 2010).
3. The most thorough, if sensationalist and controversial, account of Iranian Freemasonry is provided by Esma'il Ra'in *Faramushkhanah va Faramasonari dar Iran* (House of Forgetfulness and Freemasonry in Iran) (Tehran: Amir Kabir, 1978). See also Hamed Algar 'An Introduction to the History of Freemansonry (*sic*) in Iran', *Middle Eastern Studies* vi/3 (1970), pp. 276–96. For a more balanced survey see 'Freemasonry' in *Encyclopaedia Iranica Online*.
4. See 'Iran ra chera bayad dust dasht (Why we must love Iran)', in Afshar and Homayunpur (eds.), *Siyasatnameh-ye Zoka' al-Molk*, p. 251.
5. See for example 'Pasokh beh matbu'at-e Englis (A Response to the English Press)', in Afshar and Homayunpur (eds.), *Siyasatnameh-ye Zoka' al-Molk*, p. 91.

6. Mohammad Ali Foroughi 'The Modernization of Law', *Journal of Persianate Studies* iii/1 (2010), pp. 31–46.
7. Ibid., p. 41.
8. Mangol Bayat 'The *Rowshanfekr* in the Constitutional period', in H. E. Chehabi and Vanessa Martin (eds.), *Iran's Constitutional Revolution: Popular Politics, Cultural Transformations and Transnational Connections* (London: I.B.Tauris, 2010), p. 179.
9. See for example, Karen O'Brien, *Narratives of Enlightenment: Cosmopolitan History from Voltaire to Gibbon* (Cambridge: Cambridge University Press, 1997) (Kindle Edition), loc: pp. 46–152.
10. Foroughi's religious beliefs and antagonism towards the religion of the clergy are clear in his recently-discovered last testament to his children, reprinted for the first time in Afshar and Homayunpur (eds.), *Siyasatnameh-ye Zoka' al-Molk*, pp. 295–300; in this, Foroughi makes clear his belief in God as the essence of truth and righteousness and has nothing to do with what Hajji and Mullah so-and-so believe.
11. For a useful account of the role of Freemasonry in the Enlightenment, see Margaret C. Jacob, *The Radical Enlightenment: Pantheists, Freemasons and Republicans* (Lafayette, LA: Cornerstone, 2006), especially pp. ix–xiv and 80–151.
12. See Sami Zubaida, *Beyond Islam: A New Understanding of the Middle East* (London: I.B.Tauris, 2011), pp. 135–44.
13. See A. Albert Kudsi-Zadeh 'Afghānī and Freemasonry in Egypt', *Journal of the American Oriental Society* xcii/1 (1972), pp. 25–35.
14. Jamal al Din al Afghani 'Answer of Jamal al Din to Renan', *Journal des débats* (May 18 1883), reprinted in Nikki R. Keddie (ed.), *An Islamic Response to Imperialism* (Berkeley: University of California Press, 1986), pp. 181–7. The argument around the responsibility of the Enlightenment for the subsequent development of race theory revolves around the idea of polygenesis, which originated in the Enlightenment challenge to the religious belief in a single creation, which many considered scientifically implausible. Seeking a cosmopolitan approach, philosophers argued for multiple 'creations', It was for others to develop this further into a 'racial hierarchy'. See in this respect, Colin Kidd, *The Forging of Races* (Cambridge: Cambridge University Press, 2006).
15. G. W. F. Hegel, *The Philosophy of History* (New York: Dover, 1956), p. 173.
16. 'Iran ra chera bayad dust dasht (Why we must love Iran)', in Afshar and Homayunpur (eds.), *Siyasatnameh-ye Zoka' al-Molk*, p. 253.
17. 'Ta'sir-e rafter-e shah dar tarbiyat-e Irani (The role of the Shah in the education of Iranians)', *Maqalat-e Foroughi*, vol. 2, p. 70.
18. Ibid., p. 69. This term is repeated more emphatically in his speech entitled 'Farhangestan Chist? (What is the Language Academy)', in *Maqalat-e Foroughi*, vol.1, p. 182.

NATIONALISM IN EARLY TWENTIETH-CENTURY IRAN   25

19. See in this respect Catherine Hall, *Macaulay and Son: Architects of Imperial Britain* (New Haven and London: Yale University Press, 2012), pp. xv–xvi.
20. 'Adabiyat-e Iran (The literature of Iran)', *Maqalat-e Foroughi*, vol. 2, p. 224. The article was originally published in 1316/1938.
21. Foroughi uses the transliteration of this term, ibid., p. 225.
22. 'Farhangestan Chist? (What is the Farhangestan?)' *Maqalat-e Foroughi*, vol. 1, p. 180.
23. For a similar incident with Reza Shah see Hoseyn Makki *Tarikh-e Bist Saleh-ye Iran* (A Twenty Year History of Iran), vol. 6 (Tehran: Amir Kabir, 1982), p. 235.
24. 'Zaban va adabiyat-e Farsi (Persian language and literature)', in Afshar and Homayunpur (eds.) *Siyasatnameh-ye Zoka' al-Molk*, p. 259, first published in the newspaper *Asr-e Jadid* in 1915.
25. *Kholaseh-ye Shahnameh-ye Ferdowsi* (An Abridgement of Ferdowsi's Shahnameh) (Tehran: Majid, 1999), first published in 1313/1934, pp. 7–28.
26. The word he uses in response to a question is *asheqam*, '*Moqadame-ye Shahnameh*' (Introduction to the Shahnameh) *Maqalat-e Foroughi*, vol. 2, p. 331 See also *Moqadame-ye montakheb-e Shahnameh Bara-ye Dabirestan* (Introduction to Selections from the Shahnameh For Secondary School), op.cit. p. 351.
27. 'Maqam-e arjmand-e Ferdowsi (The Esteemed position of Ferdowsi)', *Maqalat-e Foroughi*, vol. 2, p. 310, delivered in 1934.
28. 'Khotbeh-ye Tajgozari, (Coronation Oration)', in Afshar and Homayunpur (eds.), *Siyasatnameh-ye Zoka' al-Molk*, pp. 113–15, delivered at Reza Shah's coronation in 1926. In contrast with his speech in 1934, Foroughi refers in this oration to the fact that some people would see the Pishdadians and Kayanids as legends in the fantastical sense (*afsanehha-ye bastani bekhanand*). Indeed in this oration Foroughi uses terms such as 'race' that are not echoed and are more often contradicted in his more reflective speeches and articles and one should consider whether a popular familiarity with this famous oration has unduly coloured the popular understanding of Foroughi's ideas.
29. Percy Sykes, *A History of Persia* (London: RoutledgeCurzon, 2004) (first published 1915), p. 133.
30. Mohammad Ali Foroughi 'The Modernization of Law', p. 35.
31. Mohammad Ali Foroughi *Osul-e elm va servat-e melal* (The Principles of the Study of National Wealth) (Tehran: Farzan, 1998), first published 1323/1905. Among other works, Foroughi also turned his mind to an introductory text on Physics, published in 1328/1910.
32. Mohammad Ali Foroughi *Hoquq-e asasi: ya adab-e mashrutiyat-e doval* (Fundamental Laws or the rules of Constitutionalism of States) (Tehran: 1325–6/1907–8), reprinted in Afshar and Homayunpur (eds.), *Siyasatnameh-ye Zoka' al-Molk*, pp. 5–62.
33. This term, as Foroughi notes, is translated into Persian as 'rights', see 'The Modernization of Law', p. 42.
34. Mohammad Ali Foroughi, *Hoquq-e asasi: ya adab-e mashrutiyat-e doval*, in Afshar and Homayunpur (eds.) op.cit. pp. 11–13.

35. The parallels in these laws and Foroughi's paper are striking. A translation can be found in E. G. Browne, 'The Persian Revolution 1905–1909', (Washington DC: Mage, 1995, new Edition ed. By Abbas Amanat, originally published by Cambridge University Press in 1910), pp. 372–84. See also in this respect the response of leading members of the *ulema* to Mozaffar al-Din Shah recounted in the 'General Report on Persia for the year 1906', Sir Cecil Spring-Rice to Sir Edward Grey, 29 January 1907, p. 6, reprinted in R.M. Burrell (ed.) *Iran Political Diaries*, vol. III (N.P.: Archive Editions, 1997), p. 78.
36. Foroughi, *Hoquq-e asasi*, p. 19.
37. Ibid., p. 51. By this Foroughi probably means an unwillingness to compromise.
38. Ibid., pp. 51–2.
39. Ibid., p. 56.
40. Foroughi 'The Modernization of Law', p. 33.

CHAPTER 2

SUBVERSIVE SUBALTERNS: THE BAGH-E SHAH TWENTY-TWO

Manoutchehr Eskandari-Qajar[1]

As pictorial records go, there are indeed many snapshots of the revolutionary upheaval that became known as the Persian Constitutional Revolution of 1905, but none are as telling as the photograph of the 22 Bagh-e Shah prisoners, made famous outside Iran by Edward G. Browne in his book *The Persian Revolution, 1905–1909*, which captured the imagination of the world as the most important representation in that heroic struggle of 'right versus wrong'.[2] Considering thus the Persian Constitutional Revolution in light of the role of subalterns in revolutionary outcomes, I would like to focus on this most iconic of symbols of that revolution and explore some of the reasons for the figuring of these particular 22 as representative of the struggle of the revolutionaries against the regime of Mohammad Ali Shah Qajar.

The Constitutional Revolution of 1905–9 went through three distinct phases, or five if one were to count the years of reversal of its gains from 1909–11 and from 1911 to the final defeat of the aims of the revolution with the establishment of the military dictatorship of Reza Khan in 1921. The three essential moments of the Constitutional Revolution are: the beginning, from the Tehran riots in 1905 to the proclamation of the Constitution in 1906 and 1907; the 'lesser autocracy' of 1907–9; and finally the exile of Mohammad Ali Shah and the victory of the revolutionaries with the re-establishment of constitutional monarchy on 16 July 1909, installing 12-year-old Soltan Ahmad Mirza as monarch and the Qajar elder Ali Reza Khan Azod al-Molk as regent. That year also saw the opening of the Second Majles (Parliament), in November. The photograph in question relates to the period of the 'lesser autocracy' (*estebdad-e saghir*) and the events referred to as the Bagh-e Shah events.

On 22 June 1908, the day before the bombardment of the Majles and the subsequent arrest of the Bagh-e Shah detainees, Colonel Liakhov (Liakhoff), the Russian commander of the Cossack Brigade loyal to Mohammad Ali Shah, issued a martial law proclamation for Tehran. At the same time, the Shah issued two proclamations explaining that the measures he had taken were in order to safeguard the population from political chaos and to maintain law and order, which, according to the most renowned historian of the Constitutional Revolution, Ahmad Kasravi, were for the benefit of the foreign powers to alleviate any concerns they may have had that the Shah might be overstepping the bounds of constitutional rule.[3]

On 23 June 1908, on the Shah's orders, Liakhov shelled the Majles and the next day government troops bombarded and ransacked

Figure 2.1 The Bagh-e Shah Twenty-Two in E.G. Browne's *The Persian Revolution*. (Source: E.G. Brownes', *The Persian Revolution 1905–1909*, pp. 210–11)

the princely residences of Mas'ud Mirza Zell al-Soltan, of his son Jalal al-Dowleh, and of Zahir al-Dowleh, husband of Princess Forugh al-Dowleh, daughter of Naser al-Din Shah. The reason for these actions was the Shah's accusation that they had harboured meetings of secret societies such as the *anjoman-e okhovvat* (The Society of Brotherhood) and that soldiers had been targeted and shot at from these residences.[4] On that same day, constitutionalists who had gathered in the Sepahsalar mosque, near the Majles, were violently evicted and dispersed. Those who survived the attack sought refuge, some in the home of Mohsen Khan Amin al-Dowleh, husband of Princess Fakhr al-Dowleh, daughter of Mozaffar al-Din Shah, some in the Ottoman Embassy, some in the British Legation and some in their own homes and the homes of nearby relatives. Eventually, those who had not taken refuge in the foreign embassies were apprehended and taken to the Bagh-e Shah, the summer residence of the Shah, which, since 3 June had been his command centre and subsequently became a place of detention for the losers of the confrontations three weeks later.

The first victims of the Shah were the fiery orator Hajji Mirza Nasrollah (Malek al-Motekallemin) and the editor of the journal *Sur-e Esrafil*, Mirza Jahangir Khan, who were both summarily executed on 24 June 1908.[5] The others are described below in the story of the Bagh-e Shah Twenty-Two and their other companions at the 'Shah's Garden'.[6]

There are several versions of the famous picture, five of which are known to this author.[7] The four published versions are found in E. G. Browne's *The Persian Revolution 1905–1909*;[8] in Ahmad Kasravi's *Tarikh-e mashruteh-ye Iran*;[9] in Seyfollah Vahidnia, *Dar zir-e tigh*;[10] and in a book co-edited by Abdol-Hoseyn Zarrinkub and Ruzbeh Zarrinkub.[11]

Kasravi's and Vahidnia's photos are virtually identical except for a dark spot in the upper right-hand corner of the Vahidnia version. The version in the Zarrinkub edition is different in the numbers assigned to the persons in it for identification purposes; in the information written below each number; in the angle from which the picture was taken – slightly more to the left from the frontal view in Kasravi and Vahidnia; and in the position of the distich composed for the occasion by someone sympathetic to the cause of the revolutionaries. In Zarrinkub the distich is centred at the bottom of the picture between the descriptions of the individuals in it, while in Kasravi and Vahidnia it is centred at the top and across the length of the picture. Browne's picture is different in

Figure 2.2 The Bagh-e Shah Twenty-Two, in Vahidnia's *Dar zir-e tigh*. (Source: Seyfollah Vahidnia, *Dar zir-e tigh*, Appendix, p.6)

several ways from the others: the picture is taken from a position to the right-of-centre; the prisoners are arranged in a semi-circle arching down and to the right, away from the steps and towards the photographer, and the positions of two of the prisoners have changed from standing to sitting.[12] Additionally the distich in Browne's version differs from all other versions, as does the numbering of the prisoners written in for purposes of identification. The distich in the other versions reads: *khahi ke dadad bar dard-e sad selseleh bidad ra, mennat bekesh, gardan beneh zanjir-e estebdad ra* (If you wish your cry to be heard by legions hence, bear the burden, wear the chains of tyranny). In Browne's it reads: *ankeh da'em havas-e sukhtan-e ma mikard, kash miamad va az dur tamasha mikard* (He whose constant wish for us was to burn, would that he could see us now from a distance).[13] Also, in Browne's version, at the bottom centre, the words '*fada'iyan-e mashruteh-ye Iran, 1326–1908, zendeh bad azadi, 23 jumada al-ula*' (Martyrs of the Constitutional Movement of Iran, 1326–1908, 'Long Live Liberty' 23 Jumada al-Ula) are added.

It is difficult to say with certainty which of the versions of this photograph was taken first, but it is clear that all were taken within a

THE BAGH-E SHAH TWENTY-TWO   31

short time span. This is evident from the virtually identical position of the crouching detainees, positions that could not be maintained for long or be reassumed with such similarity. It is also clear that these photographs were taken on the day of the capture of the detainees by the authorities, as indicated in all the narratives of the events.

The pictures also reveal that the prisoners had already been subjected to mistreatment by the time they were photographed, as several of the detainees are wearing bandages on their heads, covering wounds. The names of the detainees and their occupations, where listed, also indicate that the revolutionaries came from an urban population, but from a wide cross-section of that urban population, thus underlining the fact that the revolution was indeed a middle-class phenomenon of the intelligentsia, but one also supported by members of the aristocracy, the clergy, and by members of the merchant classes and of the poorer segments of society.

Though it may appear so to the casual observer, the detainees are not random, as people caught up in a *razzia* on demonstrators by authorities would be. These individuals were particularly sought for detention, though the full story of some of their specific roles as members of the opposition to the Shah's rule, their connections with larger movements and forces beyond their evident affiliations, and the Shah's actual reasons for ordering their detention and elimination may still have to be written.

After taking up residence at the Bagh-e Shah on 3 June 1908, some nine days later, on 12 June, Mohammad Ali Shah named eight individuals he wanted expelled from the capital because of their participation in the Tupkhaneh events of 16 and 17 December 1907.[14] E.G. Browne lists these individuals as follows: 'Mirza Jahangir Khan, editor of the *Sur-i-Israfil*; Sayyid Muhammad Riza of Shiraz, the editor of *Musawat*; the great Nationalist orators *Maliku'l-Mutakallimin* and Aqa Sayyid Jamal, both of Isfahan; Mirza Dawud Khan; the *Zahiru's-Sultan*, a cousin of the Shah and a prominent officer of the National Volunteers;[15] Hajji Yahya Dawlatabadi;[16] and Mirza 'Ali Muhammad *"Biradar"*.' 'In addition to the expulsion of these leaders of the popular party,' writes Browne, 'the Shah demanded control of the Press and disarmament of the people.'[17] Mangol Bayat, citing Mokhber al-Saltaneh Hedayat's *Khaterat va Khatarat*, also makes reference to this list by the Shah, but mentions other individuals left out by Browne, specifically: Jamal al-Din

Va'ez, Taqizadeh, and the editor of *'Roh al-Qods'* [sic] which, she says, also 'figured in the royal blacklist'.[18]

On the day of the raid on the constitutionalists who had gathered in the Sepahsalar Mosque and the Majles (23 June 1908), more than 250 people died on both sides.[19] Browne describes the fate of those not killed in the shelling by the Cossack Brigade as follows:

> Of the leaders of the people, Sayyid Taqi-zada, the *Mu'azidu's-Saltana* and some thirty or forty others succeeded in reaching the shelter of the British Legation, which, however, was instructed to admit only those fugitives that were in danger of their lives. The eight Nationalists whose expulsion the Shah had previously demanded, and who had taken refuge in the Sipahsalar college, fled to the house of the *Aminu'd-Dawla*, which was close at hand, but this traitor at once telephoned news of their arrival to the Cossack headquarters, and soldiers were immediately sent out to arrest them.[20] One, Hajji Mirza Ibrahim, was killed while resisting the soldiers' attempt to strip him, and the others were taken to the Shah's camp at Bagh-i-Shah, where the next day Mirza Jahangir Khan and the *Maliku'l-Mutakallimin* were strangled.[21] The Shah's cousin, Prince *Zahiru's-Sultan*, was also led out for execution, but was spared at the last moment, owing, it was said, to the declaration of his mother, the sister of the late Muzaffaru'd-Din-Shah, that she would kill herself if her son were put to death.[22] After being cross-examined, he was finally released and allowed to go to Europe. Of the remaining four, Sayyid Muhammad Riza succeeded in escaping, and wandered about, enduring extreme hardships from hunger and exposure, in Mazandaran and Gilan, but ultimately had the good fortune to reach a place of safety.[23] Aqa Sayyid Jamal also escaped from Tihran, but is believed to have been captured in disguise near Hamadan and put to death.[24] The *Mustasharu'd-Dawla*, the honest and fearless Tabriz deputy, and Prince Yahya Mirza long lay in chains and captivity at the Bagh-i-Shah, with many other prisoners ...[25]

Among those seeking refuge in the British legation was also Mirza Ali Akbar Khan, Dehkhoda, who, as Browne relates also, together with Taqizadeh and his colleague Mo'azed al-Saltaneh ultimately ended up in England and Switzerland, respectively. Taqizadeh and Moʻazed al-Saltaneh would form and support the Persia Committee on 30 October 1908, of which Browne was a founding member, and Dehkhoda in Yverdon went on to revive the *Sur-e Esrafil* from exile, where he would be joined later by Moʻazed al-Saltaneh.[26]

In a slightly different version of the events, Abrahamian states that on 23 June, 39 people were arrested of those who 'failed to escape or take sanctuary in the Ottoman embassy'.[27] He mentions by name several of the individuals in the picture being discussed, including Qazi Qazvini, Soltan al-Olama, Hajji Ebrahim and Yahya Mirza, as well as some of the individuals related to the people in the picture such as Hajji Mirza Nasrollah (Malek al-Motekallemin) and Jahangir Khan. Abrahamian also clarifies Browne's mention of 'Aqa Sayyid Jamal' as Jamal al-Din Esfahani, about whom he relates the same sequence of events as Browne. Abrahamian also mentions the preachers Abdollah Behbahani and Mohammad Tabatabaʻi as among the 39 arrested, and states that they were put under house arrest rather than being brought to the Bagh-e Shah, confirming therefore the account by Kasravi that because they were *seyyed*s and because Malekeh Jahan, the wife of Mohammad Ali Shah and daughter of Kamran Mirza (Nayeb al-Saltaneh), liked Tabatabaʻi, they were treated with more leniency.[28]

Of the persons named as part of the Shah's list and as part of the refugees in the British legation or detainees at the Bagh-e Shah, only the following are seen in the picture that is the subject of our discussion, and this is what is known of their fates.

From the Shah's list by Browne: Mirza Davud Khan (Vahidnia 15; Browne 21), the partner of Mirza Jahangir Khan Shirazi, editor of the *Sur-e Esrafil*, who was strangled together with Hajji Mirza Nasrollah (Malek al-Motekallemin). No information is given in the sources consulted as to the ultimate fate of this Mirza Davud Khan.

From the Shah's list by Mangol Bayat: Abrahamian relates that Soltan al-Olama Khorasani (Vahidnia 2; Browne 10) was tortured and poisoned at the Bagh-e-Shah,[29] but Bayat does offer some background to the reason why he was on the Shah's list to begin with. In November 1907, a month before the Tupkhaneh events, Soltan al-Olama Khorasani published a strongly worded article in *Ruh al-Qodos*, which directly threatened the Shah.[30] Bayat states that the article 'prompted the minister of the press to summon its author, Soltan al-Olama Khorasani, who was also the editor of the paper. Nevertheless, despite the explicit threat and the disrespectful tone, he was not punished. In the *Majles*, Speaker Ehtesham al-Saltana passionately defended freedom of the press, even though he readily declared articles defaming religion or the government were not to be tolerated. He successfully pushed for a resolution to issue a warning to the paper but to pardon Khorasani for his offense that time.'[31]

From the second list discussed by Browne, which does not completely match the list of the Shah he cites earlier, only Prince Yahya Mirza (Vahidnia 16; Browne 20) is featured in Browne's picture. Browne adds this about the fate of the Prince: 'Yahya Mirza, after several weeks' captivity in the Bagh-i-Shah, was at length released, and lived to be re-elected a member of the new *Majlis*, but he died shortly after it was opened (in the latter half of 1909), as a result of his sufferings during his confinement.'[32]

Of the remaining prisoners in the picture, the following are mentioned in Abrahamian's list: Sheikh Ali of Qazvin (Vahidnia 1; Browne 11), whom Browne describes as 'one of the few survivors of the twelve chosen followers' of Seyyed Jamal al-Din Asadabadi (Afghani), and was also one of the chief judges of the Supreme Court of the time of the Revolution.[33] Browne states that he was one of the prisoners in the Bagh-e Shah 'on whom the ex-Shah's wrath fell most heavily'.[34] He was tortured and then poisoned.[35] Though not mentioned by Abrahamian, Mirza Mohammad Ali Khan (Vahidnia 8; Browne 4) was the author of the article in *Taraqqi*, a work in refutation of religions (*radd-e mazaheb*), the content of which was equivalent to apostasy.[36] He was also, according to Browne, an associate of Sheykh Ali of Qazvin and also one of the chosen 'twelve disciples' of Jamal al-Din Asadabadi (Afghani).[37] From this it must be surmized that he too was killed at the Bagh-e Shah.

Additionally Abrahamian specifies that 19 of the 39 detainees were given prison sentences, adding: 'These included four merchants, one tobacconist, one tailor, two former army officers, one prince, two journalists, six civil servants, and two household servants belonging to one of the princely prisoners.'[38] Extrapolating from this statement, we can thus also account for the fates of Hajji Mohammad Taqi Bonakdar (Vahidnia 21; Browne 15) and Mashhadi Baqer (Vahidnia 9; Browne 3), two of these four merchants; Hajji Khan Khayyat (Vahidnia 19; Browne 17), the tailor; Mirza Ali Akbar Khan Mo'tamed al-Divan (Vahidnia 12;

Browne 13), one of the six civil servants; Shahzadeh Naser al-Mamalek (Vahidnia 11; Browne 1), the prince; Heshmat Nezam (Vahidnia 10; Browne 2) and Aqa Ali Sarbaz (Vahidnia 7; Browne 5), the two former soldiers; Sharif Sahhaf (Vahidnia 7; Browne 5) and Sheykh Ebrahim (Vahidnia 4; Browne 8), the two journalists; Aqa Majid Sigarforush (Vahidnia 5; Browne 7), the tobacconist; and Ali Beg (Vahidnia 20; Browne 16) and Mirza Hoseyn Gomashteh (Vahidnia 3; Browne 9), the two servants.

This leaves Sheykh Ebrahim Talaqani (Vahidnia 18; Browne 18), Mirza Bozorg Tabrizi (Vahidnia 17; Browne 19), and Nayeb Baqer Khan (Vahidnia 14; Browne 22) unaccounted for, unless they fit into one of the categories Abrahamian mentions. Mirza Bozorg Tabrizi (also called 'Aqa Bozorg Khan' by Browne) may in fact be the same person as 'Sayyid Hajji Ibrahim Aqa, the liberal deputy from Tabriz' mentioned by Abrahamian. If so, as Abrahamian relates, he was killed trying to escape from the Bagh-e Shah. Mirza Mohammad Ali (Vahidnia 13; Browne 12), the son of the fiery preacher Malek al-Motekallemin, was released after the killing of his father, as Kasravi relates in his *Tarikh*. As to the others, the assumption must be that they too received only jail sentences and thus survived the ordeal unless otherwise recorded in one of the accounts of the revolution besides the ones consulted. One who survived the ordeal was Mirza Ali Akbar Qazvini (Vahidnia 22; Browne 14), the brother of Sheykh Ali of Qazvin, who left the account of the prisoners quoted in Kasravi mentioned below in connection with Yahya Mirza's ordeal and fate.

Among the Bagh-e Shah Twenty-Two, Yahya Mirza Eskandari (Vahidnia 16; Browne 20) is of particular interest. There are only two pictures of Yahya Mirza extant: one a formal portrait taken at a photographer's studio and the other the picture of him and 21 other detainees, taken at the Bagh-e Shah on Tuesday 23 June 1908/23 Jumada al-Ula 1326, the day of their capture. To understand why Yahya Mirza Eskandari ended up as one of the prisoners in the Bagh-e Shah, we must briefly retrace the context and the intellectual influences that led him to become the prominent constitutionalist he was. To do so we must also point to the many intellectual and religious strands that came together to form the complex fabric of the Constitutional Revolutionary movement itself.

Intricate connections linked many of the revolutionaries of the Constitutional period and formed the intellectual background from which they drew inspiration and support. To give some idea about these connections and cross-connections which brought the revolutionaries together in a common cause, one could point, for instance, to the Dar al-Fonun, Naser al-Din Shah's progressive polytechnic school, where many of the prominent members of the movement were educated.[39] Then there was the Azali/Babi connection. Many of the leaders of the revolution were at least strongly influenced by the reformist and universalist ideas of this creed, if not being outright, though secret, adherents of it.[40] Another was the *anjoman* connection. Almost all of the members of the opposition belonged to one or another of the many societies that had sprung up around the time of the revolution, and some of these were more radical than others, such as that of the *fada'iyan*, a society to which the assassin of Prime-Minister Amin al-Soltan, Abbas Aqa, belonged and which had ties to Jamal al-Din Asadabadi (Afghani). Another was the Freemasonry connection, brought to Persia from the time of the first students sent by Abbas Mirza to Europe and by the first envoys of Fath Ali Shah to Europe such as Askar Khan and Abol Hasan Khan but also and closer to the time of the revolution, by Malkum Khan and his *faramushkhaneh* (House of Oblivion), which was modelled on the masonic lodges of Europe and reputedly connected to them.[41] Another connection was the link to and support by foreign powers such as Britain of individual players in the opposition. Finally there was the connection with particular individuals, such as Mirza Malkum Khan, Seyyed Jamal al-Din Asadabadi, and Hasan Taqizadeh, of various participants in the revolution, and although for many revolutionaries these connections did overlap in different combinations and configurations, a connection to one group did not necessarily entail connection to the others as well.

Several chroniclers of the events of 23 June 1908 give details on the fate of the individuals detained by the authorities and their backgrounds that help uncover some of the reasons for their detention and also show us the deeper connections just referred to. For instance, as Janet Afary states, the founder of *Sur-e Esrafil*, Mirza Jahangir Khan Shirazi who was strangled on 24 June 1908 at the Bagh-e Shah together with Hajji Mirza Nasrollah (Malek al-Motekallemin) 'was a graduate of the Dar al-Funun and an Azali Babi who had been influenced by Mirza Aqa Khan Kermani'.[42] Mirza Jahangir Khan had hired Mirza Ali Akbar Qazvini (Dehkhoda) as writer and editor for *Sur-e Esrafil* after a recommendation by Hasan Taqizadeh, one of the main leaders of the revolutionary movement. Dehkhoda himself was a graduate of the Dar al-Fonun and, as Afary relates, 'both Dehkhoda and Mirza Jahangir Khan were members of the secret National Revolutionary Committee in Tehran', which in turn had ties to one of the more radical *anjoman*s, the Organization of the Social Democrats.[43] Much the same is true of the background of Yahya Mirza Eskandari.

Yahya Mirza Eskandari was born c.1874–5. He was the eldest son of Mohsen Mirza (Kafil al-Dowleh) and grandson of Hajj Mohammad Taher Mirza, cousin and French tutor of Naser al-Din Shah, best remembered as the translator of the works of Alexandre Dumas (father), including *The Three Musketeers* and *The Count of Monte Cristo*.[44] Together with his brother Soleyman Mirza, Yahya Mirza greatly influenced the course of the Constitutional movement in the direction of secularism and progressivism, ideas to which Yahya Mirza was exposed at a young age in his family and through his education at the Dar al-Fonun. Yahya Mirza's uncle, Mohammad Ali Mirza Eskandari, known as Prince Ali Khan, was one of the instructors at the Dar al-Fonun when Soleyman Mirza and Yahya Mirza were both students at that institution. Prince Ali Khan is remembered not only for his role as a teacher at the Dar al-Fonun, but also as the translator of the most radical work of the populist French writer Eugène Sue, *Les Mystères du Peuple*,[45] and as a founding member of one of the most influential secret societies of the Constitutional era, the Adamiyat Society.[46] Prince Ali Khan's academic and political work was one of the key influences on the intellectual and political lives of both Yahya and Soleyman Mirza Eskandari. Yahya Mirza and Soleyman Mirza both joined the *anjoman-e adamiyat* in 1906. Before that they and other members of the Eskandari family were members of the more radical *komiteh-ye enqelabi*, the Revolutionary Committee, another of the prominent secret societies of the time.[47] The pair split from the Adamiyat Society in 1907, after the Tupkhaneh events of December that year,[48] to form the *anjoman-e hoquq*, the Society for Civil Rights, a more radical association with a more progressive agenda than that of the Adamiyat Society.[49]

Yahya Mirza was the deputy from Tehran in the First Majles, and served, together with Taqizadeh, as leader of its Liberal faction. The First Majles opened in October of 1906, and divided itself into roughly three factions: the Royalists, the Moderates, and the Liberals. The Royalists, representing the court, were led by princes and notables connected with the court. Two wealthy merchants, Mohammad Ali Shalforush and Hajji Ali Amin al-Zarb, led the Moderates, representing the merchant and middle classes. The Liberals, representing the intelligentsia, were led by Taqizadeh, deputy from Tabriz, and Yahya Mirza, deputy from Tehran, and they 'advocated extensive social and economic as well as political reforms'.[50] Yahya Mirza's career as deputy was interrupted when the events of 1908 – the shelling of the Majles on 23 June by the Cossack Brigade and his subsequent imprisonment and torture at the Bagh-e Shah prison – intervened. After his release from jail, Yahya Mirza was re-elected as deputy from Tehran to the Second Majles in 1909.[51] He was, however, not able to serve in his elected position and died in 1909, in his early 30s, as a result of complications from the torture he suffered the year prior. His brother Soleyman Mirza assumed his seat in the assembly, holding it until the dissolution of the Second Majles in December 1911.

Yahya Mirza's last contribution to the politics of Persia was an intellectual one in the form of the novella *Arusi-ye Mehrangiz* (Mehrangiz's Wedding). In the introduction to the publication of this novella in their journal *Iran-e now*, the editors state that Yahya Mirza personally brought the finished version of the novella to them a week before he died. Their epitaph to him reads as follows:

> *Arusi-e Mehrangiz* is a novella from the pen of deceased *mojahed* Yahya Mirza, and will be published from today on, in instalments in the pages of *Iran-e now*. A martyr in the cause of the people, and ill-fated deputy of the people, Yahya Mirza was one among those who sacrificed themselves for liberty, and whose death for the future wellbeing of the nation is a loss that cannot be replaced. Yahya Mirza is known to most of our readers and to the educated people of Iran. This is the same Yahya Mirza who during the lesser constitutional phase was editor of the journal *Hoquq*, and who in those pages would genuinely and assiduously strive to explain the intricacies of the Fundamental Law in easy to understand terms to the people of the nation. At the greater *mashruteh*, he was elected by the people of Tehran as deputy to the national assembly, but before the opening of the *Majles*, passed away from this world. The reason for his untimely death was the torture inflicted on him in the Bagh-e Shah prison of Mohammad Ali Mirza, which made his precious being ill. While

under treatment for the injuries suffered, he could not withstand the pressures of the necessary operations, and passed away. Our venerable readers are aware of the circumstances under which he passed away. The deceased brought this book one week before his death to our office and honoured us by allowing us to publish it whenever we deemed convenient. We are herewith greatly honoured to be able to comply with the wishes of this great-souled martyr.[52]

The archives of the International Institute of Social History in Amsterdam, of which Professor Touraj Atabaki is a director and senior researcher, contain the most complete files on the activities of the communist Tudeh Party of Iran during the years of exile of its leadership in Eastern Europe. It is fitting therefore to complete these archives with choice passages about Yahya Mirza Eskandari by his son Iraj Eskandari, co-founder and later secretary-general of the Tudeh Party, and with passages by Mirza Ali Akbar Khan Qazvini, as quoted in Ahmad Kasravi, who shared a cell in the Bagh-e Shah with this extraordinary champion for freedom and justice in Iran.

When looking at the photograph of the detainees of the Bagh-e Shah, some of the heads of the prisoners in the picture are bandaged from injuries sustained during arrest or subsequent beatings. Yahya Mirza's head, however, is not bandaged; he wears the garb of a mullah and this is a puzzling fact, to say the least, given that Yahya Mirza was the most secular of people and was not a preacher or in the habit of wearing this traditional garb. Another puzzling fact is the absence of Soleyman Mirza among the ranks of the prisoners at the Bagh-e Shah. Both these puzzles are explained by Iraj Eskandari, in his memoirs:

> Now that I look back at my childhood days, I see my life as it was then, deeply imbued with a host of political matters. I was one year old when my father, Yahya Mirza Eskandari, died. Of course, I cannot recall anything personally of my father, but as far back as I can recall, I heard from everyone – my mother, my paternal grandmother, my father's father (Mohsen Mirza Eskandari) and my mother's father (Ali Khan Mirza Eskandari), my paternal uncles, maternal uncles, paternal aunts, and also possibly others – that my father was a martyr for liberty under the chains of Mohammad Ali Shah at the Bagh-e Shah. He was one of the

noted Constitutionalists, a learned man and able speaker, who rose up against the autocracy of Mohammad Ali Shah, and who, as a result, had lost his life in this struggle.

My paternal grandmother, who would always remember him with the greatest respect and sorrow, would relate that one day the Silahkhor[53] surrounded our house (my paternal grandfather's house), with orders to arrest my father and my uncle (Soleyman Mirza Eskandari), who had been betrayed to the authorities by spies of the autocrats 'who had received them first but then secretly betrayed to the Bagh-e Shah'.[54]

My father and my uncle, in order to stave off the entry of the Silahkhor into our home, decided to leave the house and to save themselves in some way. For this reason Yahya Mirza put on the turban of the *akhund* who would come to the house for the instruction of my aunts (because in those days there were no public schools for women yet), wore the cloak and garment (*aba* and *reda*) of the cleric, and with this disguise left the house. At the little bazaar of Sangelaj, the children who had not seen an *akhund* with a European-style neck-tie before, began to make noise and made up this (nonsensical rhyming) verse: '*anjir-o mamchirash kon, fokoli ra zanjirash kon*' (... put *the fokoli* [literally: man with the *faux-col*] in chains). These noisy urchins thus drew the attention of the Silahkhor to my father whom they promptly apprehended.

When the four Silahkhor apprehended my father, he asked them why they were apprehending him. They answered: 'We do not know. Our chief ordered us to.' At this point Soleyman Mirza asked them: 'Well does your chief also give you money for this purpose?' They answered in the negative. Soleyman Mirza then replied 'I have thirty-five tumans money in my pocket; if you take me to a safe place I will give you that money'. The Silahkhor who were now faced with this offer, conferred among themselves and agreed on condition that he also give his pocket watch and clothes. Soleyman Mirza agreed but said 'first take me to a place where I can take off my clothes and give to you'. They agreed and took him to my maternal grandfather's home (Ali Khan Mirza Eskandari) and left after receiving the promised sum. Soleyman Mirza would remain in that home, which at that time was outside the city limits (Jey and Beryanak), until the fall of Mohammad Ali Shah.[55]

THE BAGH-E SHAH TWENTY-TWO 41

Ahmad Kasravi, in memorializing the events of the Constitutional Revolution, quotes Yahya Mirza's jail-mate, Mirza Ali Akbar Qazvini, in remembrance of Yahya Mirza's actions and words in the dungeons of the Bagh-e Shah:[56]

> From that day on persons who had been apprehended as part of the followers Tabataba'i and others, and who were innocent, one by one were taken to the room, interrogated and released.[57]
>
> Aqa Mohammad Ali, the son of Malek, was released after the incident (*hadeseh*) involving his father. Thus our numbers were greatly reduced. At this time they brought Yahya Mirza to us, whom they had captured, and it was then that they took all 22 of us in chains in the shape we were in, to take pictures of us. After that they also brought Seyyed Ya'qub Shirazi to us. We 20-some persons thus spent our days in chains that way.[58]
>
> Lunch and dinner for each person was a round bread and cucumbers, and each day, they would take us out eight by eight in chains, and one has to imagine what suffering we went through and how embarrassed we were in front of each other. In all this they would not spare us any torture or hurt, with regard to some of us in particular, especially the poor editor of *Ruh al-Qodos* and Zia' al-Soltan.
>
> The tribunal that had been set up was investigating three matters and by means of torture and pressure wanted to get information from individuals. These three matters were: 1) who had thrown the bomb at the Shah? 2) Who was the founder of the anjoman in the house of Azdelmolk?[59] and 3) Who was giving rifles to the mojaheds? These were the questions they were pursuing. Other than that they were not interested in the events of the Majles and the Mashruteh (Constitutional Movement).
>
> As they suspected that the editor of *Ruh al-Qodos* and Zia' al-Soltan had knowledge of the background to the attempt on the Shah's life, they were subjected to severe torture. Every night they would be taken out and tied to stools and beaten severely, and though their cries would resonate in the entire Bagh-e Shah, none of those generals and Ministers present would come to their rescue.
>
> The pitiful state of these unfortunate men made us forget our own dire circumstances. Finally it was Loqman al-Molk, the

physician of the Shah, who felt pity on these unfortunate ones and angrily said, 'until when do we have to tremble in fear and till when will the trouble of these poor devils continue?' As a result of his anger and complaints the torturing of these two stopped.

This Loqman al-Molk, may God bless his soul, also did us another great favour. We had no other undergarments other than the ones on our persons, which after a few days were torn and in worn out condition. al-Molk sent us each a pair of undergarments and with this act helped rescue our dignity.[60]

The head of our jailers was a lieutenant by the name of Soltan Baqer, who was also charged with torturing us. One night as always the poor editor of *Ruh al-Qodos* was taken and beaten from head to toe, and in that state of exhaustion was returned to our cell to be shackled again at the neck by Soltan Baqer. It was then that the jailer said to him 'After all this you still did not tell us?'. Despite the state he was in, he spoke up and said 'Mr. Soltan, what do I know in order to confess?' Baqer was pricked by this remark and took to whipping the poor soul another 20 or 30 blows. After that, still in anger, he turned to the others and randomly landed several blows on Hajji. To Hajji Mohammad Taqi, my brother Qazi, Yahya Mirza, Mirza Davud Khan, and Baqer Khan.

That night Yahya Mirza showed such courage that it left all of us in amazement. He would not flinch at the blows Baqer Khan was landing on his head and body. Realizing this, Baqer Khan, recoiled to collect himself and to assume a firmer position, which indicated to us that he was going to give him a terrible beating. Calmly, Yahya Mirza turned his shackled neck facing the wall, exposing his back to the coming hail of blows. Baqer Khan did not remain idle and lowered the whip some 60–70 times on the exposed back that was covered only by a shirt. We were sure he had fainted, but as soon as Baqer Khan was done landing his blows and had left the cell, Yahya Mirza turned to us and with a calm face said: 'Did that coward leave?' We were stunned at this display of courage, and his forbearance and calm was a source of consolation for all of us and our grief was as if cut in half.

He then began to talk by telling us stories of the sufferings and sacrifices of the French revolutionaries, and with his demeanour and words he calmed the fires raging in our hearts.

This Yahya Mirza was of fair complexion and handsome, and his behaviour even fairer. From the day he joined us, our singular solace was his conversations with us. His words of wisdom and the stories he related to us helped lighten our burden. That night when he suffered those blows yet did not refrain from calm conversation and story-telling, we became doubtful whether any blows had landed on him at all, and to assure ourselves we lifted his shirt, and saw that his entire back was swollen and bruised. This sight filled us with even more amazement.

We spent 12 days this way and on the 13th day they killed my brother, the judge... After this episode we still remained in jail for a while, until they had interrogated us to their satisfaction and since they did not receive any further information from us that was of use to them, they sent Yahya Mirza, Mirza Davud Khan and me to the home of Mo'ayyed al-Dowleh, the Governor of Tehran. There having received from each of us a guarantee, they released us.

Mohammad Ali Mirza[61] had a different fate in mind for Yahya Mirza, but Heshmat al-Dowleh intervened on his behalf, and for this reason he was sent to the custom-house of Astara after being released, but he did not survive long due to the injuries inflicted on him in jail, and he died soon thereafter. The editor of *Ruh al-Qodos* was taken to a cistern where they disposed of him.[62] The rest were released one by one.

In an interesting twist of fate, Iraj Eskandari, the son of Yahya Mirza Eskandari, would also spend precious years in jail under the next dictatorship, that of Reza Shah, in another jail which had previously also housed a Qajar summer palace, the Qasr Prison in the north of Tehran, and his jail-mates and companions were also some of the most prominent intellectuals of the time. Interestingly, Ahmad Kasravi, the writer of the history of the Constitutional Movement of Iran, became one of the lawyers defending this group of prisoners, who were remembered in the memoir written by Bozorg Alavi, one of the fellow prisoners and friend of Iraj Eskandari, titled 'The Fifty-Three' and published a few years after their release from Qasr prison in 1944.[63] Ervand Abrahamian's book, *Tortured Confessions* retraces in detail the years 1938–41, from the arrest of the 'Fifty-Three' in 1937, to their show trial in 1938, to the abdication of Reza Shah and their release in 1941.[64]

The influence of Yahya Mirza's example reverberated long after his untimely death, through his family. Many of the battles Iraj Eskandari fought within the Tudeh Party during his long life – from the questions about his commitment to the more radical direction the Tudeh took immediately after its founding at the house of Soleyman Mirza in 1941, to the leadership challenges in his later years and the questions about his patriotism that were inevitably raised by those who considered membership in a Communist Party *ipso facto* a betrayal of the homeland – were shaped by the memory of this exceptional father. As Abrahamian observed, Iraj Eskandari related in his memoirs that some even 'labelled him a "rightist" because he recognized the importance of individual rights, parliamentary politics, and constitutional laws'.[65]

No greater testimony to the importance of the influence of the Constitutional Movement and the impact of Yahya Mirza's life could be given than this statement by his son, that he had to 'defend' himself against the 'accusation' of being heir to the grand promise of that revolution and to that of his father's example, a promise that has yet to come to fruition in the modern Iran that was created out of the ashes of the Constitutional Revolution of 1905.

Notes

1. Parts of this article dealing with the prisoners at the Bagh-e Shah and the literary and political work of Yahya Mirza Eskandari have been published as separate articles in *Qajar Studies* vi (2006), pp. 113–43; and in *Iranian Studies* 40/4, xl (September 2007), pp. 511–28.
2. See Edward G. Browne, *The Persian Revolution of 1905–1909* (Cambridge: Cambridge University Press, 1910; Washington DC: Mage Publishers, 1995).
3. Ahmad Kasravi, *Tarikh-e mashruteh-ye Iran (History of the Constitutional Movement of Iran)*, volume 2 (Tehran: Amir Kabir, 2537/1357/1978), pp. 657–8. This is a confirming example of the thesis by Theda Skocpol that the actions of the state in pre-revolutionary and revolutionary situations are guided by its interest calculations and by external structural constraints imposed on the state by foreign powers. See Theda Skocpol, *States and Social Revolutions: A Comparative Analysis of France, Russia and China* (Cambridge: Cambridge University Press, 1979), Chapter One.
4. Kasravi, *Tarikh*, volume 2, p. 657. From his actions, it is clear that the Shah was concerned with two issues in particular: one, apprehending and punishing those who had incited people to revolutionary action through their speeches and publications; and two, apprehending and punishing those who had engaged in

THE BAGH-E SHAH TWENTY-TWO   45

actual violence against him and his government. The trigger for his ire against those who incited violence was, of course, the hand-grenade attack against his person on 28 February 1908, and a subsequent attack the next day on 1 March 1908, resulting in his first declaration of martial law on 10 June 1908.

5. See Browne, *The Persian Revolution*, Chapter Seven, pp. 196–210, for a day-to-day account of the events leading to the Bagh-e Shah photograph and the days immediately following that photograph. For reasons that are a mystery to me, despite the precise dating and day-to-day accounting that Browne gives, he miscalculates the date of 23 Jumada al-Ula 1326 as 'July 4, 1908' (p. 209). I have checked and rechecked this date. It is 23 June 1908.

6. The actual number of detainees at the Bagh-e Shah was closer to some 40, as prisoners would be brought in and released or executed. Not all of them are remembered by name or mentioned in the records of the period. As pointed out above, two of the prominent detainees were immediately executed. Two more, the preachers Behbahani and Tabataba'i, are also not mentioned or pictured among the 'Bagh-e Shah twenty-two'. Thus these 22 became symbolic of all the detainees and martyrs of the Bagh-e Shah events.

7. I have seen the original photograph, which became the template for the postcard made famous abroad through its publication by Browne, in a series of unpublished photographs accompanying an unpublished manuscript of the period. The publication of either would be a sensational addition to the study of this period of Iranian history.

8. Browne, *The Persian Revolution*, insert between pp. 210–11, states that the picture is a 'postcard' of the revolution, suggesting that it was widely circulated and bought (fn. 3, p. 209). One of these period postcards depicting the twenty-two Bagh-e Shah detainees is in my own library.

9. Kasravi, *Tarikh*, volume 2, p. 662.

10. Seyfollah Vahidnia, *Dar zir-e tigh* (*Under the Blade*) (Tehran: Dastan Publishers, 1999), Appendix, p. 6.

11. Abdol-Hoseyn Zarrinkub and Ruzbeh Zarrinkub (eds.), *Do resaleh dar bareh-ye enqelab-e mashruteh-ye Iran az Abolqasem Khan Naser al-Molk va Mohammad Aqa Iravani* (*Two Treatises on Iran's Constitutional Revolution by Abolqasem Khan Naser al-Molk and Mohammad Aqa Iravani*) (Tehran: Sazman-e Asnad-e Melli-ye Iran, 2001), p. 144.

12. Numbers 12 and 13 sitting in Browne's picture are standing as 2 and 4 in Zarrinkub's version and as 12 and 13 in Kasravi/Vahidnia.

13. Browne's list is on p. 209; Zarrinkub's is on p. 144.

14. The 'Tupkhaneh events' refer to the abortive coup by the Shah against the Constitutionalists, which centred around the main Artillery Square (Tupkhaneh) facing the Parliament (Majles). For a detailed description of these events, see among others Browne, *The Persian Revolution*, pp. 162–71 and Mangol Bayat, *Iran's First Revolution: Shi'ism and the Constitutional Revolution of 1905–1909* (Oxford: Oxford University Press, 1991), pp. 210–12.

15. This 'Zahiru's-Sultan' is Zahir al-Soltan, the son of Zahir al-Dowleh (Safi Ali Shah) and Princess Forugh al-Dowleh 'Malekeh-ye Iran', a prominent daughter of Naser al-Din Shah. Princess Forugh al-Dowleh and her daughters, Zahir al-Soltan's sisters, were also prominent Constitutionalists.
16. On the identity and background of Haji Mirza Yahya Dowlatabadi, see Abbas Amanat, 'Memory and Amnesia in the Historiography of the Constitutional Revolution', in Touraj Atabaki (ed.), *Iran in the 20th Century: Historiography and Political Culture* (London: I.B.Tauris 2009), p. 30.
17. Browne, *The Persian Revolution*, p. 204.
18. Bayat, *Iran's First Revolution*, p. 212.
19. Browne states the number of dead as 'unknown' (*The Persian Revolution*, p. 208), whereas Abrahamian gives it as 'over 250' in *Between Two Revolutions* (Princeton: Princeton University Press, 1982), p. 96.
20. This '*Aminu'd-Dawla*' was Mohsen Khan Amin al-Dowleh II, husband of Princess Fakhr al-Dowleh and son of the famous Mirza Ali Khan Amin al-Dowleh I.
21. For pictures of Mirza Jahangir Khan and Hajji Mirza Nasrollah (Malek al-Motekallemin) see Browne, *The Persian Revolution*, inserts between pp. 208–9 and 204–5, respectively.
22. See note 15 above.
23. This was the editor of the newspaper *Mosavat* (*Musawat*) mentioned in Mohammad Ali Shah's list reproduced by Browne, *The Persian Revolution*, p. 204.
24. For a picture of Aqa Seyyed Jamal al-Din Esfahani, see Browne, *The Persian Revolution*, insert between pp. 204–5.
25. Ibid., pp. 208–9.
26. Ibid., p. 264.
27. Abrahamian, *Between Two Revolutions*, p. 96. Abrahamian is the first to mention the Ottoman embassy as a place of refuge for the constitutionalists in addition to the British legation, which is located a short distance to the north-west of the Ottoman embassy.
28. Ibid., p. 97. See also Kasravi, *Tarikh*, volume 2, p. 661. For pictures of Tabataba'i and Behbahani, see ibid., volume 1, pp. 2 and 53 respectively.
29. Abrahamian, *Between Two Revolutions*, p. 96.
30. For the translation of the article, see Browne, *The Persian Revolution*, pp. 156–9.
31. Bayat, *Iran's First Revolution*, p. 211.
32. Browne, *The Persian Revolution*, p. 208, fn. 2.
33. Ibid., p. 209.
34. Browne, *The Persian Revolution*, p. 10.
35. Abrahamian, *Between Two Revolutions*, p. 96.
36. Browne, *The Persian Revolution*, p. 10.
37. Ibid.
38. Abrahamian, *Between Two Revolutions*, p. 97.
39. Founded in 1851 by Naser al-Din Shah through the efforts of his Prime Minister Mirza Taqi Khan, Amir Kabir, the Dar al-Fonun was the premier

institution of secular learning in Iran, where European and Persian instructors taught a variety of disciplines ranging from sciences to art, literature, philosophy, languages, politics and more, introducing into Persian society Western ideas in a systematic way for the first time. The Dar al-Fonun was under the direct tutelage of the Shah himself and over 1,000 students had graduated from it by 1891. The names of its instructors and students are legend in Iran to this day.

40. See in particular Abbas Amanat 'Memory and Amnesia', pp. 27–36.
41. On the Masonic connections of the Constitutionalists see Mangol Bayat, 'The Rowshanfekr in the Constitutional Period', in H. E. Chehabi and Vanessa Martin (eds.), *Iran's Constitutional Revolution: Popular Politics, Cultural Transformations and Transnational Connections* (London: I.B.Tauris, 2010), pp. 174–80.
42. Janet Afary, *The Iranian Constitutional Revolution, 1906–1911* (New York: Columbia University Press, 1996), p. 117.
43. Ibid.
44. The translations of the works of Alexandre Dumas by Mohammad Taher Mirza Eskandari were an instant sensation and created an indigenous industry of novelists copying the style of Dumas and even continuing some of his stories in the Persian context, such as the novel *Pesar-e Monte Kristo* (*The Son of Monte Cristo*). The message of Alexandre Dumas's work, particularly that of the story of Monte Cristo, was one of justice, and in this sense it joined a long tradition of morality tales already indigenous to Persian literature.
45. Eugène Sue (1804–57) was one of the most prominent writers of his time. *Les Mystères du Peuple a Travers les Ages*, a ten-volume odyssey of a 'proletarian family through the ages from ancient Gaul to the eve of the 1848 Revolution in France', written in 1849, was his most radical and controversial work.
46. Regarding the origins of the Adamiyat Society, see Bayat, *Iran's First Revolution*, pp. 165–7 and 220–1; see also Abrahamian, *Iran Between Two Revolutions*, p. 77.
47. With regard to the membership of the Revolutionary Committee and its intellectual and political bent see Abrahamian, *Iran Between Two Revolutions*, p. 79.
48. For a description of the Tupkhaneh events, as already mentioned, see among others, Bayat, *Iran's First Revolution*, pp. 210–14.
49. The *anjoman-e hoquq*, was founded first as a branch of the Adamiyat Society. See Bayat, *Iran's First Revolution*, p. 221. The organ of the Anjoman-e hoquq was the journal *Hoquq*, of which Yahya Mirza was the editor.
50. See Abrahamian, *Iran Between Two Revolutions*, pp. 88 and 103–6.
51. Mehdi Qoli Mokhber al-Saltaneh Hedayat, *Gozaresh-e Iran: Qajariyeh va mashrutiyat* (Tehran: Nashr-e Noqreh, 1984) p. 248, lists the deputies to the Second Majles from Tehran as follows: Hajj Seyyed Nasrollah, Ehtesham al-Saltaneh, Vosuq al-Dowleh, Hakim al-Molk, Sadiq Hazrat, Mostashar al-Dowleh, Taqizadeh, Zoka' al-Molk, Sani' al-Dowleh, Hoseyn Qoli Khan Navvab, Asadollah Mirza, Sheykh Hoseyn Yazdi, Yahya Mirza, Mo'tamen al-Molk, and Vahid al-Molk.

52. *Iran-e now* iii/3 (24 October 1910), p. 3. (Translation mine.)
53. *Silahkhor* or *Silahkhori* were troops of Kurdish origin in the service of the Shah and together with the Cossack Brigades were used as enforcers of the Shah's will during the Constitutional Revolution. They were greatly feared by the general population. See for instance Browne, *The Persian Revolution*, p. 201.
54. This is a reference to the betrayal by Mohsen Khan Amin al-Dowleh of the refugees in his house on 23 June 1908.
55. Iraj Eskandari, *Khaterat-e siyasi (Political Memoirs)*, ed. Ali Dehbashi (Tehran: Elmi Publishers, 1989), pp. 17–18. (Translation mine.)
56. Kasravi, *Tarikh*, volume 2, pp. 661–6. (Translation mine.)
57. The interrogators, according to Kasravi, were: Mo'ayyed al-Dowleh, Governor of Tehran, Shahzadeh Mo'ayyed al-Saltaneh, Seyyed Mohsen Sadr al-Ashraf, Arshad al-Dowleh, one individual *mir panj* from the Qazzaq khaneh, Mirza Abdol Motalleb Yazdi (editor of the *Adamiyat* newspaper), writer of the police station, Mirza Ahmad Khan (Oshtori). (This last person showed great compassion towards the prisoners, says Kasravi).
58. The recollection of the sequence of events may be faulty as Malek al-Motekallemin and Jahangir Khan were killed the day after the picture of the detainees was taken at the Bagh-e Shah, as indicated above.
59. 'Azdelmolk' is Ali Reza Khan Azod al-Molk, the elder of the Qajar clan who would become Regent of Persia for Soltan Ahmad Mirza in 1909. His residence had been the gathering place of some of these *anjoman*s, a fashion and tradition similar to many of the *salons* on the eve of the French Revolution.
60. For a picture of Hakim Loqman al-Molk, see Kasravi, *Tarikh*, volume 2, p. 665.
61. i.e. the Shah. He was referred to as Mohammad Ali Mirza by those who could not forgive him for his autocracy and cruelty in the matter of the Constitutionalists at the Bagh-e Shah.
62. According to Kasravi, the editor of *Ruh al-Qodos* was thrown into a well (cistern) where he died after days of torture, hunger and deprivation. Kasravi, *Tarikh*, volume 2, p. 666, fn. 1.
63. Bozorg Alavi, *Panjah va seh nafar (The Fifty-Three)* (Reprint, Tehran: Amir Kabir, 1978).
64. Ervand Abrahamian, *Tortured Confessions: Prisons and Public Recantations in Modern Iran* (Berkeley: University of California Press, 1999), pp. 27–48. The term 'Fifty-Three' was also later applied to the Tudeh group that was arrested and charged after the attempted assassination of Mohammad Reza Shah in 1949, for which the Tudeh was blamed, even though the actual number of the Tudeh members put on trial was 50. See Abrahamian, *Tortured Confessions*, pp. 84–5.
65. Ibid., p. 81.

CHAPTER 3

THE PLACE OF SHI'I CLERICS IN THE FIRST IRANIAN CONSTITUTION*

Janet Afary

The 1906 Constitutional Revolution, Social Democrats and the Battle to Reduce Shi'i Authority

The first 'Awakening' of the non-European world took place at the turn of the early twentieth century. Nations such as Iran (1906–11), India (1905–8), Turkey (1908), and China (1911–12) witnessed dramatic social movements and uprisings, many of which involved non-violent protests. What is so remarkable about these movements is that, contrary to common assumptions, these were not just movements challenging the imperialist incursions of the West; rather, they also called for a more democratic social and political order at home and included calls for religious reform. Most were following the example of the Russian Revolution of 1905 and aspired to having a constitution and a parliamentary political system that checked the powers of the monarchy and the clerical establishment. For obvious reasons, the royalist factions were adamantly opposed to these new constitutional orders and did everything in their power to disarm them.

Cities such as Baku and Tbilisi were home to large populations of Shi'i Muslims, including many immigrant workers and merchants who had joined the revolutionary movement in Russia but regarded Iran as their ancestral homeland. Soon they formed their own secret social democratic cells in Baku. These cells adhered to a hybrid ideology, a mélange of European socialism and indigenous Shi'i Iranian ideas. They upheld liberalism and nationalism and called for political and social reforms. They demanded a redistribution of lands to peasants, reforms in child labour, modern education for boys and girls, an eight-hour day for factory employees, and other similar social democratic reforms. Although most were practicing Muslims, they also criticized the extreme authority of Shi'i clerics as well as certain Shi'i rituals, such as the practice of self-flagellation during the month of Muharram.[1]

These movements in the north had a dramatic influence on Iran's Constitutional Revolution of 1906. After more than a year of protests in Tehran and Qom in 1905–6, supporters of a new constitutional order succeeded in gaining the country's first constitution and parliament. In August 1906 the ailing monarch Mozaffar al-Din Shah (r. 1896–1907) signed an unprecedented royal proclamation that allowed the formation of a national parliamentary assembly, known as the Majles, and the drafting of a constitution.

Popular elections were soon held and the Majles opened in October 1906. A limited male franchise was established. As elsewhere in the world, women were excluded from the electoral process, and property and language qualifications barred peasants, workers, and many non-Persian-speaking tribes and communities. Still, the heavy representation of the trade guilds of Tehran and Tabriz, and the contribution of liberal and social democratic deputies, made the First Iranian Parliament one of the most respected institutions of modern Iran. Many parliamentary deputies and journalists were secretly affiliated with social democratic centres where debates within parliament were analysed and progressive agendas formulated.[2]

In their fight against the new monarch Mohammad Ali Shah and the clerics, constitutionalists relied on two sources: first, the new grassroots institutions of the revolution: local councils, known as *anjoman*s, their volunteer military force known as Mojahedin, and the radical newspapers; and second, the support they received from three progressive grand clerics in Najaf. Indeed, many reforms could not have happened without support from Najaf.

The First Majles accomplished a number of unprecedented deeds during its short-lived existence. It ratified a constitution, set up executive, legislative, and judicial branches of the government, and substantially reduced the powers of the monarchy. Majles deputies gained the right to remove irresponsible ministers and government officials. They balanced the state budget and allocated all major expenses. This move drastically curtailed the court budget and soon led to the permanent closing of the royal harem.

The National Assembly also challenged the authority of the British and Russian governments in Iran. The new constitution decreed that all major foreign transactions had to be ratified by the National Assembly. The era when European entrepreneurs and governments gained lucrative concessions in the country by slipping handsome pay-offs to the king and his cronies had come to an end.

This chapter focuses on the process whereby the Majles tried to reduce the powers of the clerical establishment. At the time Iran was ruled by two sets of laws: shari'a religious law, which was controlled by the Shi'i ulema, and *'urf* customary law, which was administered by the state. Even clerics who supported the Constitutional Revolution in the summer of 1906 had assumed that the new political order would reduce the powers of the king and reform *'urf* law, leaving shari'a laws more or less intact. However, liberal and social democratic deputies and journalists were determined to replace the binary legal system of Iran with a more modern secular structure. Deputies such as Hasan Taqizadeh, who were influenced by liberalism and social democratic ideas from Transcaucasia, spearheaded these radical reforms. Soon the novel discourses of the Constitutional Revolution would create a paradigm shift in Iranian society. Many clerics resisted these reforms. The result was a bifurcated set of laws that institutionalized clerical authority, while also placing limits on clerics in legislative and judicial branches of the government.

Institutionalization of Shi'ism in the Constitution

In Iran, as in other pre-modern societies, the traditional notion of justice differed dramatically from our contemporary understanding of the term. Justice (*'adl*) was one of the fundamental elements of Shi'ism and a precondition for the selection of a *marja'-e taqlid* or source of emulation. A *marja'* was expected to be a mature and respectable learned man known for his devotion to the faith and his intelligence. A just *marja'* was one who scrupulously adhered to the shari'a by refraining from what was prohibited and performing all that was obligated.[3] This included strict adherence to all social and class hierarchies in a legal system where women were treated far differently from men; Sunnis and those belonging to other Shi'i schools of Islam (Ismailis and Zaidis) had fewer rights than Twelver Shi'is; non-Muslims were subject to strict segregation and had added financial obligations in the form of *jezya* religious taxes; slaves occupied a position between humans and commodities. Even those belonging to Twelver Shi'ism were not treated the same in this traditional notion of *'adl*.

Shi'i leadership was decentralized and clerics were afforded great discretion in interpreting laws. Different clerics might issue different rulings for the same transgression, and the same crime could receive vastly different punishment depending on the judge and the location. Torture, corporeal punishment, or executions were viewed as proper punishment for certain crimes. These types of punishments, carried out by the state or its representatives, were generally performed during large public ceremonial events that were approved by the clerics and served as a means of both chastising the public and entertaining them.[4]

Many of these social hierarchies would be questioned and overturned in the course of the Constitutional Revolution, when new laws were promulgated in the hopes of creating a nation state with equal rights for all male citizens. The December 1906 Constitution was a progressive document, which substantially reduced the authority of the king – he remained head of the state, but his ministers answered to the parliament and could be dismissed by its authority. Parliament also had the right to ratify all major financial transactions and concessions with foreign powers. Freedom of the press was guaranteed in the constitution and parliamentary meetings were open to the public. Members also created new secular laws and judicial codes that reduced the powers of the clerics.[5]

In the winter of 1907, progressive parliamentarians proposed a bill of rights that codified some of the civil liberties that had been gained in the course of the revolution. This became the first draft of a supplement to the 1906 Constitution, but the process of ratifying this document turned into a major political and ideological confrontation between the liberal-radical faction of the assembly and the conservatives. The final draft, known as the Supplementary Fundamental Law, was ratified on 7 October 1907. This Supplementary Law guaranteed certain basic rights for citizens, such as those of association and equality before the law for all (male) citizens, including some religious minorities, but many of its provisions also altered the secular and democratic nature of the 1906 Constitution.

With this document, constitutionalists curtailed the domain of the shari'a in several significant ways. They were also forced to grant the clerical establishment new institutional authority within the Majles. Articles 1 and 2 of the Supplementary Laws show the essence of these concessions. In Article 1, the Shi'i character of the nation was elevated over and above the national character of the Iranian people. The model for the Iranian constitution had been the Belgian constitution of 1831, but the Iranians had also borrowed elements from the Bulgarian and Ottoman basic laws. These laws had defined the geographic parameters of their respective nations and listed conditions that constituted citizenship, through birth or through naturalization. The 1907 Supplementary Laws of Iran initially followed a similar model and enumerated the country's provinces and departments:

> Article 1. The Iranian nation is composed of the following provinces and departments (followed by a list of 25 regions). Article 2. Division of provinces into local authorities. Article 3. The boundaries of the Iranian nation, its provinces and municipalities, will not change except according to law.[6]

Despite this, the final draft of the Supplementary Laws began with an entirely different premise and signalled a departure from all other official documents that had appeared in the first year of the Constitutional Revolution. The Royal Proclamation of August, the Electoral Laws of September, and the Constitution of December 1906 had been largely secular documents, making only brief references to the Qur'an, mostly when an oath was required. In contrast, the 1907 Supplementary Laws began with a declaration of the religious identity of Iran instead of the national identity, and codified one particular branch of Islam, albeit that of the majority, as the official religion of Iran. Rather than naming the country's provinces or borders, Article I stated: 'the Official religion of Iran is Islam, according to the orthodox Ja'fari doctrine of Twelver Shi'ism.'[7] The shah was also expected to 'profess and promote the [Twelver Shi'i] Ja'fari doctrine', thus emphasizing the religious underpinnings and obligations of Iranian monarchy.

Article 2 of the 1907 law called for the establishment of a council of clerics with veto power over the parliament. Under Article 2, laws ratified by the parliament could not be at variance with the shari'a. MPs were given the right to select five *mojtahed*s who sat on the council of clerics. A *mojtahed* was a high-ranking cleric who had received the authority to interpret religious laws according to his judgment. Their selection was to be made from a list of 20 candidates provided by the ulema themselves.[8] The ulema thus reasserted their role as representatives of the Hidden Imam inside the Majles and maintained their right to instruct the ruler and the government in perpetuity:

> Iranian, Article 2. At no time must any legal enactment of the Sacred National Consultative Assembly [...] be at variance with the sacred principles of Islam or the Laws of [the Prophet Mohammad]. It is hereby declared that it is for the ulema [...] to determine whether such laws as may be proposed are, or are not, conformable to the principles of Islam; and it is therefore officially enacted that there shall exist at all times a Committee composed of no less than five *mojtahed*s or other devout theologians, cognizant also of the requirements of the age [...]. This Article shall continue unchanged until the appearance of the Mahdi [the Messiah].

The architect of Article 2 was the ranking *mojtahed* of Tehran, Sheykh Fazlollah Nuri (1843–1909).[9] Nuri had studied in Najaf under the *marja'* Mirza Hasan Shirazi before returning to Tehran in 1883. In the summer of 1906, Nuri briefly supported the constitutionalists, before turning against them when the aims of the new democratic movement became clearer. He soon became its most vociferous opponent, joined Mohammad Ali Shah, and issued fatwas and wrote articles in his newspaper, *Lavayeh-e Sheykh Fazlollah Nuri*, where he accused supporters of the movement of heresy and apostasy.[10]

Article 2 was a novelty among the modern constitutions of Europe or the Middle East. Neither the Ottoman nor the Bulgarian laws had given such overt recognition and power to the religious establishment. The Sunni Ottomans had a much more extensive history of reform than the Iranians, where the sultan had claimed the authority of the caliph (supreme religious leader) since the fifteenth century. The Tanzimat reforms of the mid-nineteenth century had attempted to unite people of different religions to preserve the unity of the Ottoman Empire in the face of Western support for its dismemberment. These reforms had recognized the nominal equality of Ottoman subjects before the law 'without distinction of class and religion'.[11] Also, although Article 11 of the Ottoman Constitution made Islam the state religion, it had not given preference to a specific sect, not even the Sunni Islam professed by the majority of Ottomans. Further, this Ottoman article contained a provision for the protection of religious minorities, which affirmed that the Ottoman state would 'protect the free exercise of faiths professed in the empire'.[12]

Similarly, Article 37 of the Bulgarian Constitution stated that Eastern Orthodox Christianity was the state religion. Here again, provisions were added to safeguard the rights of religious minorities. Article 40 of the Bulgarian Constitution gave Christians and Bulgarians 'of any other religion [...] full liberty to profess their religion'.[13] The Iranian Constitution made no such explicit guarantee of rights to Iran's minorities, either Sunni minorities or non-Muslims, even though both groups were granted equal rights before state law.

It seems that Iranian constitutionalists had examined the Ottoman and Bulgarian laws to determine the authority of the clerics in the new order.[14] Following the example of the French Constitution, Articles 14, 15, and 17 of the Belgian Constitution had divested the Catholic Church and its priests of much of their authority, guaranteed freedom of opinion, religious liberty, and the right not to observe religious rituals.[15] By contrast, the Bulgarian Constitution (Articles 37 and 39) had declared the Eastern Orthodox confession the state religion of Bulgaria with vast authority.[16] Under the Ottoman Constitution (Articles 4 and 11), the sultan retained the functions of both king and caliph, and was responsible for carrying out the shari'a as well as other laws. Thus, despite attempts to limit the powers of the religious establishment, the Iranian Constitution ultimately exceeded of all its predecessors, including the Ottoman and Bulgarian examples, in the degree to which it upheld clerical authority as an independent source of power and a body of clerics to oversee the actions of Parliament.[17]

Why did this happen, despite all the attempts by the liberal constitutionalists to produce a more democratic document? There were several reasons. Shi'i clerics historically had much greater authority in Iran than their Sunni colleagues in the neighbouring Ottoman Empire. The Shi'i ulema also had a separate source of income because they collected an annual tax from their followers. This meant they could remain independent of both the shah and the new constitutional state. Clerics had also played an influential role in the early stages of the revolution. They had employed large numbers of theology students who were routinely utilized in street processions. Low-level clerics and theology students (*talabeh*s) participated in demonstrations, joined the *anjoman*s, and became influential activists. As would happen throughout modern Iranian history, Parliament could not take on the shah and the ulema at the same time, while also fighting the encroachment of two vast imperialist powers, Russian and Britain. When Great Britain and Russia signed a secret treaty in St Petersburg in August 1907 – a treaty that partitioned the country into three zones, with a northern Russian and a southern British zone, and a middle neutral zone of influence – the Western powers further weakened the constitutionalists, who now found themselves with their backs to the wall.

To be sure, there were some ranking clerics who opposed Western encroachment and supported the new constitutional order on religious and anti-colonial grounds. Among them were the three leading Shi'i *marja'-e taqlid* of Najaf, Seyyed 'Abdollah Mazandarani, Seyyed Mohammad Kazem Khorasani, and Mirza Hoseyn Tehrani. The most vocal and respected one of the three was Khorasani. Unfortunately, he and his colleagues did not write much about the revolution.

Without mentioning Nuri by name, the three clerics led by Khorasani argued that, 'support for opponents of constitutionalism, no matter the person [...] was tantamount to fighting a war against the Hidden Imam'.[18] In general they adopted what we would today call an anti-colonial Muslim discourse, one that exposed the machinations of the Western powers and placed greater limits on the authority of the monarch. They argued that to save the nation from foreign concessions, debts, and other irresponsible actions of the monarchy, greater limits had to be placed on the shah and the court. However, even these constitutionalist clerics envisioned a prominent role for shari'a and its jurists in the new order.

Soon after the ratification of the constitution in 1906, Sheykh Fazlollah Nuri and his supporters, who had maintained close ties to the court, began to air their strong disagreements with the reforms. They rejected the first draft of the Supplementary Laws for its secular orientation and accused liberal constitutionalists of heresy and apostasy. In response, the Majles agreed to the formation of a clerical council, with

THE PLACE OF SHI'I CLERICS   57

Nuri at its head. This had responsibility for comparing and contrasting the new laws with shari'a and amending undesirable and overtly secular ones which interfered with the authority of the ulema. The result was Article 2, which established a council of clerics in perpetuity.

As the dissident cleric Mohsen Kadivar, now living in exile, has argued, Nuri was in fact an early supporter of the concept of *velayat-e faqih* (rule by jurists).[19] Nuri challenged the legislative authority of parliament and opined: 'In the absence of the Hidden Imam, *velayat* is with the *faqih*s (religious jurists) and the *mojtahed*, not some grocer or clothes merchant [...]. What does it mean [for Parliament] to write laws? The laws of Muslims are Islam,' which *mojtahed*s had safeguarded.[20] Still, Nuri's and these earlier definitions of *velayat-e faqih* were far more limited in scope than the later definitions of the term developed by Ayatollah Khomeini nearly 70 years later. Neither Nuri, nor constitutionalist clerics who supported the concept of *velayat-e faqih* in 1907, challenged the authority of the shah and his executive powers, nor did they claim absolute political authority for the *faqih*s. Rather, they disapproved of the new legislative and judicial branches of the state and claimed that both functions belonged properly to the *faqih*s.[21]

In comparing the views of clerical supporters of the constitutional order in 1906–7 we see that even ranking constitutionalist clerics such as Khorasani of Najaf, who distanced themselves from the notion of *velayat-e faqih*, shared some of Nuri's views.[22] Clerics who backed the Constitutional Revolution and those who opposed it had a number of points in common. Both, for example, supported Article 2 of the Supplementary Laws, and held that parliament should be prevented from drafting legislation that conflicted with shari'a. Both insisted that the *faqih*s should control the judicial branch of government, and finally both expected that existing social hierarchies between Muslims and non-Muslims, Shi'is and Sunnis, men and women, would remain intact. Although some clerics grudgingly agreed to the representation of non-Muslims representatives in the parliament, most clerics assumed that the new constitution left shari'a laws intact and simply codified and expanded '*urf* law.[23]

Since the three grand ayatollahs wrote little on the subject, their opinions can only be gleaned from the writings of some of their most devoted students. Khorasani's perspective on these limits is best captured in the writings of Mohammad Esma'il Mahallati Gharavi.[24] Defending Article 8, which granted equal rights to all male Iranians,

Mahallati insisted that the new bill of rights of the Supplementary Laws did not interfere with the personal, familial, and religious laws of the people – areas traditionally under the auspices of the shari'a – or with the distribution of alms. These matters were entirely within the province of the religious establishment. With these assurances in place, Mahallati saw no reason to be apprehensive about Article 8. He recalled that modern European laws had also called for equality and new civil liberties, but none of these had had the effect of eradicating class or gender distinctions. Article 8 would institute a similar situation in Iran. Equality would have a very precise meaning. Citizens would be treated equally before state law and in matters such as taxation, but religious and class hierarchies would not disappear. To prove his point, he argued that indeed no nation on earth, not even Europeans, had declared the equality of all their citizens in all affairs: 'Do the king and a soldier receive the same income in England?'[25]

Khorasani's other protégé, Mohammad Hoseyn Na'ini, also believed that a constitutional government would not obviate Shi'i doctrines.[26] Na'ini was one of the *mojtahed*s who contributed to Article 2, but he also supported the election of recognized religious minorities to the parliament. In his well-known essay, *'Tanbih al-Umma va Tanzih al-Milla'* (Awakening the Muslim Community and Purifying the Nation), Na'ini states, 'If the minorities select some-one from their rank, even though they are not expected to be loyal to Islam, they will exhibit good will toward the nation (*vatan*) and others, and such qualifications will be sufficient for their participation'.[27] Na'ini assuaged his audience's concerns that the new laws might end up legitimizing the 'equality of Muslims with *dhimmi* non-Muslims' or the 'unveiling of women'. He assured them that such radical measures would not be adopted in Iran because the constitution did not call for equality between 'adults and children, sane and insane persons, healthy and sick people' and so forth. With these assurances, he convinced many other clerics that the new constitutional order, with the added Supplementary Laws, would not threaten the ulema's authority in any significant way.[28] However, after the hanging of Sheykh Fazlollah Nuri in July 1909, a shocked Na'ini changed his mind. Apparently he told his students in Najaf to collect the remaining issues of his essay and discard them, primarily because he never thought the new constitution would grant itself such far-reaching authority over the clerical establishment.[29]

Rights of the Judiciary

The struggle for a constitutional order in Iran had begun with the demand for the establishment of a House of Justice, and by 1907 many radical constitutionalists were pushing for the formation of a modern judiciary. Constitutionalist clerics were not averse to implementing some procedures like the creation of a Western-style courthouse. They assumed that a modern judiciary would revise and expand the old *'urf* law, leaving shari'a matters in their hands, but they resisted any attempt to alter or even unify sharia law. Several times constitutionalists and the new minister of justice, Mo'ayyed al-Saltaneh, called on clerics to at least unify existing shari'a laws but they were resolutely rebuffed.[30] At the same time secular constitutionalists such as Taqizadeh wanted to revamp the whole system. He and his supporters hoped to build a legal system composed of a new generation of judges trained in modern laws and independent from the clerics.

After battling clerical opposition for months, progressive constitutionalists ultimately chose to compromise. In the manner of the Ottoman Constitution, they established a two-tier judicial system that maintained the *'urf*/shari'a binary in many areas:

> Ottoman, Article 87: Affairs touching the shari'a are tried by the Tribunals of the Shari'a. The judgment of civil affairs pertains to Civil Tribunals. Iranian 1907, Article 71: The Supreme Ministry of Justice and the judicial tribunals are the places officially destined for the redress of public grievances, while judgment in all matters falling within the scope of the Ecclesiastical Law is vested in just *mojtahed*s possessing the necessary qualifications.

A similar compromise was reached over the selection of the chief prosecutor. The Ministry of Justice would appoint the prosecutor, but the shah and qualified *mojtahed*s had to approve the appointment:

> Iranian 1907, Article 83: The appointment of the public prosecutor is within the competence of the shah, supported by the approval of the ecclesiastical judge.

Civil Liberties

Civil liberties are rights that protect citizens from powers of the state, but these protections and rights often contradict religious duties and obligations. Clerical constitutionalists accepted some civil liberties, but not rights that came into conflict with religious obligations or altered family law. Through the efforts of social democrats inside and outside parliament, the struggle for civil liberties, in particular the right to equality and the right to freedom, took centre stage in this period.

The French Declaration of the Rights of Man had recognized individual liberties, as had the Belgian (Article 7) and Ottoman (Article 9) constitutions, but neither the Bulgarian Constitution nor the Iranian law of 1907 recognized individual liberties. Social democratic MPs in parliament, such as Taqizadeh and his supporters in Azerbaijan, Gilan, and Tehran, secured the principle of equality before the law in 1907 but not that of individual liberty. Article 8 states, 'the people of the Persian Empire are to enjoy equal rights before the state law'. The principal model for this right was Article 6 of the French Declaration, an abbreviated version of which had appeared in the Belgian (Article 6), Ottoman (Article 17), and Bulgarian (Article 57) constitutions. The key term in the Iranian law was that it specified 'equality before the state law', making no provision for equality before religious law. As far as the clerical establishment was concerned, religious (and therefore legal) distinctions between Muslims and non-Muslims still existed. Sheykh Fazlollah Nuri, for example, maintained that an Islamic nation cannot be a constitutional one as well, because it is impossible to have equality in Islam. He wrote that shari'a clearly separates the rights of 'a slave and a free man, a father and a son, a husband and a wife, a wealthy man and a poor man, a wise man and a fool'. Likewise it distinguished, several other categories such as 'a Muslim and an apostate, a *dhimmi*-apostate and a captive-apostate, and one who has left Islam'.[31]

Several other civil rights provisions from the Belgian Constitution were included in the Supplementary Laws. They guaranteed individual property rights, the sanctity of life and domicile, the right to privacy regarding letters and telegrams, and the right to trial. Under Article 14, no Iranian citizen could be exiled from the country or prevented from living there.[32] In addition, the state, rather than the clergy, was placed in control of the public education system (Article 19), a major achievement for Iranian constitutionalists.

A comparison of the first draft of the 1907 law and the final version demonstrates further concessions to the Shi'i clergy. Education in the fields of science, art, and crafts was permitted 'save in the case of such as may be forbidden by the ecclesiastical law' (Article 18). Freedom of the press was granted, except for 'heretical books and matters hurtful to the perspicuous religion' (Article 20). Freedom of association was granted throughout the nation, provided *anjoman*s and other such associations were 'not productive of mischief to religion or the state' (Article 21). Thirty years prior, the Ottoman Constitution had guaranteed these rights without the encumbrances that were tacked on to the 1907 Iranian law. Whereas Sultan Abdülhamid II suppressed the Ottoman Constitution soon after its birth, the conservative clerics in Iran aborted these new civil rights while they were still embryonic.

Certain progressive clauses in the Belgian and Ottoman constitutions never made it into the 1907 Iranian law. Articles 14–16 of the Belgian Constitution established freedom of religion, denied state intervention in religious matters, and required civil weddings to precede religious ones. Though Belgian Article 23 recognized its people's multilingual heritage, the Iranian Constitution included no such provision, despite Iran's similarly polyglot population.[33] In the Ottoman Constitution, Article 24 prohibited corvée labour, and Article 26 banned torture and inquisition. Article 61 of the Bulgarian Constitution banned slavery of 'either sex' and declared that slaves became free upon entering Bulgaria. None of these civil rights provisions were incorporated into the Iranian law, although constitutionalists inside and outside the Majles and European abolitionists continued to work for the eradication of the last vestiges of the Iranian slave trade, which continued in the Persian Gulf for decades.[34]

Personal freedoms were either absent from or restricted in much of the Iranian Constitution. From 1906 onward, many members of the ulema continued to oppose the concept of individual freedom (*azadi*), and the word soon took on a pejorative connotation. In some quarters the term *azadi*, including the right to be different and to act differently from other people, was equated with irreligion, immorality, lack of chastity, and licentiousness. In terms of gender, *azadi* came to have a doubly negative connotation and was directly associated with sexual immorality. A free woman (*zan-e azad*) was an immoral and sexually promiscuous one.

Equality before the law was viewed more positively. However, even in this area, equality for Sunni Muslims, non-Muslims, and women was never practiced. Women ultimately received the right to vote in 1963 and inheritance, marriage, and divorce laws have continued to remain unequal 100 years later. Religious minorities knew that they could never successfully pursue a legal action against a Shi'i Muslim. Three decades after the Constitutional Revolution, after the reforms of the Reza Shah era (1925–41), equality remained a privilege that the state granted to Iranian citizens, including women and minorities. As far as the shah, or the majority male Shi'i communities were concerned, equality before the law could also be withdrawn when women or minorities transgressed acceptable boundaries, that is to say when they demanded real freedom.

Freedom of the Press

Progressive MPs and government ministers also insisted upon freedom of the press (Article 20). They argued that if the ulema's objections to a free press were taken into account, classical works of Persian literature such as Ferdowsi's epic *Shahnameh* (*Book of Kings*) and Sa'di's *Golestan* (*The Rose Garden*) could be censored because of their perceived profanities. Taqizadeh suggested a middle ground, which involved establishing two classes of publications and two bodies to monitor them, modelling his proposal on Bulgarian Articles 79 and 80. Religious authorities would oversee the publication of religious texts, while modern educators and scholars supervised other kinds of publications.[35] The Bulgarian Constitution divided the two areas in the following manner:

> Bulgarian, Article 79: The press is free. No censorship may be instituted, and no caution may be required from authors, editors, or publishers. If the author be well known and resides within the principality, no action may be brought against the editor, the publisher, or the salesman. Bulgarian, Article 80: The Holy Scripture, prayer books, and catechisms destined for use in the churches of the Orthodox rite, as also treatises of ecclesiastical law destined for use in Orthodox schools, must be submitted for the approval of the Holy Synod.
>
> Bulgarian, Article 81: Offenses in whatever concerns the press, can be tried only under the law and by the ordinary courts.

However, Taqizadeh's suggestion for two publication committees was only partially accepted. Hence, the crisp distinctions regarding the responsibilities and capacities of the press in the Bulgarian Constitution are absent from the Iranian Supplementary Laws. Article 20 created two categories of publications: one, acceptable publications that were exempt from censorship; and two, 'heretical' works that were not. The Constitution never explained what constituted a 'heretical' work. In this way, the ecclesiastical order could label any publications that did not meet its approval as 'hurtful to religion', proceed to ban it, and prosecute its writer and publisher.

> Iranian 1907, Article 20: All publications, except heretical books and matters hurtful to the perspicuous religion [of Islam] are free, and are exempt from the censorship. If, however, anything should be discovered in them contrary to the Press law, the publisher or writer is liable to punishment according to that law. If the writer be known, and be resident in Iran, then the publisher, printer and distributor shall not be liable to prosecution.

The Battle for Equality and Liberty

In Shi'i Iranian society, maintaining social and religious distinctions was of paramount importance. A majority of Shi'i theologians included Jews and Christians, who normally held the status of *dhimmi* (protected but second class citizens) under Islamic law, in the category of infidels (*koffar*) who were ritually impure.[36] Segregation was enforced through a series of spatial, sartorial, and dietary rules and regulations. Qajar monarchs continued the Safavid policy of intolerance toward Sunni Muslims and non-Muslims.[37] Babi and Baha'i minorities, who often lived within Muslim communities and intermarried with Muslims, were denied the customary protection of the recognized religious minorities under Islam. They were at the greatest risk of violence and frequently, on one pretext or another, were attacked and even forced to convert. Mistreatment of religious minorities was not always rooted in religion and ideology. Rather, such incidents could be motivated by socioeconomic or political reasons and subsequently justified on religious and legal grounds.[38]

In the second half of the nineteenth century, Britain, France, and Russia had intervened in Iran's treatment of its minorities, often in response to *dhimmi*s' calls for protection. French and British diplomats encouraged the king to lift various restrictions on Iran's minority communities. Parsi merchants from British-ruled India also pressed the shah for protection for their Zoroastrian co-religionists in Iran, whom they were in continuous contact with. Naser al-Din Shah and Mozaffar al-Din Shah issued several edicts (*firman*s) during their reigns that outlawed some of the restrictions on Jews and Zoroastrians. However, the ulema objected to these changes in the status of Iranian minorities and ultimately ignored the edicts, which meant that religious harassment of non-Muslims continued into the early twentieth century.[39]

In the course of drafting the Supplementary Laws, Taqizadeh insisted on the inclusion of Article 8, which declared that 'the people of the Iranian state are to enjoy equal rights before the Law'. Taqizadeh and his colleagues argued, 'If this article were included in the law, but all other articles were changed, Western countries would still recognize us as a constitutional order. But if we eliminate this [Article 8] and include everything else, they will not recognize us as a constitutional order.' Taqizadeh pointed out that European consulates inside Iran had developed close contacts with Christians, Jews, and Zoroastrians. These foreign powers interfered in Iran's internal affairs by routinely taking sides in local skirmishes between Muslim and non-Muslim communities, often backing the minorities. By recognizing the rights of Iran's non-Muslims, Taqizadeh wanted to establish the foundations of a modern nation state with equality before the law for all citizens. He also believed that, by granting this right, he was removing a major excuse for imperialist meddling in internal Iranian affairs.[40] In addition, he was convinced that educated and entrepreneurial minorities were valuable assets for a modernizing Iran. Some Christian Iranians had attended missionary schools, and Iranian Jews were often educated by the more secular Alliance israélite universelle. Both were therefore more familiar with Western languages and cultures. Some had also developed extensive economic ties with their co-religionists abroad.[41] Most of all, Taqizadeh was convinced that a modern nation, with extensive commercial ties to the West, could not have a two-tier legal system, one for Muslims and another for non-Muslims and foreign visitors.

For his part, Nuri was concerned with the diminished authority of the ulema under the new order. He continued to insist that 'equality and Islam may never coexist'. Nuri characterized the MPs who pushed for the ratification of these civil rights as 'base, knavish and dishonourable people'. The shari'a had given Muslims special privileges, both as Muslims and as men, yet they wished to deny themselves and others these advantages. To Muslims who dared to move beyond such prejudices and made the astonishing claim that 'I should be equal and brother with the Zoroastrian, the Armenian, and the Jew!' Nuri had only one response: 'May God curse those who do not value themselves.'[42]

Progressive constitutionalists outside Iran also pushed hard for the inclusion of equality as a guiding precept in the constitution. From the Russian Caucasus, Abdulrahim Talebof, a strong defender of Article 8, wrote to his friend Mirza Fazl-Ali Aqa Tabrizi, a parliamentary deputy representing the clerics of Iranian Azerbaijan:

> My Dear: Bad news arrives from Tabriz. In Tehran, a major fight has developed over two articles of the Constitution. With regard to the first one [Article 8], I hope that by now the honourable clerics have accepted this principle and thus have not shamed our Muslim honour. The Christians, Zoroastrians, and Jews pay taxes to the government. This tax is their *jezya* [poll] tax. I don't understand the problem. Are the ulema demanding that, as in the old days, the Christians not leave their houses in humid weather? Are they expecting them to fly over a muddy alley to avoid ritually polluting the earth? The fact is that fifty years before the constitution was written, social needs resulted in the disappearance of such artificial traditions that were unknown to the Prophet. If the purpose of this debate is to allow Muslims to confiscate the property [of non-Muslims], trample upon their rights as human beings (*hoquq-e ensan*), and deny them justice, then [it should be noted that] we have no such shari'a law that would allow Muslims the right to trample other people. If the purpose of this argument is to prevent [non-Muslim] members from being elected [to Parliament] or the popular councils, then why should this be the case? If we select one representative for every 300,000 persons, then we should do the same for the Christians and the Jews. Moreover, Zoroastrians are our ancestors in Iran. How could we in good conscience not include them in our midst and deprive members of this honest and decent nation of their rights as citizens?[43]

Zoroastrian merchants inside Iran joined this discussion. They complained about repeated prejudice and harassment and demanded the ratification of Article 8 to receive both legal protection and recognition. 'Is the sacred word equality for all the people of the nation, or is it only for some people?' they wrote in one such petition.[44] Armenians threatened to seek sanctuary at the European legations if Article 8 was not ratified.[45] The Azerbaijan Central Committee of the Dashnak Armenian Party demanded that Parliament establish 'equality before the law without distinction of faith and nationality'.[46]

Others, such as Sheykh Salim from Azerbaijan, were more aware of the ramifications of the pending changes. A constitutionalist cleric from Tabriz with social democratic tendencies, Salim was known for his fierce support of the poor and the peasants. He realized that the new constitution would gradually undermine the old boundaries between civil and religious laws, and initiate a series of events that would revise the shari'a. Salim feared that if equal legal rights were granted to non-Muslims, the conservative opposition would turn completely against the new constitutional order. Unwilling to discuss these conclusions publicly, he suggested to a colleague in parliament that the Supplementary Laws' language of equal rights be thinly veiled to conceal and safeguard the potential for future progressive reform:

> On the matter of equality, it is better if you do not frame the issue as the rights of Muslims vs. heathens [non-Muslim Iranians]. Rather, you should frame it as the rights of Iranians vs. foreigners. After all, there are Muslims who live abroad as well. Then, if [the conservatives] complain, we can say that we are dealing with equal rights of Muslims who live abroad. In the end, it is better if the issue of Muslim and heathen Iranians remains dormant. It will be less of an obstacle.[47]

Note that even a fierce constitutionalist such as Salim, who defended Article 8, used the highly derogatory term 'heathens' (*koffar*) to refer to non-Muslims in his private correspondence. In public proclamations, constitutionalists including Salim used the more polite term *dhimmi* or the newly-coined one *melal-e motefarreqeh* (various faith communities). The point is that even constitutionalists who fought for Article 8 avoided mention of non-Muslim Iranians in the law because the conservative

THE PLACE OF SHI'I CLERICS

Shi'i clerics would have recognized such a reference as a threat to their authority, rendering ratification impossible. As a result, there were at least three public positions on the proposed civil rights legislation:

(i) Conservatives such as Sheykh Fazlollah Nuri argued that a secular civil code was irreconcilable with the shari'a. Nuri supported the shah during the Minor Autocracy (1908–9) when royalist forces closed down the parliament, executed several leading constitutionalists, and drove others into exile. After the restoration of the constitutional order in the summer of 1909, Nuri was tried and executed for his role in the murder of several constitutionalists.

(ii) Moderate clerics, such as Na'ini and Mahallati, argued that the domain of the civil and religious law would remain separate as they had been under *urf* and shari'a laws. The new laws would neither interfere in matters traditionally adjudicated by the ulema (such as collecting of *jezya* taxes) nor subvert existing principles of the shari'a. After the execution of Nuri and the rise of the more secular Democrat Party, which openly called for separation of religion and state, supporters of this view became disillusioned with the new political order. They joined the more conservative Moderate Party in the Second Majles (1909–11) or abandoned politics altogether.

(iii) More secular and left-wing MPs denied that there were any contradictions between the proposed secular laws and shari'a law in their public pronouncements. None dared enumerate the critical differences between religious and secular law. Repeated reassurances from progressive MPs that parliament would neither interfere in the daily affairs of citizens nor regulate religious and family matters helped push through the Supplementary Laws in the autumn of 1907, though in a more modified version than the one proposed by Nuri and his supporters. Article 8 survived this acrimonious debate. Equal rights for minorities were also quietly incorporated in articles dealing with the nation's finances. These articles nominally outlawed the practice of collecting *jezya* taxes from non-Muslims and paved the way for future reforms in this area:

Iranian 1907, Article 97: In the matter of taxes there shall be no distinction or difference among the individuals who compose the nation.

Iranian 1907, Article 99: Save in such cases as are explicitly excepted by Law, nothing can on any pretext be demanded from the people save under the categories of state, provincial, departmental, and municipal taxes.

In 1909, supporters of this group formed the Democrat Party in the second parliament and briefly pushed their more secular agenda, including a party programme that called for separation of religion and state.

Conclusion

With the ascendence of Mohammad Ali Shah to the throne in early 1907, the revolution entered a more perilous stage. Mohammad Ali shah detested the limits placed on his powers and recognized that the easiest way to challenge the new order was to accuse it of undermining the shari'a. The shah was backed by conservative clerics, especially Nuri, who also realized that the new constitution undermined their authority.

The Iranian Constitutional Laws of 1906–7 went far beyond the Belgian, Bulgarian, and Ottoman constitutions, as well as those of Germany, Japan, and Russia in reducing monarchical powers. The Iranian parliament was a legislative body, vested with many of the rights that had previously been the province of European or Japanese monarch. The constitution established the principle of national sovereignty and introduced the notion that the shah was a representative of the people, stating unequivocally, 'all the powers emanate from the nation' (Article 26).

When progressive constitutionalists proposed a series of amendments to the 1906 constitution that guaranteed broader civil rights, Nuri and his backers confronted the Majles and demanded that the new laws conform to religious laws. Ultimately progressive constitutionalists reached a compromise with Nuri and his royalist backers. The Supplementary Laws granted basic civil rights. The 1907 Supplementary Laws also curtailed the vast authority of the shah by mandating regular consultations with his cabinet ministers. These ministers were in turn responsible to the parliament for their actions and those of the shah.

Clerical authority was also restricted in three major ways: first, by creating a new legislative body; second, by dividing the judiciary into religious and secular units, wherein the *mojtahed*s controlled the religious and family law, whereas civil courts dealt with other matters (Article 27);

THE PLACE OF SHI'I CLERICS   69

and third, by establishing the principle that the state, and not the clerics, controlled the educational system.

The 1907 law granted new rights to Sunnis and *dhimmi*s, including Christians, Jews, and Zoroastrians, but not Babis or Baha'is, by stating that all (male) citizens were equal before the state law. Here the language of the law was less precise and transparent than that of the Belgian, Bulgarian, or Ottoman laws. When universal male suffrage was adopted in Iran in 1911, once again the ethnic, linguistic, and educational diversity of the nation was not taken into account, because all voters were required to read and write in Persian.

Regarding gender rights, as feminist scholars have shown, the strict demarcation of private and public realms in the aftermath of modern democratic revolutions had often resulted in codifying existing patriarchal traditions, inventing new ones, and ultimately giving men greater control over women's lives in modern institutions. The same scenario played out during the Iranian Constitutional Revolution.[48] The electoral laws of 1906 barred women from participation in the new political process by denying them the franchise. Family law remained fully under the aegis of the *mojtahed*s, a harbinger of the fact that the battle to establish more secular laws concerning gender and the family would be a long and bitter one. In the decades that followed, Iranian women did gain new rights to education, employment, and political participation, but the state continued to incorporate many religious and patriarchal practices into the newly-created modern laws.[49]

The Supplementary Laws also recognized the Twelver branch of Shi'i Islam as the official religion of the country and gave a council of clerics substantial rights and privileges that directly violated the earlier liberal spirit of the constitution. National identity was subsumed under the Shi'i Ithna 'Ashari religious identity. The ulema gained veto power over the parliament and retained control of the religious courts. Some of the civil liberties that were granted in 1906, such as freedom of press or association, were curtailed in the 1907 laws. Other civil liberties that were introduced in the 1907 law were restricted by religious qualifications.

The council of clerics briefly functioned during the Second Majles (1909–11). In future decades secular constitutionalists hampered the formation of this council on the grounds that some MPs were ranking clerics hence there was no need for an additional council of clerics.

Yet the very existence of Article 2 in the constitution, the fact that in a democratically-elected parliament, the clerics could insist on forming their own council of clerics with veto powers over all parliamentary deliberations, dampened the secular intellectuals' enthusiasm for a more democratic political order and robbed the process of its original liberal spirit.

Notes

*. An early draft of this article was published in *Critical Research on Religion* i/3 (2013): pp. 327–346.
1. For a discussion of Muharram rituals in Iran, see Peter Chelkowski (ed.), *Taziyeh: Ritual and Drama in Iran* (New York: NYU Press, 1979) and Yann Richard, *Shi'ite Islam* (Oxford: Blackwell, 1995).
2. For details, see Janet Afary, *The Iranian Constitutional Revolution, 1906–1911: Grassroots Democracy, Social Democracy, and the Origins of Feminism* (New York: Columbia University Press, 1996), especially Chapters Three and Four.
3. Moojan Momen, *An Introduction to Shi'i Islam* (New Haven: Yale University Press, 1985), p. 202.
4. See, for example, the description by Ja'far Shahri of some of these public executions. He writes that 'after the execution, the public's reaction depended on the circumstances of the case and of the punishment. If they felt the hanging was excessive or unjust, the crowd wept and cried for the poor soul, but if the condemned was a cruel murderer, and the punishment was deemed justified, they "expressed their joy and clapped hands" as the man's body dangled in air'. Ja'far Shahri, *Tehran-e Qadim*, vol. 1 (Tehran: Entesharat-e Mo'in, 1978), pp. 418–9.
5. For a text of the 1906 constitution, see Edward Granville Browne, *The Persian Revolution of 1905–1909* (Cambridge: Cambridge University Press, 1910), pp. 362–71.
6. For a text of the first draft, see Iraj Afshar, *Qabaleh-ye Tarikh* (Tehran: Talayeh Press, 1989).
7. For a text of these laws, see Browne, *The Persian Revolution*, pp. 372–84.
8. Mohammad Torkaman, 'Nezarat-e Mojtahedin-e Taraz-e Avval', *Tarikh-e Mo'aser-e Iran* 1 (Winter 1994), p. 33. The council of clerics operated briefly during the Second Majles (1909–11) but remained dormant for the next 70 years. Still, clerical deputies such as Hasan Modarres examined new laws and rejected those they deemed in violation of the shari'a.
9. As Torkaman has pointed out, in Nuri's original proposal: (i) the clerical committee operated outside the parliament and therefore established a parallel structure of authority; (ii) the exact number of members of this committee was not determined; (iii) the selection process for the committee was undefined; and (iv) the stipulation that committee members should be fully aware of contemporary worldly concerns was not indicated; see Torkaman, 'Nezarat'.

THE PLACE OF SHI'I CLERICS 71

10. When constitutionalist forces regained the capital in July 1909, Nuri was tried for the murder of several constitutionalists and found guilty. After receiving permission from some of the Najaf clerics, and allowing the public to check with Najaf through open telegraph lines, the constitutionalists publicly hanged Nuri. He was rehabilitated after the Islamic Revolution of 1979 and is considered one of the early martyrs of Islamism.
11. Bernard Lewis, *The Emergence of Modern Turkey* (London: Oxford University Press, 1968), p. 134.
12. Suna Kili, *Turkish Constitutional Development* (Istanbul: Mentes Matbaasi, 1971).
13. For the text of the Bulgarian law, see Albert Blaustein and Gisbert Flanz (eds.) *Constitutions of the Countries of the World* (Dobbs Ferry, NY: Oceana Publications, 1992).
14. While in exile in London, Hasan Taqizadeh gave a speech to the Central Asian Society on 11 November 1908, where he explained that he and his colleagues had based the Supplementary Constitutional Laws 'largely on the Belgian (Constitutional) laws, partly on the French, and partly on the laws prevalent in Bulgaria', quoted in Edward Granville Browne, 'The Persian Constitutionalists', *Proceedings of the Central Asian Society* (1909), pp. 1–16. We are unaware of the language in which the Bulgarian law was initially examined.
15. I have used the French text of the Belgian Constitution that appears in J. J. Thonissen, *La Constitution Belge* (Bruxelles: Bruylant-Christophe, 1879).
16. See the text in Blaustein and Flanz (eds.), *Constitutions*.
17. Kili, *Turkish Constitutional Development*, pp. 1501–62. Bulgaria was part of the Ottoman Empire for five centuries before it became a Russian protectorate in 1878. The Bulgarian Constitution gave its king dictatorial powers in times of emergency. See Blaustein and Flanz (eds.), *Constitutions*.
18. Davud Feyrahi, 'Mabani-ye Feqhi-ye Mashruteh Khahi az Didgah-e Akhund-e Khorasani', in: Azarmeh Sanjari (ed.) *Majmu'eh-ye Maqalat-e Hamayesh-e Barrasi-ye Mabani-ye Fekri va Ejtema'i-ye Mashrutiyat-e Iran: Bozorgdasht-e Ayatollah Mohammad Kazem Khorasani* (Tehran: Mo'asseseh-ye Tahqiqat va Olum-e Ensani, 2005), pp. 195–218.
19. In the early nineteenth century, the *faqih* Molla Ahmad Naraqi (1771–1829) elaborated on the concept of *velayat-e faqih* (Rule of Jurists). Naraqi claimed that the most learned *faqih* also acquired the imams' divine inspiration, and therefore had both the exclusive right to interpret and administer the shari'a and the ability to exercise political power until Judgment Day. In this more expansive view of the role of the *mojtathed*, the leading jurist acquired nearly the authority of the Mahdi and was entitled to certain political powers. However, the concept of *velayat-e faqih* remained a minority position in Usuli Shi'ism and gradually faded away until Ayatollah Khomeini resurrected it in the 1970s in a still far more expansive view, giving the jurist the authority of both the *faqih* and the king.
20. Sheykh Fazlollah Nuri's essay in in Gholam-Hoseyn Zargarinezhad (ed.), *Rasa'el-e Mashrutiyyat* (Tehran: Kavir Press, 1995), p. 155. For an inside view

into these discussions and whether Jews, Armenians, and Zoroastrians should be granted equal rights, see the letter by Abdulrahim Talbof to Mirza Fazlali Aqa, 21 Jamdi 1325, in Gholam-Hoseyn Mirza Saleh (ed.), *Bohran-e Demokrasi dar Majles-e Avval* (Tehran: Homa Press, 1993), pp. 505–1.

21. Mohsen Kadivar, 'Andisheh-ye Siyasi-ye Akhund-e Khorasani', in A. Sanjari (ed.), *Barrasi-ye Mabani-ye Fekri va Ejtema'i-ye Mashrutiyat-e Iran* (Tehran: Tehran University, 2005), p. 254.
22. Ibid, pp. 240–3.
23. Ahmad Kasravi captures this outrage in his classic study of the Constitutional Revolution. For example, the cleric Ahmad Tabataba'i writes to this son-in-law, 'You do not know how destructive this Parliament has been to people's livelihood and religion... [People] have stopped reading the Qur'an and praying, and instead read the newspapers, which are full of blasphemy and insult our sacred religion'. Ahmad Kasravi, *Tarikh-e Mashruteh-ye Iran* (Tehran: Amir Kabir, 1984), p. 101.
24. See Mohammad Esma'il Gharavi Mahallati's essay in Zargarinezhad (ed.), *Rasa'el*, pp. 495–549.
25. Ibid., p. 518.
26. Mohammad Hoseyn Na'ini was a close associate of the two constitutionalist clerics in Najaf – Mazandarani and Khorasani – but was more conservative than Khorasani – see Sohrab Yazdani *Kasravi va Tarikh-e Mashruteh-ye Iran* (Tehran: Nashr-e Ney, 1997), pp. 134–5. As Mohsen Kadivar points out, some constitutionalist clerics supported the concept of *velayat-e faqih*. Na'ini, for example, believed in a limited form of *velayat-e faqih*, which might explain why he was more conservative than Khorasani or Mahallati. For more details see the outstanding work by Kadivar, 'Andisheh-ye Siyasi-ye Akhund-e Khorasani', pp. 240–1.
27. Mohammad Hoseyn Na'ini Gharavi, *Tanbih al-Umma va Tanzih al-Milla* (Tehran: Sherkat-e Chapkhaneh-ye Ferdowsi, 1995), p. 89. See also Farzin Vahdat, *God and Juggernaut: Iran's Intellectual Encounter with Modernity* (Syracuse: Syracuse University Press, 2002), p. 70. I thank Farzin Vahdat for e-mail exchanges in the autumn of 2006 for further clarification on this point.
28. Na'ini, *Tanbih al-Umma*, pp. 36–7.
29. See Abdul-Hadi Hairi, *Shi'ism and Constitutionalism in Iran: A Study of the Role Played by the Persian Residents of Iraq in Iranian Politics* (Leiden: Brill Press, 1977), p. 240.
30. For details see Mehdi Malekzadeh, *Tarikh-e Enqelab-e Mashrutiyat-e Iran*, vol. 3 (Tehran: 'Elmi Press, 1984), p. 628 and Yahya Dowlatabadi, *Hayat-e Yahya*, vol. 2 (Tehran: Ebn-e Sina Press, 1952), pp. 2202–21.
31. Nuri, 'Hormat-e Mashruteh', in Zargarinezhad (ed.), *Rasa'el-e Mashrutiyat*, pp. 1591–600.
32. This article might have been a response to Article 113 of the Ottoman Constitution, which gave the sultan the right to exile those violating state security. Sultan Abdülhamid dissolved the parliament, suspended the

constitution in 1878, and expelled liberal reformers from the country; see Kili, *Turkish Constitutional Development*, p. 15.
33. Religious minorities (including Sunnis) comprised about 10 per cent of the population.
34. Mostashar al-Dowleh had called for an end to torture and slavery in his 1871 book, but these issues were not addressed in the 1906–7 Constitution. Domestic slavery, mostly by tribal brigands, persisted through the 1920s, and even later in the Persian Gulf area. For details, see Thomas M. Ricks, 'Slavery and Slave Trading in Shi'i Iran, AD 1500–1900', in Maghan Keita (ed.), *Conceptualizing/Re-Conceptualizing Africa: The Construction of African Historical Identity* (Leiden: Brill, 2002), pp. 778–8. The slave trade continued on a much smaller scale in the opposite direction. In 1929, some 250 Baluchis were sold across the Persian Gulf. See the letter by Arthur Henderson, 9 November 1929, in Foreign Office 248/1387.
35. See *Mozakerat-e Majles*, 7 Rajab 1325 (17 August 1907), p. 212.
36. By the late nineteenth century one could find more than 50 types of such restrictions imposed on Jews, Christians, or Zoroastrians. Jews, for example, could not walk on the streets when it was raining because 'water and moister transferred their uncleanliness' to Muslims. Jews also could not enter a Muslim's house or store if per chance they entered in the company of a Muslim; they were not allowed to touch anything inside a store, though ironically their money was considered clean (see Issawi, Charles (ed.) (1971) *The Economic History of Iran, 1800–1914*. (Chicago: University of Chicago Press), p. 64 and Daniel Tsadik, *Between Foreigners and Shi'is: Nineteenth-Century Iran and its Jewish Minority* (Stanford: Stanford University Press, 2007), p. 17.
37. On this issue, see Yusef Sharifi, *Dard-e Ahl-e Zemmeh* (Los Angeles: Ketab Corporation, 2009). For the treatment of minorities in the Safavid and Qajar eras, see, among others: Hasan Taremi, *'Allameh Majlesi* (Tehran: Tarh-e Now, 1996); Walter Fischel, 'The Jews of Persia under the Kajar Dynasty', *Jewish Social Studies* xii (1950), pp. 119–60; Rudi Matthee, 'Between Aloofness and Fascination: Safavid Views of the West'. *Iranian Studies* xxxi/2 (1998), pp. 219–46; and Tsadik, *Between Foreigners and Shi'is*.
38. For a detailed discussion of these issues, see Eliz Sanasarian, *Religious Minorities in Iran* (Cambridge: Cambridge University Press, 2006); Mehrdad Amanat, *Jewish Identities in Iran: Resistance and Conversion to Islam and the Baha'i Faith* (London: I.B.Tauris, 2011); Houri Berberian, *Armenians and the Iranian Constitutional Revolution of 1905 1–911* (Boulder: Westview Press, 2001); Habib Levy, *Tarikh-e Yahud-e Iran*, vol. 3 (Beverly Hills: Sazeman-e Farhangi-ye Iranian-e Yahudi-ye Kalifornia,1989); and Habib Levy, *A Comprehensive History of the Jews of Iran: The Outset of the Diaspora* (Costa Mesa: CA: Mazda Press, 1999).
39. Napier Malcolm, *Five Years in a Persian Town* (Charleston: BiblioLife, 2009), p. 50; Tsadik, *Between Foreigners and Shi'is*, pp. 33–177.

40. Mehdi Mojtahedi, *Taqizadeh* (Tehran: Tehran University Publications, 1979), pp. 58–9. Mehdi Mojtahedi and others have indicated that Taqizadeh played a key role in these debates.
41. Homa Nateq, *Karnameh-ye Farhangi-ye Farangi dar Iran* (Paris: Khavaran Press, 1996).
42. Nuri's essay in Zargarinezhad, *Rasa'el*, pp. 1591–610.
43. Abdulrahim Talebof to Mirza Fazl-Ali Aqa, 21 Jumadi I, 1325, published in Mirza Saleh (ed.), *Bohran-e Demokrasi*, pp. 505–1. Some educated members of the elite no longer observed practices such as avoiding all bodily contact with non-Muslims, but Talebof's claim that such conduct was abandoned in the 1860s is an exaggeration. See Janet Afary, 'From Outcasts to Citizens: Jews in Qajar Iran', in Homa Sarshar (ed.), *Esther's Children: A Portrait of Iranian Jews* (Los Angeles and Philadelphia: The Center for Iranian Jewish Oral History & The Jewish Publication Society, 2002), pp. 137–57.
44. See *Mozakerat-e Majles* Rabi' II, 6, 1325 (14 May 1907), p. 169. See also *Mozakerat-e Majles*, Jamadi 1, 5, 1325 (17 June 1907). Zoroastrians did not align themselves with Jews and Christian Armenians, perhaps because they ranked higher in the religious hierarchy of Iran.
45. Mojtahedi, *Taqizadeh*, p. 60.
46. Thanks to Houri Berberian for providing me with a copy of this statement. See also Berberian, *Armenians*.
47. See the 1907 private letter of Sheykh Salim to Mirza Fazl-Ali Aqa Tabrizi that appears in Mirza Saleh, *Bohran-e Demokrasi*, pp. 85–6.
48. For a classic treatment of the subject, see Jean Bethke Elshtain, *Public Man, Private Woman: Women in Social and Political Thought* (Princeton: Princeton University Press, 1996) and Patricia Boling, *Privacy and the Politics of Intimate Life* (Ithaca: Cornell University Press, 1996).
49. For a discussion of gender-related changes during the Pahlavi era, see Parvin Paidar, *Women and the Political Process in Twentieth-Century Iran* (Cambridge: Cambridge University Press, 1995) and Janet Afary, *Sexual Politics in Modern Iran* (Cambridge: Cambridge University Press, 2009).

PART II

TRANSNATIONAL CONNECTIONS

CHAPTER 4

IRANIAN NATIONALISM AND GLOBAL SOLIDARITY NETWORKS, 1906–18: INTERNATIONALISM, TRANSNATIONALISM, GLOBALIZATION, AND NATIONALIST COSMOPOLITANISM[1]

Mansour Bonakdarian

Nationalist thought and politics have been pervasive themes in studies of Iran since the nineteenth century. Some of the studies dealing with the formative stages of Iranian nationalisms have also commented on the extent to which different expressions of Iranian nationalism borrowed from, corresponded to, or diverged from *past* historical models of nationalism in other parts of the world (paradoxically often in reference to those European/Western countries where the emergence of nationalism coincided with the rising imperialist ascendancy of those countries, contrary to the Iranian experience). Conspicuously absent in most of these studies is the extent to which the emergent nationalist ideologies and practices in Iran also dialogically engaged with *contemporary* nationalist movements and ideas in other parts of the world, and in the colonized and semi-colonized territories in particular. This study only briefly highlights a few instances and attributes of the manifold, multidirectional interactions between Iranian nationalisms and other contemporary nationalist movements in the framework of global anti-imperialist solidarity networks during the period from the Iranian Constitutional Revolution to the end of World War I – with this period marking the rapid proliferation of broad-based and organized anti-imperialist nationalist struggles in Iran, albeit with roots in earlier episodes such as the 1891–1892 tobacco protest movement. Above all, this account contributes to ongoing attempts at de-provincializing the historiography of Iran in general.[2]

Although no single, truly global, all-encompassing, anti-imperialist solidarity network existed at that time (or even after the formation of the League Against Imperialism in 1927 for that matter) – and many of the nationalist movements and groupings participating in the different networks subscribed to exclusionary constructs of nationality, civilization, and/or race, these networks nonetheless were at some level 'global' in their reach, if for no other reason than the fact that each of them broadly or marginally overlapped with other networks, making them links in a wider chain of an incontrovertibly global web.[3] Given the available space, this chapter does not address the particular definitions of nation, nationalisms, and varying nationalist platforms in the Iranian context at the time; nor their limitations and discontents. Suffice it only to mention the obvious fact that, in addition to domestic factors, Iranian nationalisms developed in reaction to actual or perceived outside intervention in Iran and in contrasting Iran's progress with that of other countries – and hence from the moment of conception were by definition developmentally grounded in a trans-Iranian framework – and to also underscore a central theme of this chapter: that Iranian nationalists ideologically both borrowed from and also contributed to nationalist thought and movements elsewhere through observation as well as direct and indirect interaction with one another. Of course, by definition, the very 'universality' of the project of nationalism pursued by these Iranians was in essence, albeit not in its particular imagined and unfolding local contours, a *worlding* process. Iranian nationalists (regardless of their varying platforms) were part of a worldwide phenomenon of nationalisms; more precisely, they belonged to the tier of nationalists from the colonized and semi-colonized regions of the world.

By the time of the outbreak of the Iranian Constitutional Revolution in 1906, Iran was already deeply immersed in a wide spectrum of international affairs and globalization processes, including economic, technological and diplomatic; was engaged in literary, fashion, intellectual,[4] and artistic interactions; participated at the Permanent Court of Arbitration in the Hague and was represented at international moral and educational congresses and in international geographical societies; alongside the transmission and exchange of expert knowledge (ranging from education[5] to journalistic, medical, and scientific, including attendance at the International Congress of Orientalists beginning with the organization's fourteenth meeting in Algiers in 1905), or such other developments as participation at the Great Exhibition at the Crystal Palace in London in 1851 and in other international exhibitions in Europe and the United States; not to mention Iranian collections at various museums and archives around the world and the global reach of Iranian literature (classical Persian in this case), to name only a very few random examples.[6] Many of these globalization processes and global interactions in the case of Iran, with varying accompanying attributes of 'mordernity', can in fact be traced back to the Safavid era (1501–1722), if not earlier.[7] Beginning in the nineteenth century, nationalism was a further ingredient in Iran's immersion in the contemporary globalization processes.

This fragmentary general overview of some of the global solidarity networks *apropos* Iranian nationalists during the period primarily focuses on selected examples drawn from the cross-currents of Iranian, Indian, and Irish nationalist struggles, as well as a host of other contemporary nationalist movements and struggles from territories beyond the range of the Ottoman Empire, the Russian Caucasus, and Central Asia, which have been receiving greater attention in recent years.[8] This summary outline also does not devote much attention to the leading and most effective organized activity in the West in support of the Iranian constitutional and nationalist struggle before World War I in the form of the Persia Committee in London (1908–14), which included a number of Irish nationalists.

Locating Iran in the Global Solidarity Networks

A good starting point is an event that has captured my imagination ever since I stumbled across a very brief summary account of it nearly two decades ago, and to which I have already referred in passing in an earlier publication.[9] This event, a gathering of mostly nationalist groups from colonized and semi-colonized regions of the world, was nothing extraordinary by itself. Numerous such gatherings, many with much larger attendance, had already taken place in European cities and in other parts of the world for decades. Yet this event, of which only a few very cursory contemporary accounts are available, offers a number of heuristic openings and outlines some of the key themes that pertain to the main topic of this chapter. This was a gathering on 10 March 1912 at the Hôtel des Sociétés Savantes in Paris, just over two months after the termination of the Iranian Constitutional Revolution of 1906–11 as a consequence of Russian and British machinations that led to the closure of the Second Majles (Iranian parliament) in late December 1911. The gathering was 'to honour and congratulate The Chinese Republican Committee' following the successful 1911–12 republican Xinhai Revolution in China. A report of this event appeared in the radical pan-Indian nationalist paper *Bande Mataram*, published in Geneva and edited by the Paris-based militant pan-Indian nationalist and feminist Madame Bhikhaji Rustom Cama, who was of Parsi ethno-religious background and occasionally introduced herself at international anti-imperialist and feminist gatherings as an Indian of Iranian ancestry.[10] According to the paper, this gathering was organized 'solely by The Orientals', adding enigmatically that it was also 'purely on oriental lines'. Those attending the event, the report continued, 'were representatives of all the different nationalities of Asia and Africa, such as [t]he Hind[ustanis], Egyptians, Persians, Algerians, Caucasians, Arm[e]nians[,] Turks, Japanese, Chines[e], and even men from Syria & Arabia', along with sympathizers from around Europe. The programme also included a dance performance by Madame Armen (also spelt Armène) Ohanian, the 'Russian'-born, Paris-based, Armenian-Iranian dancer, who was already emerging as an international dance sensation with extensive press coverage of her performances.[11] Although Cama did not mention it, the gathering was most likely organized by the Chinese Republican Committee of Europe, which was chiefly comprised of Chinese students (many of them with anarchist leaning), given that this committee, in conjunction with the Sino-French Union, would organize other receptions in Paris throughout the month in celebration of the establishment of the Chinese Republic.[12]

The rare reports of the event that I have so far managed to locate do not identify the Iranian delegates attending this gathering, nor is there any reference to this event in the available memoirs and published correspondence of leading Iranian nationalist personalities in Paris at the time, who included Mohammad Qazvini, Hoseyn Kazemzadeh (Iranshahr), and the young students Ebrahim Pourdavoud and Mirza Mahmoud Khan Ashrafzadeh; all of whom would subsequently be involved in the German-backed Iranian nationalist activities during World War I. Among their range of activities in defence of Iran's sovereignty and calls for the restoration of the Iranian Majles, Qazvini, Kazemzadeh, and Pourdavoud would shortly join the newly-founded International League for Defending the Rights of People based in Paris (Ligue internationale pour la défense du droit des peuples, 1912), with Pourdavoud being selected by his colleagues to represent Iran at the League's first congress in August of that year.[13] Having arrived in Paris in 1910 to pursue his studies in law, by 1912 Pourdavoud had already made the acquaintance of Madame Cama.[14] For the Iranians attending the March 1912 gathering in Paris, the celebration of the success of the Chinese Revolution and the establishment of the Chinese Republic could only have been replete with a bittersweet sentiment of camaraderie and festivity accompanied by a mood of melancholia and a sense of nationalist trauma at the memory of the recent suppression of the Iranian constitutional movement, as well as the nostalgic recollection that not long ago the Iranian revolution had served as an inspiration for some nationalist struggles elsewhere, particularly in Asia. Yet, the gathering must also have afforded an occasion for renewed nationalist hope and inspiration for these Iranians, particularly with the enthusiastic response of the crowd to the declaration by an Egyptian delegate of 'Long live the independence of China! Long live the independence of Persia! Long live the independence of Egypt! Long live the independence of India! Long live all the nationalities struggling for liberation!'[15] The Iranian delegates, and possibly many of the representatives of other nationalities present at this event, would likely have been present at an earlier 12 February public mass meeting that had also taken place at the Hôtel des Sociétés Savantes. That meeting, organized under the auspices of the (French) Human Rights League (La Ligue des droits de l'homme, established in 1898) with an estimated attendance of around 800 individuals, had been arranged to protest against the so-called Anglo-

Russian 'partition' of Iran as one of the many such recent protest gatherings in Paris and other European cities.[16]

The Chinese revolutionaries, notwithstanding the many differences between the Iranian and Chinese revolutions in their local, regional, and international settings and their objectives, and despite the ongoing threats faced by the new Chinese state, were now at a juncture resembling a combination of both the August 1906 and July 1909 time frames in the Iranian constitutionalist-nationalist memory. The Chinese, too, had staged a revolution directed against both imperialist intervention and the native autocracy, albeit also with overtones of ethnic hostility toward the ruling Manchu dynasty (a phenomenon lacking in the Iranian context, certainly on a similar level or intensity), as well as having established a republican government following the ouster of the Chinese Emperor in February 1912 (as opposed to the continuation of monarchy in Iran).[17] Iranians had staged a successful revolution in the summer of 1906 (albeit without recourse to armed struggle) and had eventually ousted an autocratic monarch, Mohammad Ali Shah, in July 1909, replacing him with his son following a civil war in 1908–9. The Iranian delegates at the 1912 gathering would also have been amply cognizant that others in attendance perceived them as envoys of a once buoyant, but now defeated, revolution. For the Chinese nationalists the Iranian revolution, which once had served as a beacon, now also loomed as a cautionary tale of the potential dangers ahead, particularly given the continued armed hostilities by groups opposed to the new revolutionary government and the ongoing imperialist meddling in Chinese affairs.[18] The Iranian experience since 1906 was itself now clearly an instance of *worlding* other nationalist and parliamentary reformist struggles (both historicizing and analysing them by way of referring to the Iranian example).

The 1912 gathering at the Hôtel des Sociétés Savantes, among many other gatherings during the early years of the twentieth century that brought together representatives of various nationalist movements from around the world or afforded them alternative fora of international or transnational audiences (certainly not limited only to events in European/Western locations), also points to a number of key analytical themes, including the interplay between nationalism, cosmopolitanism, internationalism, and transnationalism in the global solidarity networks. Moreover, the 1912 event directs our attention to the broad spectrum and diversity of the global networks. These ranged from independent voluntary associations, as in the case of this gathering, to hierarchical and deferential associations arranged through the patronage of other states, as in the case of the collaborations between the German-backed Iranian Nationalist Committee in Berlin (and other Iranian nationalist groupings) during World War I with the German- or Ottoman-backed nationalist groups from other parts of the world. Expressions of solidarity also varied from the short-term, even if intermittent, token displays among nationalists from different parts of the world (as in the case of Iranians and Chinese) to protracted and more substantial forms of collaboration (as in the case of armed co-operation between groups of Iranians and Indians during World War I). Among the many other features of these networks, there were reciprocal and unreciprocated expressions of solidarity, as well as particular types of articulated affinities (discussed later). Furthermore, gatherings similar to the 1912 one also help us situate the organization by non-Europeans of such geographically and ideologically diverse (yet inclusive) gatherings within the framework of the globalization processes underway at the time – as opposed to similar events organized and hosted by Europeans/Westerners, such as the annual meetings of the International Socialist Congress (the Second International, 1889–1916; and operating under the aegis of the International Socialist Bureau after 1900), which around this time was rapidly extending its membership to non-Western/non-European regions (as organized socialist movements began to form in those other parts of the world around the turn of the twentieth century). There were myriad other similar gatherings in Western countries and in other parts of the world during this period devoted to anti-autocratic, anti-colonial, and anti-racist struggles, in which Iranian nationalists of different orientations participated. These ranged from banquets to mass meetings and congresses – including gatherings inside Iran itself and in India, the Russian Caucasus, the Ottoman Empire, and Egypt – with some of them devoted specifically to the Iranian nationalist struggle.[19] By then, many non-European/non-Western groups already had been organizing their own cross-solidarity conferences in European/Western locations in pursuit of wide-ranging objectives, as in the case of the African Association formed in London in 1897 (which also included people of African descent from Western territories), or the Indian nationalists affiliated with the India House in London (1905–10), or the pan-Islamic La Fraternité Musulmane (founded in Paris in 1907 and led by the Young Turks, with which Iranian nationalists were in contact), among other examples. There were also other types of gatherings with broader target audiences (than just the nationalist or particular pan-groupings) which afforded additional alternative venues for nationalists from the colonized and semi-colonized regions to champion their own causes. Examples of such settings included the congresses of the Second International (especially after 1907) or a host of other types of assemblies that did not even formally endorse anti-imperialist struggles, as in the case of the statements made by the veteran Iranian nationalist Yahya Dowlatabadi during the Universal Races Congress in London in July 1911.[20]

Madame Cama's highly enthusiastic and hyperbolic statement in her report of the March 1912 gathering in Paris in reference to the spectrum of 'nationalities' represented at the event – 'It looked as if The Ideal International Republic was established in this world'[21] – is highly suspect in its elision of the frequently parochial nature of many anti-imperialist nationalist platforms at the time. The statement disregarded the limitations, if not antagonistic disenchantments, of the interplay between most nationalisms and platforms of internationalism or transnationalism, as in the case of the conflicting Armenian and Ottoman nationalist aspirations at the time, with delegates from both groups being present at the 1912 meeting (even while nationalists representing such conflicting national agenda may in unison have expressed solidarity with *other* nationalist groups). This is not to say that the anti-imperialist solidarity networks did not often also include individuals committed to multiple international and transnational platforms and struggles, regardless of the confines of their allegiances; among them individuals actively engaged in facilitating the nationalist campaigns of other groups. Madame Cama herself, also an ardent champion of global feminism, had already lent direct assistance to the Iranian revolutionary cause, as well as to the activities of Irish and Egyptian nationalists. Among other examples, she assisted with the September 1910 meeting of the Egyptian Congress in Brussels, at which time she also arranged for 'a telegram to be sent by the Persians of Paris condemning Russo-British aggression in Persia', in addition to encouraging many Indian letters of protest in support of Iran's independence over the years.[22] An Iranian example of individuals committed to a broad spectrum of nationalist and transnational commitments and engaged in different solidarity networks was Seyyed Jalal al-Din Kashani (Mo'ayyed al-Eslam), the proprietor of the Calcutta *Habl al-Matin*, who simultaneously advocated Iranian nationalism, and pan-Indian nationalism (somewhat incongruously alongside the activities of Indian Muslim nationalists after 1906), together with a non-sectarian pan-Islamic platform, while also championing the rights of Iranian Zoroastrians, greater educational opportunities for Iranian women, and other religious and social reforms. He and a number of his Iranian nationalist associates in India worked closely with the Indian Muslim nationalist organization the All-India Muslim League (ML; founded in 1906), with Mirza Shuja'at Ali Beg (the Iranian vice-consul in Calcutta, also identified as 'Khan Bahador Hajj Moulavi Mirza Shuja'at Ali Khan') being elected as a vice-president of the Bengal branch of the ML in 1910, and Agha Seyyed Hussein Shustary also serving as a vice-president of the same branch of the ML.[23] The ML, in turn, utilized its various branches in India and in Britain in support of the Iranian Constitutional Revolution.[24] Yet another example of an individual with multiple commitments was the Bulgarian Vladikoff Panoff, a careerist internationalist revolutionary with anarchist-socialist and feminist leanings and a participant on the constitutionalist side in the Iranian civil war of 1908–9, which pitted the constitutionalist-nationalist forces against the royalist forces of the autocratic Mohammad Ali Shah and his Russian backers, with the latter enjoying London's implicit consent. Panoff also reported for a host of Russian liberal press on the Iranian revolution and facilitated contacts between the Istanbul-based Iranian anjoman-e sa'adat (Society of the Welfare of Iranians) and the International Socialist Bureau – the latter in co-operation with the Iranian socialist Dr Abdullah 'Qara Bey,' with both of them joining the anjoman-e sa'adat in 1909,[25] and 'Qara Bey' and one of his Iranian socialist associates Rahimzadeh later travelling to Paris, London and other locations to elicit greater international socialist support for the beleaguered Iranian revolutionaries.

The examples of Mo'ayyed al-Eslam and the Iranian anjoman-e sa'adat in Istanbul also highlight the participation of Iranians from the émigré and diaspora communities, including women's organizations, in the global nationalist solidarity networks. The émigré and diaspora organizations ranged, for example, from the anjoman-e vefaq-e iraniyan (Society of Iranian Alliaance) in Egypt[26] to anjoman-e okhovat-e iraniyan (Society of Iranian Fraternity) in Baghdad, Ottoman Iraq,[27] and the anjoman-e mosavat (Society of Equality) in Karbala, Ottoman Iraq.[28]

Nationalist Cosmopolitanisms

Such contacts and exchanges between Iranian nationalists and anti-imperialists or reformist and other similar groups or individuals from other parts of the world, alongside ideological cross-influences, further underscore the unquestionably cosmopolitan foundations and formations of miscellaneous Iranian nationalisms, whether secular or religious in their orientation. These nationalist platforms were conceived, articulated, re-articulated, and staged through engagement with different circuits of global solidarity networks from the early phases of Iranian nationalism in the nineteenth century.[29] Examples of these contacts prior to the Constitutional Revolution, even if often in much less organized forms, ranged from those between the pan-Islamist Seyyed Jamal al-Din Asadabadi (a.k.a., 'al-Afghani') and Egyptian nationalists in the late nineteenth century, to Asadabadi's and Mirza Malkum Khan's direct collaboration in London with British critics of their government's official Iranian policy during the Iranian tobacco protest movement of 1891–2,[30] to contacts (beginning in the late-nineteenth century) between Iranian and Indian nationalists, or various forms of association between members of the Iranian émigré communities in the Russian Caucasus and Russian socialist organizations, or between Iranian dissidents in the Ottoman Empire and members of the Young Ottoman and Young Turk organizations. These previous contacts were mostly initiated by members of the Iranian émigré and diaspora communities in territories primarily adjoining Iran (Egypt being the exception), and just prior to the Constitutional Revolution included the earliest examples of organized collaborations, as in the form of Iranian social-democratic groups in the Russian Caucasus (e.g., the formation of the Iranian ejtema'iyun-e 'ammiyun 'Social Democratic Party' in Baku in 1904). These decades also marked the birth of the Iranian press with varying nationalist propensities, launched by members of the émigré and diaspora communities and constituting the earliest forms of Iranian nationalist press prior to the outbreak of the Constitutional Revolution, leaving aside other types of Iranian nationalist publications inside Iran itself, such as the *shahnamah* ('nocturnal letters').[31]

This nationalist cosmopolitanism was much more evident both inside and outside Iran after the outbreak of the revolution in 1906, and particularly following the 31 August 1907 Anglo–Russian Agreement that divided Iran into Russian, British, and neutral spheres of influence, while also delineating the British and Russian reach of influence in Afghanistan and Tibet. In fact, it was in Iran itself that the widest scope (if not the most decisive overall consequence) of interaction between Iranians and non-Iranians occurred within the global solidarity networks, in so far as not only bringing groups from other territories into direct contact and collaboration with Iranian nationalists, but also exposing these groups to a broad range of Iranian social classes (urban and rural/tribal) – including Iranians from different religious background and women in some cases – particularly during the nationalist armed operations against the Iranian autocracy and its Russian military backers in 1908–9. A similar pattern of contacts inside Iran would take place during World War I in opposition to Russian and British occupation of the country and would continue after 1918 in the case of ongoing nationalist armed uprisings, such as the Jangal (forest) insurgency in the Caspian littoral (1914–21).[32]

Among many other examples, the non-Iranian participants in these collaborations during the Constitutional Revolution included hundreds of Armenians, Georgians, Azeris, and other 'Russians' mainly from the Caucasus, as well as Bulgarian volunteers and mercenaries, and the occasional German, American – i.e. Howard Baskerville, who was killed in his first armed engagement and was widely eulogized and memorialized,[33] and the team of American Treasury advisers led by William Morgan Shuster, whose policies led to the final showdown between the Second Majles and Russia and Britain – or the few Ottoman (Young Turk) sympathizers, even as the Ottomans engaged in their own territorial aggression against Iran. In addition, a few members of the British consular staff in Iran, such as Claude B. Stokes, also provided assistance to the Iranian revolutionary camp. The Irish journalist Arthur Moore, reporting for the Persia Committee in London, which championed the Iranian revolution, and the author of *The Orient Express* (1914), briefly joined the Iranian nationalist forces in the besieged city of Tabriz during the Iranian civil war of 1908–9, before growing disillusioned with Iranian nationalists. The socialist, republican Irish-nationalist William J. Maloney served as a reporter for Reuters in

Iran and was in contact with Iranian nationalist circles, whose views he echoed in his reports. Without wishing to exaggerate their overall role or influence in the fate of the Iranian nationalist struggle, these collaborations were at times extremely significant in both determining the outcome on the battlefield and in generating international expressions of solidarity with Iranian nationalists. It is no surprise that during the Iranian civil war of 1908–9 the nationalist revolutionary Hoseyn Kasma'i, also a participant in the future Jangal armed uprising against Russian and British occupation of Iran during World War I (which again attracted non-Iranian combatants and advisers to its ranks), would casually write to the Tabriz constitutionalist-nationalist paper *Anjoman* that the revolutionary fighters in the city of Rasht at the time 'could be characterized as "international"'.[34] Among numerous other examples, after the constitutionalist-nationalist victory in the civil war, the Calcutta *Habl al-Matin* would express gratitude to those individuals and groups in other parts of the world who had been assisting the Iranian nationalist cause ('freedom-nurturers of the worlds of humanity', 'nurturers of justice in Europe', and 'the humanitarian European press, of France and England in particular').[35] Similarly, during World War I the Berlin-based Iranian nationalist mouthpiece *Kaveh* would write in an obituary for the former prominent nationalist leader Sardar As'ad Bakhtiari: 'In the history of the revolution in Iran no more than four or five individuals can be considered as venerated men in the full sense of the word. Sardar As'ad, [and] Yeprim Khan [the Armenian émigré nationalist and a prominent figure in the Iranian constitutionalist-nationalist victory in the 1908–9 civil war] from Iran, and the American [W. Morgan] Shuster are the most shining examples of our recent history.'[36] These and many other such contemporary commentaries by Iranians and non-Iranians were incontrovertible acknowledgment of the considerable extent to which the Iranian nationalist struggle had assumed an international dimension, with an international support base and international participants; in fact, it was the first revolution of its kind in Asia to become so internationalized.

While there was a long history of non-Iranians (including Europeans) being employed in the service of the Iranian state or by regional strongmen as military advisers or mercenary fighters, the Constitutional Revolution marked the first occasion that outside groups joined ranks with Iranian *nationalists* in armed struggle. This pattern would continue during World War I and subsequently, just as there would be abundant appeals for solidarity issued by Iranian nationalists to their sympathizers and the public at large around the world during the coming years. Among other contemporary indications of the worlding and cosmopolitan framing of the Iranian Constitutional Revolution by Iranians themselves are the frequent historical contextualizations of Iranian developments, cast in world-historical frameworks, appearing in the pages of the Iranian nationalist press and in other range of nationalist commentaries. These included comparative references to nationalist movements and revolutions in other parts of the world past and present,[37] once again with parallels during World War I and subsequently; just as Chinese, Indian, Egyptian, and other revolutionaries referred to Iranian developments among their assortment of historical examples. Events such as the March 1912 meeting at the Hôtel des Sociétés Savantes provide alternative means of plotting, grounding, discussing, and analysing Iranian nationalisms during the period and offer avenues for further heuristic engagement with the historiography of the evolution of nationalist ideologies and movements in Iran.

Contact Zones

Paris, London, New York, Berlin, and other 'Western' cities during the period served as what can be termed *third contact zones*[38] for Iranian and other nationalists from the colonized and semi-colonized regions of the world. In such locations, these nationalists could come into direct contact, in ways they could not do through mere correspondence. These contact zones served as alternative spaces of direct interaction between these nationalists *outside* the parameters their own designated 'national' territories, as opposed to, for example, direct Iranian and Indian nationalist contacts in Calcutta or Shiraz, or between Iranian and Egyptian nationalists in Cairo – although exceptions will have to be made in the case of the Irish and other groups from 'colonized' territories within Europe itself when, for instance, we discuss locations such as London or Manchester as the contact zones, given that there was a long-established and sizeable Irish community presence in such places (although places such as Paris, for example, still qualified as a third contact zone for Irish nationalists).[39] In the case of imperial capitals, such as London and Paris – and here for the sake of a narrower focus excluding such imperial capitals as Istanbul and Tokyo, which also served as third contact zones for certain groups – the imperial metropolises were transformed (at least for the duration of such gatherings, and often with the assistance of sympathetic [non-colonial] individuals from the imperial metropolises themselves) into combined spaces of *trans*-imperial convergence and anti-colonial, anti-imperialist, or anti-racist solidarity campaigns, and redefined as 'heterotopic' spaces, to borrow Michel Foucault's concept of alternative, non-hierarchic spatial configurations.[40] These meeting places were simultaneously both divested of, and yet distended with, their pre- and post-event 'imperial' attribute for the duration of the gatherings. To borrow Mircea Eliade's concepts of 'sacred' and 'profane' time and space, albeit here applied in a drastically different sense and context than that intended by Eliade, the locations of such gatherings by anti-imperialist nationalists within the imperial metropolises transformed these places from imperialist or profane to anti-imperialist or sacred spaces for the duration of the meetings, or vice versa if viewed through an imperialist lens. Anti-imperialist nationalist groups from within and outside each of the imperial dominions were brought together in these alternatively-configured spaces of the third contact zones in ways that were distinct from, and also less hegemonic than, the more regular nationalist activities of, say, Indians, or Irish, or Egyptians in London (since those nationalists hailed from British imperial territories). Such gatherings could range in their articulation of anti-imperialism from the most progressive forms of radical nationalism to the most chauvinistic forms of ethno-nationalism. In 1917, in the midst of World War I, Stockholm too would serve as such a third contact zone for Iranian nationalists attending a congress of the Socialist International.

Participation in these gatherings with vastly diverse attendance was marked by prior or on-location linguistic, historical, social (including class), and cultural 'translation' (at times not too successfully),[41] as well as by instances of political-ideological navigation, and national self-inscription and self-affirmation; underscoring the particular *accented* presence of different participants. Another development in these third contact zones was the publication of journals devoted to the coverage of worldwide anti-colonial/anti-imperialist struggles produced by nationalists from those regions – as in the case of one of the earliest such Iranian papers, Malkum Khan's *Qanun* (London, 1890–98). In addition, there were numerous articles endorsing these nationalist movements that appeared in the sympathetic European/Western press in these contact zones, including in some of the socialist, feminist, or theosophical press, as well as in publications specifically devoted to anti-imperialist struggles, such as the monthly *Egypt* published in London from 1911 to 1913 by the renowned British conservative anti-imperialist Wilfrid Scawen Blunt and edited by the internationalist, socialist, feminist, republican Irish-nationalist Frederick Ryan, which also championed the Iranian nationalist struggle. Individuals from the colonized and semi-colonized regions of the world also contributed to such articles appearing in the Western/European press (with their equivalents in other locations such as Calcutta or Tokyo). Among many other examples of such forms of anti-imperialist journalism in the third contact zones were *The African Times and Orient Review* (founded in London in 1912 by the purportedly 'Egyptian' anti-imperialist, pan-Islamist, pan-Asianist, and pan-Africanist Dusé Mohamed Ali), which provided coverage of Iranian affairs, to the New York-based militant Irish nationalist newspaper the *Gaelic American* (1903–51), the militant pan-Indian papers *Indian Sociologist* (London, 1905–10; and Paris subsequently), *Bande Mataram* (Geneva, 1910–14), *Free Hindustan* (Vancouver, 1907–8; Seattle, 1908–10), and *Ghadar* (San Francisco, 1913–15), all of which also advocated the Iranian nationalist agenda. Iranian specimens of this type of nationalist press from the period included the short-lived *Iranshahr* (Paris, 1914) and the much better known Berlin-based and German state-funded *Kaveh* during its early publication years (1916–18), when it also functioned as a German propaganda outlet during World War I (and, of course, steered clear of castigating German imperialism).[42] These contact zones appeared in diverse works of fiction in various languages, ranging from the Japanese Shiba Shirō's *kajin no kigū* (*Serendipitous Encounters with Beautiful Women*, 1885–97) to the African-American W.E.B. Du Bois' *Dark Princess* (1928) or the Jamaican Pan-Africanist Claude Mckay's *Banjo* (1929).

Nationalist Solidarities: From Sympathy to Armed Cooperation

The third contact zones also served as locations of safety and exile for nationalists from the colonized and semi-colonized regions. For Iranian nationalists, places such as Paris and London had served as locations of refuge since the latter decades of the nineteenth century, alongside the often more convenient and more traditional locations of safe haven for Iranians fleeing different forms of persecution in their country, even before the emergence of nationalism, as in the case of the Indian subcontinent, the Russian and Ottoman empires, or Egypt.[43] Iran itself, in turn, came to serve as a place of refuge for persecuted nationalists from other territories (whether or not functioning as a third contact zone in this context), such as groups from the Caucasus. In 1909, a group of Indian nationalist refugees fleeing British persecution arrived in Iran, with Seyyed Abdullah 'Mujtahid' (Baladi-i Bushehri) evidently being one of their first Iranian benefactors after they reached Bushehr, before finally taking refuge in the city of Shiraz. These Indians included Ajit Singh, Sufi Amba Parsad, Rishikesh Letha (a.k.a. Rikhikesh, who later assumed the alias 'Zia al-Din'), Thakur Das, and Zia-ul-Haq. While Ajit Singh and three of his companions eventually left Iran, Sufi Amba remained in Shiraz and continued collaborating with Iranian nationalists, with their range of collaborations including the publication of a nationalist newspaper by the name of *Hayat*. Sufi Amba, who also helped found a school with a 'modern' curriculum in Shiraz and served as its principal, was eventually killed in Iran or committed suicide after capture in 1916 (accounts of his death vary), following his participation in the joint Iranian and Indian nationalist armed operations against the British forces in World War I. By then, he had been joined by other militant Indian nationalists arriving in Iran during the war.[44] He was also known in Iran as 'Agha Sufi-ye Hendi', or by his Iranian aliases 'Mohammad Hoseyn Sufi' and 'Mohammad Hoseyn "Khadem-e Shari'at"', while Thakur Das went by the alias 'Gholam Hussein', and Ajit Singh adopted the Persian name of 'Mirza Hassan Khan' and would travel throughout Europe, with the assistance of Iranian nationalists at various locations along the way and under his assumed Iranian name and with a forged Iranian passport, before eventually settling in Brazil.[45] The Calcutta *Habl al-Matin*, in its report of Ajit Singh's and Sufi Amba's refuge in Shiraz, wrote that they were under the protection of a notable cleric in that city, Hojat al-Islam Agha Mirza Ibrahim Mahallati, and were said to be publishing a paper by the name of *Hayat*, which reportedly denounced British imperialism and Anglo–Russian belligerence in Iran. The report added that their Iranian patron had thwarted attempts by the British consulate to apprehend the Indian refugees.[46] Briefly settling in Lucerne, Switzerland, in 1912–13, Ajit Singh would later comment on the anti-imperialist solidarity networks in that city and in various other European locations before the outbreak of World War I, including Iranian participation in these networks. Of the groups in Lucerne, he wrote: 'Here I could come in frequent touch with Iranians, Egyptians, [and] Morocc[a]ns. I held an Iranian passport and students, travellers, [and] tourists used to visit this place and I had the chance of coming into at least social contact.' He continued: 'I got in touch with the youth – Finns, Turks, Egyptians, Russians, [and] Irish. After a short time a society of the oppressed of the world was organised [...]. The aim of the society was mutual sympathy in each other's cause of liberty, and if possible, co-operation and help.' He then added, 'There was another society of Oriental people of which no European could become a member. There Moroccans, Tunisians, Algerians, Egyptians, Turks, Persians, [and] Indians [were] its members [...]. People from Geneva also used to attend [these] meetings. Sometimes we went to Geneva to meet our sympathisers.'[47] One of the Iranians assisting Ajit Singh during his stay in Switzerland was Seyyed Mohammad Ali Jamalzadeh, who according to Singh 'showed much interest in India'.[48]

There had been contacts between Indian and Iranian nationalists since the late nineteenth century, with varying degrees of political co-operation as noted already. However, it was during World War I that the first instance of armed collaboration between certain segments of the two groups occurred. The Iranian and Indian nationalist armed collaboration in Iran during World War I, with German backing and funding, had been facilitated through earlier contacts between the veteran Iranian nationalist Seyyed Hasan Taqizadeh and militant Indian nationalists in the United States affiliated with the Ghadar Party (founded in San Francisco, 1913). According to Taqizadeh, who had met a member of Ghadar in New York state (on this occasion the Catskill Mountains serving as an anti-imperialist nationalist third contact zone), it was also the Ghadar members who after the start of World War I had recommended him to the German authorities for establishing what became the Berlin-Based Iranian Nationalist Committee (1916–18).[49] Iranian nationalists, too, had been expressing sympathy with the Indian nationalist resistance to British imperialism for some time.[50] The Indian militants operating in Iran or in the adjoining territories (including

Afghanistan) during World War I were all affiliated with the Indian Independence Committee founded in Berlin in 1915 by Ghadar members (as the successor to the 1914 Indian Committee in Berlin), with Kedar Nath Sondhi as the initial direct representative of the Berlin committee in Iran. Abd al-Hoseyn Sheybani (Vahid al-Molk), the official representative in Germany during the war of the nationalist provisional government of Iran (1915–17), mentions meeting an Indian nationalist in Berlin who had recently arrived from Iran and went by the assumed name of 'Zia al-Din' (which was the alias adopted by Rishikesh Letha, possibly taken from the name of one of the Iranians who had assisted him and his fellow Indian refugees during his first stay in Iran in 1909, who included Seyyed Zia al-Din Tabataba'i).[51] The small band of Indian nationalists operating in Iran during the war fought alongside the Iranian Democrat Party activists, the Tangestani and Qashqa'i tribes, other groups of Iranian nationalists, German agents (including the legendary Wilhelm Wassmuss), and the Swedish staff of the Iranian gendarmerie. The campaigns of the Indian Independence Committee in Iran and in neighbouring Afghanistan ultimately met with failure, including the objectives of the Provisional Government of India formed in December 1915 in Kabul.

Cross-nationalist collaborations in the solidarity networks also at times yielded corollary 'non-political' forms of co-operation and association. A case in point is the founding of the Sufi Society (anjoman-e-sufieh) in Shiraz in 1914 by Sufi Amba Prasad and one of his Iranian benefactors, Shaykh Mohammad Rahim, evidently as part of the worldwide theosophical movement established by Madame Blavatsky and Henry Steel Olcott in New York in 1875 and the first such lodge founded in Iran, by which time the Theosophical Society had attained a wide global reach and was under the presidency of the Irish-British feminist and anti-imperialist Annie Besant (who, incidentally, would be elected as the annual president of the Indian National Congress in 1917).[52] Although not much information is available about the activities and the popular reach of the lodge, this was yet another minor example of Iran's broader engagements with globalization processes at the time within Iranian borders, facilitated on this occasion also through participants in the global solidarity networks. Collaboration between segments of militant Iranian and Indian nationalists would continue in the post-World War I era, albeit in other forms and largely through the Moscow-controlled Third/

Communist International (1919), while Indian nationalists at large continued to comment on Iranian affairs, including their condemnations of the abortive Anglo–Iranian Agreement of 1919.[53]

Centres and Margins of Anti-imperialist Solidarity Networks

Not all expressions of solidarity were reciprocal; nor did all 'nationalities' always directly participate in the solidarity networks that championed their cause. An example of a one-way expression of solidarity with the Iranian nationalist cause is that of the wide-ranging activities of Irish nationalists (belonging to the parliamentary Home Rule, the more militant Home Rule, or the separatist republican camps) in advocacy of the Iranian constitutionalist-nationalist struggle before World War I.[54] Overt Iranian expressions of solidarity with Irish nationalists (the more militant factions specifically) occurred only during World War I and largely as a consequence of the German-backed wartime propaganda directed against Britain and Russia. Similar to the Iranian, Indian, and Egyptian committees in Berlin, Germany had also set up a republican Irish nationalist committee in co-ordination with the Irish Republican Brotherhood and its affiliate organizations in Ireland and in the United States, as well as attempting to establish an Irish Brigade in the German prisoner of war camps, which proved a dismal failure.[55] The 15 August 1916 issue of the Iranian nationalist paper *Kaveh* (Berlin) included an anonymous article (written by Seyyed Mohammad Ali Jamalzadeh) on 'The Hanging of Sir Roger Casement'. Casement, the republican Irish nationalist representative in Germany and a former British diplomat, was arrested by British authorities shortly after landing in Ireland just ahead of the failed 1916 Easter Rising in Dublin and was subsequently executed on charges of treason, despite substantial international calls for clemency.[56] Incidentally, Casement had failed to secure German approval for dispatching units of the Irish Brigade to 'the Turkish war front', believing that such a step would be of immense 'political importance, particularly in India, Persia and Afghanistan' and with 'an undoubted political effect on the Eastern mind'.[57]

In the immediate years following the end of World War I, Iranian nationalists of differing proclivities would devote much greater attention to the Irish Question (not forgetting that by then Ireland was in the throes of what came to be called the Irish War of Independence or the Anglo–Irish War of 1919–21, leading to the creation of the Irish Free State in 1922).[58] Moreover, after the end of the war – by which time Tsarist Russia had collapsed and Britain was the uncontested imperialist power in the region and British forces were fighting the Jangal insurgency in northern Iran – some Iranian nationalists had also begun to cluster Iran with India, Egypt, and Ireland in their struggle against British imperialism; thereby, consciously or inadvertently, placing Iran in the same category as the British colonies.[59] This was the sort of categorization of the Iranian nationalist struggle which militant Indian and Irish nationalists had conducted for some time, and more so during World War I and after. In 1920 (following the abortive 1919 Anglo–Iranian Agreement and in the midst of the Irish War of Independence), Eamon de Valera, the president of the self-proclaimed Irish Republic, stated at a gathering of the Friends of Freedom for India in New York: 'Our cause is a common cause. We swear friendship tonight; and we send our common greetings and our pledges to our brothers in Egypt and in Persia, and tell them also that their cause is our cause.'[60]

As in the case of those segments of the so-called subaltern male population of Iran who were directly or indirectly involved with, or in other ways affected by, the nationalist global solidarity networks – including the rank-and-file recruits in nationalist armed units in Iran who fought alongside non-Iranian nationalist combatants – very little is still known about the gendered dimensions of the encounters and engagements with these solidarity networks by Iranian women of different social classes, and those of rural or tribal, as well as urban lower-classes, in particular.[61] There is certainly ample evidence that during these years Iranian nationalist women of the educated higher urban classes inside Iran, and especially women's rights activists among them, as well as some women in the Iranian diaspora and émigré communities, participated in a wide range of political activities and international communications and exchanges with the global nationalist solidarity networks, alongside contacts with the international women's rights movements, including the British suffragists. The latter range of exchanges was in pursuance of both the Iranian women's nationalist objectives and their promotion of women's rights.[62] Other Iranian women, most of whose social backgrounds remain unknown, participated in nationalist armed conflicts.[63] By the turn of the twentieth century,

Iranian women's rights activists (women and men) were establishing contact with international suffragist/feminist organizations and these nexuses would be utilized by the nationalist women after the outbreak of the Iranian Constitutional Revolution to solicit feminist, as well as broader public, support in other parts of the world for the preservation of Iran's sovereignty and constitutional government. These women's nationalist and reformist agencies inside Iran at the time, with analogous activities during World War I and the Jangal and other uprisings, gained rapid recognition and praise from their cohorts in the colonized and semi-colonized regions of the world, as well as from the sympathetic segments of Western feminists and other observers.[64] However, the available evidence indicates that the feminist activities of Iranian nationalists in the global networks occurred largely in isolation from the more usual (male-dominated) Iranian nationalist undertakings and global circuits, even if on occasion these campaigns occurred in conjunction with one another and through a number of intersecting global solidarity networks and agents. The rights and conditions of Iranian women at the time were the subject of a talk given by the Iranian nationalist Mirza Ali Agha 'Mujtahid' at a gathering of a Russian women's club in St Petersburg in early 1909, with the Bulgarian Panoff serving as the translator and also commenting on Iranian women's conditions himself.[65] Meanwhile, a number of other proponents of the Iranian revolution in Europe tended to accentuate the women's question in the Iranian revolution in different settings, notably the French Marylie Markovitch (née Amélie de Néry).[66] In June 1910, the British suffragist paper *Common Cause* noted that 'Prince [F]irouze [later a.k.a. Nosrat al-Dawleh], the cousin of the Shah, will give a lecture on "Persian Women"' at the 1910 gathering of the Congrès Permanent du Féminisme International in Paris.[67]

Women's organizations elsewhere also rushed to assist the Iranian revolutionary struggle and extended various forms of assistance, as in the case of the Ottoman women's (Muslim and Christian) relief fund for the constitutionalist fighters in Tabriz during the 1908–9 civil war.[68] Once again, little is known of the range of direct exchanges between Iranian and Ottoman nationalist women during the period prior to the end of World War I (i.e., Turkish, Arab, and other ethnic women from the Empire before 1918), even if women from both territories were in contact with international women's rights organizations, and not forgetting the Ottoman Empire's dual status as both an empire and a territory under assault by European imperialist powers. Iranian women in émigré and diaspora communities also lent assistance to the Iranian nationalist struggle, including Iranian women in India and in the Ottoman Empire.[69]

The outbreak of World War I was to disrupt direct communications between Iranian women and the various global networks, including the international feminist organizations, just as the war also fractured many of the existing anti-imperialist and nationalist solidarity networks, as well as the international feminist and socialist movements, despite efforts by the International Socialist Bureau or by the Women's International League for Peace and Freedom (1915) – which at the time did not have Iranian representation or a formal monitor for that country – to promote peace and international solidarity.[70]

Direct Indian and Iranian nationalist collaborations inside Iran during World War I occurred under drastically different conditions than before, accompanied moreover by major transformations in the basic feature of the global solidarity networks in which Iranians had participated. These transformations were also indicative of the extent to which Iranian nationalisms and the global solidarity networks were interlocked with global developments. Just to offer a few examples of the transformations affecting the Iranian nationalist struggle and leaving aside the ongoing factionalism among Iranian nationalist camps – including the nationalist provisional government established in late December 1915 and headed by Reza-Qoli Mafi (Nezam al-Saltaneh) and those affiliated with the Iranian Nationalist Committee in Berlin[71] – with the outbreak of the war many former advocates of the Iranian cause in countries such as Britain and France curtailed their Iranian campaign to focus on their own 'national' survival, or they were simply unable to participate in the former networks due to the new circumstances; even if there still existed small-scale dissenting organizations and voices in Britain and France that condemned the war and their own governments' continued violations of other countries' sovereignty, such as the Union of Democratic Control in Britain (1914). The war had ushered in the armed confrontation of 'imperial nationalisms' of the major powers alongside transfigured 'anti-colonial nationalist struggles' (including in Central and Eastern Europe and in Ireland). As far as some of the nationalist solidarity networks that had endorsed the Iranian struggle before the war were concerned, now the mainstream Indian

National Congress (INC) or the (Home Rule) Irish Nationalist Party, even if they continued to be vigilant about Iranian affairs during the war, followed their own organization's official policy of supporting the Empire during the war. In the case of India, the All-India Muslim League and most leading Parsi defenders of Iran's independence, whether or not they were affiliated with the INC, also opted to support the British war effort for their own wartime and postwar calculations. Similarly, the likes of Mo'ayyid al-Islam, while certainly not dismissive of Iranian developments during the war and facing greater wartime British press restrictions in India, also chose to curb the Calcutta *Habl al-Matin*'s attacks against British policy.[72] Former allies of Iranian nationalists in the Russian Caucasus, even if willing to challenge Russian aggression in Iran during the war, were now caught in the frontier region in the war between Russia and the Ottoman Empire or exposed to more brutal Russian policy. Others, such as the main Armenian nationalist organizations, opted to side with Russia against the Ottoman Empire; while the Iranian nationalists who openly challenged British and Russian occupation of Iran chose to directly side with the enemies of their enemies – i.e. Germany and the Ottoman Empire – even if many Iranian nationalists distrusted the Ottomans.[73]

Whereas the solidarity networks in which Iranian nationalists had participated prior to the war consisted of non-state entities and championed the Iranian struggle on its own terms, even if other participants in these networks ultimately hoped that Iranian success could be beneficial to their own struggles (e.g., by damaging British imperial prestige or denting Tsarist Russia's regional influence), a major transformation took place during the war. Iranian and Indian nationalists operating in Iran during the war had become players in a new type of solidarity network that prioritized German and Ottoman war aims above those of Iranian or Indian nationalist struggles, seeing the latter as a secondary objective, if not merely a form of diversion tactic adopted against the imperial rivals of Berlin and Istanbul in the war (the same can be said of German policy toward the militant Irish nationalists who opted to ally themselves with Germany). These were different axial modalities of the Iranian nationalist struggle in the global networks: from anti-imperialist nationalist solidarity to nationalist dependence on imperial powers, even if it was under the new circumstances that Iranian nationalists received their most substantial outside material aid (having enjoyed funding from such non-state sources as members of India's Parsi community, among others, during the Constitutional Revolution – although some members of the Iranian opposition before 1906 had on occasion relied on British or Russian funds). In fact, by 1917 Indian and Iranian nationalists in Berlin were independently growing concerned with the extent of Germany's genuine sympathy for, and commitment to, their respective nationalist objectives.[74] As far as cross-affinities went, there were now horizontal affinities among Indian and Iranian nationalists (which is not to say these groups too did not regard one another as a means to their own specific ends), with both sides occupying a subordinate part in a vertically hierarchical organizational network with Germany at the top, in addition to being materially and financially subservient to Germany (and to the Ottoman Empire, albeit more begrudgingly than in the case of Germany).[75] Similarly, Berlin during the war did not function as a third contact zone between the anti-imperialist nationalist groupings operating there, given that their activities were monitored and regulated by the German authorities, who also funded these nationalist groupings' propaganda machinery and sanctioned what could and could not be published by them.

Although many Iranian nationalists had been gravitating toward Germany even before the outbreak of the war, as an ostensibly disinterested imperial counterweight to British and Russian aggression in Iran, the war had now completely transformed circumstances. Just as before the Constitutional Revolution, Iran was now once again an instrument of great power rivalry in the region – having been so since the nineteenth century in the framework of the Russo–British rivalry prior to the 1907 Anglo–Russian Agreement, and from 1907 to 1914 sporadically turned into a site of low-intensity rivalry between Britain and Russia, on the one hand, and Germany, on the other. The difference was that now the rival imperial powers had militarily clashed in Iran and around the world, further imperilling Iran's independence. This is not to say that Iranian nationalists defying British and Russian occupation of Iran at the time had much of a choice in their available options for resistance, unless they were willing to adopt a completely different policy of accepting foreign occupation, or resort to non-violent tactics of non co-operation with the objective of building a mass-based nationalist movement for future large-scale popular confrontation with the imperial powers (by which time Iran could very well have been fully colonized). But these are mere conjectures.

The end of the war in 1918 saw the termination of Iranian nationalist propaganda in Germany and in the Ottoman territories, along with the collapse of much of the Iranian armed resistance against the Allied occupation of Iran, with Britain as the unprecedented dominant European imperialist power in the region now, in light of the Allied victory in the war and the collapse of Tsarist Russia in 1917 (followed by the rise to power of the Bolshevik government later that year). Germany, the imperial ally and patron of Iranian nationalist resistance during the war, was defeated and divested of its Empire, with the Ottoman Empire also having collapsed and largely been partitioned into new Arab territories as British and French mandate protectorates, including the British mandate in Iraq, neighbouring Iran to the West. Meanwhile, the young Bolshevik state to the north of Iran was engaged in a civil war for its very survival, in which some of its opposing factions also received military assistance from Britain, France, the United States, and Japan. The Bolsheviks, in turn, were extending support to the continued Jangal uprising in northern Iran, which was now solely directed against the British imperial presence in the country, leaving aside the domestic reform agenda of the insurgency movement. To the east of Iran, Britain was attempting to expand its influence in Afghanistan; a plan that would fail by 1919, the same year in which London pushed for the signing of the ultimately abortive Anglo–Iranian Agreement. These and many other regional and international developments, including the nationalist uprising in Egypt in 1919, the resumption of the mainstream Indian nationalist campaigns of the INC against Britain with an unprecedented mass participation after the 1919 British massacre in Amritsar, and the Irish War of Independence, as well as the emergence of a new Moscow-centred Communist International, to name only a few global developments in the immediate postwar period, would all impact the ideological, organizational, and tactical features of Iranian nationalisms and their future participation in the new solidarity networks. These new circumstances would again underline the global contingency of, and constraints on, Iranian nationalisms, alongside related internal developments that interacted with the global transformations in a dialogic mode – with some of the major internal transformations in Iran by 1921 that impacted the contours of nationalist ideologies and movements including a slate of other nationalist armed uprisings in different provinces, in addition to the ongoing Jangal insurgency, as well as a coup by Reza Khan that would set in motion his subsequent rapid rise to power.

Notes

1. This chapter draws on material from two of my ongoing book projects, respectively titled *Confluences of Nationalism, Internationalism, and Transnationalism in Early 20th Century Anti-Imperialist Struggles: India, Iran, and Ireland 1905–1921* and *Éirinn & Iran go Brách: Iran in Irish-nationalist historical, literary, cultural, and political imaginations from the late 18th century to 1921*. I have presented earlier drafts of segments of the longer projects at various invitational conferences and lectures. My thanks to the following for the opportunities to share these earlier drafts: Firoozeh Kashani-Sabet (University of Pennsylvania, 2006), Hamid Akbari (Northeastern Illinois University, 2006), Ahmad Ashraf (Columbia University, 2006), Nasrin Rahimieh (University of California, Irvine, 2007), and Firoozeh Papan-Matin (University of Washington, Seattle, 2009). I would also like to thank Houchang Chehabi for his meticulous editing of the final draft of this chapter.
2. For some other examples focusing on this time period, see also Janet Afary, *The Iranian Constitutional Revolution, 1906–1911: Grassroots Democracy, Social Democracy, and the Origins of Feminism* (New York: Columbia, 1996); Houri Berberian, *Armenians and the Iranian Constitutional Revolution of 1905–1911: The Love for Freedom has No Fatherland* (Boulder: Westview Press, 2001); Touraj Atabaki, 'Constitutionalism in Iran and its Asian Interdependencies', *Comparative Studies of South Asia, Africa and the Middle East* xxviii/1 (2008), pp. 142–53; the essays by Touraj Atabaki, Charles Kurzman, Yidan Wang, Kamran Rastegar, Farzin Vejdani, and Mansour Bonakdarian in H. E. Chehabi and Vanessa Martin (eds.), *Iran's Constitutional Revolution: Politics, Cultural Transformations, and Transnational Connections* (London: I.B.Tauris, 2010); Nader Sohrabi, *Revolution and Constitutionalism in the Ottoman Empire and Iran* (New York: Cambridge University Press, 2011); Fariba Zarinebaf, 'From Istanbul to Tabriz: Modernity and Constitutionalism in the Ottoman Empire and Iran', *Comparative Studies of South Asia, Africa, and the Middle East* xxviii/1 (2008), pp. 154–69; Sabri Ateş, *The Ottoman-Iranian Borderlands: Making a Boundary, 1843–1914* (New York: Cambridge University Press, 2013); Mansour Bonakdarian, *Britain and the Iranian Constitutional Revolution of 1906–1911: Foreign Policy, Imperialism, and Dissent* (Syracuse: Syracuse University Press, 2006); Iago Gocheleishvili, 'Georgian Connections of the Iranian Constitutional Revolution of 1905–1911', *Central Eurasian Studies Review* v/1 (2006), pp. 10–14; and Mansour Bonakdarian, 'India: IX. Political and Cultural Relations: Qajar Period, Early 20th Century', *Encyclopaedia Iranica*, vol. XIII, fascicle 1 (2004), pp. 32–44.

3. In addition to the sources cited in the previous endnote that focus specifically on Iran, for a few other examples of wide-ranging studies of international, transregional, and transnational solidarity networks in different historical settings, see also Margaret E. Keck and Kathryn Sikkink, *Activists Beyond Borders: Advocacy Networks in International Politics* (Ithaca: Cornell University Press, 1998); James Goodman and Paul James (eds.), *Nationalism and Global Solidarities: Alternative Projections to Neoliberal Globalization* (New York: Routledge, 2007); David Featherstone, *Resistance, Space and Political Identities: The Making of Counter-Global Networks* (Malden: Wiley-Blackwell, 2008); idem, *Solidarity: Hidden Histories and Geographies of Internationalism* (London: Zed Books, 2012); Ilham Khuri-Makdisi, *The Eastern Mediterranean and the Making of Global Radicalism, 1860–1914* (Berkeley: University of California Press, 2010); Maia Ramnath, *Haj to Utopia: How the Ghadar Movement Charted Global Radicalism and Attempted to Overthrow the British Empire* (Berkeley: University of California Press, 2011); Cemil Aydin, *The Politics of Anti-Westernism in Asia: Visions of World Order in Pan-Islamic and Pan-Asian Thought* (New York: Columbia University Press, 2007); Emily S. Rosenberg (ed.), *A World Connecting: 1870–1945* (Cambridge: Harvard University Press, 2012); Benedict Anderson, *Under Three Flags: Anarchism and the Anti-colonial Imagination* (London: Verso, 2005); Elmo Gonzaga, *Globalization and Becoming-nation: Subjectivity, Nationhood, and Narrative in the Period of Global Capitalism* (Quezon City: University of Philippines Press, 2009); James L. Gelvin and Nile Green (eds.), *Global Muslims in the Age of Steam and Print* (Berkeley: University of California Press, 2014).
4. Ali Gheissari, *Iranian Intellectuals in the Twentieth Century* (Austin: University of Texas Press, 1998), Chapters One and Two; Ali Mirsepassi, *Intellectual Discourse and the Politics of Modernization: Negotiating Modernity in Iran* (New York: Cambridge University Press, 2000), Chapter Two; Farzin Vahdat, *God and Juggernaut: Iran's Intellectual Encounter With Modernity* (Syracuse: Syracuse University Press, 2002), Chapter One.
5. On the introduction of 'modern education' in Iran, see Monica Ringer, *Education, Religion and the Discourse of Cultural Reform in Qajar, Iran* (Costa Mesa: Mazda, 2001).
6. On the 'worlding' of Iran in this context, see also Charles Kurzman, 'Weaving Iran into the Tree of Nations', *International Journal of Middle East Studies* xxxvii/2 (2005), pp. 137–66; Amir Arsalan Afkhami, 'Defending the Guarded Domain: Epidemics and the Emergence of an International Sanitary Policy in Iran', *Comparative Studies of South Asia, Africa and the Middle East* xix/1 (1999), pp. 122–34; and Hasan Javadi, *Persian Literary Influence on English Literature: With Special Reference to the Nineteenth Century* (Costa Mesa: Mazda Publishers, 2005).
7. See also Rudolph P. Matthee, *The Politics of Trade in Safavid Iran: Silk for Silver, 1600–1730* (Cambridge: Cambridge University Press, 1999); Willem Floor and Edmund Herzig (eds.), *Iran and the World in the Safavid Age* (London: I.B.Tauris,

2012); Kirti N. Chaudhuri, *Asia Before Europe: Economy and Civilisation of the Indian Ocean from the Rise of Islam to 1750* (Cambridge: Cambridge University Press, 1990); Andre Gunder Frank, *ReOrient: Global Economy in the Asian Age* (Berkeley: University of California Press, 1998).

8. For a sampling of studies focusing on the regional solidarity networks in the Caucasus and Central Asia during the period, see also Touraj Atabaki, 'Constitutionalists *Sans Frontières*: Iranian Constitutionalism and its Asian Connections', in Chehabi and Martin (eds.), *Iran's Constitutional Revolution*, pp. 341–356; idem., 'Constitutionalism in Iran and its Asian Interdependencies'; Firuz Kazemzadeh, *The Struggle for Transcaucasia (1917–1921)* (Oxford: George Ronald, 1951); Mansoureh Ettehadieh (Nezam-Mafi), *Peydayesh va Tahavvol-e Ahzab-e Siyasi-ye Mashrutiyat* (Tehran: Gostareh, 1982/1983); Janet Afary, 'Armenian Social Democrats, the Democrat Party of Iran, and *Iran-i Naw*: A Secret Camaraderie', in Kambiz Eslami (ed.), *Iran and Iranian Studies: Essays in Honor of Iraj Afshar* (Princeton: Zagros Press, 1998), pp. 239–56; Houri Berberian, *Armenians and the Iranian Constitutional Revolution*; Abd al-Hay Habibi, *Jonbesh-e Mashrutiyat dar Afghanestan* (Kabul, 1984); Cosroe Chaqueri, *The Soviet Socialist Republic of Iran, 1920–1921: Birth of the Trauma* (Pittsburgh: University of Pittsburgh Press, 1995); G.L. Dmitriev, *Indian Revolutionaries in Central Asia* (Delhi: Hope India Publications, 2012).

9. Bonakdarian, *Britain and the Iranian Constitutional Revolution*, p. xx.

10. For instance, in June 1913 Cama participated at the 'International Women's Congress' in Paris, representing both India and Iran and stating in her address to the delegates: 'Hindustan is the land of my birth, and Iran is the country of my ancestors!' *Bande Mataram* (Geneva) iv/11 (July 1913), pp. 1–2.

11. *Bande Mataram* (Geneva) iii/8 (April 1912), p. 1. It should be noted that among the countries listed in this article, Japan itself was an imperialist power and an ally of Britain at the time, even if many contemporary nationalists from China to Iran, Egypt, India, and elsewhere praised Japan as the paragon of parliamentary democracy, reform, and resistance to European/Western imperialism in Asia.

12. Louis Laloy, 'Voix de l'Asie', *Journal des débats* (Paris), 22 March 1912, p. 538. See also Alexander Major, 'Revolutionaries and Republicans: The French Press on Sun Yat-sen and the Xinhai Revolution', in Lee Lai To and Lee Hock Guan (eds.), *Sun Yat-sen, Nanyang and the 1911 Revolution* (Singapore: Institute of Southeast Asian Studies, 2011), pp. 289–90. For accounts of other similar celebrations and banquets in Paris and other parts of Europe, see also M.T.Z. Tyau, 'Celebration of the Chinese Republic', *Chinese Students' Monthly* (Boston) vii/8 (10 June 1912), pp. 660–2; *Republican Advocate of China* (Shanghai) i/5 (4 May 1912), pp. 165–6; *The Sun* (New York), 15 Match 1912, p. 3, c.a; *New-York Tribune*, 15 March 1912, p. 4, c.f; *The Singapore Free Press and Mercantile Advertiser*, 1 May 1912, p. 3, c.b; and Union sino-française, *La République chinoise et la paix universelle* (Paris: Ponroy et Cie, 1912). Shortly before the meeting on 10 March 1912, Louis Laloy, a noted French musicologist and expert on Chinese

music, had published an article in which he praised Armen Ohanian. See Laloy, 'Danses d'Asie', *La Revue musicale S.I.M.* viii/1 (15 January 1912), pp. 39–40.
13. See Pourdavoud to Seyyed Hasan Taqizadeh (12 August 1912) in Iraj Afshar, (ed.) *Namehha-ye Mashrutiyat va Mohajerat* (Tehran: Nashr-e Qatreh, 2006/2007), pp. 384–7; *Ligue Internationale pour la défense du droit des peuples* (Paris) i–ii (November and December 1912), pp. 141–5. For other coverage of Iranian affairs by the league see the subsequent issues of its journal for the years 1913 and 1914. The outbreak of World War I terminated the League's activities.
14. See the editors' introductory essay on Pourdavoud in Rustom P. Masani, et al. (eds.), *Professor Poure Davoud Memorial Volume. No. 2* (Bombay: The Iran League, 1951).
15. Louis Laloy, 'Voix de l'Asie', p. 538.
16. See *Le Figaro* (Paris), 13 February 1912, p. 4, c.f-p. 5, c.a. The largest of such protest meetings in Europe took place in London on 15 January 1912, with an estimated crowd of reportedly up to 6,000. In France, in addition to the likes of the socialists Jean Jaurès and Jean Longuet, or Marylie Markovitch and other proponents of the Iranian constitutionalist-nationalist struggle, the Union Franco-Persane had been formed in Paris in July 1909, with its steering committee consisting of Samad Khan Momtaz al-Saltaneh (the Iranian representative in Paris) as honorary president, and the renowned explorer and archaeologist Marcel-Auguste Dieulafoy as its president. On Union Franco-Persane, see also the organization's journal (*Bulletin de l'Union franco-persane*); *Habl al-Matin* (Calcutta) xvii/10 (27 Sha'ban 1327 [13 September 1909]), pp. 7–8; ibid., xvii/17 (17 Shawwal 1327 [1 November 1909]), pp. 21–2. Following the Iranian civil war of 1908–9, an Iranian organization named markaz-e ettehad va taraqqi (the Union and Progress Centre) was established in Paris, later also using the name komiteh-ye ettehad va taraqqi (Union and Progress Committee). This organization was in regular communication with the Union Franco-Persane. *Habl al-Matin* (Calcutta) xvii/32 (17 Safar 1328 [28 February 1910]), pp. 1–6; ibid. xvii/46 (5 Jamadi al-Thani 1328 [13 June 1910]), pp. 17–19; ibid., xviii/9 (16 Sha'ban 1328 [22 August 1910]), pp. 17–19; ibid., xviii/11 (30 Sha'ban 1328 [5 September 1910]), pp. 10–12; ibid., xviii/23 (2 Dhu al-Hajja 1328 [5 December 1910]), pp. 12–13. For broader coverage of the Iranian revolution and some of the sympathetic campaigns in France, see Mariam Habibi, *L'interface France-Iran 1907–1938: Une diplomatie dévoilée* (Paris: L'Harmattan, 2004).
17. On the Chinese press coverage of the Iranian Constitutional Revolution of 1906–11 and the Chinese nationalist interest in the Iranian developments at the time, see Yidan Wang, 'The Iranian Constitutional Revolution as Reported in the Chinese Press', in Chehabi and Martin (eds.), *Iran's Constitutional Revolution*, pp. 369–79. For an example of an early reporting of the nationalist-reformist movement in China in the pages of the Iranian press, see 'The Awakening of the Chinese', in the Calcutta *Habl al-Matin* xv/21 (10 Dhi-Qa'da 1325 [16 December 1907]), – p. 11, c.b to p. 12, cc.a-b. This article, which

dealt with the reforms advocated by the Confucian scholar Kang Youwei, also mentioned the participation of Chinese women in the nationalist movement and the expanding educational opportunities for girls in China and in Japan, as well as the publication of journals devoted to improving women's conditions and books for reforming their educational training, attempts to end the practice of foot-binding, which the article erroneously presumed was a universal practice among all Chinese women, and other social and military reforms. The article then called on Iranians to pursue modern education and undergo armed training for defending their country's sovereignty against British and Russian aggression through the formation of volunteer militias.

18. See, for example, the *Republican Advocate of China* (Shanghai) ii/17 (26 July 1913), p. 670.
19. The many examples of such gatherings range from the meeting in Istanbul on 28 October 1910, protesting against a British ultimatum to the Iranian constitutional government, with participants at the meeting including 'Iranians, Ottomans [i.e., Ottoman Turks], Arabs, Turks [i.e., from outside the Ottoman Empire and Iran], Tatars, and others', (*Habl al-Matin* (Calcutta) xviii/20 (11 Dhi-Qa'da 1328 [14 November 1910]), pp. 21–2), to the 'extraordinary meeting of the Persia's Defence Society' in Calcutta, which drew up a resolution submitted to the Government of India (22 February 1912, F.O.371/1423, no.153614 [National Archives, United Kingdom]).
20. See Hadji Mirza Yahya (Dowlatabadi), 'Persia' in Gustav Spiller (ed.), *Papers on Inter-Racial Problems. Communicated to the First Universal Races Congress Held at the University of London July 26–29, 1911* (London: P.S. King & Son, 1911), pp. 143–54; Mansour Bonakdarian, 'Negotiating Universal Values and Cultural and National Parameters: Iran and Turkey at the First Universal Races Congress (London, 1911)', *Radical History Review* xcii (Spring 2005), pp. 118–32; and idem, 'Iran at the Universal Races Congress of 1911: Nationalist Agenda, Cosmopolitan Platform, & Global Networks', in Ian Christopher Fletcher, Yaël Simpson Fletcher, and Mansour Bonakdarian (eds.), *The First Universal Races Congress of 1911: Empires, Civilization, Encounters* (forthcoming).
21. *Bande Mataram* (Geneva) iii/8 (April 1912), p. 1.
22. Among other works, see Panchanan Saha, *Madam Cama (Bhikaji Rustom K.R.): 'Mother of Indian Revolution'* (Calcutta: Manisha, 1975), pp. 36–8; Khorshed Adi Sethna, *Madame Bhikhaiji Rustom Cama* (New Delhi: Ministry of Information and Broadcasting, 1987). On Cama and her activities in Europe, see also Nawaz B. Mody, 'Madame Bhikhaiji Rustom Cama: Sentinel of Liberty' in Mody (ed.), *The Parsis in Western India: 1818 to 1920* (Bombay: Allied Publishers, 1998), pp. 46–79.
23. Along with Mo'ayyid al-Islam, both Shuja'at Ali Beg and Shustary were also active in the founding of the Indian Red Crescent Society in 1911. Matiur Rahman, *From Consultation to Confrontation: A Study of the Muslim League in British Indian Politics, 1906–1912* (London: Luzac, 1970), pp. 78, 229, 242. See also Syed Sharifuddin Pirzada (ed.), *Foundations of Pakistan. All-India Muslim*

League Documents: 1906–1947. Volume I: 1906–1924 (Karachi: National Publishing House, n.d.), p. 191; Azmi Özcan, *Pan-Islamism: Indian Muslims, the Ottomans and Britain (1877–1924)* (New York: Brill, 1997), p. 139.
24. See Bonakdarian, 'India: IX. Political and Cultural Relations: Qajar Period, Early 20th Century'. For another example of ML's expression of solidarity with Iranian revolutionaries (during the Iranian Civil War of 1908–9 in this case), see the Calcutta *Habl al-Matin* xvi/20 (5 Dhi-Qa'da 1326 [30 November 1908]), p. 5.
25. On contacts between the Istanbul-based anjoman-e sa'adat and Dr Abdullah 'Qara Bey' and Panoff, see Iraj Afshar (ed.), *Mobarezeh ba Mohammad Ali Shah* (Tehran: Tus, 1980/1981), p. 390 (doc.216). See also *Labour Leader* (London), 15 December 1911, p. 789, c.c; *Justice* (London), 16 December 1911, p. 2, c.d. For Persian translations of some of the reports Panoff wrote in the Russian newspaper *Reych*, see *Habl al-Matin* (Calcutta) xvi/28 (16 Muharram 1327 [8 February 1909]), pp. 17–18. On the paper's further coverage of Panoff's activities, see ibid., xvi/32 (15 Safar 1327 [8 March 1909], pp. 5–6; xvi/42 (26 Rabi' al-Thani 1327 [17 May 1909]), pp. 20, 22; xvi/44 (11 Jamadi al-Awwal 1327 [31 May 1909]), pp. 20–1; xvi/46 (25 Jamadi al-Awwal 1327 [14 June 1909]), p. 11; xvii/9 (20 Sha'ban 1327 [6 September 1909]), p. 19.
26. *Habl al-Matin* (Calcutta) xvii/1 (16 Jamadi al-Thani 1327 [5 July 1909]), p. 20; ibid., xvii/10 (27 Sha'ban 1327 [13 September 1909]), pp. 9–11; ibid., xvii/32 (17 Safar 1328 [28 February 1910]), p. 18–20.
27. Ibid., xvii/11 (4 Ramadan 1327 [20 September 1909]), pp. 9–12; ibid., xviii/27 (30 Dhu al-Hajja 1328 [2 January 1911]), pp. 8–9.
28. Ibid., xvii/37 (1 Rabi' al-Thani 1328 [11 April 1910]), p. 17.
29. On 'cosmopolitanism' and universalism v. particularism, see also Robert J. Holton, *Cosmopolitanisms: New Thinking and New Directions* (Houndmills: Palgrave Macmillan, 2009); Maria Rovisco and Magdalena Nowicka (eds.), *The Ashgate Research Companion to Cosmopolitanism* (Burlington, Vermont: Ashgate, 2011); Sam Knowles, 'Macrocosmopolitanism? Gilroy, Appiah, and Bhabha: The Unsettling Generality of Cosmopolitan Ideas', *Postcolonial Text* iii/4 (2007), pp. 1–11; Şeyla Benhabib, *Another Cosmopolitanism* (New York: Oxford University Press, 2006).
30. See also my forthcoming 'Presenting Dissident "Iranian Modernity" to European Audiences: Malkum Khan and Sayyid Jamal al-Din Assadabadi ("Afghani") and the British Debates on the Iranian Tobacco Protest of 1891–92'.
31. These newspapers included *Akhtar* (Istanbul, 1875–96), *Soraya* (Cairo, 1898–1900), *Irshad* (Baku, 1905–6), or *Habl al-Matin* (Calcutta, 1893–1930), not to mention the earliest Iranian reformist-nationalist press in Europe (i.e., *Qanun*, published by Malkum Khan in London from 1890 to 1898), and not counting here the reformist pan-Islamist paper published by Assadabadi and his Egyptian associate Muhammad 'Abduh in Paris (*al-'Urwa al-Wuthqa*, 1884). See also Pardis Minuchehr, 'The Exile Persian Press and the pro-constitutionalist 'Ulamā of the 'Atabāt', in Robert Gleave (ed.), *Religion and Society in Qajar Iran* (New York: Routledge Curzon, 2005), pp. 393–400. On the Iranian constitutional

press in general, see Pardis Minuchehr's and Negin Nabavi's essays in Chehabi and Martin (eds.), *Iran's Constitutional Revolution*.
32. On the latter movement, see also Fred Halliday, 'Revolution in Iran: was it possible in 1921?', *Khamsin* (London) vii (1980), pp. 53–64; Pezhmann Dailami, 'The Bolsheviks and the Jangali Revolutionary Movement, 1915–1920', *Cahiers du monde russe et soviétique* xxxi/1 (January-March 1990), pp. 43–59; idem, 'Jangali Movement', (http://www.iranicaonline.org/articles/jangali-movement); Chaqueri, *The Soviet Socialist Republic of Iran*. The insurgency's newspaper, *Jangal*, would be replete with references to non-Iranian comrades joining the uprising or supporting it in other ways.
33. See for instance S. Rezazadeh Shafaq, *Howard Baskerville* (Cambridge, MA: Tŷ Aur Press, 2012).
34. Kasma'i wrote '(anternassional) [i.e., the Persian pronunciation of the French word] va (beyn-al-melal)', *Anjoman* (Tabriz) iii/40 (6 Safar 1327 [27 February 1909]), p. 3, c.b
35. *Habl al-Matin* (Calcutta) xvii/7 (6 Sha'ban 1327 [23 August 1909]), p. 8.
36. *Kaveh* ii/24 (7 Shahrivar 1287 [15 January 1918]), p. 8.
37. For a few examples, see Mansour Bonakdarian, 'A World Born through the Chamber of a Revolver: Revolutionary Violence, Culture, and Modernity in Iran, 1906–1911', *Comparative Studies of South Asia, Africa and the Middle East* xxv/2 (2005), p. 325.
38. As opposed to the alternative contact zones within a nationalist group's own 'national' territory, even if this territory was formally designated as part of the dominions of an imperial power (as in the case of India, Ireland, or Algeria, for example), or the contact zones within the 'national' territories of other colonized/semi-colonized groups (as in the case of, for example, Irish nationalist contacts with Egyptian nationalists in Egypt, or Iranian nationalist contacts with Indian nationalists in India).
39. I am using the term 'third contact zones' here in a distinct manner from Homi K. Bhabha's Third Space Theory, which deals with the concept of cultural hybridity; even though the two categories need not be mutually exclusive. On theorizing 'contact zones' in general as cross-cultural 'social spaces', see Mary Louise Pratt, *Imperial Eyes: Travel Writing and Transculturation* (New York: Routledge, 1992). For a few other examples of the more general discussion of anti-imperialist and/or anti-racist contact zones at large, see also Jonathan Schneer, *London 1900: The Imperial Metropolis* (New Haven: Yale University Press, 1999), Felix Driver and David Gilbert (eds.), *Imperial Cities: Landscape, Display and Identity* (Manchester: Manchester University Press, 1999), and Khuri-Makdisi, *The Eastern Mediterranean and the Making of Global Radicalism*, among a wide array of such studies.
40. For an alternative discussion of heterotopic spaces in the context of Iranian modernities, see Mohamad Tavakoli-Targhi, 'Modernity, Heterotopia, and Homeless Texts', in Tavakoli-Targhi, *Refashioning Iran: Orientalism, Occidentalism, and Historiography* (Houndmills: Palgrave, 2001).

41. On the concept of translation in such settings, see also Brent Hayes Edwards, *The Practice of Diaspora: Literature, Translation, and the Rise of Black Internationalism* (Cambridge: Harvard University Press, 2003).
42. *Kaveh*, the best known German-subsidized Iranian nationalist paper during the war, did not have the distinction of being the first such paper financed by German authorities. The first German-funded Iranian nationalist newspaper appears to have been *Khavar*, which began publication in Istanbul in September 1914. On the German financing of *Khavar*, see *The Sun* (New York), 30 May 1915, p. 8, c.g. On the publication and format of the paper, see Mohammad-Mehdi Mashhuri, 'Ruznameh-ye Khavar va Naqshi an dar Komiteh-ye Melliyun-e Berlin", *Payam-e Baharistan* ii/1–2 (2014), pp. 690–6. On the publication of another war-time anti-Allied nationalist newspaper *Rastakhiz* (Baghdad and Kermanshah, 1915–6), see Nassereddin Parvin, 'Rastkiz' (http://www.iranicaonline.org/articles/rastakhiz).
43. See also Mansour Bonakdarian, 'Iranian Constitutional Exiles and British Foreign-Policy Dissenters, 1908–1909', *International Journal of Middle East Studies* xxvii/2 (May 1995), pp. 175–91.
44. See Pardaman Singh and Joginder Singh Dhanki (eds.), *Buried Alive: Autobiography, Speeches, and Writings of an Indian Revolutionary Sardar Ajit Singh* (New Delhi: Gitanjali, 1984), pp. 47–58. Among other Indian nationalists killed in Iran during World War I were Kedar Nath Sondhi (alais 'Syed Kadar Ali'), Dadachanji Kershasp (alias 'Hassan Ali Khan'), and Basanta Singh (Chounda Basant Singh; alias 'Abdul Aziz') in 1917. Although the accounts vary, other Indian nationalists fighting the British forces around Shiraz and Bushehr, or engaged in other operations at different points during the war in collaboration with German agents and the German-backed Iranian nationalists, evidently included Amin Chaudhry, Rishikesh Letha, Pramathanath Dutta (alias 'Dawood Ali Khan'), Pandurang Khankhoje, Agashe (alias 'Mohammad Ali'), Kandubai Kumarji Nayik (alais 'Ali Bin Hassan'), Amin Sarma (A.C. Sharma?; alias 'Mubarak Ullah'), Chait Singh (alias 'Jan Mahamed'), Mandayam Parthasarathi Tirumala Acharya, and Mirza Abbas in addition to the likes of Mulavi Abdul Hafiz Mohammad Barakatullah and Mahendra Pratap who travelled through Iran from the Ottoman Empire en route to Afghanistan along with German agents. It is most certain that the individual identified in an Iranian government war-time correspondence as 'Mohammad Ali Khan Hendi' (i.e., Mohammad Ali 'the Indian') was Agashe. For the text of the correspondence, see Kaveh Bayat (ed.), *Iran va Jang-e Jahani-ye Avval: Asnad-e Vezarat-e Dakheleh*, second edition (Tehran: Sazman-e asnad-e melli-ye Iran, 2002), p. 182. On Indian nationalist activities in Iran, see Ganesh Prasad Sinha, *The Man and the Scientist: Essays in Honour of Professor Balbhadra Prasad* (New Delhi: People's Publishing House, 1979), p. 251; M. P. Tirumala Acharya, *Reminiscences of an Indian Revolutionary*. Bishamber Dayal Yadav editor (New Delhi: Anmol, 1991), pp. 28–36; Uma Mukherjee, *Two Great Indian Revolutionaries: Rash Behari Bose & Jyotindra Nath Mukherjee* (Calcutta: Firma K. L. Mukhopadhyay, 1966), pp. 85–9; Laxman Prasad Mathur, *Indian*

Revolutionary Movement in the United States of America (New Delhi: S. Chand & Co., 1970), pp. 78–9; Tilak Raj Sareen, *Indian Revolutionary Movement Abroad (1905–1921)* (New Delhi: Sterling. 1979), Chapter seven; Richard J. Popplewell, *Intelligence and Imperial Defence: British Intelligence and the Defence of the Indian Empire 1904–1924* (London: Frank Cass, 1995), pp. 176–85; Emily C. Brown, *Har Dayal: Hindu Revolutionary and Rationalist* (Tucson: University of Arizona Press, 1975), pp. 183, 205, 210; Nirode K. Barooah, *Chatto: The Life and Times of an Indian Anti-Imperialist in Europe* (New Delhi: Oxford University Press, 2004), pp. 65–6; the text of the account given to Dr Bhupendranath Dutta by Pandurang Khankhoje at Calcutta, 7 June 1949, appearing in the 1 November 1995 and 7 April 1996 issues of *Heritage: Bulletin of the History Sub-Committee of Desh Bhagat Yadgar Committee*, as partially reproduced in the following website: http://www.rebelsindia.com/ViewArticle.aspx?ai=327; letter from Pandurang Khankhoje to Bhagwan Singh Gyanee, 7 October, 1953 (http://www.saadigi talarchive.org/item/20120723-824).

These Indian nationalists were on what proved to be an abortive mission for entering India through Iranian Baluchistan after forming an independent Indian army by means of recruiting captured or deserting Indian soldiers serving in the British forces in Iran. They were also anticipating the naval landing of a large contingent of Ghadar fighters, a plan that was foiled by the British. For an account by Pandurang Khankhoje on the activities of Indian nationalist in Iran during the war and their contacts with Iranian nationalists inside Iran and in Europe during and after the war, see Savitri Sawhney, *I Shall Never Ask for Pardon: A Memoir of Pandurang Khankhoje* (New Delhi: Penguin, 2008), pp. 153–210. Khankhoje went by the alias 'Mohammed Khan' (later also posing as a Bakhtiari named 'Hadji Aga Khan', as well as on occasion evidently using the Persian-Turkish rendering of his last name in the form of 'Khan Khoja'). Incidentally, by his own account, Khankhoje's outlook on nationalism had been shaped considerably by contacts with Chinese nationalist students while he was studying in Japan before the war. Khankhoje entered Iran by way of Ottoman territory sometime around early February 1915 in the company of Agashe, P. Dutta, and the German Wilhelm Wassmuss, among others. See ibid., pp. 156–7.

45. Among many other sources, see P. Singh and J. Singh Dhanki (eds.), *Buried Alive*, pp. 47–70; *Indian Sociologist* (Paris), September 1910, p. 35; *Bande Mataram* (Geneva) i/12 (August 1910), pp. 1–2; ibid., iii/1 (September 1911), p. 4; Shiri Ram Bakshi and Rashmi Pathak (eds.), *Punjab Through the Ages*. Volume 4 (New Delhi: Sarup and Sons, 2007), pp. 115–16; Mukherjee, *Two Great Indian Revolutionaries*, pp. 87–8 and passim; Edward Granville Browne, *The Press and Poetry of Modern Persia. Partly Based on the Manuscript Work of Mirzâ Muhammad Ali Khân "Tarbiyat" of Tabriz* (Cambridge: University Press, 1914), p. 79 (Browne assumed that the Sufi and 'Mohammad Hussein' were two different individuals); 'P928/1916 Persia: Indian anarchist Sufi Amba Parshad and newspaper "Intiqam" (Revenge) (no ref.), 26 December 1915 to 28 March 1916" [IOR/L/PS/11/103, India Office Records-The National Archives,

United Kingdom]; 'P2181/1916. Persia: Sufi Amba Parshad, Indian anarchist, at Shiraz (no ref.), 6 June 1916 to 17 July 1916' [IOR/L/PS/11/106, India Office Records-The National Archives, United Kingdom]; Mohammad Hoseyn Roknzadeh Adamiyat, *Fars va Jang-e Beyn al-melal*. Vol. 2 (Tehran: Elmi, 1948/9), pp. 25–9. As evident from the different sources, there is much confusion and uncertainty about the various details of Sufi Amba's life. On the interactions between Indian and Iranian nationalists during the period, see also Bonakdarian, 'India: IX. Political and Cultural Relations: Qajar Period, Early 20th Century', *Encyclopaedia Iranica*, vol. XIII, fascicle 1, 2004, pp. 32–44. For examples of other Indian militants operating in different parts of the world and using false Iranian names and/or posing as Iranians, as in the case of those involved in the German-backed Indo–Irish activities in the United States, see also French Strother, *Fighting Germany's Spies* (Garden City, New York: Doubleday Page, 1919), pp. 234–6. On Irish and Indian nationalist activities in the United States during the war, see Matthew Erin Plowman, 'Irish Republicans and the Indo-German Conspiracy of World War I', *New Hibernia Review* vii/3 (Autumn 2003), pp. 80–105.
46. *Habl al-Matin* (Calcutta) xviii/2 (26 Jamadi al-Thani 1328 [4 July 1910]), p. 24. The paper identified another Indian refugee in Shiraz accompanying Ajit Singh and Sufi Amba as 'Zia al-Din', which was the alias adopted by Rishikesh Letha; whereas it must have meant 'Zia-ul-Haq', given that the paper stated this Indian individual was a Muslim and had formerly served as the editor of the Indian (Urdu) newspaper *Peshwa* (mistyped as 'Peshawar' in this report). The *Peshwa* was one of the newspapers published by the Bharat Mata Society (a.k.a., Anjuman-i Muhibaan-i Watan) founded by Ajit Singh and Sufi Amba, among others, with Sufi Amba as the paper's chief editor and Zia-ul-Haq as a member of its editorial staff. Given that *Habl al-Matin* had to tread a careful line with the British censors in India, the paper went on to add that it had examined a copy of *Hayat* and found in it no indication of its alleged Indian editors, nor any sign of antagonism toward Britain. On Sufi Amba's residence in Shiraz, see also Mohammad Dabir-Siyaqi (ed.), *Rah-aghaz-e Hekmat: Yaddashtha-ye Ruzaneh-ye Mirza Ali Asghar Khan Hekmat Shirazi*. Two volumes (Tehran: Khojasteh: 2006), passim.
47. Singh and Singh Dhanki (eds.), *Buried Alive*, pp. 63–4.
48. Ibid., p. 68; Seyyed Mohammad Ali Jamalzadeh, *Khaterat-e Seyyed Mohammad-Ali Jamalzadeh*. Iraj Afshar and Ali Dehbashi editors (Tehran: Sokhan, 1999/2000), pp. 239–43. Following the outbreak of World War I, Jamalzadeh would travel from Switzerland to Berlin, to join the Iranian nationalists gathered in that city, accompanied on his journey to Berlin by the Indian nationalist Virendranath Chattopadhya. In Berlin, he and other Iranian nationalists would also make the acquaintance of the Indian nationalist leader Har Dayal. Jamalzadeh would subsequently travel from Berlin to Iran, along with a group of other Iranian nationalists, to join the armed nationalist insurgency against the British and the Russians. His companions on the leg of

the journey to Baghdad in the Ottoman Empire included the Indian nationalist Mulavi Abdul Hafiz Mohammad Barakatullah, who was travelling to Afghanistan via Iran along with a group of Afghan nationalists and Germans. Ibid., pp. 71–2, 74.

49. Seyyed Hasan Taqizadeh, *Zendegi-ye Tufani: Khaterat-e Seyyed Hasan Taqizadeh*, Iraj Afshar (ed.) (Tehran: Elmi, 1988/9), pp. 175–6, 183–4. Taqizadeh wrote that Iranian nationalists recruited by Berlin were initially expected to work under the supervision of the Indian committee, but that Taqizadeh and his colleagues insisted and managed to obtain German approval for setting up their own separate Iranian nationalist committee. On the US-based Ghadar party and its international activities, see Ramnath, *Haj to Utopia*; Mathur, *Indian Revolutionary Movement in the United States*; Ramesh Chandra Majumdar, *History of the Freedom Movement in India*. Vol. 2 (Calcutta: Firma K. L. Mukhopadhyay, 1963). On Ghadar and its world-wide activities after the outbreak of World War I, see also Harish K. Puri, *Ghadar Movement: Ideology, Organization, & Strategy* (Amritsar: Guru Nanak Dev University Press, 1983); Prem Bahadur Sinha, *Indian National Liberation Movement and Russia (1905–1917)* (New Delhi: Sterling, 1975), pp. 100–2; Harald Fischer-Tiné, 'Indian Nationalism and the "world forces": transnational and diasporic dimensions of the Indian freedom movement on the eve of the First World War', *Journal of Global History* ii/3 (November 2007), pp. 325–44.

50. Among the many examples, the Iranian constitutionalist paper *Majles* (Tehran) periodically reported on political developments in India, such as debates surrounding the arrest and internal exile of the militant Indian nationalists Lajpat Rai and Ajit Singh by the British authorities in 1907 (*Majles* i/109 [10 June 1907], p. 4; ibid., i/120 [21 June 1907], p. 3; ibid., i/141 [20 July 1907], p. 4). See also the brief notice of the twentieth annual meeting of the Indian National Congress in Allahabad appearing in *Iran-e Now* (Tehran) 73 (21 January 1911), p. 4; Afary, *The Iranian Constitutional Revolution*, pp. 306–7. The satirical *Molla Nasr al-Din*, published in Azeri Turkish in Tbilisi, Georgia, and distributed in Iran, also printed a cartoon depicting different stages in British subjugation of India and the Indian nationalist uprising, the imminent victory of which the paper predicted (no. 34, 23 August 1909, p. 2).

51. Abd al-Hoseyn Sheybani, *Khaterat-e Mohajerat: az Dowlat-e Movaqqat-e Kermanshah ta Komiteh-ye Melliyun-e Berlin*, Iraj Afshar and Kaveh Bayat (eds) (Tehran: Shirazeh, 1999/2000), p. 304. On the assistance the Indian refugees had received in 1909 from Tabataba'i, Mahmud Pahlavi (later Mahmud Mahmud), and other Iranian nationalists during their stay in Iran, see Singh and Singh Dhanki (eds.), *Buried Alive*, pp. 47–58. It is claimed that following the end of the war, the Iranian government awarded Rishikesh Letha a scholarship for continuing his university studies in the United States in recognition of his war-time service to the Iranian nationalist cause. See 'Latta, Rikhikesh', in Jagdish Saran Sharma, *Encyclopaedia Indica*, Vol. 2, second edition (New Delhi: S. Chand, 1981), p. 669.

52. 'We are very glad to place on record the founding of our first Lodge in *Persia*. It is in Shiraz, and is called the Anjuman-i-Sufieh. The President is Sheikh Muhammad Rahim, and the Secretary is Amba Prasad Sufi'. *The Theosophist* (Adyar) xxxv/6 (March 1914), p. 797. Many leading Indian and Irish nationalists had ties to the Theosophical Society, as did many prominent Parsis, whether or not engaged in Indian nationalist politics. On efforts by the Theosophical Society to expand its activities into Iran, see also E.G. Hart, 'The Persian Order of Service', *The Theosophist* (Adyar) xxxv/2 (November 1913), pp. 316–18. See also *Herald of the Star* (Liverpool) iii/1 (1, January 1914), pp. 57 and 58. Earlier moves to introduce the teachings of the Theosophical Society in Iran reportedly included the dissemination of its doctrines by Ardeshir Edulji ('Reporter'; also spelled Ardeshir Edalji), the Indian Parsi representative overseeing the affairs of the Zoroastrian community in Iran. See *Lucifer* (London) xiii/78 (15 February 1894), p. 22. For a few random reports on Edulji during the Iranian Constitutional Revolution, see *Neda-ye Vatan* (Tehran) i/14 (20 Muharram 1325 [5 March 1907]), pp. 6–7; ibid., i/15 (24 Muharram 1325 [9 March 1907]), pp. 5–6; *Habl al-Matin* (Calcutta) xvi/38 (27 Rabi' al-Awwal 1327 [18 April 1909]), p. 10; Joseph Maunsell Hone and Page L. Dickinson, *Persia in Revolution. With Notes of Travel in the Caucasus* (London: T. Fisher Unwin, 1910), pp. 126–7. Incidentally, after World War I, the Iranian nationalist Hoseyn Kazemzadeh(-Iranshahr) would devote much of the remainder of his life to teaching his own brand of theosophy in Europe. See Kazem Kazemzadeh-Iranshahr (ed.), *Asar va Ahval-e Kazemzadeh-Iranshahr* (Tehran: Eqbal, 1984/5).
53. See, for example, Surendra Karr, 'The Passing of Persia', in the Ghadar Party publication *Independent Hindustan* (San Francisco) i/1 (September 1920), pp. 5–9, 11; Lajpat Rai, 'The New Anglo-Persian Treaty: An Asiatic View', *New Republic* (Washington, DC), 3 September 1919, pp. 152–3. The veteran Indian nationalist Lajpat Rai was among the founders of the League of Oppressed Peoples (New York, 1919), the executive committee of which included Arthur Upham Pope, the future controversial expert on Iranian antiquities and art. See, for example, *Public: A Journal of Democracy* (New York), 22 November 1919, p. 1098. Pope, who also served as the league's temporary secretary, was already active in Irish nationalist campaigns and belonged to the Protestant contingent of the Friends of Irish Freedom, founded in March 1916 during the gathering of the Irish Race Convention in New York, organized by republican Irish nationalists. In this capacity, he engaged in lecture tours across the US on behalf of the organization. See, for example, *News Letter of the Friends of Irish Freedom National Bureau of Information* (Washington, DC) i/36, 5 March 1920, p. 7. On Pope, see also Noel Siver 'Pope, Arthur Upham' (http://www.iranicaonline.org/articles/pope-arthur-upham).
54. Bonakdarian, 'Erin and Iran Resurgent: Ireland and the Iranian Constitutional Revolution of 1906–1911', in Chehabi and Martin (eds.), *Iran's Constitutional Revolution*, pp. 291–318.

55. Among the Iranian nationalists in Berlin, we know that in 1917 Abd al-Hoseyn Sheybani (Vahid al-Molk), who was personally acquainted with the leading Irish nationalist representative in the German capital at the time (Georges Chatterton-Hill), attended at least one of the meetings organized by the German Irish Society in that city (on 2 December 1917), during which speakers called for the independence of Ireland. Sheybani was also present at another gathering organized by that society on March 17 1918 (in celebration of St Patrick's Day). Sheybani, *Khaterat-e Mohajerat*, pp. 416, 463, 500. Sheybani, who had arrived in Germany in early September 1916, had also been meeting with representatives of German-backed Arab and Indian nationalist groups there. See ibid., p. 136. On the 1918 St Patrick's Day celebration by the German Irish Society in Berlin and the presence of Iranian representatives, and Chatterton-Hill's special greetings to Indian, Egyptian, and Iranian nationalists, see also *Documents Relative to the Sinn Féin Movement* (London: H.M. Stationary Office, 1921), pp. 41–5; 'Vigilant', 'Sinn Fein and Germany', *Quarterly Review* (London) ccxxx/456 (July 1918), pp. 232–3.
56. '"Dar-zadan-e Ser Roger Kezment", *Kaveh* (Berlin) i/11 (1916), pp. 71–3. The article quoted material from the Swiss *Le Journal de Genève*. Jamalzadeh is identified as the author of this article by Iraj Afshar in Afshar (ed.), *Zendegi-ye Tufani: Khaterat-e Seyyed Hasan Taqizadeh*, second edition (Tehran: Elmi, 1993/94), p. 497. On Jamalzadeh's life and political activism, see also Jamalzadeh, *Khaterat-e Seyyed Mohammad-Ali Jamalzadeh*; Iraj Afshar, 'Mohammad-Ali Jamalzadeh', *Nameh-ye Farhangestan* (Tehran) iii/3 (1997), pp. 9–49; Nahid Mozaffari, 'Jamalzadeh, Mohammad-Ali. i. Life' (http://www.iranicaonline.org/articles/jamalzadeh-i).
57. Reinhard R. Doerries, *Prelude to the Easter Rising: Sir Roger Casement in Imperial Germany* (London: Frank Cass, 2000), pp. 172–3.
58. In this regard, see also 'The Irish Movement' in the Iranian literary/cultural journal *Bahar* (Tehran) ii/6 (November 1921/Rabi' al-Awwal, 1340), pp. 349–54. The journal also published an article on Gandhi and the Indian nationalist movement.
59. See, for example, 'A Letter from Persian Nationalists: The Passing of Persia under the British Yoke', in the *Independent Hindustan* (San Francisco) i/8 (April 1921), pp. 6–7, signed by 'S. Jafar Khan and Sha[h] Jehanian'. It also should not be forgotten that by 1919, unlike in Iran, there were mass protest movements underway against British domination in Egypt, India, and Ireland.
60. Eamon De Valera, *India and Ireland* (New York: Friends of Freedom for India, 1920) (speech delivered on 28 February 1920 at the Central Opera House, New York City), p. 24.
61. See also Badr ol-Moluk Bamdad, *From Darkness into Light: Women's Emancipation in Iran*. F.R.C. Bagley translator and editor (Hicksville: Exposition Press, 1977); Eliz Sanasarian, *The Women's Right Movement in Iran* (New York: Praeger, 1982); Janet Afary, *The Iranian Constitutional Revolution*, Chapter 7; idem, 'On the Origins of Feminism in Early 20th-Century Iran', *Journal of Women's History* i/2

(1989), pp. 65–87; Abd al-Hoseyn Nahid, *Zanan-e Iran dar Jonbesh-e Mashruteh* (Saarbrücken: Navid, 1989); Afsaneh Najmabadi, '*Zanha-yi Millat*: Women or the Wives of the Nation?', *Iranian Studies* xxvi/1–2 (1993), pp. 51–71; Parvin Paidar, *Women and Political Participation in Twentieth-Century Iran* (Cambridge: Cambridge University Press, 1995).

62. For the text of the telegram (dated 5 December 1911) from the Tehran-based anjoman-e mokhaderat-e vatan (Society of the Women of the Homeland) to the Society for Women's Suffrage in London (an affiliate of the Women's Social and Political Union), which was transmitted to the National Union of Women's Suffrage Societies, as well as the list of the Iranian signatories of this telegram, see *Common Cause* (London), 14 December 1911, p. 633. The telegram called on British suffragists to assist in safeguarding Iran's independence in light of the latest Russian ultimatum to the Iranian government. It is not clear whether the English text of this telegram was prepared by one of the Iranian signatories or one of the American missionary women in Tehran who frequented the gatherings of this particular Iranian women's society (Mary Park Jordan and Annie Woodman Stocking being the most regular American attendees of these gatherings). On These American women, see Bamdad, *From Darkness into Light*, p. 30; Afary, *The Iranian Constitutional Revolution*, p. 185.

The publication of the American W. Morgan Shuster's *The Strangling of Persia* in 1912 would play a major part in highlighting the role of Iranian women in the Iranian revolution and the endeavours on the part of some of the women to improve women's conditions in Iran. See also W. Morgan [Shuster], 'Shuster's Own Story: Persia's Fight for Life', *Hearst's Magazine: The World Today* (New York) xxi/11 (May 1912), pp. 2234–43, among Shuster's other press commentaries that devoted special attention to the participation of women in the Iranian revolution. The heroic deeds of Iranian women during the Constitutional Revolution, alongside Chinese women's participation in the 1911–12 Xinhai Revolution, would come to epitomize the rapid 'awakening' of Asian women in Western feminist commentaries and frequently appeared in their discussion of women's world-wide struggles for greater rights. See, for example, the American-born British suffragist and author Elizabeth Robins' *Way Stations* (Leipzig: B. Tauchnitz, 1913), p. 264; or the feminist fiction of the American Ella W. Peattie (*The Precipice* [Boston: Houghton Mifflin, 1914], p. 224). One of the most detailed accounts of Iranian women's participation in the revolution prior to the publication of Shuster's book appeared in the renowned Indian 'world journalist' Saint Nihal Singh's 'The Persian Woman at the Parting of the Ways', *Englishwoman* (London), February 1911, pp. 173–81. See also Annie Woodman Stocking, 'The New Woman in Persia', *Modern World* (New York) ii/4 (October 1912), pp. 567–72.

63. In a report for the liberal Russian newspaper *Reych* from Tabriz on 29 November 1908, the Bulgarian revolutionary Panoff mentioned the participation of women in the armed defence of the city against the Russian-backed royalist

forces, stating that among the revolutionary casualties following a major deadly military confrontation with the royalist forces on that date the corpses of 67 women were discovered, who had dressed as men and participated in the battle, although not stating whether all of the women were Iranian or whether they also included women who had accompanied the male volunteers and mercenaries from the Caucasus who were fighting on the side of the Iranian revolutionaries. *Habl al-Matin* (Calcutta) xvi/23 (26 Dhi-Qa'da 1326 [21 December 1908]), p. 4.

64. Mansour Bonakdarian 'British Suffragists and Iranian Women', in Ian Fletcher, Philippa Levine, and Laura Nym Mayhall (eds.), *Women's Suffrage in the British Empire: Citizenship, Nation, and Race* (London: Routledge, 2000), pp. 157–74. At the International Women's Congress in Paris in June 1913, Madame Cama appears to have acted as the representative of both Indian and Iranian women, although it is not clear whether Iranian women had solicited their representation by her at the event. *Bande Mataram* (Geneva) iv/11 (July 1913), pp. 1–2. For additional examples of the international coverage of Iranian women's activities, see also 'Feminism in Persia' in the New York *Literary Digest* xv/19 (7 May 1910), p. 914.

65. *Habl al-Matin* (Calcutta) xvi/32 (15 Safar 1327 [8 March 1909]), p. 19.

66. In March 1909, for example, Markovitch gave a presentation ('La Femme dans la Révolution persane') on the role of Iranian women in the revolution at the first meeting of Congrès Permanent du Féminisme International in Paris. *Women's Franchise* (London), 4 March 1909, p. 431. Markovitch, also regularly commented on other aspects of the Iranian revolution, including journalism in Iran. During the civil war of 1908–9 a Tabriz constitutionalist paper published an article from Paris (very likely written by Mohammad Qazvini) that particularly highlighted Markovitch's efforts on behalf of the Iranian revolutionaries, among other European supporters, and mentioned that she had assisted in organizing a recent 'conference' in Paris on the Iranian revolution, which was attended by prominent French journalists and personalities, as well as members of the Young Turks and Iranians, among other groups. *Naleh-ye Mellat* i/35 (7 January 1909 [14 Dhu al-Hajja 1326]), pp. 1–2. This article was reproduced in the Calcutta *Habl al-Matin* xvi/31 (8 Safar 1327 [1 March 1909]), pp. 20–1. Markovitch herself reportedly gave a two-hour long presentation at this gathering. For an example of Markovitch's direct journalistic collaboration with Iranians in Paris, see Markovitch and 'Mirza Djafar', 'Le bonheur de Djemchid', *Revue des Français* vii/1 (25 January 1912), pp. 62–9.

See also Markovitch, 'La Femme et la Révolution persane', *La Revue [Mondiale]* (Paris) lxxv/4 (July-August 1908), pp. 148–56. For examples of the global circulation and coverage of Markovitch's articles and commentaries on Iran, and Iranian women in this case, see the mention or reproduction of the above article in the following: 'The Revolt of Women in Persia', *Review of Reviews* (British edition, London) xxxviii/ (August 1908), p. 168; 'Woman and the Persian Revolution', *American Review of Reviews* xxxviii (September 1908), pp. 374–5; 'Women and the Persian Revolution', *Oamaru Mail* (New Zealand), 5 December 1908, p. 3. Or, see the Calcutta *Modern Review*'s coverage of an article by Markovitch that had appeared earlier in the *Hindustan Review* (Calcutta), painting a bleak picture of the existing conditions of Iranian women, while suggesting there was a glimmer of hope for the improvement of their conditions because of greater contacts with Europeans. 'Women in Persia', July 1915, pp. 110–12. Among Markovitch's many other publications and commentaries on Iranian women, see also 'La vie des femmes en Perse', *Revue des Français* (Paris) iv/2 (February 1909), pp. 108–14.

67. 9 June 1910, p. 138. Among its other coverage of Iranian women's conditions, the same paper, which was only one of the British suffragist papers at the time commenting on Iranian developments, mentioned (based on a report appearing in the *Times* of London) later in the same year a 'large meeting in Teheran' by women in April 'to discuss educational problems', emphasizing the role of American women missionaries in the process. *Common Cause*, 1 September 1910, p. 334.

68. *Habl al-Matin* (Calcutta) xvi/28 (16 Muharram 1327 [8 February 1909]), pp. 16–17.

69. Among these were the women's anjoman-e vefaq-e iraniyan (Society of Iranian Alliance) in Hyderabad, India, which consisted of Iranian women and Indian Parsi women and sent appeals to various groups and individuals in Britain in support of Iran's independence. This organization also contacted Queen Mary, the wife of the British monarch George V, requesting her 'to show her great kindness of heart in relieving the distress of women in Persia by preventing the inroad of Russia in Persia'. See the telegram of 9 December 1911, in *F.O.371/1423* (The National Archives, United Kingdom). On the international appeals of Istanbul-based Iranian women's organizations, including those addressed to the German empress and the French feminists, see also *Habl al-Matin* (Calcutta) xvi/29 (23 Muharram 1327 [15 February 1909]), pp. 17–18. Some Iranian women in India were already engaged in international women's rights activities prior to the Constitutional Revolution. See, for example, the report of the 1903 gathering of 'the Calicut Ladies' Association' by Mrs. C. Besley ('What Women Are Doing in India') in *Womanhood* (London) xii/53 (February 1904), p. 161 (note that the author mentions Indian Parsi women and Persian women separately).

70. The 1917 International Socialist Conference in Stockholm, which was attended by an Iranian delegation and was also intended to affect peace by reaching out to the various 'national' chapters of the International Socialist Bureau, was a good indicator of the fractured solidarity networks during the war. For the report on Iran during the conference, see Camille Huysmans (ed.), *Stockholm* (Stockholm: Tidens Förlag, 1918), pp. 394–403. The session devoted to Iran, Turkey, India, and Egypt took place on 13 July, with Taqizadeh and Sheybani (Vahid al-Molk) as

representatives of the Iranian delegation (see ibid., pp. xiv–xv). Many chapters of the Second International were either unable or unwilling to attend the gathering (the first of its kind during the war) or were prohibited from doing so by their governments. A report of this conference appeared in the Berlin *Kaveh* ii/22 (24 Mordad 1296 [15 August 1917]), pp. 1–5. See also Yahya Dowlatabadi's recollection of the event and his mention of the representatives of Egyptian, Indian, and other nationalists. Dowlatabadi, *Hayat-e Yahya*, Vol. 4, reprint (Tehran: Attar, 1983), pp. 40, 46–54, 57–64. Dowlatabadi also claimed that, despite his opposition to Russian and British aggression in Iran, he was impartial toward the major belligerent powers in the war. Ibid., pp. 53, 63.

71. This factionalism was evident also in the presence of Sheybani (Vahid al-Molk) as the direct representative in Berlin of the Iranian nationalist provisional government, acting alongside Taqizadeh and other members of the Iranian Nationalist Committee in the German capital, who primarily represented the minority social-democratic wing of Iranian nationalists affiliated with the Democrat Party, with also intermittent clashes between the armed partisans of the two camps inside Iran, not to mention the rivalries between various tribal groups that had joined the nationalist armed struggle against the Allied forces in Iran, or their periodic displays of political autonomy from the Iranian provisional government – all of which had earlier pre-war precedents and were by no means unique to Iranian nationalism. See also Mansoureh Ettehadiyyeh, 'The Iranian Provisional Government', in Touraj Atabaki (ed.), *Iran and the First World War: Battleground of the Great Powers* (London: I.B.Tauris, 2006), pp. 9–27; Iraj Tanhatan Nasseri, 'The Muhajirat and the National Government of Kermanshah 1915–1917' (unpublished dissertation: University of Edinburgh, 1980); Michael J. Lustig, 'The Muhajerat and the Provisional Government in Kermanshah, 1915–1917: Conflict and Co-operation between the Political Parties' (unpublished dissertation: New York University, 1987).

72. See also Nassereddin Parvin, 'Habl al-Matin' (http://www.iranicaonline.org/articles/habl-al-matin).

73. On Iran and World War I, among many other works, see Atabaki (ed.), *Iran and the First World War*; Kaveh Bayat (ed.), *Asnad-e Jang-e Jahani-ye Avval dar Jonub-e Iran: Marhaleh-ye Avval, 1333–1334 Hijri-Qamari/1915–1916 Miladi* (Qom: Hamsayeh, 1998); idem (ed.), *Iran va Jang-e Jahani-ye Avval*; Behruz Qotbi, *Asnad-e Jang-e Avval-e Jahani dar Iran* (Tehran: Vezarat-e Farhang va Ershad-e Eslami, 1991); William J. Olson, *Anglo-Iranian Relations During World War I* (London: Frank Cass, 1984).

See also Yahya Dowlatabadi's account of developments during the war in *Hayat-e Yahya*, vol. 3, reprint (Tehran: Attar, 1983), pp. 268–74; from ibid., p. 282 to p. 102 in idem, *Hayat-e Yahya*, volume 4, reprint (Tehran: Attar, 1983). It should be kept in mind that Dowlatabadi, similar to Sheybani and others, may have subsequently revised his impressions and opinions, as he clearly had done with the account of the 1911 Universal Races Congress in his memoir. He composed his recollection of the war-time events much later. See pp. 268–74 in *Hayat-e Yahya*, vol. 3. On the activities of the Berlin Committee, see ibid., p. 289 as well as the *Hayat-e Yahya*, vol. 4, pp. 41, 43–6, 59, 62–3. On the dependence on Germany of the Iranian government of national defence (i.e., the provisional government), including financial reliance, see *Hayat-e Yahya*, vol. 3, pp. 330, 332; *Hayat-e Yahya*, vol. 4, pp. 32–4, 62–3. On the Jangal movement, see ibid., pp. 93–4. On Dowlatabadi's personal objection to the 'pan-Islamic' propaganda of the Ottoman government [which only enjoyed Berlin's lukewarm endorsement], see *Hayat-e Yahya*, vol. 4, p. 35; and note his discussion of the war-time Ottoman persecution of Armenians and his references to the Armenian nationalist organization the Dashnaksutiun party's anti-Ottoman campaigns, without any hint in this case of the Dashnaksutiun solidarity with the Iranian constitutional movement prior to the war (*Hayat-e Yahya*, vol. 4, pp. 17–19).

74. See, for example, the Indian nationalist leader, and a founding member of the Ghadar party in 1913, Har Dayal's *Forty-four Months in Germany and Turkey, February 1915 to October 1918: A Record of Personal Impressions* (London: P. S. King & Son, 1920), passim; Ilse Itscherenska, 'Taqizadeh dar Alman-e Qeysari', *Iran Nameh* xxi/1–2 (2003), pp. 49–76. In this article, note in particular 1) the discussion of Taqizadeh's later reticence to comment on the period he spent in Berlin during the war, and 2) the dissimilar accounts by Taqizadeh and Reza Afshar concerning Berlin's position on the question of aiding Iran's independence as part of Germany's Eastern policy during the war. Note also the 1917 telegram sent by Taqizadeh and Sheybani to President Wilson, appealing to Wilson's advocacy of the principle of national independence in his Fourteen Points. Irish nationalist representatives in Berlin would also voice similar disgruntlement with Germany's sincerity in assisting to bring about a republican uprising in Ireland.

75. On Iranian nationalists and Germany, see also Jennifer Jenkins, 'Weltpolitik on the Persian Frontier: Germany and Iran 1906–1918', 2012, unpublished paper; Itscherenska, 'Taqizadeh dar Alman-i Qeysari'; idem, 'Heydar Hán, das Berliner Persische Komitee und die Deutschen. Interkulturellen Begegnungen im Ersten Weltkrieg', in Gerhard Höpp und Brigitte Reinwald (eds.), *Fremdeinsätze: Afrikaner und Asiaten in europäischen Kriegen, 1914–1945* (Berlin: Das Arabische Buch, 2000), pp. 57–78; Oliver Bast, *Almaniha dar Iran*, trans. Hoseyn Bani-Ahmad (Tehran: Shirazeh, 1998); Mas'sumeh Arbab, *Ravabet-e Iran va Alman dar Jang-e Jahani-ye Avval, 1332–1336* (Tehran: Motale'at-e Tarikh-e Mo'aser-e Iran, 2004).

CHAPTER 5

'THE PARIS OF THE MIDDLE EAST': IRANIANS IN COSMOPOLITAN BEIRUT*

H.E. Chehabi

By the end of the nineteenth century, the Ottoman Empire and Iran were the only two remaining fully sovereign states in the Muslim world and faced similar problems in their relations with the Western powers. The Ottoman Empire, however, was geographically closer to Europe, contained much larger populations of non-Muslims, and had a geographical lay-out — long coastlines, as opposed to Iran's more continental topography — more favourable to interaction with the outside world; European ideas, tastes, and cultural practices tended to reach it earlier than Iran. What Iranians associated with 'modernity' was thus informed and mediated by developments in the Ottoman Empire, although the Caucasus played a major role as well.[1] While the influence of the Ottoman experience on the intellectual and cultural development of Iran has been studied, much of the existing literature concentrates on Istanbul and the presence there of large numbers of Iranians who, upon returning to Iran, became advocates of change.[2] The cultural interactions between the Ottoman Empire's Arab lands (including Egypt) and Iran have been studied much less.[3] In the Arab parts of the Ottoman Empire, Beirut played a major role as a commercial and educational centre for the Eastern Mediterranean beginning in the 1860s, a centrality that was given official recognition when in 1888 it became the centre of an

Ottoman *vilayet*. It had a religiously diverse population, hosted numerous foreign consulates, and attracted both foreign and Ottoman entrepreneurs, as well as missionaries and students.[4]

The duality of European and Ottoman influence in Beirut 'insured a certain political and social openness that remained characteristic of the city in modern times'.[5] Beirut came, like Alexandria, to embody a certain cosmopolitanism, by which I mean a geographic milieu where different cultures, languages, and religions co-exist and interact, and where a sizable portion of the inhabitants have a psychological disposition to be interested in other cultures and be curious and inspired by developments and innovations in the wider world.[6]

Beginning in the nineteenth century, Beirut also attracted many Iranians. This chapter offers a cursory look at the part some of these individuals played in the spreading of modern ideas and practices to Iran; it has no claim to be comprehensive.

Two Early Visitors

The earliest Iranian account of the wonders of Beirut I know of are those of Rezaqoli Mirza, a nephew of the then ruling Mohammad Shah Qajar (r. 1833–48) and Haj Mohammad Ali Pirzadeh (1835–1903), a Sufi master who travelled widely in India, the Middle East, and Europe.[7]

Reza-Qoli Mirza visited the Levant in 1837 on his way to London.[8] Beirut was a small town then, surrounded by gardens and orchards, but even at this time people from many parts of the world were residing in the town, Rezaqoli Mirza notes, and consuls from 18 countries were stationed there. Nonetheless, when the Persian prince entered Beirut, 'young and old, women and men, stopped whatever they had been doing, and surrounded us, gawking at us as if they had never seen a Persian'.[9] There were also things to be learned. On 26 March he visited the Reverend Eli Smith, an American missionary, who regaled him with his scientific knowledge:

> [Smith] had hung up a map of the world, and we carefully looked at different countries' borders. Then he brought two spheres which were so masterfully crafted that one did not tire of beholding them. One was the planet earth. The surrounding sea, the seven continents, and the borders of all countries were very cleanly

drawn on it. The second was the celestial sphere, on which the twelve signs of the zodiac and the fixed stars had been placed just as the traditional Iranian astronomers imagined them to be. And it was his reasoned opinion that the sea does not surround the planet but that [...] it surrounds the land-mass and that the new world is on the other side of the water and lies opposite this side of the earth and that, contrary to what is commonly believed, it is planet earth that moves and it is the celestial sphere that is fixed. Since he did not speak Turkish, Persian, or Arabic well, I did not fully understand what he meant and we therefore could not engage in a proper debate.[10]

Smith then proceeded to prove to the Qajar prince that air had weight, after which he demonstrated the power of electricity to him.[11]

Haj Mohammad Ali Pirzadeh spent a week in Beirut in late May 1888, and in his account of that visit mentions that he had been there 20 years earlier as well. He was impressed by the progress that had been accomplished since then:

Beirut has become an important city. In the whole Ottoman Empire there are few other cities as animated and prosperous as Beirut. Izmir is prosperous too, but there prosperity developed over time, whereas in Beirut it has come only in the last twenty years. I was here twenty years ago, and none of the buildings existed then. Now there are schools, hospitals, and military academies in the European style, and excellent hotels have been opened. The streets are wide and have gas lights; filtered water is conveyed in leaden pipes to all households. There are beautiful gardens and public spaces.[12] People regularly come from Europe to Beirut to enjoy its attractions and its weather, and stay for three to four months.[13]

In 1888, he tells us, there were only 20 Iranians living in Beirut. These included Haji Mahmud of Tabriz, an antique dealer who procured old objects and coins in Damascus, Tyre, Sidon, and Baalbek, and sold them to Europeans at high prices. He had married a Lebanese woman and settled in Beirut. Another resident of Beirut, Mirza Baqer from Fars, knew English, French, Hebrew and Arabic in addition to his native

Persian. As a young man he had converted to Christianity, but after realizing that the Gospels were not God's revelation, he had become a Jew. This religion disappointed him too, and he became an atheist. But then the Prophet Muhammad appeared to him in a dream, and he became a Muslim. He went to London as a missionary for Islam, but returned to Beirut after five years, marrying a local Arab woman.[14]

Reza-Qoli Mirza and Haji Pirzadeh only passed through Beirut, but soon Iranians came to Beirut to study, attracted by its modern schools.

Beirut's Educational Role

In 1875, French Jesuits founded the Université Saint-Joseph in Beirut. In 1866, American missionaries founded the Syrian Protestant College, which was renamed the American University of Beirut (AUB) in 1920. In addition to these two universities there was a plethora of colleges and schools, both religious and secular.[15] The presence of these educational establishments led to the appearance of other institutions connected to international networks of knowledge and trade so that by the end of the nineteenth century Beirut had become the major educational metropolis of West Asia.

Soon Beirut attracted the attention of Iran's elite families, for as the Iranian writer Sa'id Nafisi put it in his memoirs, 'in those days many Iranian families that wanted their children to get a modern education did not send them to Europe but enrolled them in the French schools in Beirut, most of which had been founded by Christian missionaries, preferring that their offspring get acquainted with modern culture in a Muslim country'.[16] It helped that since the middle of the nineteenth century Ottoman–Iranian relations at the state-to-state level had improved markedly. Iran maintained consulates in Beirut, Sidon, and Tripoli, and while in Sidon the Shi'ite Osseiran family acted as consular agents, in Beirut this role devolved on the Greek-Orthodox Sursock family,[17] one of the top merchant dynasties of the city.[18]

The Iranians who studied in Beirut or passed through the city regularly sang its praises. Mehdi-Qoli Hedayat (Mokhber al-Saltaneh), a leading statesman of the early twentieth century who was prime minister for six years, wrote that 'Beirut {was] an important publishing centre, and its schools and hospitals [drew] attention from far and near'.[19] Yunes Afrukhteh, an Iranian who began studying at the Syrian Protestant

College in 1909, called Beirut *Dar al-Elm-e Mamlekat-e Osmani* (the abode of learning of the Ottoman Empire).[20]

One of the pioneers of Iranian modernity who received his early education in Lebanon was Mirza Hasan Tabrizi Roshdiyeh (1851– 1944), the son of a high-ranking cleric who, as was customary for young men from clerical families, studied to be a cleric himself. He initially intended to go to Najaf for further training, but then changed his mind and decided to acquire a secular education when he became aware of the huge gap in literacy rates between Iran and Europe. He went first to Istanbul and then to Cairo, but it was in Beirut that he found what he was looking for. He stayed in Beirut from 1881 to 1883, during which time, in his son's words, he 'learned the principles and methods of modern education from French-trained teachers'.[21] In 1888 he founded Iran's first modern elementary school in Tabriz, followed in 1898 by one in Tehran. These schools met with a lot of hostility from traditionalist circles and were occasionally destroyed by clerically-instigated mobs. But in the end they became the model for Iran's public education system, and when Mirza Hasan adopted a family name he chose Roshdieh, after the Ottoman Rüşdiye schools.[22]

Another key figure in Iranian cultural modernity was Mohammad Ali Jamalzadeh (1892–1997), the founder of modern Persian prose literature whose short stories have become classics.[23] His father was very active in the constitutional revolution of 1906, and sent his son to Beirut in 1908, together with two sons of a member of Parliament. Jamalzadeh attended the Lazarist school in Antoura, where he published a hand-written school newspaper called *La Devise* with a fellow student named Wajih Khoury. The priests at Antoura liked what he wrote and encouraged his literary endeavours. They offered him a scholarship to study in Lille with the possibility of going on to write for *La Croix*, but then the students had to write an essay about a person whom they admired, and Jamalzadeh ruined his chances by choosing Voltaire. It was in Beirut that Jamalzadeh learnt about the execution of his father in Iran, and shortly thereafter he went to Europe, eventually settling in Geneva, where he worked for the League of Nations and later the United Nations.[24]

In the medical field, too, Beirut's educational establishments were renowned throughout the entire Middle East.[25] One man who left us a detailed account of his years in Beirut was Qasem Ghani (1893–1952), who arrived in that city in 1914. In the first volume of his reminiscences, which is devoted almost entirely to Beirut, he tells us that 'in those days Beirut had a great reputation in Iran and was considered a centre of learning', adding that books published in Beirut were read a lot in Tehran. When he arrived in Lebanon there were about 200 Iranian students there.[26] After his return to Iran, Ghani had a distinguished career as educator and diplomat.[27]

Another Iranian graduate who stands out was Zabih Ghorban (1903–2006), who graduated from AUB in 1931. Upon his return to Iran he became the director of a small hospital in Shiraz. Once there, he found that they had no nurses, and so his sister and another relative were sent to Beirut, where they received training as nurses and midwives. When they returned to Iran, they trained other nurses. These modern women went to work unveiled, and on one occasion the governor had to provide them with police protection against mob-assault. In due course Ghorban became the founder and dean of the Medical School of Shiraz University and finally chancellor of that university.[28]

In the sciences, there was Mahmud Hesabi (1903–92), who attended a Catholic school and AUB. He worked for a French construction company near the Syrian border and then obtained a doctorate in France. Upon his return to Iran he took a leading role in the founding of the University of Tehran and became minister of education in one of Mohammad Mosaddeq's cabinets. He is now sometimes referred to as 'the father of Iranian physics'.

Beirut as a Commercial Hub

As Beirut consolidated its position as the main port-city of West Asia, European commodities became widely available, and the new middle class increasingly adopted a Western lifestyle, consuming European-style foods, dressing in European-style clothes, furnishing their homes in the European way, and adopting European manners;[29] under the French mandate after 1920 these trends intensified and Beirut became known as the 'Paris of the Middle East'.[30] Beirut was now a major commercial centre, and naturally many Iranian imports originated there. One of pre-revolutionary Iran's most distinguished businessmen and industrialists, Habib Sabet (1903–90), started his career there, and expressed admiration for the city in his memoirs:[31]

> My first trip to Beirut [in 1925], the capital of Lebanon, that beautiful and historic city built on the slopes of Mount Lebanon and on the shores of the Mediterranean, was very enjoyable and caused me unprecedented excitement. I had heard about the history of this port city which contained remains from pre-historic times and which had been a major trading and cultural centre during the Phoenician, Roman, and Islamic civilizations and finally under the Ottoman Empire. I had heard that in the present century its civil cultural development had reached the highest levels both in its Islamic and Arab, and in its Western and Christian aspects. But hearing is not like seeing.

He continues that everything he had known and heard about Beirut was palpable when he beheld the civilization of Lebanon:

> I enjoyed looking at the city's markets and shops, which were filled with European goods, chairs, furniture, elegant fabrics, graceful clothes, and dishes made of crystal and china; I would spend hours in the streets and clothes [...] buying gifts that would be easy to carry. I particularly remember a pair of black patent leather shoes that I bought for my sister, which back in Iran attracted a lot of attention since no one had seen patent leather shoes in our country. All my relatives and acquaintances asked that on my next trip I should buy them similar fashionable shoes.

After a few days of sightseeing, Sabet set out to buy a car. 'All European and American car makers had representatives in that magnificent city, which, as one of my friends put it, was the Paris of the Middle East.' After some deliberation, he decided to buy a Ford, and went to see the local Ford dealer. That turned out to be Charles Corm, whom Sabet remembered as a 'respectable and well-mannered poet and scholar, [who] was very elegantly dressed, always wearing beige silken shirts and high-quality suits'.[32] With this car, Sabet started a passenger service between Tehran and various cities in Iraq, then went into the import business, and finally became an industrial magnate and one of Iran's richest men by 1978.

Another business pioneer whose activities have left their mark on Iran was a Lebanese immigrant to Iran, Michel Gemayel (1893–1974). A cousin of Pierre Gemayel, the founder of the Kataeb, he bought the fleet of lorries of the French Armée du Levant when World War I ended. Encouraged by a former Iranian schoolmate at Antoura, he went to Iran, where he persuaded the new strongman Reza Khan to buy the lorries. While in Iran, he received a monopoly for the importation of alcoholic beverages, and then hired demobilized French soldiers to transport the bottles to Tehran in the vehicles. Throughout the 1920s and 1930s Gemayel imported alcoholic beverages and represented French car and lorry manufacturers in Iran. World War II put an end to this business, and in 1942 he set up a cardboard factory in a village south of Tehran. When his son Louis expanded the factory to produce paper as well, he invented an ingenious recycling scheme to provide the raw materials: with the approval of the Tehran municipality he paid the capital's dustmen to separate the paper and cardboard they found in household rubbish and deliver it to the factory. The system started in the 1950s with 300 kg per day but by 2003 the factory was receiving 1,500 tons a day, providing some extra income for sanitation workers.[33] Unlike Sabet, whose assets were expropriated after the revolution because he was a Baha'i, the business activities of the Iranian branch of the Gemayel family continued into the twenty-first century.

Beirut and Iran's Political Elite

I would now like to turn to Iran's prerevolutionary political elite. One of the most prominent political figures of the first third of the twentieth century, Firuz Mirza Firuz (Nosrat al-Dowleh) (1889–1937), was educated in Beirut, as were some of his brothers. As foreign minister in the years following World War I, he worked hard behind the scenes to ensure Iran's continued territorial integrity at the Paris Peace Conference in 1919.[34]

The last Shah's longest-serving prime minister, Amir Abbas Hoveyda (1919–79), was profoundly affected by his Beirut childhood. He was two years old when his father was named consul in Damascus, but in 1928 the family moved to Beirut after it transpired that Iranian consular business in that city was too heavy to be conducted from Damascus. Hoveyda attended the Lycée Français in Beirut, a secular institution whose students were steeped in French culture. A polyglot who enjoyed speaking Arabic, he was in the words of his biographer 'the first true cosmopolitan [...] to reach the pinnacles of power in Iran.'[35] His brother

Fereydoun (1924–2006) was a distinguished francophone man of letters who served as Iranian ambassador to the United Nations in the 1970s.[36] He wrote a *roman à clef* after the revolution about his generation of Iranians and Lebanese and their interaction in the Middle East.[37]

The monarchy's last prime minister, Shapur Bakhtiar (1914–92), also attended the Lycée Français in the 1930s. From his post-revolutionary exile in Paris, Bakhtiar remembered 'Lebanon of the happy years, the marvellous and peaceful country that practised coexistence between different religious communities'. The war-torn Beirut of the 1970s was for him a 'Paradise lost'.[38]

Cosmopolitan or Merely Multicultural?

One must ask the question as to whether the Iranian students in Beirut were part of a cosmopolitan milieu, or whether they just took advantage of Western educational facilities without interacting with the locals. Obviously, like all foreign students they probably stuck mostly to themselves. But they also learned Arabic: both Nosrat al-Dowleh and Amir Abbas Hoveyda had private tutors for that language to supplement the education they were getting at the Western institutions.[39] It must be remembered that before Reza Shah's de-Arabizing policies of the late 1920s and 1930s, educated Iranians were familiar with and respected Arabic language and literature, and if they were lucky enough to be from Azerbaijan they knew Turkish as well and had direct access to Ottoman publications before the Turks changed their script in 1928. Thus Seyyed Hasan Taqizadeh, a major statesman and polyglot scholar of the late Qajar and early Pahlavi eras, remained in Beirut for 49 days. 'Beirut had printing houses with Arabic libraries,' he wrote, before adding that he used these with great profit.[40] Some of the books published in Beirut found their way to Iran, for the aforementioned Sa'id Nafisi remembered that his first Arabic primers, 'printed beautifully in Beirut', had impressed him in high school.[41]

It is precisely this regional cosmopolitanism that made it easier for parents to send their offspring to Beirut. Moreover, the famed educational institutions of Beirut were frequented by Arabs too, and Amir Abbas Hoveyda recalled that in one of Lebanon's cabinets 'of the twelve ministers, seven had been [his] classmates'.[42] Ali Javaherkalam, a man of letters who translated Jurji Zaydan into Persian, was Beirut-educated.

In Beirut no religious community dominated, and a university like AUB catered to students of all religious backgrounds. Many non-Muslim Iranians attended AUB, especially Baha'is, who were drawn to it because of the proximity of Acre and Haifa, where the religious leadership of the religion resided.[43] Baha'is encourage cosmopolitanism,[44] which is one reason so many Iranians view them with suspicion.[45]

That people of different religious backgrounds interacted, at least occasionally, can be seen from the following vignette, which appeared in the AUB president's report for 1934–5:

> The last event of the academic year showed how complicated the religious problems of Beirut can be. A young Zoroastrian from Persia received his medical diploma. Before going to work at Kermanshah, he desired to marry a Russian Orthodox girl, who came from Bulgaria to study nursing. Although the girl's parents cabled their consent, it was difficult to know how to conduct the wedding. Finally, all were satisfied when a recent graduate of Union Theological Seminary read a simple Protestant service in the presence of the Persian consul, who is a Shi'ite Muslim.[46]

For elite Iranians, then, Beirut constituted a milieu far more cosmopolitan than their own country, and this cosmopolitan spirit was part of the modernity they consciously or unconsciously wished to develop in Iran. No wonder then that in the first utopian novel written in Persian, titled *The Assembly of Lunatics* and published in 1924,[47] the capital of a politically unified world 2,000 years in the future is located in Mount Lebanon.[48]

The Beirut-trained Iranians who chose a career in culture and education fared better than those who entered politics. Jamalzadeh and Ghorban lived over 100 years, the educator Roshdiyeh died at the age of 93, and the physicist Hesabi lived to be 89. The politicians were much less fortunate. Nosrat al-Dowleh was arrested on Reza Shah's orders in 1936 and assassinated in 1937,[49] having used his time in jail to translate Oscar Wilde's epistle *De Profundis* into Persian.[50] Hoveyda was betrayed by Mohammad Reza Shah and executed soon after the revolution, and Bakhtiar was murdered by agents of the Islamic Republic in 1992, an earlier attempt on his life by a hired Lebanese terrorist in 1980 having failed.[51]

On the whole these Iranians admired Beirut's cosmopolitanism, but there were some who were not convinced. Qasem Ghani, upon returning to Beirut in the autumn of 1947, found that the Lebanese elites were superficially Westernized and did not value their own cultural heritage: they 'constantly talk about Lamartine, Alfred de Musset, and Victor Hugo and these sort of average people, and do not utter one word about Abu 'l-'Ala Ma'arri and Mutanabbi and others like these venerable figures, who compare to the French writers as the pure world compares to dirt'.[52]

Epilogue: Anti-cosmopolitan Reaction

With the Islamic revolution of 1979, cosmopolitan sophistication became suspect in the eyes of the new rulers. The new regime was unabashedly populist,[53] and for the new power holders cosmopolitanism was anathema not only because they identified it with 'inauthenticity, rootlessness and moral corruption',[54] but also because it was practised by the elite.

Quite a few of these new power-holders had personal connections to Lebanon, and in light of their nativism it is not astonishing that what had made Beirut so attractive in the eyes of many members of the pre-revolutionary elite, namely its easy-going synthesis of East and West, was precisely what displeased them: they manifested a deep dislike for all that the erstwhile 'Paris of the Middle East' represented, equating the city with corruption and decadence. Let us end by quoting from the memoirs of Ali Akbar Mohtashami, an early acolyte of Ayatollah Khomeini who, as Iran's ambassador to Syria in the 1980s, played a key role in the foundation of Hezbollah.[55] About Lebanon in general he writes:

> Since the country was for a long time a French colony and has many different religions, it lacks demographic homogeneity and therefore suffers from social disintegration.

But Beirut is particularly terrible:

> For one who enters Beirut for the first time, what attracts one's attention is socio-cultural corruption, which makes one think for a moment that one is in a European country [...]. One can see numerous centres of prostitution, cabarets, wine shops, dance halls,

theatres, and cinemas showing degenerate programmes and films, and sexy publications. It is a society totally alienated from Islamic and even Eastern culture and customs, and it wallows in the corrupt culture of the West. The nudity of the bodies and souls of women and men, of girls and boys, torments the eyes of the beholder.[56]

Notes

* I thank John Gurney, Ilham Makdisi, Naghmeh Sohrabi, and Sami Zubaida for their help.
1. See Afshin Matin-asgari, 'The impact of Imperial Russia and the Soviet Union on Qajar and Pahlavi Iran: Notes toward a revisionist historiography', in Stephanie Cronin (ed.), *Iranian-Russian Encounters: Empires and Revolution Since 1800* (London; New York: Routledge, 2013), pp. 11–46.
2. Anja Pistor-Hatam, *Iran und die Reformbewegung im osmanischen Reich: Persische Staatsmänner, Reisende und Oppositionelle unter dem Einfluß der Tanzimat* (Berlin: Klaus Schwarz, 1992); Thierry Zarcone and Fariba Zarinebaf-Shahr (eds.), *Les Iraniens d'Istanbul* (Tehran: Institut Français de Recherches en Iran and Istanbul: Institut Français d'Etudes Anatoliennes, 1993).
3. Kamran Rastegar, 'Literary Modernity between Arabic and Persian: Jurji Zaydan's *Riwayat* in Persian Translation', *Comparative Critical Studies* iv/3 (2007), pp. 359–78; Kamran Rastegar, '*Mashruteh* and *al-Nahda*: The Iranian Constitutional Revolution in the Iranian Diaspora Press in Egypt and in Arab Reformist Periodicals', in H.E. Chehabi and Vanessa Martin (eds.), *Iran's Constitutional Revolution: Politics, Cultural Transformations and Transnational Connections* (London: I.B.Tauris, 2010), pp. 357–68 and 484–6; and H. E. Chehabi, 'Iran and Iraq: Intersocietal Linkages and Secular Nationalisms', in Abbas Amanat and Farzin Vejdani (eds.), *Iran Facing Others: Identity Boundaries in a Historical Perspective* (New York: Palgrave Macmillan, 2012), pp. 191–216.
4. Philip Mansel, *Levant: Splendour and Catastrophe in the Mediterranean* (London: John Murray, 2010), pp. 91–101, 148–55. See also Jens Hanssen, Fin de Siècle *Beirut: The Making of an Ottoman Provincial Capital* (Oxford: Clarendon Press, 2005) and Leila Tarazi Fawaz, *Merchants and Migrants in Nineteenth-Century Beirut* (Cambridge, MA: Harvard University Press, 1983).
5. Leila Fawaz, 'Foreign Presence and Reception of Ottoman Rule in Beirut', in Jens Hanssen, Thomas Philipp, and Stefan Weber (eds.), *The Empire in the City: Arab Provincial Capitals in the Late Ottoman Empire* (Würzburg: Ergon Verlag, 2002), p. 93.
6. My definition is inspired by Sami Zubaida, 'Cosmopolitans, Nationalists and Fundamentalists in the Modern Middle East', in his book *Beyond Islam: A New Understanding of the Middle East* (London: I.B.Tauris, 2001), pp. 131–55.
7. On Pirzadeh see Naghmeh Sohrabi, *Taken for Wonder: Nineteenth-Century Travel Accounts from Iran and Europe* (Oxford: Oxford University Press, 2012), pp. 107–16. A map of his travels is on p. 104.

8. Asghar Farmanfarma'i Qajar (ed.) *Safarnameh-ye Reza-Qoli Mirza Fath-Ali Shah darbareh-ye ahval-e khod va amuha va baradaranash dar Iran va Orupa* (Tehran: Entesharat-e Daneshgah-e Tehran, 1967).
9. Ibid, pp. 269–70.
10. Ibid., pp. 274–5.
11. Ibid., pp. 275–7.
12. See Samir Kassir, *Histoire de Beyrouth* (Paris: Fayard, 2003), 'Une vitrine de la modernité ottomane', pp. 158–91.
13. Hafez Farmanfarma'iyan (ed.) *Safarnameh-ye Haji Pirzadeh* (Tehran: Entesharat-e Babak, 1981), vol. 2, p. 204.
14. *Safarnameh-ye Haji Pirzadeh*, vol. 2, pp. 206–15.
15. For an overview see Theodor Hanf, *Erziehungswesen in Gesellschaft und Politik des Libanon* (Bielefeld: Bertelsmann Universitätsverlag, 1969), pp. 6–74 and Kassir, *Histoire de Beyrouth*, pp. 215–41, 'Entre Rome et Boston'. For a discussion of non-Western schools see Hanssen, *Fin de Siècle Beirut*, pp. 163–89, 'Provincial Classrooms'.
16. Ali-Reza E'tesam, *Beh revayat-e Sa'id Nafisi: Khaterat-e siyasi, adabi, javani* (Tehran: Nashr-e Markaz, 2002), p. 64.
17. Johann Strauss, 'La présence diplomatique iranienne à Istanbul et dans les provinces de l'Empire Ottoman, 1848–1908', in Zarcone and Zarinebaf-Shahr (eds.), *Les Iraniens d'Istanbul*, pp. 28–32.
18. On the Sursocks see Mansel, *Levant*, pp. 152–3, 167–8, 194–5, 284–5, 291, 296–9, 303, 307.
19. Mehdiqoli Hedayat, *Safarnameh-te tasharrof beh Makkeh-ye mo'azzameh* (Tehran: Chapkhaneh-ye Majles, n.d.), p. 180.
20. Doktor Yunes Afrukhteh, *Khaterat-e noh saleh*, reprint (Los Angeles: Kalimát Press, 1983), p. 493.
21. Shams al-Din Roshdiyeh, *Savaneh-e 'omr* (Tehran: Nashr-e Tarikh, 1983), pp. 12 and 23.
22. See David Menashri, *Education and the Making of Modern Iran* (Ithaca: Cornell University Press, 1992), pp. 60–3; and Monica M. Ringer, *Education, Religion, and the Discourse of Cultural Reform in Qajar Iran* (Costa Mesa: Mazda, 2001), pp. 155–62.
23. His first collection of short stories, on which his fame rests, is available in English as Mohammad Ali Jamalzada, *One Upon a Time*, translated by Heshmat Moayyad and Paul Sprachman (New York: Bibliotheca Persica, 1985).
24. Paul Sprachman, 'The Post-Revolutionary Jamalzadeh', in Mohammad Mehdi Khorrami and M. R. Ghanoonparvar (eds.), *Critical Encounters: Essays on Persian Literature and Culture in Honor of Peter J. Chelkowski* (Costa Mesa: Mazda, 2007), pp. 36–45.
25. See for instance Nigarendé, 'Beyrouth, centre médical', *Revue du Monde Musulman* vii/1-2 (1909), pp. 39–52.
26. *Yaddashtha-ye Doktor Qasem-e Ghani*, vol. 1 (London: Ithaca Press, 1980), pp. 75 and 101.

27. H.E. Chehabi, 'An Iranian in First World War Beirut: Qasem Ghani's Reminiscences', in H.E. Chehabi (ed.), *Distant Relations: Iran and Lebanon in the Last 500 Years* (London: I.B.Tauris, 2006), pp. 120–33.
28. Zabih Ghorban, *Medical Education in Shiraz: A Personal Memoir* (n.p.: n.p., n.d.), pp. 3 and 5.
29. Toufoul Abou-Hodeib, 'Taste and Class in Late Ottoman Beirut', *International Journal of Middle East Studies* xliii/3 (2011), pp. 475–92; and idem, 'The Material Life of the Ottoman Middle Class', *History Compass* x/8 (2012), pp. 584–95.
30. Kassir, *Histoire de Beyrouth*, pp. 301–90.
31. Habib Sabet, *Sargozasht-e Habib-e Sabet* (Costa Mesa: Mazda, 1993).
32. Ibid., pp. 94–5. Corm was the founder of the *Revue Phénicienne* and a leading Phoenicianist. See Asher Kaufman, '"Tell Us Our History:" Charles Corm, Mount Lebanon and Lebanese Nationalism', *Middle Eastern Studies* xl/3 (2004), pp. 1–28. See also idem, *Reviving Phoenicia: In Search of Identity in Lebanon* (London: I.B.Tauris, 2004), pp. 87–96.
33. Personal interview with Louis Gemayel, 6 July 2003, Tehran.
34. Oliver Bast, 'La mission persane à la conférence de Paix et l'accord anglo-persan de 1919: Une nouvelle interprétation', in Oliver Bast (ed.), *La Perse et la Grande Guerre* (Teheran/Paris: Institut Français de Recherche en Iran/Peeters, 2002), pp. 375–426.
35. Abbas Milani, *The Persian Sphinx: Amir Abbas Hoveyda and the Riddle of the Iranian Revolution* (Washington, DC: Mage, 2000), pp. 44, 50, 175.
36. He is the author of a classic history of the police novel: Fereydoun Hoveyda, *Histoire du roman policier* (Paris: Les Editions deu Pavillon, 1965).
37. Fereydoun Hoveyda, *Les nuits féodales: tribulations d'un persan au Moyen Orient* (Paris: Scarabée & Co/A.M. Métailié, 1983).
38. Chapour Bakhtiar, *Ma fidélité* (Paris: Albin Michel, 1982), p. 22.
39. *Majmu'eh-ye mokatebat, asnad, khaterat va asar-e Firuz Mirza Firuz (Nosrat al-Dowleh)*, vol. 2, *Khaterat-e mahbas*, Mansureh Ettehadieh (Nezam-Mafi) and Sirus Sa'dvandian (eds.) (Tehran: Nashr-e Tarikh-e Iran, 1996), p. 71, where Nosrat al-Dowleh fondly remembers a 'Monsieur Khoury'; Milani, *The Persian Sphynx*, p. 50.
40. Iraj Afshar (ed.), *Zendagi-ye tufani: khaterat-e Seyyed Hasan Taqizadeh* (Teheran: Mohammad Ali 'Elmi, 1989), p. 45.
41. E'tesam, *Khaterat*, 710–11.
42. Milani, *The Persian Sphinx*, p. 60.
43. See Richard Hollinger, 'An Iranian Enclave in Beirut: Baha'i Students at the American University of Beirut, 1906–1948', in Chehabi (ed.) *Distant Relations*, pp. 96–119.
44. Margit Warburg, *Citizens of the World: a History and Sociology of the Baha'is from a Globalisation Perspective* (Leiden: Brill, 2006).
45. H.E. Chehabi, 'Anatomy of Prejudice: Reflections on Secular Anti-Baha'ism in Iran', in Dominic Parviz Brookshaw and Seena B. Fazel (eds.), *The Baha'is of Iran: Socio-historical Studies* (London: Routledge, 2007), pp. 184–99.

46. 'Report of the President of the American University of Beirut for the Sixty-Ninth Year, 1354-5', Typescript, Beirut 22 July 1935, p. 3.
47. San'atizadeh Kermani, *Majma'-e divanegan* (Tehran: Ketabkhaneh-ye Mozaffariyeh, 1924), pp. 25–6.
48. On this novel see Claus V. Pedersen, 'The novel in early modern Persian literature', in Maria Szuppe, Anna Krasnowolska, and Claus V. Pedersen (eds.), *Mediaeval and Modern Iranian Studies: Proceedings of the 6th European Conference of Iranian Studies, Held in Vienna on 18-22 September 2007 by the Societas Iranologica Europaea* (Leuven: Peeters Press, 2011), pp. 141–2.
49. Mansoureh Ettehadieh, *The Lion of Persia: A Political Biography of Prince Farmān-Farmā* (Cambridge, MA: Tŷ Aur Press, 2012), p. 199.
50. *Majmu'eh-ye mokatebat*, pp. 42–3, 51.
51. Jean-Yves Chaperon and Jean-Noël Tournier, *Enquête sur l'assassinat de Chapour Bakhtiar* (Paris: Edition1, 1992).
52. *Yaddashtha-ye Doktor Qasem-e Ghani*, vol. 8 (London: Ithaca Press, 1980), pp. 4–5.
53. Ervand Abrahamian, *Khomeinism: Essays on the Islamic Revolution* (Berkeley: University of California Press, 1993), Chapter One.
54. Zubaida, *Beyond Islam*, pp. 131–2.
55. H.E. Chehabi, 'Iran and Lebanon in the Revolutionary Decade', in Chehabi (ed.), *Distant Relations*, pp. 201–30.
56. Seyyed Ali Akbar Mohtashami, *Khaterat-e siyasi*, vol. 2 (Tehran: Khaneh-ye andisheh-ye javan, 2000), p. 136.

PART III

SOCIAL HISTORY

CHAPTER 6

FOREIGN GOODS, NATIVE CONSUMPTION: POPULAR REACTIONS TO FOREIGN ECONOMIC DOMINATION IN IRAN (1921–3)

Serhan Afacan

If we do not open schools our children will remain illiterate. If we do not establish companies, develop and promote our industries and wear home-made clothes we will need to foreigners for everything from match to paper. We will then send orders to their factories every day and we will promote foreign goods none of which is among the necessities of our lives.[1]

By the turn of the twentieth century the greater portion of the foreign imports into Iran consisted of consumption items of which textiles, tea, and sugar were the leading articles. Only 1 per cent could be classified as capital goods, mostly of minor significance.[2] The negative consequences of the geographical challenges characterized by the inhospitable landscape were doubled by the low customs duties, lack of a countrywide market and unpopular economic policies. In the early nineteenth century the Treaties of Golestan (1813), and Turkmanchai (1828), which were signed with Russia after two bitter defeats, had set up a standard 5 per cent *ad valorem* duty for imports and exports between Russia and Iran. Britain soon obtained the same privileges in 1841, and in this it was followed by other countries in the next few years.[3] Against this 5 per cent customs duty for foreigners, an Iranian was supposed to pay 7.7 per cent on textiles and 14 per cent on sugar while he was also subject to road tax (*rahdarlik*) every time his goods passed through an Iranian town.[4] In the beginning, Iran partly benefited from the tariffs, especially in its trade with Russia, for it was regarded as a source of raw materials rather than a market for ready-made products. Yet gradually Iran became an open market for relatively cheap foreign commodities to the detriment of home industries. There are several reports, both by Iranians and foreign observers, about the 'decline' of domestic manufacturing in Iran. Although by the mid-nineteenth century Iranian craft industries recovered from the shock and managed to find alternative ways to compete with ready-made imports, such as employing an inexpensive female and child labour and using aniline dyes and yarns, Iranian producers were still in eminent need of effective state protection in order to fight the unequal battle.

Importation was controlled by Iranians and non-Iranians as well as Muslims and non-Muslims alike. Yet foreigners enjoyed a lion's share in Iran's foreign trade through the offices they opened and their agents in the country. The British were active in southern Iran where, according to Lord Curzon, six large British firms were actively involved in mercantile activities in the late nineteenth century.[5] He reports that 'a good deal of trade [was] done by native merchants; but the bulk of mercantile transactions passed through the hands of what may indisputably be described as English firms whose activity here is in pleasing contrast with the apathy that has been displayed in other parts of Central Asia'.[6] In time this foreign control reached such an extent that 'many prosperous Persian traders were converted into the agents of Russian and British commercial firms and lost their independence'.[7] In the north, the Russian influence was so obvious that in 1906 E. Grant Duff, the secretary of the British Legation in Tehran, commented with a marked exaggeration that 'the end of Persia as an independent state [was] not far off'.[8] Following this he argued that such regions of Iran as Azerbaijan, Gilan, Mazandaran, and Khorasan lay 'within the shadow of Russia, and commercially [were] practically part of that Empire'.[9] Apart from foreigners, non-Muslim Iranians greatly benefited from their contacts with Europe and were involved in foreign trade in large numbers. For example, in the early twentieth century Iranian Jews were prominent in the import of cotton textiles from Manchester though Baghdad. It is reported that at least 80 per cent of Kermanshah and Hamadan trade was in the hands of Iranian Jewish traders.[10] In a few trades, however, Muslim Iranian merchants and traders dominated. The tea trade, for example, was almost entirely controlled by Muslim merchants;[11] this was largely true for the export of carpets and opium too. The carpet trade as, especially, as Iran's main export item during the late nineteenth century was almost completely controlled by Tabrizi merchants.[12] Towards the end of the nineteenth century Iranian merchants started purchasing directly from Europe instead of buying from the foreign firms established in Iran.[13] Some Muslims, such as Hajj Hasan Amin al-Zarb, the famous nineteenth-century Iranian merchant, made huge fortunes out of foreign trade.

The ever-increasing imports drew attention early in the nineteenth century. In the subsequent decades two main attitudes prevailed: prohibitive and developmental. Prohibitionists suggested that the importation of foreign goods, especially luxuries, should simply be forbidden. They used two different arguments to support their cause. According to some, Iran had enough productive capacity to meet domestic demand, for which reason there was no need for foreign goods. Others argued that Iranians did not need those imported items simply because they were unnecessary and created bad consumption habits. This view was voiced by some in particular in the early twentieth century, and its supporters held big merchants responsible for the inflow of the unnecessary foreign items. By contrast, developmentalists admitted, though bitterly, that Iran did not have enough productive capacity, which paved the way for the inflow of foreign goods. However, as far as a remedy was concerned, they divided into two groups. Some argued that Iranian craft industries could meet the nation's needs if effectively promoted and supported by sound protective measures. Others opted for factory-based large-scale industrialization and claimed that the established methods of production were obsolete and unable to meet even the domestic need properly. There were in many cases no clear-cut boundaries between these two attitudes, but in any case they proved ineffective in curtailing the imports throughout the nineteenth century.

Importers, whether foreign or native, became the immediate target of the opposition. Foreign and non-Muslim shops selling foreign products were regarded as the agents of European economic hegemony.[14] On various occasions, such as the Russian ultimatum of 1911 against the

Iranian Parliament, foreign goods were boycotted, though not always successfully. Muslim Iranian merchants were equally resented for the excessive imports, as will shortly be discussed. Curtailment of imports and the development of native industries preoccupied diverse classes of Iranian society. From the beginning, there has always been popular attention to and demand for balancing the Iranian trade in order to counteract the decline of crafts industries. For example, during Fath Ali Shah's reign manufacturers were reported to have petitioned for the prohibition of further importation.[15] The subsequent effort of the Shah, who commanded his subjects to wear clothes made of native fabrics, was to no avail and was soon given up. Similarly, the British consul K.E. Abbot writes in 1844 that the traders and manufacturers of Kashan presented a memorial to Mohammad Shah Qajar 'praying for protection to their commerce which they presented as suffering in consequence of the introduction of European merchandize into their country'.[16] Iran was practically deprived of any real tariff autonomy throughout the nineteenth century, as a result of which attention was paid to the development of home industries. For instance Abbas Mirza, the heir apparent and governor of Azerbaijan, sent students to Britain in 1811 declaring 'they shall study something of use to me, themselves and their country'.[17]

During the administration of Mirza Taqi Khan, Amir Kabir, the powerful yet ill-fated minister of Naser al-Din Shah, more vigorous steps were taken. Several factories were established, schools were founded, and domestic production was encouraged. The underlying aim of Amir Kabir's economic policy was import substitution.[18] Also, in order to check the continuous outflow of money, the shah made repeated efforts to achieve a European type of industrialization.[19] Despite the extensive human and material capital mobilized for such projects, they fell far short of the expected outcome. Although several state-owned and private factories continued to be established, they were soon shut down. Thus when Curzon wrote in 1890 that 'factories as the term is understood and used in Europe do not exist in Persia and the multiplication and economy of labour-force by the employment of steam power or even water-power is hardly known', he was hardly exaggerating.[20] The same observation was voiced by the wealthy Amin al-Zarb, who at a meeting between the shah and a group of merchants in 1893 pointed out the lack of industries in Iran and the country's dependence on Western imports: '[...] what do we have for manufactories and industries that we can say:

we don't want the European commodities?'[21] Such observations apparently took factory-based production as the only viable manufacturing method and disregarded cottage industries and explicitly considered craft industries incapable of meeting domestic demand. Yet, although the greater part of production was undertaken in small workshops and cottages, the changing consumption habits constituted another challenge for native producers. People increasingly preferred more colourful and relatively cheaper foreign goods, particularly textiles, to the native manufactures. Lamenting the situation, Mirza Hoseyn Tahvildar makes the following observation about the weavers' guild in Isfahan in the 1870s:

> For the past few years the cheap red and yellow European fabrics have been popular. Whenever their textile fabrics have had a new design, and have appeared different to the eyes the people of Iran have given up their body and soul and have pursued the colour and scent of others. In doing this they have incurred losses which they do not realize. Especially now they are crazy about inexpensive clothes which, looked at wisely, are not at all economical or lasting. On the other hand when the merchandise of the weavers' guild lost the market, it began imitating European wares. Weavers paid more attention to appearance than to quality. It was for the sake of elegant appearance and easy handling that they employed European yarn in weaving qadaks.[22] Their work became ugly and, as a result of mixing European and Iranian materials, it became progressively defective and tore and went to pieces while worn: it also lost its stiffness, fluff, and durability. Spinners lost their jobs and gradually perished.[23]

This situation consequently presented the bazaars with a common enemy – the foreigner.[24] However, to this common enemy some added the 'traitorous' native merchants. For example, a petitioner from Azerbaijan in the early 1920s made the following observation: 'those traitorous merchants import into our glorious country the kinds of articles which are domestically produced at a scale enough to meet people's demands and by whose production craftsmen are saved from misery'.[25] Yet imports persisted while industrialization attempts remained largely unsuccessful. By the turn of the twentieth century, Iran had only a negligible number of large-scale factories with ten or more workers. Mohammad Ali Jamalzadeh gives a list of 29 factories established in Iran but he believes that these factories, whether owned by foreigners or Iranians, had not provided the expected outcome 'out of inexperience, lack of persistence and especially due to the competition of the two evil neighbours' (i.e., Britain and Russia).[26] Notwithstanding these obstacles, the production of such items as carpets, shawls, woollen and cotton fabrics, silk-stuffs and leather goods recorded a major increase and accounted for nearly one quarter of the value of Iran's total visible exports.[27] Despite this, the perennial trade deficit remained a hot matter of debate. The ineffective economic policies during the first two decades of the twentieth century and World War I further deteriorated Iran's economic condition, prompting concerns about excessive imports to resurface. A nocturnal from central Iran dated about 1911–12 clearly illustrates this point. The letter claimed in an explicitly dramatized language that destitute Iranian subaltern women suffered enormous hardships at carpet-weaving factories and even suffered miscarriages. This, argued the letter, was only so as to enable them to buy tea and sugar or spurious imported cloths.[28] According to the letter, merchants were to be blamed for this misery, since the poor would not have heard of such items and could very well live without them had the merchants not imported them into the country. Unsurprisingly, the solution they proposed was to prohibit the importation of such items and to rid people of 'the captivity of the ungodly neighbour's oppression'.[29]

Anti-import Discourse and Class Alliances

European economic domination in Iran has mostly been discussed based on a narrow understanding of economics and within the confines of a markedly modernist approach. This suggests a linear path of negative influence due to European domination, which steadily destroyed Iranian crafts. Not only were regional differences not adequately addressed, but little distinction was made between specific industries. This approach was also tainted by its insufficient elaboration of the popular perceptions and voices of the people involved in manufacturing, trading, and consumption processes. Economics has always acted in Iran, as elsewhere, as the stimulating force behind major developments. Economic concerns gave way to class-crossing alliances which more often than not clouded socioeconomic boundaries for many of the later historians. Rather than ascribing them to the simplistic, and long-abandoned, idea of lack of proper class consciousness on the part of the lower classes of society, such alliances could very well help problematize the established view of class as a self-interested constituency. A discussion of such a major economic phenomenon as excessive imports and the resultant trade deficit enable us to more closely investigate the ways in which these alliances were made, and the discursive tools employed for this purpose.

Although the influx of foreign commodities supplied Iranians with relatively cheaper and diversified products, it particularly ran to the disadvantage of urban-based domestic production, as a result of which the wider populace remained concerned about the protection, promotion and development of native industries. Such concerns were expressed in literary works, religious writings, and petitions sent from the public to the parliament. *Ahmad's Book or the Talebian Vessel*, written in the late nineteenth century by Abd al-Rahim Talebof, an Iranian intellectual and social reformer, is a good literary example. In the fictional conversations between the author and his fictional son Ahmad, Talebof warns Ahmad that if Iranians did not establish companies, develop and encourage their own industries, and wear clothes produced in their own country, they would need foreigners for everything 'from matches to paper'. In this case, he continues, Iranians would send orders to foreign factories every day and would promote foreign goods 'none of which [was] among the necessities of our lives'.[30] Indeed, during the late nineteenth and early twentieth centuries, several companies were established with the explicit objective of stimulating native industry. Textile production was particularly important for such initiatives since it was believed that Iran had enough productive capacity in textiles. In order to support such efforts, Seyyed Jamal al-Din Va'ez Esfahani, a cleric and promoter of one such company, named Sherkat-e Islami, wrote a treatise in 1900 titled *Libas al-Taqwa*. Esfahani starts his work by calling upon his fellow countrymen to wake up from the heedless sleep and to unite in order to not need foreigners to supply their textile needs.[31] He then goes on to argue that supporting this effort was identical to helping Islam and the Prophet Muhammad. He also asks his treatise to be taught to children at schools to make them conscious of this vital issue. The following two verses from the Qur'an play particularly important roles in Esfahani's argumentation.

O ye who believe! shall I lead you to a bargain that will save you from a grievous Penalty? That ye believe in Allah and His Messenger, and that ye strive (your utmost) in the Cause of Allah with your property and your persons: that will be best for you, if ye but knew! (61/10–11).[32]

Based on the metaphor of trade, Esfahani argues that there are two distinct types of capital. The first, which is also the basis of all merit, is faith in God and the Prophet. It is the second type which Esfahani defines so as to serve his argument: a *jehad*, it entails fighting against the enemies of Islam after one improves one's own faith. Nonetheless, he cautions his audience that *jehad* should not be taken in the narrow sense of armed struggle and literal fight. Quite the contrary: according to him the real *jehad* is to work to uplift the message of Islam and increase its authority, and to remove the dependence on the enemy.[33] On this common objective Esfahani bases a de-stratifying argument which suggests that all Muslims are servants of Islam and there are no such classifications as poor vs. rich or master vs. servant. Overall, Esfahani's work presents an impressive argument in which religious, nationalist, and patriotic discourses are effectively blended together in order to attract as large an audience as possible. In this sense the work successfully reflects the eclectic discourse used by many nineteenth- and twentieth-century Iranian reformists.

To the Sublime Parliament: State, Society, and Economy in Iran

Not only politicians and intellectuals, but also ordinary people were concerned about excessive imports. We shall now turn our attention to petitions sent to the Iranian parliament from various classes asking for the adoption of measures against the perceived trade deficit. First, however, a brief analysis of petitioning culture and petitions in Iran is in order. A petition can be defined as 'demands for a favour or for the redressing of an injustice directed to some established authority'.[34] Petitioning, both written and verbal, has a long history in Iran and it has been considered throughout the centuries an indispensable part of a just kingship, as in other parts of the world. In pre-Islamic Iran the king would personally appear before the public, mostly in bazaar squares, at periodic intervals to attend to people's grievances and demands. Islam further reinforced this practice and petitions continued to be one of the most effective channels of communication between the rulers and the ruled. During the nineteenth century, particularly during Naser al Din

Shah's reign, several measures were taken for the institutionalization of petitioning. In 1860 the shah declared by a decree that he saved Mondays exclusively to give audience to the aggrieved and to the supplicants. It was further added in the decree that the shah would not meet any of his ministers on those days to attend exclusively to the issues of his subjects.[35] Apparently this practice did not last long. More than a decade later, in 1874, another decree announced the establishment of the Box of Justice in Tehran in which supplicants could drop their petitions, a practice that was one year later extended to the provinces.[36] Protected by special guards to secure the necessary comfort and trust of the supplicants, the boxes were to be emptied twice a week by a trustee of the shah who would deliver them to him in a sealed bag. The guard would even suffer the death penalty if he denied the petitioners access.[37] Any petitioner submitting false petitions would suffer execution too.[38] In 1882 the more institutional and structured Council for the Investigation of Grievances (Majles-e Tahqiq-e Mazalem) was founded for the administration of justice.[39] The petitions from this council provide invaluable information about the period, particularly regarding the societal aspects of it. Yet they are mostly summaries of the original letters which apparently have not survived to this day. It is not possible, therefore, to see the original wordings of the supplicants and the many details a typical petition contains. However, in the ones sent to the Iranian parliament after the Constitutional Revolution we see the original petitions along with the invaluable details included in them.

Petitioning was established as a legal right in the Iranian constitution of 1906. The new parliament found an enthusiastic public that eagerly presented cases to it both in person and through letters and telegraphs, so much so that 'even a greengrocer thought of himself as a commander; everybody has problems with everybody else and wants to scare him by saying: "do you want me to go and present this to the parliament?"'[40] Especially in the First Parliament (1906–8), people, both spectators and petitioners, poured into the parliament building in such large numbers that Seyyed Hasan Taqizadeh, a deputy and a leading constitutionalist from Tabriz, commented: 'not even *rowzeh* can be recited here.'[41] Petitions were mostly handwritten in *nasta'liq*, but typed petitions also existed. It is not always possible to determine who wrote a petition but apparently in most cases those who did not know how to write received help for the writing. Sent by men and women, rich and poor, workers and employers, peasants and urban dwellers, petitions could be individual or collective, with in some cases tens or even more than 100 names, signatures, or stamps on them. A supplicant typically started his or her petition by showing his or her respect to the authority in question, often the Parliament, with a clearly obedient and deferential attitude. They then introduced themselves, providing detailed information about the environment and the social and political settings in which they lived. Following this, they submitted their cases. The petition ended with a statement requesting a favour or the redressing of an injustice. In order to prove the accuracy of their claims and increase the chance of attendance to their cases, petitioners sometimes included a supporting document called Letter of Testimony (*Esteshhad Nameh*). This could be a letter from a prominent person such as a leading merchant, a governor or a clergyman. In a few cases photos were attached as testimonies. This was particularly used in order to prove physical damage, such as a lost limb, for which the supplicant asked compensation or alternatively a pension. Petitions were handed in personally but those who did not show up sent their petitions directly to parliament, even when the issues concerned specific ministries or directorates. Several announcements were made urging the petitioners to address their grievances and demands to the relevant bodies, but apparently to no avail. The amount of petitions soon reached such a level that a Commission of Petitions was founded for the sole purpose of administering supplications and forwarding them to the relevant ministries. The parliament building was destroyed in the bombardment of 1908, so we have only a few petitions left from the First Parliament. Starting with the Second Parliament in 1909, however, the amount of extant evidence is quite abundant.

The significance of petitions continued during the authoritarian modernization of the Pahlavi period. Upon his rise to power, Reza Khan, Iran's future shah and the founder of the Pahlavi Dynasty, made the following declaration which attests to the significance of petitioning in Iranian culture: 'I am obliged to look after the oppressed and to liberate them from the oppressors. I will permit all my countrymen to bring their complaints directly to me and to request redress directly from me.'[42]

Petitions are an original source of information for twentieth-century Iranian history for a number of reasons. First, as Jim Sharpe observes, 'social and economic historians are becoming increasingly used to employing types of documentation whose very usefulness as historical evidence lies in the fact that its compilers were not deliberately and consciously recording for posterity'.[43] The problem is that in order to strengthen their cases and lend them greater urgency, petitioners often made false and baseless statements in their supplications, which requires us to crosscheck them with other sources such as official documents, private collections, newspapers, and so on. Second, petitions can also help us to better construct the relationship between the centre and the provinces. With the inception of the constitutional system, provincial administration also experienced a gradual transformation to the delight or the dissatisfaction of people, as the case might be. Through the petitions sent from the provinces one can see the extent to which laws or decrees were implemented, along with their local consequences. Third, since the parliament and other official bodies responded to petitions, one can construct through these sources a different pattern of state–society relations and how the two interacted through a discursive engagement. The internal correspondence between these official bodies also provides details about the working of the parliamentary system in Iran, for which reason popular perceptions about it can be derived from petitions as well.

To the Sublime Porte: Petitioners and their Petitions

Although Iran remained neutral in World War I, it suffered extensively from its consequences both as a battlefield of belligerent powers, such as Russia, Britain, and the Ottoman Empire, and because of the political instability the war brought about in the country. Also, the increased unemployment under wartime conditions had a nagative impact on the lives of the lower classes and the businesses of the well-to-do. Thus, prohibitive and developmental approaches to economic development resurfaced once again. Prohibitionists took a firm stand against imports, particularly consumption items, and argued that the economic collapse and the perennial trade deficit could only be reversed by an effective ban on them. Developmentalists, in contrast, argued that such a ban was not only against the basic principles of a free market economy but also practically unworkable since home manufactures did not have enough productive capacity to substitute imports. Hence they called for far-fledged economic planning and development. It appears that in the early

1920s the prohibitive approach was rather widespread. In October 1921 the Merchants Union of Tehran sent a petition to the Majles in which they attracted the attention of the deputies to the distressing economic conditions in the country[44] where they cautioned about the *inescapability* of an irreversible devastation should the economic situation continued as it was. Based on an analysis of the customs statistics they further argued that the reason for widespread poverty and economic disaster was the inflow of imports, contrasting with the scarcity or even the absence of exports. As a remedy they came up with a list containing luxuries and decorative items to be prohibited from importation. It consisted of 81 articles such as candles, cacao, sugar, tea, carpets, felt, eggs, biscuits, cheese, salt, fish, meat, vegetables, wax, oil, gramophones, and glass and crystal products. The list also contained many textile articles such as woollen fabrics, cotton fabrics, silk fabrics, linens, and the combinations of all these were separately specified in the list. As a matter of fact there was a chronic deficit in Iran's visible trade throughout 1910s which by the end of the decade added up to at least $30 million and which was mainly financed by the outflow of precious metals, i.e., gold and silver.[45] This alarmed many producers and traders as well as wholesalers.

Upon the first petition eliciting no reaction, the union sent a second one in November 1921 to the same effect.[46] Only two days after the second petition the Ministry of Agriculture, Commerce and Public Welfare (MACPW) informed the head of the parliament that during the government of Moshir al-Dowleh between July 1920 and October 1920 the matter had been investigated and a commission had been set up at that ministry in order to consider the prohibition of the importation of luxuries and a report along with a list of such items had been sent to the Prime Ministry.[47] It appears from the MACPW letter that no effective measure could be taken on the issue of excessive imports chiefly due to the economic treaties signed with such countries as Britain and Russia. Merchants in the provinces soon joined the Tehran merchants in their prohibitionist attitude. The Merchants Union of Hamadan was the first to support Tehran merchants by a petition sent in late November 1921. They argued that notwithstanding the good intention of the state, the law regarding the prohibition of the outflow of gold and silver from the country did not produce the expected outcome due to the smuggling activities of those people who '[did] not care about the benefits of the country'.[48] By this they were referring to the law passed by parliament on 8 May 1915 which prohibited the outflow of gold and silver from the country. According to the merchants, prohibiting the importation of luxurious and 'unnecessary' items would be the most effective means by which to maintain the balance of trade. The discussion was further continued by Tehran merchants in a third petition sent in mid-December 1921, in which they explicitly criticized the ineffectiveness of the parliament to attend to the issue.[49] They stated that their proposal for a ban on imports was in fact to the detriment of merchants. It is only out of a feeling of patriotism (*vatan dusti*), and a sense of altruism, argued the merchants, that they preferred the common good to that of themselves. Therefore, the deputies too, they stated, were supposed to give more attention to the matter than they had done so far. In the rest of the petition merchants directed the attention of the deputies to the possible risks of widespread poverty and deprivation, warning that with each day passing with the current trade deficit, the risk of widespread poverty was growing terrifyingly. Moreover they added an intimidating warning by suggesting that no powerful force could stand against the devastating flow of widespread poverty and depravity. In an atmosphere of grave political instability and regional insurgencies this was a major warning.

A series of correspondence between parliament and the various state bodies followed this last petition. In February 1922 the Ministry of Finance sent parliament a report prepared by the commission set up at the Administration-General of Customs (AGC).[50] The report began by referring to the law concerning the banning of the outflow of previous metals from the country. According to the report, although the law aimed at protecting the Iranian currency against the unfavourable wartime conditions, any country which was incapable of reciprocating in kind to imports was obliged to pay in cash. It then stated that as Joseph Naus, the former administrator of customs, had forecast that as long as Iran's imports remained more than its exports and as long as Iran failed to develop its industry and expand its exports, according to the principles of economics it was inevitable that it would spend its gold and silver stocks, which would result in poverty and bankruptcy. In another report, the AGC summarized its views under three articles.[51] First of all, it was proposed that the government should consider the treaties to check whether the prohibition of imports was compatible with them. Second, the Iranian government had the right to adopt countervailing measures in order to decrease the imports and balance its trade through which it would protect and promote its national industries. According to the report, in the previous few years many European states had put extraordinary taxes on imports for various reasons but primarily to protect the value of their money. By these measures they aimed at increasing their customs revenues and developing their industries. Third, as the AGC had suggested in earlier years, the government could put extortionate taxes on some of the luxuries, and apply prohibition to others.

From early 1922 onwards, merchants, guildsmen, and workers in the provinces were more actively involved in the discussions. In January 1922 Hajj Muhammad Taqi Vakil al-Ro'aya of Hamadan, one of the prominent constitutionalist-merchants and the sponsor of the *bast* at Abd al-Azim in 1906, sent a private petition to parliament in which he brought a new dimension to the issue.[52] After highlighting the importance of maintaining the balance between imports and exports, Vakil al-Ro'aya called the attention of the deputies to the significance of free trade and the possible problems that could originate from its violation. Based on this, he proposed that a law should be passed according to which those who wanted to import foreign manufactures into Iran should first export Iranian goods at the same value as their imports. Vakil al-Ro'aya was also the head of the Hamadan Merchants Union and his argument should have influenced other merchants too. In the second petition, sent to the Majles on 7 February 1922, the Union argued that prohibiting the import of luxuries could not save more than 4 million tomans.[53] Furthermore, due to the principle of free trade as an important clause of international trade, such a measure would not produce the expected outcome. The Union then argued that balancing trade through encouraging and increasing exports was the only viable way to rescue the country and its people from devastation and to bring wealth. However, the merchants were aware of the fact that to achieve such an economic leap forward in the near future was near to impossible since it would require the development and dissemination of trade, agriculture, and industry, building streets and roads, exploitation of mines such as those in Kerman province, building a dam at Ahvaz, opening an agricultural bank and companies, and establishing and supporting factories and making several other fundamental arrangements. In order to achieve these developments, added the merchants,

Iran would need too much time, which made this option impractical. As an interim solution, Vakil al-Ro'aya's proposal was reasserted.

Nonetheless it appears that both Vakil al-Ro'aya and the Union abandoned this rather complicated solution and turned back to the simple one proposed by the merchants of Tehran. This shift becomes clear in a petition sent to parliament on 12 January 1923.[54] After reiterating their account as to the economically harmful consequences of the trade deficit, they pointed out the significance of the balance of trade. Following this, the merchants described the socially devastating consequences of excessive imports, which hurt every sensible person. According to them, the inflow of foreign goods into the country had gradually destroyed 1,000s of Iranian families living off craft industries. These people who tirelessly worked throughout long years to meet the demands of the country resisted the unfavourable conditions as for as they could. However, because they were deprived of any state protection they gradually disappeared and were still disappearing. The marks of this decadence and misfortune, they argued, could be seen in such craft centres as Kerman, Isfahan, Kashan, Yazd, and other towns. The merchants then warned the deputies that should they keep on tolerating this situation the predominance of imports over exports would be enough to turn the country into a large poor house where everybody would fall short of finding a solution. Based on this, they reaffirmed their proposal as to the prohibition of the importation of luxuries and decorative items to Iran. According to them, after inspecting national manufactures and textiles, which could become productive with little support, a law prohibiting the import of goods also produced in the country should be passed.

Due to the lack of adoption of any measures by parliament, more aggressive petitions were sent from the provinces such as the one dispatched by the Merchants Union of Malayer in November 1922.[55] After criticizing the deputies for not paying attention to their previous petitions and not discussing them openly in parliament, they stated that the balance of trade was a matter of life and death. Thus, the petition argued, instead of discussing issues of minor significance the deputies were supposed to consider the trade of the country and ways to balance trade. Individuals were also involved in the discussions. In December 1922, a certain Mahmud M. Ramez, a textile entrepreneur from Tehran, sent a petition in which he argued that the only way out of the widespread poverty and depravity was to use national textiles and manufactures. To this end he proposed a law called 'the encouragement of industrialists' be passed by parliament.[56] According to Ramez, this law would consist of three articles. First, the state would, through MACPW, allocate 10,000 tumans in order to develop the textile industry. Second, the ministry would make sure that no penny would be wasted. Third, 15 months after a factory operations were fully functional, the entrepreneurs would pay back 500 tumans annually to the ministry with a certain percentage of benefit that the government would determine.

A close analysis of the prohibitive and developmental opinions reveals that there was an observable accord of views as to the vitality of curtailing imports. Yet opinions do not appear to be clear enough in on how domestic demand could be met once imports were effectively curtailed. On the one hand, one has the impression from the prohibitive approach that the ability of the then-existing home manufactures seemed self-evident. Put differently, it was suggested that foreign manufactures did not fill a gap in the market but competed with home-made goods. Consequently the sole prohibition of imports should have appeared to them sufficient as a solution. On the other hand, the developmentalist approach acknowledged the insufficiency of home production but disagreed on how to overcome it. According to some, the encouragement of craft industries would serve this end while others urged for large-scale industrialization supported by projects in transportation and other infrastructural fields. In the main, however, the issue of the ban on imports and the promotion of home-made production was as much an emotionally-charged discursive debate as it was an informed negotiation on the productive capacity of the country. As different classes other than the merchants became involved in the discussions, this discursive aspect became more visible. In December 1922 the Guilds Union of Tehran sent a petition to the Majles in which they reproduced the account as to the negative consequences of the disastrous economic situation and argued that guilds' members were the most immediate victims of this unfavourable economic situation.[57] Following this, they expressed their support in favour of the then-discussed bill making it obligatory for those who lived on the treasury of Muslims, to wit state employees, to wear clothes produced in Iran. The law passed on 19 February 1923. We will touch upon this law later. According to the Union, an article introducing a penalty for the violators should also be added to the law. Finally they stated that through this law some needs of the country would be met and new employment opportunities would be created for the jobless. In the meantime, religious groups brought a new dimension to the issue. On 6 December 1922, the Society of Religion (Jame'eh-ye diyanat) and the Society of Free Muslims (Jam'iyat-e Ahrar-e Islami) petitioned the Majles. On the top of the petition sent by the former, a prophetic saying was quoted which goes, 'Islam is always higher and nothing goes above it' (*al-Islamu ya'lu wa la yu'la alayh*). By ascribing the deteriorating economic situation of the country to the excessive imports and the scarcity of exports, the petition affirmed its support for the above-mentioned bill which would save the people and the helpless workers from misery. It was also stressed that use of national textiles and other goods was an effective means to combat imports. The Society of Free Muslims also supported the proposal of the merchants regarding the prohibition of the importing of luxuries.

In the meantime, the Merchants' Union of Tehran continued to pressure parliament to adopt its proposal. The Majles argued in a petition sent in January 1923 that although their proposal as to the prohibition of the importation of unnecessary articles had been met positively and with good intentions by the deputies, during the two years no measures had been taken to heal the economic situation of the country.[58] Moreover, obstacles were created for exports while imports were facilitated. Therefore they asked their proposal to be loudly read in parliament and to be put into practice if considered useful. If the deputies did not find it useful, added the merchants, they should come up with a better solution and inform the merchants about that too. The responsibility of parliament to improve country's economy and to develop native industries was further highlighted by the petitions sent from the merchants unions of Golpayegan (6 February 1923),[59] Kermanshah (11 February 1923),[60] Ardabil (22 February 1923),[61] Astara (27 February 1923)[62] and Khorasan (5 March 1923),[63] all of which shared the same determination as to the significance of trade protection. According to the Kermanshah merchants, the textiles produced in Isfahan and Khorasan could save the country from foreign products if effectively encouraged by the state. The petitions sent from Astara and Ardabil, two of Iran's northern cities close to the Russian border, rendered Russian merchants responsible for the grave economic situation. Speaking on behalf of 'the people and the merchants of the town', the petition of the Merchants'

Union of Ardabil directed deputies' attention to the deputies to the assaults on and the monopolization of Iran's economy by Russian merchants. The merchants of Astara took a rather aggressive stand against their foreign competitors. After referring to the widespread poverty in Iran, the petition stated that Iran's unjust and inhumane civilized neighbours were 'by various tricks and unbearable devices busy destroying Iran's future and fortune, monopolizing its trade, and turning Iranians into servants and captives'. Thus, the supplicants expressed their support for a ban on imports. In this way Iran should make it clear to foreigners as soon as possible that Iranians were no longer willing to submit to their pressure and monopolization of their trade and would no longer be subjects to their unjust and greedy objectives. In any case, added the petition, the merchants, the notables as well as the toilers and the farmers of Astara would practically put the proposal into effect and refrain from using foreign goods as much as possible.

The 'Law for the use of national clothes' *(qanun-e este'mal-e albaseh-ye vatani)* passed in February 1923 should be considered against this background. It made it compulsory for all state employees, including the military, to wear clothes produced from native fabrics and of Iranian make. In a collective petition dated December 1922, the supplicants expressed their gratitude to the deputies for their sensitivity to native textiles and discussing the bill at parliament.[64] According to them, this law was the only way to guarantee the honour and the future of religion and the country *(din va dowlat)*. Another petition, dated 4 January 1923, argued that the encouragement of national textiles, which would result in the balance of trade, would also save the Muslim nation from being in need of foreigners.[65] On the other hand, however, as far as those people who lived on other sectors were concerned the law caused a frustration and resentment. For instance, on 4 March 1923 shoemakers expressed their considerations about the law in a petition which they asked to be read at the parliament to be a sign of the deputies' attention to the situation of a handful of toilers.[66] The petitions read as follows:

> Before we begin our petition we request the retainers of the President of the Majles, may God endure his power, and the honourable deputies to read this petition loudly in the Majles and to pay due attention to the situation of these craftsmen. Admittedly the purpose behind the establishment of this national

regime and the basis of the constitutional system is to attain the means of security and welfare for all as well as to obtain advantages and dispose disadvantages to Iranians. This can only be obtained by making laws for the good of the country and for providing peace and revenues to people from which the general populace will benefit without discriminating between various crafts therein. You should not forget the principle of egalitarianism (*mesdaq-e vaqi'-ye musavat*). As the shoe makers we have always made sacrifices and become forerunners for the establishment of the sacred constitutional while at the same time we have, in the last years, significantly developed our craft and made our handicraft far more beautiful and attractive. However, in return for our efforts some of the deputies totally disregarded this craft in their debates concerning the use of native fabrics and home manufactures and they were oblivious to our craft and showed a humiliating attitude towards us on. Their pretext was that home-made shoes hurt and injured their feet and produced [?]. Of course our words are about a number of deputies who wear foreign shoes and not those who from the beginning of their lives wore home-made shoes. In the meanwhile we urge those deputies who did not help us to study history in order to see what the Japanese Emperor did and said. You should have already heard that the Emperor, Mikado, declared that until shoes were produced in his country he would go around barefooted which he really did for a while until shoes were produced in his country. This is how a great men and persons who are interested in promoting and developing a nation do. We like to attract the attention of you gentlemen and request that as you pay attention to the native shoes like you did to native textiles. This way we request you to add an article about native shoes to the supplement of the law and to promote this craft too.

The petition is an interesting example of how workers engaged with the ruling establishment. On the one hand the workers used every discursive tool at their disposal and criticized the deputies but on the other were careful not take a negative attitude against all of the deputies and they distinguished the deputies who wore foreign shoes and those who used domestic ones. However, there were also those who were critical of the actual value of the law which allegedly aimed at appeasing the popular excitement due to the insufficient production capacity of the industry. In a petition dated 4 March 1923, Taqi Daneshvar (Alam al-Saltaneh) stressed the unintended consequences of this law.[67] He argued that although there was much excitement among the populace about the promotion of craft industries in general and handmade textiles in particular, it was not possible to meet the demand of the market with handmade textiles and manually-washed cotton and wool. Moreover, he argued, the native wool fabrics passed on anthrax to 100s of people. Furthermore, if the industry were unable to meet demand, then prices would rise considerably, in turn promoting the cheap foreign fabrics. Following these considerations, Daneshvar emphasized that mechanization of the textile industry was the only feasible solution. Taking into account the devaluation of the German mark, he proposed the purchase of factories from Germany at low prices, to be established in Iran. The issues raised by Daneshvar were not the only problems that the law revealed. In the main the law was a notable means to promote the weaving industry. However, it also exposed the state's inability to introduce any effective prohibition on imports.

Conclusion

A chronic trade deficit continued to exist in Iran's visible trade throughout the 1920s; by the end of the decade it added up to at least $30 million and was mainly financed by the outflow of gold and silver.[68] Lack of a country-wide market and the virtual absence of transportation facilities were compounded by the hostile economic policies of Russia and Britain. Invisibles, such as the remittances by Iranians working abroad, pilgrimage expenditure, and exports made by illegal means might have partly offset the trade deficit. To this balance sheet, the increasing oil revenues, especially from 1920s onwards, should also be added. In the late 1920s and early 1930s a number of measures were adopted in order to balance Iran's foreign trade as well as to develop its manufacturing capacity. In 1928 full tariff autonomy was attained, at least on paper, and in 1925 a law was passed which exempted industrial and agricultural machines and instruments and their component parts from import duties for ten years.[69] Before 1930, several monopolies were formed starting with sugar and tea which extended to other goods until foreign trade was fully monopolized by the state in 1931. Throughout the

1930s, Iran experienced a major industrial leap forward which was also supported by infrastructural and transportation projects. Nonetheless, debates and complaints around trade deficit, real or imaginary, persisted as a channel to express diverse economic concerns. Under the guise of these concerns, the ailing artisan expressed his resentment over losing his livelihood; the small-scale industrialist sought a bigger share of the blessings of the growing country-wide market; and the nascent worker looked to improve his working and living conditions. To put it bluntly, all resented the foreign goods which, they believed, constituted the source of all evils. Beyond their sheer economic significance, discussions around trade deficit and foreign commodities in the late 1910s and early 1920s tell us a great deal about the grassroots perceptions of economic development, as well as about state–society relations during this period.

Notes

1. Abd al-Rahim Talebof, *Ketab-e Ahmad ya Safineh-e Talebi* (Tehran: Sazman-e Ketabha-ye Jibi, 1967), p. 98.
2. Julian Bharier, *Economic Development in Iran: 1900–1970* (London: Oxford University Press, 1971), pp. 9–10.
3. Charles Issawi, 'European Economic Penetration: 1872–1921', in Peter Avery, Gavin Hambly and Charles Melvilla (eds.), *The Cambridge History of Iran Vol. 7* (Cambridge: Cambridge University Press, 1991), p. 596.
4. Issawi, 'European Economic Penetration', p. 600.
5. George N. Curzon, *Persia and the Persian Question* (London: Longmans, Green, and Co, 1892), p. 13. Quoted in Ahmad Ashraf, 'Historical Obstacles to the Development of a Bourgeoisie in Iran', in M.A. Cook (ed.), *Studies in the Economic History of the Middle East from the Rise of Islam to the Present Day* (London: Oxford University Press, 1970), p. 326.
6. Curzon, *Persia*, p. 41. Quoted in Ashraf, 'Historical Obstacles', p. 326.
7. Ashraf, 'Historical Obstacles', p. 326.
8. FO 371/111 'Situation in Persia, July 1906'.
9. FO 371/111 'Situation in Persia, July 1906'.
10. MacLean Report, A and P 1904, pp. 36–9 quoted in Charles Issawi, *The Economic History of Iran: 1800–1914* (Chicago: The University of Chicago Press, 1971), p. 62.
11. FO 248/1029 (1911).
12. Willem Floor, *Guilds, Merchants and Ulama in Nineteenth-Century Iran* (Washington, DC: Mage Publishers, 2009), p. 39.
13. Floor, *Guilds, Merchants and Ulama*, p. 42.
14. For example, based on an unauthenticated letter which allegedly arrived from the great mullahs of the Atabat (Najaf and Karbala) in 1903, Hajj Mirza Hasan

of Tabriz urged the governor of Tabriz abolish the tariffs and close the European and Armenian shops. The forgery soon became clear and Hajj Mirza Hasan of Tabriz was expelled from the city. E.G. Browne, *The Persian Revolution, 1905– 1909* (London: Frank Cass & Co. Ltd, 1966), p. 107.
15. Willem Floor, *The Persian Textile Industry in Historical Perspective 1500–1925* (Paris: L'Harmattan, 1999), p. 98.
16. Issawi, *The Economic History of Iran*, p. 259.
17. Willem Floor, *Traditional Crafts in Qajar Iran, 1800–1925* (California: Mazda Publishers, 2003), p. 14.
18. Floor, *Traditional Crafts*, p. 16.
19. Floor, *Traditional Crafts*, p. 16.
20. Bharier, *Economic Development*, p. 13.
21. Quoted by Floor, 'The Merchants (tujjar) in Qajar Iran', *Zeitschrift der Deutschen Morgenländischen Gesellschaft* cxxvi (1976), p. 131.
22. A tightly woven cotton fabric of fast colour which was once quite a popular fabric.
23. Issawi, *Economic History of Iran*, pp. 280–1.
24. Ervand Abrahamian, *Iran between Two Revolutions* (Princeton: Princeton University Press 1982), p. 58.
25. LMDCIP, dore4-k25-j12-p52, 19 March 1923.
26. Hojjat Fallah Tootcar, 'Faa'leyatha-ye ejtemai va seyasi-ye asnaf va pishavaran az enghlab-e mashrutiyat-e Iran ta ruy-e kar amadan-e Reza Shah' (Social and Political Activities of Guilds and Artisans from the Iranian Constitutional Revolution to the Rise of Reza Shah, 1906–1925). PhD diss., (in Persian), Tarbiyat Modarres University, 2003, 26.
27. Bharier, *Economic Development*, p. 170.
28. Kurosh Nowruzmoradi, 'Varaqah-ye Entebahiyeh: Shabnameh'i az Eraq-e Ajam', *Payam-e Baharestan* ii/3 (2009), p. 371.
29. They mean the Russians as the main exporters of the above items.
30. Talebof, *Ketab-e Ahmad*, p. 98.
31. Seyyed Jamal al-Din Va'ez Esfahani, *Libas al-taqwa*, Homea Rezwani (ed.) (Tehran: Nashr-e Tarikh-e Iran, 1985), pp. 10–11.
32. A. Yusuf Ali, *The Holy Qur'an: Text, Translation and Commentary* (Brentwood: Amana, 1983), 1541–1542.
33. Esfahani, *Libas*, pp. 23–4.
34. The definition is taken from: Lex Heerma Van Voss, 'Introduction', *International Review of Social History* xlvi, Supplement 9, 'Petitions in Social History' (2001), pp. 1–10, here p. 1. Petitions are among the least exploited sources of Middle Eastern scholarship. Although there are some studies about petitions they have not duly been used as sources of information on Middle Eastern, and particularly Iranian, history writing. The most detailed work on nineteenth-century petitions from Iran is Irene Schneider, *The Petitioning System in Iran: State, Society and Power Relations in the Late 19th Century* (Wiesbaden: Harrassowitz Verlag, 2006). Schneider focuses on the petitions sent between

1883 and 1886 to the Council for the Investigation of Grievances (Majles-e Tahqiq-e Mazalem), founded in 1882. As Schneider also points out, some of these petitions had previously been published in Fereydun Adamiyat and Homa Nateq (eds.), *Afkar-e Ejtema'i va Siyasi Eqtesadi dar Asar-e Montesher Nashodeh-e Dowran-e Qajar* (Essen: Nima Verlag, n.d.). Mansoureh Ettehadieh Nezam-Mafi also has an article which focuses on the Council for the Investigation of Grievances: Mansoureh Ettehadieh Nezam-Mafi, 'The Council for the Investigation of Grievances: A Case Study of Nineteenth Century Iranian Social History, *Iranian Studies* xxii/1 (1989), pp. 51–61. On the Constitutional Period I have come across two Persian articles: Ali Tatari, 'Barrasi-ye Jayghah-e Arizeh dar Pazhuheshha-ye Asnadi', *Payam-e Baharestan* ii/4 (2009), pp. 465–76 and Siavash Shohani, 'Gozari bar Arayez-e E'anat", *Payam-e Baharestan* ii/no. 3 (2009), pp. 315–29. While Tatari analyses petitions in terms of their place in conventional documentation categories, Shohani investigates demands, financial and otherwise, as a specific type of petitions.
35. Sohrabi, *Revolution and Constitutionalism in the Ottoman Empire and Iran* (New York: Cambridge University Press, 2011), p. 297.
36. Ibid., 297. Schneider gives 1864 as the date of the establishment of these boxes both in Tehran and in the provinces. *The Petitioning System*, p. 35.
37. However, apparently in the provinces the practice was far from without troubles. According to Lord Curzon, the governors in the provinces 'ordered a watch to be kept on those boxes; the bastinado was freely administered to any indiscreet person dropping in a petition'. Schneider, *The Petitioning System*, p. 35.
38. Schneider, *The Petitioning System*, p. 36.
39. Ettehadieh Nezam-Mafi, 'The Council', p. 52.
40. Mansureh Ettehadiyeh Nezam-Mafi, *Majles va Entekhabat* (Tehran: Nashr-e Tarikh-e Iran, 1996), p. 23.
41. Adamiyat, *Ide'olozhi*, 371. *Rowzeh khani* is a Shi'ite ritual sermon that recounts for a mourning public the tragedy of Karbala in AD 680, when one of the grandsons of the Prophet Muhammad, Hoseyn ibn Ali, was killed along with some of his family members and supporters.
42. Habib Ladjevardi, *Labor Unions and Autocracy in Iran* (New York: Syracuse University Press, 1985), p. 12.
43. Jim Sharpe, 'History from Below', in Peter Burke (ed.), *New Perspectives on Historical Writing* (Cambridge: Polity Press, 1991), p. 30.
44. Library, Museum and Document Center of Iran Parliament (henceforth LMDCIP), d4-k25-j12-p14, 31 October, 1921.
45. Massoud Karshenas, *Oil, State and Industrialization in Iran* (Cambridge: Cambridge University Press, 1990), p. 70. According to Moghadam, this $30 million was the deficit on the visible account including the oil sector. The invisible account was also in deficit during this period. See G.R. Moghadam, 'Iran's Foreign Trade Policy and Economic Development in the inter-War Period' (Unpublished PhD dissertation, Stanford University, 1956), p. 60, as quoted in Kershenas, *Oil, State and Industrialization*, p. 70 footnote 11.

46. LMDCIP, d4-k25-j12-p14, 15 November 1921.
47. Ibid., 18 November 1921.
48. Ibid., 20 November 1921.
49. Ibid., 1 December 1921.
50. Ibid., 14 February 1922.
51. Ibid., n.d.
52. Ibid., 2 January 1922.
53. Ibid., 7 February 1922.
54. Ibid., 11 January 1922.
55. Ibid., 23 November 1922.
56. Ibid., 2 December 1922.
57. Ibid., 2 December 1922.
58. Ibid., 16 February 1923.
59. Ibid.
60. Ibid., 11 February 1923.
61. Ibid., 22 February 1923.
62. Ibid., 27 February 1923.
63. Ibid., 5 March 1923.
64. Ibid., 6 January 1923.
65. Ibid., 4 January 1923.
66. Ibid., 'From the Shoe-Makers', 4 March 1923. Library Museum and Document Center of Iran Parliament.
67. Ibid., 4 March 1923.
68. Massoud Karshenas, *Oil, State and Industrialization in Iran* (Cambridge: Cambridge University Press, 1990), p. 70.
69. There were already similar proposals for the development of industry in the country. For example, in June 1922, Hajj Mohammad Mo'in al-Tojjar Bushehri, a prominent merchant and constitutionalist and deputy to the First and the Third Parliaments, sent a petition to the Majles to this effect. After emphasizing the significance of removing the need to foreign goods he proposed a similar law for the exemption of machines from import fees. dore4-k25-j12-p31 'moin al-Tojjar', 30 June 1922. Taqizadeh, too, made a similar proposal. Asked about the ways to develop industry in the country he proposed, inter alia, the abolition of import dues on machinery. FO 307/10158. The law ultimately passed in 1925 did not apply to many small-scale capital goods such as sewing and knitting machines, printing and engraving machines, etc. (Bharier, *Economic Development*, 176), which, as Floor rightly observes, shows the state's biased attitude towards large-scale industries. Floor, *Labour and Industry in Iran*, p. 124.

CHAPTER 7

HIDDEN FROM HISTORY? WOMEN WORKERS IN MODERN IRAN: A THEME REVISITED[1]

Valentine M. Moghadam

Some 40 years ago, British feminist historian Sheila Rowbotham asked why women were 'hidden from history' and helped to found the field of women's history. Years later, Gayatri Spivak asked, 'Can the subaltern speak?' and added a new dimension to the field of subaltern studies. Throughout, Marxists have inquired into the relationship between the sexual division of labour and the mode of production, although Engels's cogent commentary about family, private property, and the state – and the 'world-historical defeat of the female sex' – was subsequently eclipsed by analyses that focused on capital and (the male working-) class. These questions are used to frame this chapter, which examines the history and historiography of working-class women in Iran.[2]

The field of Iranian historical studies has grown considerably, but one is struck by the paucity of studies on working-class women, the dearth of data on women workers, and the absence of working women's voices in the major English-language studies of social, economic, and political history (e.g., works by Lambton, Issawi, Bharier, Keddie, Abrahamian, Ladjevardi and Bayat). Subaltern women – as distinct from elite women – barely speak, and are indeed hidden from history. Despite this, we know from studies of women and work in other parts of the Middle East and from references in what is a fugitive literature, that the women of the popular classes have always been engaged in the spheres of production and reproduction, in such key areas as carpet production, food production, personal services, and all manner of household labour.

Iran's first national census of population and housing was conducted in 1956; data and information for periods before then are inadequate or scattered and difficult to obtain. It is possible that archives in Iran could shed light on the history of women workers, but I am not aware of any such archival research. This is in contrast to developments in Middle East social history, especially in connection with the Ottoman Empire. Research on women in the Safavid era shows that elite Iranian women engaged in political activities, while Fariba Zarinebaf-Shahr has described the *waqf* contributions of elite Safavid women in the shrine-city of Ardabil.[3] But we are still largely in the dark with respect to non-elite and subaltern women.

Theoretical and Historical Overview: Capitalist Development and Female Labour

In the introduction to the 1884 edition of his classic text, *Origin of the Family, Private Property and the State*, Engels argued that the first division of labour was the sexual division of labour. With the rise of private property and the state, maternal clans and matrilocal arrangements gave way to the patriarchal family. Over the millennia the sexual division of labour has shown remarkable consistency, despite some variations. Marxist-feminists have noted the salience of material production and biological reproduction, theorized its links to the social position and economic roles of women, analysed the relationship between culture and sex (including cultural reproduction and the social control of women and their sexuality), and examined the critical role of women's labour in social reproduction. Equally important are the ways in which women's economic roles correspond to modes of production within complex social formations across historical periods, the dialectical (interactive) relationship between gender relations and class structure, class/gender arrangements and modes of production, and the effects of state formation and state policies on the position of women. Insights from world-systems theory also show how the global system affects relations, institutions, and processes within core, peripheral, and semi-peripheral societies, and the ways in which women's paid and unpaid labour contributes to capital accumulation.[4] In Iran, too, women's economic roles and their social positions – or their subordination and subjectivity – have been shaped by the world-system, the mode of production, the state, and class location. The Iranian social formation, like that of many late-developing countries, has been characterized by a combination of modes of production, which have co-existed – and sometimes conflicted – with each other. What appears to have remained constant across pre-capitalist and capitalist production relations is the patriarchal nature of gender relations and the sexual division of labour.

As feminist anthropologists, historians, and sociologists have noted, the pre-industrial economy was organized on a household/family basis, whereby each member of the household/family was expected to make some contribution to the joint resources.[5] Household enterprises contributed to the family's subsistence as well as to the surplus mobilized for the landlord or king. Not only were families (or households) the basic social units of pre-industrial society, they were also patriarchal. For Weber, patriarchy or 'patriarchalism' was a system of power common in traditional societies, 'where, within a group which is usually organized on both economic and a kinship base, as a household, authority is exercised by a particular individual who is designated by a definite rule of inheritance'. As Bradley points out, Weber saw patriarchy as closely related to the feudal system that linked a lord and his male vassals in a power relationship.[6] Feminist scholars, for whom patriarchy is male domination within the household and the broader culture/society, have examined the implications of these historical processes and social structures for female labour, the legal status of women, and women's agency.

Women have worked throughout history and in all kinds of productive systems. And yet, at certain times in history an ideology of domesticity has emerged, tying women to family roles and defining productive labour as exclusively masculine. I have referred to this arrangement as the 'patriarchal gender contract'.[7] Historical analysis shows that this division of labour is hardly confined to Islam but is in fact a cross-cultural characteristic of gender relations; British historians, for example, have noted the rise of an ideology of domesticity with the development of capitalism in England. And yet the deployment of female labour has shifted with changes in the mode of production and state ideology. In what follows we sketch those patterns in distinct periods of capitalist development: the late Qajar period, the period of early modernization under Reza Shah, rapid industrialization under Mohammad Reza Shah Pahlavi, and the Islamic Republic.

Capitalist Development and Female Labour in Qajar Iran

In the late Qajar period, Iran experienced a slow transition from a pre-industrial, traditional, and predominantly feudal society and economy to one where capitalist relations were emerging along with the appearance of modern factories. Issawi's economic history of Iran documents the kinds of factories that were built during this period, including many that failed. Women played an important economic role in the late Qajar period, in ways that benefited the family/household, owners of enterprises, and the state. In rural areas they were largely unpaid workers, though they produced rice, butter, dried fruits, and tea, and had an important role in the production of wheat, burley tobacco, cotton, hides, skins, raw and manufactured silk, drugs, dyes, wool, and cotton.[8]

The first modern European-type textile factory was established in the 1850s, but the textiles branch continued to be dominated by home-based and small-scale activities. Spinning wool and cotton at home and in the new factories was a largely female working-class occupation. Women were centrally involved in the production of cotton and silk for household consumption and for the market in Gilan, Mazandaran, Kashan, Yazd, and Isfahan.[9] Prior to the discovery and production of oil in 1911–14, Iran's main exports were agricultural products and handicrafts, and thus women's products were sold in national and international markets. Iran's export trade consisted of 'one-half or more, raw vegetable products' (e.g., dried fruits, raw cotton, rice), 'one-fourth, raw animal products' (e.g., silk cocoons, skins, wool), 'one-fourth or less, manufactures' (e.g., carpets, other textiles of silk, cotton, and wool, leather).[10] Thus women's labour contributed significantly to Iran's export trade. However, the predominantly female and child workers in such sectors were paid a wage below subsistence and controlled neither the raw material nor the finished product.[11]

Toward the end of the nineteenth century, carpet-weaving became an important manufacturing industry for both domestic and international markets, employing a large urban workforce. The most common form of organization, however, remained small-scale domestic production, where women were the main labour force. Issawi cites Russian observers of the time who wrote that carpet-weaving in late nineteenth century Azerbaijan was done exclusively by women, at home. Despite this, when carpet factories emerged, it was young boys who were sent to work in them.[12] In 1912 a carpet factory with 150 looms in two buildings was founded by the Sharq Company, staffed mainly by men and young boys, but the raw wool was spun into thread by women working at home, and the dyes were prepared by nomadic women.[13]

In his study of women in the Qajar period, Boshra Delrish emphasizes the important role of women in productive labour for both the home market and for export. Iran's rice was in large part produced by women in Gilan, while Gilaki women also cultivated silk-worms and spun silk. Among the Turkomans, widows were in demand for remarriage due to their expertise in rug-making and animal husbandry. Delrish cites contemporary observers who commented on, for example, Kermani women's production of shawls, caps, and even rifles; Qazvini women's production of crochet needles; Isfahani women's work in the production of clothing, embroidered articles, textiles, and rope; Assyrian and Armenian women's arduous work in the fields; and Hamadani women's involvement in ribbon-making. In 1906–7, some 3,000 workshops producing velvet (*makhmal bafi*) could be found in people's homes, almost entirely operated by women. As in other pre-capitalist or early capitalist societies, where the household economy prevailed, a marriageable woman's 'worth' was determined by her expertise in handicrafts. Rug-making was particularly valued, and Delrish points out that the carpets produced by women in Tabriz, Hamadan, Isfahan, and Mashhad for export markets via Istanbul were of very high quality. But he also mentions the onerous work conditions and paltry incomes earned by women carpet weavers. In villages, the profit from the sale of carpets often accrued to the landlord, while in many cities the women would be forced to sell their carpets cheaply to bazaaris. 'It was not difficult to exploit female labour, considering the absence of state regulation.'[14]

In the late nineteenth century, many Iranian handicrafts began to be replaced by Western manufactured goods, and this resulted in both the deterioration of the guilds and loss of women's livelihood. An Isfahani tax collector reported: 'At least one-tenth of the guilds in this city were weavers; not even one-fifth have survived. About one-twentieth of the needy widows of Isfahan raised their children on the income they derived from spinning for the weavers; they have now lost their source of livelihood.'[15] This was, however, not the case with carpets. '[B]y far the most important craft benefiting from expanded foreign markets was carpet weaving, which attracted a substantial amount of foreign and domestic capital and by 1914 was exporting goods worth £1 million.'[16]

In her study of the Constitutional Revolution, Janet Afary notes that Iran's social democrats wondered whether they should agitate among the workers, organize them, struggle for higher wages, and force the capitalists and managers to adopt a more modern system of production.[17] There is, however, no record of the organizing of women workers, even though women were among the early proletarians, semi-proletarians, and petty commodity producers. Women's labour surely varied by social class, but we have little information on how it varied by ethnicity or religion. In a document on the economic condition of the Armenians of Julfa in 1881, women are mentioned among the artisans: 'A great majority of the women weave socks, and many men are employed in weaving.' The document also attests to Armenian women's household labour and childcare in a laudatory fashion that highlights their 'wise household management'. Armenian women did not use wet nurses but did 'only on necessary occasions call hired women' to do some work.[18] Who were the hired women?

What the available evidence certainly suggests is that the late Qajar era, characterized by the transition from pre-capitalism to capitalism, saw the formation of a class of semi-proletarians, or a reserve army of labour – women. That reserve army became available, to some extent, for factory labour. For the most part, however, women remained situated in rural or household production of rugs and foodstuffs or were found in more traditional occupations such as bathhouse attendants, wet nurses, and birth attendants. Some midwives also assisted women with abortions.[19] Such work roles for women, along with prostitution, were found elsewhere in the Middle East.[20]

Available evidence suggests that prostitution in the Qajar era may have been increasing in scale. Certainly it was a 'social problem' tied to poverty and a 'moral problem' associated with the Qajar court that was widely commented upon, not least by Constitutionalists and reformers. According to Delrish, 'E'temad al-Saltanah mentions the problem of prostitution, while Amin al-Saltanah was said to 'spend half his time with prostitutes'. Prostituted women – some of whom may have been singers and dancers in the Qajar court – were sometimes widows or abandoned women from the lower classes, and thus poverty was certainly one cause. Under the Qajars, prostitution seems to have been alternately tolerated, encouraged, and punished. Some narratives suggest harsh punishments for the prostitutes and for their soldier-customers; the prostitutes had their heads shaved and were paraded in the streets.[21] At the same time, prostitution may have had an economic function, providing a source of revenue and cheap labour for the Qajars. Prostitutes were sometimes arrested and fined, after which they returned to work. Under Naser al-Din Shah, some 14,000 tumans were collected annually from prostitutes. Delrish cites Curzon to the effect that local authorities generated much revenue from prostitutes; extortion by unscrupulous officials is also mentioned. A 'House of Detention' existed to ostensibly reform prostitutes, but in fact engaged the women in the production of clothing for mullahs and soldiers, while older women were deployed to wash the dead in preparation for burial.[22] Prostituted women were also politically manipulated by the royalists in their campaign against the Constitutionalists, as we shall see below.

The Constitutional Revolution: Political Opportunities and Economic Constraints

Afary's study highlights women's collective action in the Constitutional Revolution in favour of nationalism and women's rights. Dramatic news accounts of women's patriotic support included a November 1906 account in *Majlis* that 'widows were contributing their earrings and bracelets' to help accumulate the necessary capital for the establishment of a national bank and that 'each was competing against the other' to make the largest contribution. Bamdad wrote about a washerwoman who came to the courtyard of the Majles, paid one tuman, and asked to subscribe to the bank. *Majlis*, *Anjuman*, and *Neda-ye Vatan* all printed a woman's letter from Qazvin to the Majles deputy Sa'd al-Dowleh, who had helped write the new constitution. The woman offered to contribute the jewellery she had saved for hard times, while her destitute neighbour, a widow and mother of a small child, brought in some of her household articles. One woman turned in her inheritance of 5,000 tumans; others made similarly generous deposits.[23] Afary also describes how nationalist women became involved in the movement to wear native fabrics and to stop the purchase of imported European textiles, in a manner similar to the Indian Swadeshi boycott of British goods (1904–11). School children proudly began to wear native garments, while in Tabriz women organized meetings around the boycott and pleaded with others 'to wear their old clothes for some time', hoping that the nation would soon produce its own textiles.[24]

Women were manipulated, too. Afary describes how Mohammad Ali Shah's collaborator Sa'd al-Dowleh devised several strategies to disgrace *Majlis* and attack the advocates of women's rights, who were being accused of promoting immorality and prostitution. In one such action, he orchestrated a demonstration by a group of prostitutes who marched unveiled in the streets of Tehran chanting, 'The constitution has given us freedom to abandon our religious obligations and live as we wish'.[25]

One of the battles of the Constitutional Revolution revolved around the expansion of modern schools (*madrasa*) to replace the traditional religiously-based schools (*maktab*). In particular, there was a battle over schooling for girls. Afary explains that the opponents of the new schools claimed that they were concerned with women's presumed loss of honour. In response, proponents pointed out that girls who attended the traditional schools were often sexually molested by the male relatives of the female instructor. The new schools not only provided women with a decent education but also protected them from such advances. They argued, too, that schooling would prevent the further expansion of a contemporary social problem – destitute, illiterate, and widowed women with little means of support who ended their lives in begging and prostitution. Taj al-Saltanah, a daughter of Naser al-Din Shah, spoke and wrote about veiling, prostitution, and loveless arranged marriages. She argued that in an urban working-class family the meagre income of a man was never adequate to cover all the expenses of his extended family; if women could remove their veils and be employed in various professions, they could avoid prostitution and earn a living in an honourable way, with the family living in comfort and dignity.[26] The weekly newspaper for women, *Danesh*, drew attention to problems such as the extreme age differences between men and women in most urban marriages, where husbands were sometimes decades older than their wives; pregnant women and their abandoned babies; sexual harassment of women on the streets; and the lives of some urban middle-class women who could be 'regarded by their husbands as virtual slaves'.[27]

As women became more publicly visible during the Constitutional Revolution, their subordinate and oppressed status became a matter of public debate. In August 1907 when a group of destitute widows whose pensions had been postponed for many months took sanctuary (*bast*) at the Artillery Square, near parliament, the journal *Habl al-Matin* devoted an editorial to their plight. According to the editorial, '[t]he most miserable and innocent people of the world are Iranian women, especially the residents of large cities, and particularly, the women of Tehran, to whom every door of refuge is closed'.[28] These women had neither an education nor a profession through which they could earn a living, the editorial went on, and so they were completely dependent on their husbands. Due to their precarious lives, they accepted their husbands' abuses and obeyed all their petty demands. Still, 'the unjust men act as if women were not human beings'. Entitled 'The Most Dishonoured People', the editorial argued that the nation, by virtue of its treatment of women, had been disgraced. *Habl al-Matin* pledged to start a fund for the destitute women who had taken sanctuary in Artillery Square if the ministers and the wealthy members of the community refused to attend to their plight immediately.[29]

Modernization, Industrialization and Proletarianization

The discovery of oil in 1908 began to change Iran's political economy. Britain took advantage first, exploiting Iran's oil through the Anglo-Persian Oil Company. At this time, however, Iran's economy was still dominated by agriculture, carpets, and handicrafts produced largely by women. Halliday writes that the socially dominant classes were the tribal leaders, larger landowners, merchants, and aristocrats at the court and in the civil service – a pattern that changed very little up to the 1940s, 'though the actual membership of the landowning class was altered by Reza Shah's acquisitions in the 1920s and 1930s'.[30] Iran had joined the International Labour Organization as early as 1914, and in 1920–1 this organization informed the government of its concern over working conditions in the carpet industry in Kerman. This led to a series of decrees designed to improve working conditions with respect to length of the workday, the minimum age of employment for girls and boys, safety, sanitation, and health. According to Floor, two articles of the decree of 17 December 1923 read in part: 'boys and girls shall work in separate workshops; mixed workshops are absolutely forbidden,' and 'foremen (those who dictate the pattern to the workers) shall not enter the girls' workshop, where forewomen shall be employed.' It is not clear what motivated the call for segregation, or whether it was enforced. We have no information on sexual harassment of female carpet weavers during this period.[31]

Prostitution remained an occupation for destitute women without family supports and in demand by men of various backgrounds. Kashani-Sabet writes of the authorities' concern about the spread of venereal disease, which was associated with prostitution. She discusses a report on sanitary conditions, completed by health officials and presented to the Ministry of the Interior, which stressed that compulsory military service, mandated in 1925, would contribute to the spread of venereal disease to rural and tribal communities. A recommendation was made to create health services throughout the country for the inspection of prostitutes, while municipal authorities would be required to register prostitutes in order to regulate them as well as treat them for any venereal disease. One treatment centre evidently was set up in Shahr-e Now, the locale that for decades came to be associated with prostitution. In another report, editor Roshanak Nowdoust writes in her women's magazine that 'prostitutes were generally poor and hard-working women', distinguishing them from 'the minority of skilled and wealthy women'.[32]

We need to know more about working women in Azerbaijan – a centre of culture, political movements, and the labour movement during the first few decades of the twentieth century – and within the communist movement. An article in a 2002 (1381) issue of the feminist journal *Fasl-e Zanan*, which provides a summary overview of working women's conditions and their role in the workers' movement, mentions that in 1925, Ja'far Pishehvari appointed a woman to the Azeri Assembly's labour committee.[33]

The 1930s saw the first stage of Iran's industrialization, as well as a concerted effort in state-building and modernization under Reza Shah Pahlavi. Roads, telephones, automobiles, a railway line, and state-owned factories were introduced, as well as modern schools, a university, some education for girls, unveiling, and new legal codes. In this period women were encouraged to attend university, become teachers, and work for the growing state sector. The state bureaucracy grew relatively quickly and absorbed the small number of modern middle-class women.[34] It also modernized certain practices and occupations traditionally associated with women, such as birth attendant and healer, and thus expanded the middle class. In 1930 the government set up a midwifery school under the supervision of the Ministry of Health, and nursing received a boost when the Women's Hospital (Marizkhaneh-e Nesvan) opened in 1935 and included a College of Midwifery.[35] Where American missionaries and their medical associates were earlier responsible for the training of nurses and doctors, many of them members of the Christian minority groups, it was now the Iranian government that was training midwives and nurses.

Production practices were similarly modernized. Floor describes industrialization, the formation of an industrial proletariat, and trade union activity during the 1930s. Some 29 large-scale textile mills were built between 1931 and 1939, both by state and private capital, and mainly in Isfahan, Yazd, Kerman, and Shahi. Urbanization, industrialization, and proletarianization were limited, however, thus limiting the growth of an urban or modern female labour force. Moreover, the 1936 law banning labour unions curtailed working-class action. Estimates of the size of the industrial labour force in the late Reza Shah period vary, with Floor estimating a 1.2 million-strong active male workforce and a 'considerable female workforce, the size of which is unknown'. Much of this female labour force was no doubt concentrated in the carpet industry, the total of which was some 250,000.[36] As late as 1946, some 75 per cent of the economically-active population was agricultural – a figure based on a report indicating the existence of 2.5 million farm families.[37]

Whether in urban or rural areas, wages and working conditions were abysmal, and they were particularly atrocious in private-sector establishments. Factory owners often vilified workers, withheld wages, or physically punished them for perceived infractions. In addition to child labour, bonded labour was prevalent, again mainly in the private sector, although Floor reports that a state silk factory in Chalus in 1933 coercively recruited Yazdi silk weavers. In the carpet industry, workers (predominantly women and children) often lost their eyesight, developed physical deformities, and experienced stunted growth.[38]

Despite industrialization during the Reza Shah era, the significant contribution to Iran's economy until the 1950s came from agriculture, where women played an important role in the production of food and labour-intensive goods in household-centred industries. Textiles and carpets also absorbed women workers, in both rural and urban workshops. And in the urban areas, one group of women continued to be engaged in private or personal services, working as domestics, bathhouse attendants, hair removers (*band-andaz*), washerwomen, fortune-tellers, and prostitutes.

Rapid Industrialization after the 1950s

On the eve of the second stage of industrialization in Iran, the 1956 census counted 573,000 women in the economically-active population. It also showed that half the country's population lived in rural areas and that child labour, especially of young girls, was prevalent. Official statistics showed a high concentration of women in cottage industries, mainly in the rural areas.[39] Women were mostly employed in carpet-weaving, textile and spinning factories; in factories making matches, glass and cardboard boxes; in tea factories, cotton cleaning and gunnysack factories; and in the embroidery industries. In the service sector they remained in the lowest grades of cleaning and catering, where they were categorized as unskilled labourers and received wages that were lower than those given to men. Textiles and food processing had leading positions in this period. Women represented 34 per cent of manufacturing workers in 1956 and 40 per cent in 1966.[40] This was no doubt an undercount, considering the extent of home-based productive work in the rural areas.

According to Mehdi Partovi, in 1953 the daily wage for men in a Qazvin factory was 25–36 rials whereas the daily wage for women was 8–10 rials. In a factory in Semnan, a male labourer's wage was 41 rials and the woman worker earned 36 rials. Partovi adds that later the male wages at that factory were reduced to 31 rials and female wages to 20 rials. In a weaving factory, children were paid three to four times less than men, and women's wages were two to three times less than men's. Another problem that women workers faced was lack of access to health services.[41]

Official statistics undercounted women's rural economic activity but showed that women's employment in Tehran fell between 1956 and

1966, probably the result of rising incomes or of rural–urban migration. Women's employment then rose, from 9 per cent of the total non-agricultural work force in the early 1960s to 11 per cent in 1971. The expansion of schooling and healthcare helped spur the growth in female employment. By 1970, Iran had 16 nursing schools, three of which operated in Tehran; assistant nurses (*behyar*) 'received rudimentary training in health and hygiene, usually a two-year course of study after completing the ninth grade'.[42] Such new occupations allowed young women from lower-income or lower-middle-class families to receive training and earn an income. Halliday writes that the rate of urban female employment was expected to rise to 25 per cent by the early 1990s.[43] It should be noted that this percentage was achieved in the late 1990s in the Islamic Republic.

In the early 1970s, some 13 per cent of all women over the age of 12 (1.4 million) were employed, and most were in the countryside. A total of 70 per cent of all cloth weaving and 72 per cent of carpet-weaving was done in the rural sector, mostly by women and girls.[44] They were either underpaid family workers or received very low wages; they worked in very poor conditions and were at the mercy of the middlemen who employed them. In 1970 in Yazd textile mills, women were paid 90 rials per day, which was below subsistence level.[45] Iran therefore had the 'paradoxical pattern of a substantial female industrial labour force in the rural sector', whereas in the urban areas women made up a much lower proportion of those employed in industry.[46]

Despite conditions, women workers were not always passive. In 1960 and 1962, women workers at the Shahnaz Factory protested; in 1971, a group of 500 women workers from Ziba Factory took part in a demonstration; in 1973 there were three protests by women workers from Pars Electric Factory; and in 1976 protests by women workers at the Melli Shoe Factory and the Shahi Weaving Factory.[47]

During the 1970s, Iran became a major oil exporter and an emerging semi-peripheral country. As industrialization expanded and factories grew, more women were hired as production workers and other kinds of employees in the modern manufacturing sector. On the eve of the Revolution, women earning wages and salaries in public and private sector manufacturing made up between 20 and 27 per cent of the total.[48] This proportion shrank considerably after the Revolution, as factory work came to be deemed inappropriate for Muslim women. But even before the Revolution, factory work for women could be morally hazardous, and some factories seemed to attract troubled women. Faranak, a left-wing activist, recalls trying to organize factory workers, only to find that 'in the locker room I would find women who prostituted themselves after work or were drug addicts or subjects of violence – all so common and so justified'.[49]

Faranak's experience with organizing women industrial workers was different from that of Poya, who engaged in trade union activities in 1979 when the workers' councils were at their peak. She explains that she tried to organize women in four factories – two pharmaceutical, one biscuit-making, and one textile factory – and that some of the women with whom she worked or whom she interviewed were members of the workers' councils (*shura*), although she does not provide figures or other detailed information. She writes that health issues such as the use of chemicals in the pharmaceutical industry or the harsh conditions of work in the textile industry were especially important to the women workers. Another important issue, according to one worker, was 'the child care problem. Most women leave their jobs when they become pregnant. Some will come back to work when their babies are older. They usually leave their children with their family, relatives or even sometimes with neighbours.' The women wanted a child-care centre, literacy classes, more showers, sinks, and soap, and a work environment with less dust and noise pollution.[50]

Home-based work continued throughout the country, including the major cities. Often this home-based work was linked to the bazaar, which in turn was networked with the adjoining neighbourhoods in a complex pattern of economic and social relations that relied in part on female domestic labour. The wives of many bazaaris created collectives of women that included their daughters, relatives, and neighbours, mobilized to engage in piece-work for the bazaar merchants. Often these women sewed clothes for sale in the bazaar, or worked on duvet covers (*lahaf*) that were subsequently finished in the bazaar workshops. Such arrangements were made possible by the kinds of housing that existed around the bazaars; large multi-family compounds.[51] As such, the homes were sites of production and the bazaar was the site chiefly of distribution in what was a reflection of the sexual division of labour and of capitalist and pre-capitalist work relations.

Many urban women, however, did not take part in income-generating activities. Rural migrants to Tehran, in particular, seem to have experienced 'housewife-ization', a phenomenon also noted in Turkey and Egypt, and theorized by Maria Mies as part of capitalist modernization and rural–urban migration.[52] A survey conducted in Isfahan in the 1960s found very low economic activity among women, especially among migrants, although child labour seemed high among the sons and daughters of migrants.[53] The poor women that Janet Bauer studied in South Tehran 'spent most of their day behind their compound walls or those of their neighbours'. Several of the women in the neighbourhood were engaged in waged labour outside the home, some of it at the women's centre that was run by the Women's Organization of Iran. The poorest women were employed as domestic workers or at the women's centre doing cooking and cleaning. Janet Bauer's interviews with women in south Tehran shed light on their lives, identities, sense of the constraints they faced, and aspirations for themselves and their daughters.[54]

Rural Women: Exploitation and Alienation

As noted, rural women have contributed substantially to the production process and to capital accumulation. Research by Erika Friedl, Lois Beck, Haleh Afshar, and Maryam Poya on rural women's labour during the Pahlavi eras and in the Islamic Republic showed the separation of women from the fruits of their labour (alienation), their inability to control the income from their production (exploitation), and their social status (subordination) in what has been a pre-capitalist, patriarchal, social, and economic structure. A strict gender division of labour is predicated on the valorization of men's work and the devaluation of women's work. Moreover, as women over the decades were denied control and autonomy of decision over their products, they could not turn their activities into sources of power, whether public or domestic. Tapper, for example, has described the sexual division of labour among the Shahsavan nomads and characterized gender relations as domination by the men and obedience by the women.[55] Similarly, in her discussion of the different rural production systems she studied over several decades, Friedl dispelled 'romantic' notions of rural women's autonomy and mobility. With respect to nomads and tribes, Friedl explains that according to tribal custom, women do not inherit, they do not hold offices, do not carry weapons, and are expected to perform services for the men responsible for them. Legally, a woman has no rights to any of her products, economic or reproductive. The resulting economic dependency of women on men, however, was somewhat balanced by the women's access to a large group of people, which affords them not only more occasions for input into the discussion of the many issues that emerge in the life of a populous village, but also some occasions to create mutually interdependent power relationships with a wide net of relatives.[56]

In the agricultural system, women spend much of their day in the courtyard with other women, save for mealtime visits from their husbands, fathers, brothers, or sons. Most of the quintessentially female tasks of preparing food, processing wool and milk, and caring for infants are carried out there in close proximity to other women. Village lanes, shops, and the surroundings of the village, especially the fields, are largely male domains. Women are not prohibited from being outside the house, but they must have a legitimate reason to be out: carrying water, walking from one house to another, and performing an urgent errand are acceptable reasons. In rare cases, desperate young widows with children may plough fields, harvest a wheat crop, or cut grass for a cow at home. More frequently, however, women engaged in the cultivation of cash crops like tobacco, opium, and sugar beets.

Inequalities by gender and age are among the defining features of rural households. In her study of the sexual division of labour and gender ideology in a rural area of Kerman that specializes in pistachio cultivation, Shahrashoub Razavi found that a lower value was assigned to women's work (pistachio processing) compared to men's work (ploughing, irrigating, pruning, tractor-driving, land repair) and thus to the marriage of a girl as compared to a boy. For infants and children under six years old, nearly twice as much was spent on healthcare for boys compared to their female siblings. On average boys had completed six years of schooling, compared to the 3.5 years that the girls had achieved. Nearly twice as much was spent on clothing for teenage boys as for their female counterparts. And while the father, who earned more, was responsible for providing the necessary expenses for a son's wedding, provision of a daughter's trousseau was the responsibility of the mother, who earned much less. Whereas the boys were given pocket money, any earnings by the girls were handed over to their mothers. Moreover, while the rural men allocated part of their earnings for tobacco and opium, the women spent their earnings on the household. This situation of intra-household inequality was the result of the 'removal of women from field labour and their gradual confinement to the domestic sphere', even though their wages from seasonal work in the harvest and post-harvest operations, not to mention their cooking, cleaning, care-giving, and so on, were important to household survival.[57]

Haleh Afshar provides an account of women's work and status in the village that she studied. Women cultivated the household plot of herbs, tended the animals, and made cheese, butter, ghee, yogurt, and bread; they also spun, wove, sewed, cooked, and did all the housework. Women did not usually work as waged cultivators, and they were excluded from the *boneh* (a traditional farming collective) and from receiving *nasaq* (a customary entitlement paid to the peasant) by the rural customary barriers to women's inheritance. Occasionally women were employed for a wage to pick fruit or cotton, but their wages were negotiated by, and paid to, the male head of their household.[58]

Whereas boys joined the process of cultivation at the age of 12, as fruit pickers, and began working the land at 14, girls stayed at home to help with the housework, and prepared for marriage. Until the early 1970s they were married off at about 14 years of age. After the Revolution, and despite Khomeini's endorsement of early marriages, the growth of carpet-weaving raised the marriage age of daughters to about 18 or 19. As unwaged workers, they had become too valuable an asset to the family to be parted from it at an early age.[59]

Despite the constraints on their autonomy, rural women did find ways of exercising a degree of control over their labour, products, and income. For example, Afshar describes how the women in the village she studied used to sell their yarn to the Shahsavan tribal women who stayed in the nearby hillsides for the winter months. The small income made by this transaction was used by the women to buy materials and sometimes spells or potions from travelling salesmen; thus they had carved out a small sphere of money relations entirely under their own control. Moreover, the Shahsavan women wove *jajim*, a rough peasant rug which they sold to the villagers.[60]

Maryam Poya writes of how the product of women's labour is sold by the men of their families in the market. She quotes Golrang, a carpet-weaver and agricultural worker, who told her:

I have been a carpet-weaver and an agricultural worker since I was seven years of age. I help my father in animal husbandry and my mother in agricultural work and carpet-weaving. Women do not get paid. In a good year, when my father returns from selling the goods in the market, he gives my mother a sack or two of rice to sell within the village. With this money my mother buys gold, silver, household materials and appliances for me and my sister's *jahazieh* (trousseau). Similarly for carpet-weaving; my father sells the carpets in the market or sometimes he gives my mother a carpet to sell in the neighbourhood and she spends the money for me.[61]

Conclusion

This exploration into Iranian women's labour history in Iran's 'long twentieth century' is an initial attempt to highlight women's changing economic participation across historical periods, modes of production, and state formations. The available evidence certainly suggests that Iranian peasant and working-class women have constituted a vast reserve of cheap labour that has contributed to capital accumulation generated from manufacturing and agriculture, which capital in turn has accrued to landlords, merchants, industrialists, and the state. They have contributed to use value, surplus value, and the reproduction of labour power and the labour force. Despite this, historical and economic accounts have been largely silent on women's contributions to production and the generation of wealth, or the ways in which the state and the economy have combined with patriarchal gender arrangements to shape women's economic status and roles. At the same time, Iranian social historiography is largely silent about the extent of women's involvement in non-productive activities – whether domestic labour, servitude, or prostitution – that appear to have subsidized families, rich households, landlords, and the state.

My cursory review of the social and labour history of Iran shows that much more research is needed on 'subaltern women' and in particular on women's labour history. For without it, we face an incomplete and distorted view, at best, of Iranian history, social structure, the labour force, and collective action. There are numerous questions that cannot be answered given the current historiography and methods and priorities of research. These questions pertain to the dynamics of the relations between the bazaar and working-class households; gender differentiation within the working class and the peasantry; the generation of surplus value and women's labour; export trade and women's labour, especially in the carpet industry; migration and female economic participation; changes in the form and functions of the family; the ways in which women's domestic labour subsidized the formation of a male proletariat; and the gendered patterns of collective action. In the meantime, the gaps in Iranian social, economic, and labour history are slowly being filled by the works of feminist scholars in Iranian studies, male and female, who have drawn attention to both the structural constraints and the agency of half the country's population.

Notes

1. This paper first appeared in *Iranian Studies* as 'Hidden from History? Women Workers in Modern Iran', xxxiii/3–4 (Summer/Fall 2000 [actual publication date 2002]), pp. 377–401, and was an extended version of a paper prepared for the workshop 'Twentieth Century Iran: History from Below', which took place at the International Institute of Social History, Amsterdam, 25–26 May 2001, organized by Touraj Atabaki. It has been updated to account for new studies and information.
2. Sheila Rowbotham, *Hidden from History: Rediscovering Women in History from the 17th Century to the Present.* (New York: Pantheon Books, 1975); Gayatri Spivak, 'Can the Subaltern Speak?' in Cary Nelson and Lawrence Grossberg (eds.), *Marxism and the Interpretation of Culture* (Urbana: University of Illinois Press, 1988), pp. 271–313; Friedrich Engels, *The Origin of the Family, Private Property, and the State* (New York: Pathfinder Press, 1972).
3. Kathryn Babayan, 'The 'Aqa'id al-Nisa:' A Glimpse at Safavi Women in Local Isfahani Culture', in Gavin Hambly (ed.), *Women in the Medieval Islamic World*, (London: St. Martin's Press, 1998), pp. 349–82; Ronald W. Ferrier, 'Women in Safavid Iran: the Evidence of European Travellers', in Gavin Hambly (ed.), *Women in the Medieval Islamic World*, (London: St. Martin's Press, 1998), pp. 383–406; Fariba Zarinebaf-Shahr, 'Economic Activities of Safavid Women in the Shrine-City of Ardabil', *Iranian Studies* xxxi/2 (1998), pp. 247–61.
4. Wilma A. Dunaway, 'The Double Register of History: Situating the Forgotten Woman and Her Household in Capitalist Commodity Chains', *Journal of World-Systems Research* vii/1 (2001), pp. 2–29.
5. Rayna R. Reiter (ed.), *Toward an Anthropology of Women* (New York: Monthly Review Press, 1975).
6. Max Weber and Talcott Parsons, *The Theory of Social and Economic Organization* (New York: Free Press, 1964), p. 346; Harriet Bradley, 'Changing Social Structures: Class and Gender', in Stuart Hall et al. (eds.), *Modernity: An Introduction to Modern Societies* (London: Blackwell, 1996), p. 125.

7. Valentine M. Moghadam, *Women, Work, and Economic Reform in the Middle East and North Africa* (Boulder: Lynne Rienner Publishers, 1998), and idem, *Modernizing Women: Gender and Social Change in the Middle East*, 3rd edition, (Boulder: Lynne Rienner Publishers, 2013).
8. Charles Issawi (ed.), *The Economic History of Iran 1800–1940* (Chicago: University of Chicago Press, 1971), p. 47 and Chapter Six.
9. Willem M. Floor, *Industrialization in Iran, 1900–1941* (Durham: University of Durham, Centre for Middle Eastern and Islamic Studies, 1984), p. 30; Ahmad Seyf, 'Iranian Textile Handicrafts in the Nineteenth Century: A Note', *Middle Eastern Studies* xxxvii/3 (2001), pp. 49–58.
10. Issawi, *The Economic History of Iran 1800–1940*, p. 136.
11. Boshra Delrish, *Zan dar dowreh-ye Qajar* (Tehran: Howzeh-ye Honari-ye Sazman-e Tablighat-e Eslami, 1997); Maryam Poya, *Women, Work and Islamism: Ideology and Resistance in Iran* (London: ZED Books, 1999), p. 30.
12. Issawi, *The Economic History of Iran 1800–1940*, p. 303.
13. Ibid., pp. 271, 297, 302, 303.
14. Delrish, *Zan*, pp. 44–9, my translation.
15. Mansoor Moaddel, 'Shi'i Political Discourse and Class Mobilization in the Tobacco Movement of 1890–92', in John Foran (ed.), *A Century of Revolution: Social Movements in Iran* (Minneapolis: University of Minnesota Press, 1994), p. 9.
16. Issawi, *The Economic History of Iran 1800–1940*, p. 259.
17. Janet Afary, 'Social Democracy and the Iranian Constitutional Revolution of 1906–1911', in Foran (ed.), *A Century of Revolution*, pp. 21–43.
18. Issawi, *The Economic History of Iran 1800–1940*, p. 60.
19. Firoozeh Kashani-Sabet, *Conceiving Citizens: Women and the Politics of Motherhood in Iran* (Oxford: Oxford University Press, 2011), p. 41.
20. As described by Donald Quataert, 'The Social History of Labor in the Ottoman Empire 1800–1914', in Ellis Jay Goldberg (ed.), *The Social History of Labor in the Middle East* (Boulder: Westview Press, 1996), p. 27; Suraiya Faroqhi, *Subjects of the Sultan: Culture and Daily Life in the Ottoman Empire* (London: I.B.Tauris, 2000), pp. 120–1; Judith E Tucker, *Women in Nineteenth-Century Egypt* (Cambridge: Cambridge University Press, 1985).
21. Delrish, *Zan*, pp. 53–4.
22. Ibid., pp. 55–7.
23. Janet Afary, *The Iranian Constitutional Revolution, 1906–1911: Grassroots Democracy, Social Democracy and the Origins of Feminism* (New York: Columbia University Press, 1996), p. 179.
24. Ibid.
25. Ibid., p. 133; also see Delrish, *Zan*, pp. 56–7; Mangol Bayat-Philipp, 'Women and Revolution in Iran, 1905–1911', in Lois Beck and Nikki Keddie (eds.), *Women in the Muslim World* (Cambridge: Harvard University Press, 1978), pp. 301–2.
26. Afary, *The Iranian Constitutional Revolution, 1906–1911*, pp. 191–6.

27. Ibid., p. 200.
28. Ibid., p. 201.
29. Ibid.
30. Fred Halliday, *Iran: Dictatorship and Development* (Harmondsworth: Penguin, 1978), p. 14.
31. Floor, *Industrialization in Iran, 1900–1941*, p. 88.
32. Kashani-Sabet, *Conceiving Citizens*, p. 82.
33. Mehdi Partovi, 'Women's Status in the Working Class', in *Fasle Zanan {The Season of Women}: A collection of Feminist Articles*, in Nooshin Ahmadi Khorasani and Parvin Ardalan, (eds) vol. 2 (Tehran: The Women's Cultural Centre, 2002).
34. Afsaneh Najmabadi, *The Story of the Daughters of Quchan: Gender and National Memory in Iranian History* (Syracuse: Syracuse University Press, 1998), p. 54.
35. Kashani-Sabet, *Conceiving Citizens*, p. 108.
36. This and preceding statements from Floor, *Industrialization in Iran, 1900–1941*, pp. 27–31; see also Willem M Floor, *Labour Unions, Law and Conditions in Iran (1900–1941)* (Durham: University of Durham, Centre for Middle Eastern and Islamic Studies, 1985).
37. Julian Bharier, *Economic Development in Iran, 1900–1970*. (London: Oxford University Press, 1971), p. 34.
38. Floor, *Labour Unions, Law and Conditions in Iran (1900–1941)*, p. 111.
39. Kaveh Mirani, 'Social and Economic Change in the Role of Women, 1956–1978', in Guity Nashat (ed.), *Women and Revolution in Iran* (Boulder: Westview Press, 1983), p. 78.
40. Bharier, *Economic Development in Iran, 1900–1970*, p. 188.
41. Partovi, 'Women's Status in the Working Class', pp. 148–53.
42. Kashani-Sabet, *Conceiving Citizens*, p. 191.
43. Halliday, *Iran: Dictatorship and Development*, p. 192.
44. Ibid., p. 191.
45. Poya, *Women, Work and Islamism*, p. 47.
46. Halliday, *Iran: Dictatorship and Development*, p. 192.
47. Partovi, 'Women's Status in the Working Class'.
48. Moghadam, *Modernizing Women* (2013), Chapter Six.
49. Faranak, cited in Zohreh T. Sullivan, *Exiled Memories: Stories of Iranian Diaspora* (Philadelphia: Temple University Press, 2001), p. 135.
50. Quoted in Poya, *Women, Work and Islamism*, p. 127.
51. Mohamad Tavakoli, personal communication, January 2001.
52. Maria Mies, *Patriarchy and Accumulation on a World Scale: Women in the International Division of Labour* (London: Zed, 1998).
53. John Gulick and Margaret E. Gulick, 'The Domestic Social Environment of Women and Girls in Isfahan, Iran', in Beck and Keddie (eds.), *Women in the Muslim World*, pp. 510–511.
54. Janet Bauer, 'Poor Women and Social Consciousness in Revolutionary Iran', in Nashat (ed.), *Women and Revolution in Iran*, pp. 141–70.

55. Nancy Tapper, 'The Women's Subsociety Among the Shahsevan Nomads of Iran', in Beck and Keddie (eds.), *Women in the Muslim World*, pp. 376–7.
56. Erika Friedl, 'The Dynamics of Women's Spheres of Action in Rural Iran', in Nikki Keddie and Beth Baron (eds.), *Women in Middle Eastern History* (New Haven: Yale University Press, 1991), p. 197. See also Lois Beck, 'Women among Qashqai Nomadic Pastoralists in Iran', in Beck and Keddie (eds.), *Women in the Muslim World*, pp. 51–73.
57. Shahrashoub Razavi, 'Women, Work and Power in the Rafsanjan Basin of Iran', in Haleh Afshar (ed.), *Women in the Middle East: Perceptions, Realities and Struggles for Liberation* (London: Macmillan, 1993), p. 133.
58. Haleh Afshar, 'The Position of Women in an Iranian Village', in Haleh Afshar (ed.), *Women, Work and Ideology in the Third World* (London: Tavistock, 1985), pp. 70–1.
59. Ibid., p. 71.
60. Ibid., pp. 74–5.
61. Poya, *Women, Work and Islamism*, pp. 83–4.

CHAPTER 8

A GENERATION'S MYTH: ARMED STRUGGLE AND THE CREATION OF SOCIAL EPIC IN 1970s IRAN

Peyman Vahabzadeh

The 1960s is rightly characterized as the age of national liberation movements in post-colonial Asia and Africa as well as in many Western states. These and other movements (women's, civil rights, gay, student, etc.) of the 1960s continue to inform today's social movements and politics alike.[1] Fredric Jameson captured the essence of this decade when he averred, 'for a time, everything was possible [...] this period, in other words, was a moment of universal liberation'.[2] *Historically*, the idea of popular armed uprising rose in such historical events as the American War of Independence (1775–83) or the Haitian Revolution (1791–1804) while *conceptually* it can be traced back to the nineteenth century revolutionary violence of the Russian anarchists or Narodniks and French socialists. In exploring the conceptual lineage of armed struggle, this chapter focuses on Georges Sorel's theory of revolutionary violence and measures it against the rise of the People's Fada'i Guerrillas in Iran in order to offer a *dialectical* reading of theory and practice pertaining to rebellious action and popular-revolutionary myth.

Social life in 1970s Iran is characterized by a political binary due to the concentration of power in the hands of Mohammad Reza Pahlavi (r. 1941–79), the shah and the country's ruling elite, on the one hand, and the rise of a new generation of left-leaning university students in the 1960s (both Marxist and radical, liberationist Muslims), on the other. In the absence of the institutional means for genuine political participation and increased securitization of society, student activists adopted militant approaches that – *à la* radical student and urban guerrilla movements of the 1960s – aimed at instigating a popular uprising to overthrow the Iranian monarchy. This binarism permeated the collective psyche of the Iranian people and *inadvertently* prepared them for the Islamic Revolution of the 1979 led by the clerics.[3]

The fact that the small networks of militant intellectuals and university students could elusively but effectively challenge one of the most powerful states in the world, known for widespread abuses of human rights and mistreatment of political prisoners,[4] is often rightly attributed to the dedication of the activists and the influx of support they continually received.[5] This study of the psychological and cultural aspect of armed struggle in Iran focuses on the way the Iranian People's Fada'i Guerrillas propagated the image of the immortal fighter who embodied the everlasting struggle for justice in the face of an oppressive machine countless times stronger: the Fada'i Guerrillas gained a significant social and political presence while paradoxically their organizational presence was declining due to the regime's security measures. The paper argues that the Fada'i Guerrillas created *a constructed cultural myth (of dissent) that succeeded in creating a political weight that was unattainable politically*. This argument is supported through a content analysis of selected relevant pieces. Sorel's concept of the 'myth of general strike' will be utilized in this context to show that popular depiction of the guerrillas gave them an ineradicable mythic presence that celebrated their dedication, heroism, and justness, thereby making revolutionary violence comprehensible, even desirable, in the eyes of dissident Iranians.

Founded in April 1971 following a number of armed operations in Tehran and Tabriz, Cherikha-ye Fada'i-ye Khalq or the People's Fada'i Guerrillas (PFG; later, the Organization of Iranian People's Fada'i Guerrillas, OIPFG; or Fada'iyan, plural of Fada'i) emerged as two militant groups unified. They both largely consisted of university students and graduates, and young writers and educators.

The founders of the older formative group (Group One) had the experience of activity with the Tudeh Party of Iran in the early 1950s, but they were disillusioned with the Party due to its inaction regarding the August 1953 coup that overthrew Premier Mohammad Mosaddeq and his National Front government. Bizhan Jazani (1937–75), a social sciences graduate, and Hasan Zia Zarifi (1939–75), a lawyer, both became active as university students with the rise of the Second National Front in 1960–3, when under the pressure from the Kennedy administration, the shah had relaxed political restrictions in order to receive the US aid package for his ambitious developmental plans. Political parties and activities flourished during this period until the state's heavy-handed repression (particularly of the religious opposition to land reform and women's suffrage) in June 1963 that took the country back to autocratic rule. The two repressive waves within a decade convinced the group to prepare for guerrilla warfare in Iran. A network of 20 militants had been created by 1967 when Jazani, Zarifi, and the majority of the group were arrested, tried, and received heavy sentences.

Group One's surviving members regrouped, recruited, planned, and carried out a soon-to-be-key operation when, on the evening of 8 February 1971, nine militants attacked the Siahkal Gendarmerie Post in the Caspian Province of Gilan. With the subsequent arrest of the revolutionaries and their support network, 13 militants were summarily tried by a military court and executed on 18 March 1971. Although parochial in its extent, this operation provided Iranian dissidents with a myth of gallantry and resistance against a brutal regime. A handful of survivors of Group One, led by Hamid Ashraf (1946–76), co-founded the PFG.

The younger formative group (Group Two) came from the experience of the Second National Front and the flow and ebb of the movement in 1960–63. Mas'ud Ahmadzadeh (1947–72) and Amir Parviz Puyan (1947–71) met Abbas Meftahi (1945–72) at the University of Tehran. They formed a group and gradually adopted Marxism-Leninism. Influenced by the Cuban revolution, Che Guevara's book, Uruguay's Tupamaros, Brazilian Carlos Marighella, and Frenchman Régis Debray, they chose armed struggle as the group's strategy in 1969–70. The group's success in rapidly building underground networks became its curse when SAVAK raided them by late 1970.

Ahmadzadeh, Meftahi, Puyan, and Ashraf founded the People's Fada'i Guerrillas (PFG) in April 1971. Within a few months, the first two were arrested (and executed in 1972) and Puyan was killed (1971), leaving Ashraf to become the elusive leader of the group until his death in June 1976. The Fada'iyan had been pushed to the verge of annihilation by 1972, but they grew back to gain the upper hand in their psychological warfare against the state between 1973 and 1975.[6] They owe their success to the vast support they received from university students and intellectuals inside the country, the Confederation of Iranian Students, National Union abroad, and the weapons and funds they received from Libya and Democratic Republic of Yemen as well as the People's Front for the Liberation of Palestine (led by George Habash).[7]

Marxism-Leninism was the group's ideology, but the Fada'iyan relied heavily on Ahmadzadeh's *Armed Struggle: Both Strategy and Tactic* (Summer 1970), which argued that because the objective conditions of the revolution were ripe, armed struggle would be short-lived, and the masses would join the popular uprising soon after the initiation of guerrilla warfare.[8] Until the time of his assassination in prison, Jazani wrote several important treatises on the issues of armed struggle and popular movement. He saw armed struggle as the first step at political organization and preparation for a popular movement.[9] His writings were smuggled to the PFG leadership, leading to a new direction for the PGF (by 1974), one that was nonetheless abandoned due to the near-eradication of the group in the spring of 1976 and later in the wake of the 1979 Revolution that largely led to the rejection of armed struggle by the Left.

During their original phase between 1971 and 1979, the Fada'iyan carried out sporadic but carefully chosen operations, the most prominent of which was the assassination of Lieutenant-General Zia Farsiu, chief prosecutor of the Military Court, deemed responsible for handing down the death sentences for the Siahkal guerrillas (April 1971). In addition to clashes with police and security, the militants bombed power-lines, military posts, and police stations. This is how the guerrillas grabbed newspaper headlines and permeated the Iranian social psyche to the extent that those years of heightened urban guerrilla activity in Iran later became retrospectively known as the 'guerrilla period'.

Between 1971 and 1979, a total of 237 Fada'i cadres and activists lost their lives.[10] After the revolution, the OIPFG grew into Iran's most popular leftist group, thanks to the 'mythic' image of Fada'iyan in the people's memories.[11] The OIPFG soon split into numerous factions: some factions opposed the new regime and tried to fight it militantly, while others supported a theocratic state. By the mid-1980s, all factions had been brutally repressed, and thousands of Fada'i activists and supporters were killed between 1981 and 1988, while thousands more were forced into exile.

We should stress the generational aspect of Fada'iyan as becoming the *raison d'être* of the Fada'i Guerrillas rests with a rebellious generation of Iranians coming of age in the 1960s and 1970s. This connection is made through the student movement. Like the student movement in almost any country in the late 1960s, including Western countries,[12] the Iranian student movement (leftists and Muslims) was greatly inspired by the revolutionary spirit of the 1960s,[13] especially by the urban guerrilla wave initiated by leftist Latin American intellectuals in the aftermath of Che Guevara's death in Bolivia in 1967. Extensive social and economic development under severe political repression by the state alienated the growing student population that filled the emerging university and colleges set up to train the professionals needed for developmental plans. Stark class inequalities gave the students grounds for questioning the regime's developmental ambitions.

Thus, the guerrilla movement in Iran, spearheading the student movement, should be regarded as an attempt at reinstitutionalizing politics in the country, since due to the existence of the rentier state a curious form of 'repressive development' pushed for economic modernization while simultaneously closing doors on political participation. Revolutionary violence captured this generation's protest against its non-responsive parent-generation.

Siahkal and the 'Myth' of Revolutionary Uprising

To construct my argument, I will show how the inceptive operation of the PFG was transformed into the foundational 'myth' of a rebellious generation, although PFG's guerrilla warfare was not the first armed movement in Iran. Two years prior to the Siahkal operation, a vast Kurdish armed uprising took place in western Iran – a movement that militarized an entire region and lasted for 18 months. But the Kurdish movement left no impression on the Iranian collective memory due to the lack of a constructed social narrative. On the contrary, the Fada'iyan succeeded in leaving a cultural-psychological impact on Iranian society. Before exploring this aspect further, let us pause for a moment and clarify what is meant by 'myth'.

In *Reflections on Violence* (orig. 1906), George Sorel offers a 'philosophy of violence',[14] and he asserts that 'the term *violence* should be employed only for acts of revolt,' aiming at 'the destruction of the old order'.[15] He likens violence to calculated military campaigns in classical warfare,[16] a pure form of violence he calls the 'general strike'. But since the 'general strike' is yet to come, it can only live on as an image of social change. Participants in a 'social movement always picture their coming action as a battle in which their cause is certain to triumph', he observes. 'These constructions [i.e., pictures], I propose to call myths; the syndicalist "general strike" and Marx's catastrophic revolution are such myths.'[17] The key component of the ontological aspect of the myth is *action*. For Sorel, 'action' means to *leave the present* in a 'way [that] our freedom becomes perfectly intelligible'.[18] Since action is future-oriented, it involves 'the framing of a future, in some indeterminate time'.[19] The myth of general strike, therefore, captures the essence of genuine social transformation. Thus the 'question whether the general strike is a partial reality, or only a product of popular imagination, is of little importance. All that it is necessary to know is whether the general strike contains everything that the socialist doctrine expects of the revolutionary proletariat.'[20] By conjuring up images, desires, and expressions, I evoke a Freudian interjection: the myth of general strike replaces the comprehensive knowledge of the revolution with a condensed, symbolic version. The myth, therefore, prepares for this (future) moment of liberation and makes sense of all preceding and existing forms of action that push the existing system to its ruins and create room for future innovation. But this moment needs to be registered in the knowledge of the working class and its vanguards. So we arrive at the epistemological aspect of the myth: the general strike becomes a way of conceptualizing the proletarian violence.[21]

Sorel's 'myth of general strike' came to life in the 1960s and, specifically, within a generation that founded in Iranian politics something utterly new: Marxist-Leninist, urban, intellectual-based, guerrilla warfare. The Fada'i Guerrillas became one of Iran's most popular political parties primarily due to their vast and talented supporters' success in creating a new 'myth', the myth of immortal and selfless fighter for freedom and justice, and toward the final, future moment of deliverance.[22]

In particular, the Siahkal operation enabled a foundational-generational 'myth', that enabled a subsequent era (1971–9) overshadowed by armed struggle and laden with collective perceptions of the immortal, omnipresent, and elusive freedom fighter. To substantiate these claims we need a brief account of the Siahkal operation, its context, and the consequent depictions of it.

The Siahkal operation was carried out in the context of the security preparations for the shah's ostentatious celebration of 2,500 years of monarchy in Iran, beginning on 20 October 1971 at the ruins of Persepolis, and at a cost of $200 million. To create the calm necessary for the event, in the years leading up to the lavish celebration, SAVAK launched a major crackdown on all opposition. To show off the power of Iranian security, the head of Internal Security of SAVAK, Parviz Sabeti, staged a televised briefing on 23 December 1970. In this briefing, he showcased one of the most able SAVAK agents, Abbas Ali Shahriyarinezhad (Shahriyari), who was responsible for several high-profile sting operations that led to the arrest of dozens of revolutionaries in the 1960s (including Group One). Shahriyari (assassinated by the PFG in 1975) appeared on television with his face obscured, posing as a foreign agent, now exposed by SAVAK. Sabeti introduced him as Eslami or 'the man with a thousand faces'. Sabeti bragged about SAVAK's (supposed) one million agents and informants. In this 'island of stability,' he asserted, nothing moved without the knowledge of Iranian security. Just a month and a half after this televised power-talk, a small team of guerrillas attacked the Gendarmerie Post in the township of Siahkal, smashing the image of 'island of stability' and ridiculing Iranian security. The Caspian region's lush ecology provided natural cover for the guerrillas, and historically Gilan was home to the Jangali movement and the short-lived Soviet Socialist Republic of Iran in 1920–1.[23]

The operation was rushed in reaction to SAVAK's raiding of the team's logistics networks and arresting several members on the evening of 6 February 1971. Eight out of the nine militants of the mountain team, led by Ali Akbar Safa'i Farahani, took part in the attack, with two being killed. The team engaged with, and was chased by, the army from 9 to 28 February. With seven militants finally arrested and two killed,

Figure 8.1 The posters of Iran's most wanted men, members of the PFG, Spring 1971. (Source: Mahmud Naderi, Cherikha-ye Fada'i-ye Khalq: az nakhostin konesh ta Bahman-e 1357, jeld-e avval, vol 1).

the authorities claimed the quick 'eradication' of the 'insurgents and saboteurs'. The military court rushed the trial and appeal proceedings of the 14 arrestees (of mountain and logistic teams), and the death sentences of 13 guerrillas were hastily carried out on 18 March 1971. The regime declared its conclusive success in eliminating the guerrilla networks in a press release dated 27 March 1971, but only ten days later, on the morning of 6 April 1971, a team of militants gunned down chief military prosecutor, Lieutenant-General Zia Farsiu in Tehran. The assassination not only made a mockery of the security forces; it left the impression of the presence of a large, well-organized, and elusive underground movement.

Iranian security conceded a psychological defeat in May 1971 when SAVAK issued and distributed the posters of Iran's most-wanted men, nine PFG members with the bounty of 100,000 Tumans (roughly $15,000) for information leading to the arrest or death of each (see Figure 8.1). Contrary to SAVAK's intentions, the posters reinforced the social perception of the PFG as an elusive, hermetic, and impermeable organization. The posters, in fact, increased the popularity of the heroic militants in the eyes of dissident Iranians.

According to the partial publications of the interrogation records of the Siahkal militants, the operation was far from accurate or successful. The attack on the Siahkal post was rushed to force the release of a militant captured earlier that day (8 February) by the villagers and handed to Gendarmerie personnel. The eight men seized an old Ford van and took its passengers hostage in the post, under the watch of one of them. In the five-man attack on the post, an officer and a civilian were killed, and a militant was injured by friendly fire. Two militants were supposed to simultaneously attack the nearby forest ranger's base (unarmed), but they did not. The team seized the rifles in the post without taking ammunition. They had planned to blow up the post but forgot their explosives in the building in their haste to get out of the area.[24]

On the Shah's orders, Iranian military descended on the region in disproportionate numbers: Gilan Gendarmerie Regiment, Provincial police force, SAVAK counter-insurgency unit, and several helicopters were deployed to suppress just eight guerrillas. Lieutenant-General Oveysi, the commander of National Gendarmerie, directed the operation.[25] Strangely, however, the remaining militants did not move away from the region, as they had planned. It was chiefly the freezing temperature and exhaustion that defeated them. During the next three weeks, three insurgents were captured by the villagers of Chehel Sotun, who took the liberty of torturing their captives before handing them to the authorities. Other militants engaged with the army on several occasions. One militant, having fled the scene alone, ended up being captured by an unarmed villager eight days later, totally exhausted. When the remaining four tried to surrender, two were shot by the frightened gendarmes.[26]

Despite these facts that show the operation's failure, the mere audacity to rise up in arms and in small numbers to challenge the Iranian state fascinated dissident Iranians. The operation was celebrated as an epic turning point: it was now called the 'Siahkal Resurgence' (*Rastakhiz-e Siahkal*). Clandestine circles of dissident university students were quickly mobilized to support the elusive guerrillas. Thus, the operation marked the birth of a 'myth:' after Siahkal, revolutionary action became possible, even necessary.

Armed Propaganda: the Myth of a New Age

We have seen that Sorel's theory of the 'myth of general strike' is intended to *render revolutionary violence intelligible* within proletarian politics of his day. It *constructs a utopian horizon* toward which the minute and mundane activities of his contemporary syndicalists and socialists were to be directed. In the 1960s and 1970s Iran, I argue, the Iranian militants had *inadvertently* understood the power of Sorel's 'myth' in their own experiential way. The 'Siahkal Resurgence' immediately became a source of inspiration for a defiant generation, as it rendered guerrilla insurgency intelligible, constructing a generation's unifying utopian horizon of liberation. Haloed with gallantry, the Siahkal guerrillas were gradually elevated to the status of hagiographized liberators in underground publications and in the hearts and minds of educated dissidents. The surprising chain of events that followed the execution of the 13 guerrillas reinforced their mythic status.

While reflecting (in prison) on the increasing popularity of Fada'iyan, Bizhan Jazani, who deemed the PFG as his brainchild, offered the concept of 'armed propaganda' to capture the mythic presence of the guerrillas. Although he borrowed the *term* from Che Guevara's *Guerrilla Warfare* (1961), Jazani actually transformed it into a *concept*. For Che Guevara, 'armed propaganda' meant the presence of the guerrillas in the liberated or conflict area, involving the guerrillas' explaining their actions and trying to win the support of the peasants.[27] Drawing on the similarities between Iran and Latin America,[28] Jazani employs 'armed propaganda' (*tabligh-e mosallahaneh*) to emphasize the *symbolic and metonymic* character of guerrilla operations. He understands the concept as such: one, carefully chosen targets allow the guerrillas to send a *clear* message to a specific public, state functionaries, or movement supporters (the communications effect); two, an operation should make the guerrillas *appear* as larger and more capable than they actually are (the metonymic effect); and three, the operation should render the regime vulnerable and confused in the eyes of the people (the political effect). Armed propaganda, therefore, involves activities that can be easily decoded by the public.[29] Thus, Jazani's take on 'armed propaganda' is fit for urban guerrilla warfare where there cannot be any rebel-controlled zone (e.g., the Cuban case).

'Armed propaganda', therefore, has *certain conceptual affinities* with the 'myth of general strike'. Whereas Sorel's theory belongs to the time of rising working class movements in the West, 'armed propaganda' reconstructs the 'myth' in the age of postcolonial national liberation. Jazani's observation of the metonymic effect of the rather parochial guerrilla operations, however, was already experientially and intuitively at work in the minds of the activists of the time. In Jazani's words: 'Although these [guerrilla] groups are extremely small in comparison to the forces of the regime, their militancy and immortality [*fananapaziri*] in the face of the regime's great power puts an end to the one-sided and absolute reality of the regime.'[30]

It was in the collectively constructed and vehemently publicized mythic and epic depiction of the guerrillas that, despite state censorship, the news about insurgents circulated in the country. The following excerpt exemplifies the metonymic presence of the guerrillas in popular view. In an issue of short-lived publication, *Nabard* (published in Europe), there is a follow-up 'report' on the Siahkal operation:

Continued Armed Struggle in the Caspian Jungles

Currently in the Caspian jungles, outside [the towns of] Shahsavar, Sari, and Amol, the guerrillas, in bands of three, are fighting against the armed forces. Due to the continued attacks of the guerrillas, frightened Forest Rangers and the Gendarmerie Forces have evacuated parts of the wooded areas and this has caused the local residents to be able to use the jungles at will.

To take away the guerrillas' ability to use natural camouflage, the regime has sprayed the region using poisonous chemicals that destroy green vegetation and tree leaves.[31]

The 'report' is completely fabricated. Those who recall televised images of the Vietnam War will recognize the source of the claim about spraying chemicals to destroy the guerrillas' natural camouflage. It never happened. Reports like these, drafted and distributed without the Fada'iyan's knowledge but never denied by them, helped the guerrillas attain a mythic and metonymic presence. Those who knew the facts did not speak out about fabrications because they regarded these 'reports' as a part of psychological warfare against the regime. The Fada'iyan never engaged in such unrealistic hyperboles in the official literature of the PFG, but they certainly enjoyed being surrounded by such superhuman depictions of their activities.

It was the Siahkal affair that allowed fables of heroism and epic guerrilla presence to surface in arts and poetry.[32] These sentimental depictions within the emerging public discourse of a rebellious generation did not escape Jazani, who reflected in prison on the 'immortality' of the guerrillas, seeing in these widespread, collectively shared fables the materialization of his theory of 'armed propaganda'.

> The people have taunted the regime by communicating news and hundreds of rumours in favour of the guerrillas. Every fallen guerrilla has left behind him- or herself tales of heroic deeds. Following the attack on the Siahkal Post and even after the execution of the thirteen [militants], the jungles were filled with guerrilla bands. After the execution [assassination] of [General] Farsiu and announcing the rewards for [information on] the nine guerrillas, the people made fun of the regime through jokes. After his death, [Amir Parviz] Puyan came back to life many times. In his clashes [with security forces] [Mohammad] Saffari [Ashtiani] attained super-human powers and at the time of his martyrdom [death] he had been fighting the enemy single-handedly for hours. Mehrnush [Ebrahimi] jumped from one rooftop to another, killing enemy agents with her machine gun... These are the positive signs of the sympathy and love of the people toward armed struggle.[33]

Jazani's observation is sound. The social and communications mechanisms of propagating such depictions by dissidents go beyond our focus here. So let us revisit Sorel's theory in light of our case study.

Conclusions

Using the case of the Fada'i Guerrillas enables us to see how the post-colonial mode of armed struggle, typical of the 1960s liberation movements, *enacts in a concrete manner, but without heeding it*, the Sorelian 'myth'. Under the conditions of repressive development, Iran's ruling class produced a new social stratum of trained professionals, expected to man the ambitious developmental projects intended to situate Iran in the periphery of international capitalism. Yet this ambitious class of professionals – university students and graduates – was impeded from genuine political participation. Political disenfranchisement of this prosperous middle class alienated Iran's younger generation. The rise of armed struggle in Iran should be understood as an attempt at imposing political opening in the country. Against the background of the country's brutal security forces, the selfless actions of the militants invoked in the Iranian collective psyche age-old fables of gallantry and heroism. Such cultural dispositions shaped the political behaviour of the Iranian leftist movement.

The sacrifices of young men and women – who otherwise could have had a comfortable life but had instead chosen to fight for political inclusion and justice – did not go unnoticed in the eyes of a vast array of Iranians who ridiculed the state-propagated version of modernization. As such, without knowledge of literature on revolutionary violence (e.g., Sorel), this generation *instinctively and existentially created* its own liberationist 'myth of general strike'. They did so in a manner amazingly reminiscent of Sorel's theory. This myth, in turn, became part of the Iranian social psyche and culture. That a significant part of this generation turned to Marxism-Leninism and guerrilla warfare (*à la* Latin America) must be understood in the context of the 1960s.[34] The ideological inclinations and violent methods of this generation must be viewed as secondary to the 'myth' they created. The Fada'i Guerrillas re-emerged after the Revolution as one of Iran's largest leftist groups not due to their ideology or violent methods but because of the cultural impression they had left on society as selfless lovers of the oppressed.[35] While acknowledging their brutal suppression in post-revolutionary times, I argue, the Fada'iyan lost their popularity as the myth attached to them withered away.

Here is the issue: in every moment of an intended revolutionary change, as Sorel recognized, it is necessary, even inevitable, *to create a myth that unifies diverse experiences of different groups and renders revolutionary violence indispensable and justifiable*. To understand this 'myth' as an ideological façade, while not quite incorrect, will detract from the importance of what is at the heart of Sorel's vision: that acting needs to be linked, in perception, to a life-altering experience, while in fact the action remains connected to its intended object (e.g., subversion of capitalist state in the syndicalist tradition). This is when we notice the cohort of images (surrounding the Fada'i Guerrillas) that are capable of instigating 'the noblest, deepest, and most moving sentiments'[36] of the revolutionaries and their supporters.

To be precise, let me point out Sorel's refusal to consider the myth in terms of any measurable step. 'In employing the term myth I [...] put myself in a position to refuse any discussion whatever with the people who wish to submit the idea of a general strike to a detailed criticism.'[37] Understandably, his refusal to 'concretize' the myth arises from safeguarding the myth against endless factional debates among socialists. By refusing to allow the 'myth' to become the subject of concrete discussions, Sorel conceptualizes the myth as a super-ideological point of convergence of all revolutionary socialists. A utopia, as an image of a desire and a measure of a demand,[38] need not have 'realistic' aspects but it still exercises power over us.[39]

To explore the full merit of Sorel's concept dialectically in light of our case study, let us consider the fact that concrete actions (e.g., Siahkal) created the basis for the disproportionately epic presence of the guerrillas in society and thus for the creation of the myth as the unifying horizon of liberation. I argue that the social construction of the myth allows possible spontaneous movements to be attached to the perceived, but not yet actual, liberation movement. In as much as the myth is 'utopian', it will need to be extracted from the actual events. This is when the specific acts of real-life activists bestow upon the myth an appearance of reality. This is also precisely where this study differs from Sorel. The fact that the failed Siahkal operation was popularized as a generation's heroic resurrection in the eyes of dissident Iranians demonstrates that, theoretically, the actual event already embeds the myth. The 'myth' is an image, but it is not merely an image: it is a possible modality life as it unfolds before our waiting eyes. Social movements rise to significance because they show that concrete acts are tied to the mythic presence of a unifying, alternative future. What invites and enables the myth is the futurity of human existence. The construction of these myths, studied from the point of view of sociological analysis and cultural studies, are key to social movements' success, as the case of the Fada'i Guerrillas shows us in relation to Sorel's theory of the myth.

Notes

1. See: Regis Debray, *Revolution in the Revolution? Armed Struggle and Political Struggle in Latin American* (New York: Monthly Press Review, 1967); George Katsiaficas, *The Ideology of the New Left: A Global Analysis of 1968* (Boston: South End Press, 1987); Jeremy Varon, *Bringing the War Home: the Weather*

Underground, the Red Army Faction, and Revolutionary Violence in the Sixties and Seventies (Berkeley/Los Angeles: University of California Press, 2004).
2. Fredric Jameson, *The Ideologies of Theory: Essays 1971–1986*. Vol. 2 (Minneapolis: University of Minnesota Press, 1988), p. 207.
3. Peyman Vahabzadeh, *A Guerrilla Odyssey: Modernization, Secularism, Democracy, and the Fadai Period of National Liberation in Iran, 1971–1979* (Syracuse: Syracuse University Press, 2010), p. 215.
4. Ali Reza Nobari, *Iran Erupts* (Stanford: Iran-American Documentation Group, 1978).
5. Maziar Behrooz, *Rebels with A Cause: The Failure of the Left in Iran* (London: I.B.Tauris, 2000), p. 50; Vahabzadeh, *A Guerrilla Odyssey*, p. 214.
6. Ibid., p. 63.
7. See: Anonymous, 'Goruh-e Ahmadzadeh-Puyan-Meftahi pishahang-e jonbesh-e mosallahaneh-ye Iran' [The Ahmadzadeh-Puyan-Meftahi Group: Vanguard of Armed Movement in Iran], *19 Bahman-e Te'orik* 7 (June 1976); Anonymous, 'Goruh-e Jazani-Zarifi pishtaz-e jonbesh-e mosallahaneh-ye Iran' [The Jazani-Zarifi Group: The Vanguard of Armed Movement in Iran], *19 Bahman-e Te'orik* 4 (April 1976); Anonymous, *Tarikhcheh-ye sazmanha-ye cheriki dar Iran* [*A History of the Guerrilla Organizations in Iran*] (n.p., n.d.).
8. Mas'ud Ahmadzadeh, *Mobarezeh-ye mosallahaneh: ham estratezhi, ham taktik* [*Armed Struggle: Both Strategy and Tactic*] (Omeo, Sweden: Organization of Iranian Students, 1976).
9. Bizhan Jazani, *Cheguneh mobarezeh-ye mosallahaneh tudeh'i mishavad* [*How Armed Struggle Becomes A Mass Movement*] (n.p.: OIPFG, 1976).
10. For statistics on deaths of the Fada'i militants see: Vahabzadeh, *A Guerrilla Odyssey*, pp. 16–77; 257–9.
11. One account claims that in Iran's only free parliamentary election (March 1980), the OIPFG candidates received approximately 10 per cent of the total ballots. See: OIPF-M [Organization of Iranian People's Fada'iyan-Majority] 'The Organization of Iranian People's Fada'ian (Majority): 1971–2001', available at: http://w1.315.telia.com/~u31525377/english/his01eng.htm (accessed 28 April 2009).
12. See: Varon, *Bringing the War Home*.
13. Afshin Matin-asgari, *Iranian Student Opposition to the Shah* (Costa Mesa: Mazda Publishers, 2002); Matthew Shannon, '"Contacts with the Opposition": American Foreign Relations, the Iranian Student Movement, and the Global Sixties', *The Sixties* IV:1 (2011), pp. 1–29.
14. George Sorel, *Reflections on Violence* (Nineola: Dover Publishings Inc., 2004), p. 56.
15. Ibid., p. 171; original emphasis.
16. Ibid., p. 115.
17. Ibid., pp. 41–2.
18. Ibid., p. 48.
19. Ibid., p. 124.
20. Ibid., p. 127.

21. Ibid., p. 119.
22. For an extended history of the group see: *A Guerrilla Odyssey*, Chapter Two.
23. See: Cosroe Chaqueri, *The Soviet Socialist Republic of Iran, 1920–1921: Birth of the Trauma* (Pittsburgh: Pittsburgh University Press, 1995).
24. See: Seyed Hamid Rohani, *Nehzat-e Emam Khomeini Jeld 3* [*Imam Khomeini's Movement, vol. 3*] (Centre of the Islamic Revolution Documents, 1993), pp. 293–5; Mahmud Naderi, *Cherikha-ye Fada'i-ye Khalq: az nakhostin konesh ta Bahman-e 1357, jeld-e avval* [*People's Fada'i Guerrillas: From Their First Acts until February 1979, vol. 1*] (Tehran: Political Studies and Research Institutes, 2008), pp. 191–9.
25. Hamid Ashraf, *Jam'bandi-ye seh saleh* [*The Three-Year Summation*] (Tehran: Gam Publisher, 1979), p. 105.
26. See: Rohani, *Imam Khomeini's Movement*, pp. 296–303; Naderi, *People's Fadai Guerrillas*, pp. 199–221.
27. Ernesto Che Guevara, *Guerrilla Warfare* (Lincoln: University of Nebraska Press, 1998), p. 87; Debray, *Revolution in the Revolution?*, p. 47.
28. Bizhan Jazani, 'Jam'bandi-ye mobarezat-e si saleh-ye akhir dar Iran' [*Summation of the Struggles of the Past Thirty Years in Iran*], *19 Bahman Te'orik*, nos. 5–6 (1976), p. 92.
29. Bizhan Jazani, *Nabard ba diktatori-ye Shah* [*War Against the Shah's Dictatorship*] (n.p.: OIPFG, 1978), p. 47. The PFG 'operationalized' this concept in its manual: OIPFG, *Amuzeshha-yi baray-e jang-e cheriki shahri* [*Instructions for Urban Guerrilla Warfare*] (n.p.: OIPFG, n.d.), which reveals the influence of Carlos Marighella's 'Mini-Manual of the Urban Guerrilla' (available at: http://www.marxists.org/archive/marighella-carlos/1969/06/minimanual-urban-guerrilla [accessed 10 September 2013]) on Jazani's theory.
30. Jazani, *War Against the Shah's Dictatorship*, p. 43.
31. *Nabard* (Information Bulletin of the National Liberation Movement of Iran), no 1 (April–May 1971), p. 4.
32. See: Peyman Vahabzadeh, 'Rebellious Action and the "Guerrilla Poetry": Dialectics of Art and Life in the 1970s Iran', in Kamran Talattof (ed.), *Persian Language, Literature and Culture: New Leaves, Fresh Looks* (London/New York: Routledge: 2015).
33. Jazani, *War Against the Shah's Dictatorship*, p. 78.
34. See: Katsiaficas, *The Imagination of the New Left*.
35. See: Vahabzadeh, *A Guerrilla Odyssey*, pp. 244–5.
36. Sorel, *Reflections on Violence*, p. 366.
37. Ibid., p. 43.
38. Ibid., p. 126.
39. Ibid., p. 126.

CHAPTER 9

OIL AND PERSIAN FICTION: LITERARY DEPICTIONS OF COPING WITH MODERNITY AND CHANGE

M.R. Ghanoonparvar

By the late 1940s and early 1950s, when Iranian Prime Minister Mohammad Mosaddeq was spearheading efforts to nationalize Iranian oil, the so-called 'black gold', and the oil industry had gained tremendous importance for all Iranians of various strata and socio-economic backgrounds, both those who still adhered to a more traditional outlook and way of life and those who advocated and yearned for the creation of a more modern society, since the oil revenues were supposed to help the country's development. But oil, which had been discovered in abundance earlier in southern Iran, was perhaps also the cause of the first direct clash of Western and Iranian cultures and ways of life in the early twentieth century, which occurred subsequent to the granting of the concession for the exploration for oil to the British. With the construction of an oil refinery by 1913 in the small port town of Abadan, soon to be the largest in the world, Abadan began to grow. It did so because it also became the residence of a relatively large number of British nationals, who lived in the affluent part of the town in newly-constructed comfortable Western-style houses, and poor labourers, who had mostly migrated from other parts of Iran in search of jobs and who lived either in crowded, small oil company housing or in shantytowns. Hence, the clash was not only cultural but also economic, and increasingly political. This situation also extended to other cities and towns of the province where the oil company had exploration and extraction projects.

The first half of twentieth century also gave rise to modernist Persian literature, which from its inception in the wake of the Iranian Constitutional Revolution (1906–11) had been more socially and politically conscious and engaged, and in a sense more mundane than the literature of the previous centuries. The events in the early 1950s that resulted in a coup d'état with the help of the British and American intelligence services, and subsequently another period of dictatorial rule, were the source of disillusionment and despair for the generation that had witnessed them, including the literary artists who named the post-Mosaddeq era 'the Age of Night'. True, as the famed novelist Simin Daneshvar observed in an interview in 1987, 'the fall of Mosaddeq was a harsh slap in the face by history that we [the intellectuals] and the oppressed people of Iran suffered together', and, therefore, a major preoccupation for writers of that generation.[1] While social reactions to those events were quickly and successfully crushed, literary reactions were rather slow, as if the writers were all in a state of shock. Severe censorship also helped curtail any direct and open treatment of those events, and hence, writers who dared to write about them in most cases disguised the time, place, and characters of their stories, resorting to some sort of literary subterfuge.[2] In chronological order, in this chapter, we shall explore several works of fiction that in various contexts deal with the story or history of the encounter of Iranian society with oil and the oil industry, and because of this, also with Iranians' encounters with Europeans and Americans, referred to earlier as the clash of cultures. So important are the effects of these encounters on the country and its people, as reflected in these fictional accounts, obviously, the impact of these encounters was nationwide and ran for the course of many decades; hence, the novelists and short story writers discussed here are from various parts of Iran with different experiences and understandings of this impact. While the works of the southern writers and those of the so-called 'Khuzestan School of Fiction writing', who were born and raised in regions with an arguably different cultural environment, often provide us with firsthand experiences of living in 'oil towns' and with many characters, events, scenes, and themes that are in various respects unique and different to those by writers from other regions. Writers from other parts of Iran usually present a broader, perhaps even at times more abstract, perspective. One of the early examples of such a broad perspective approach, which I also referred to as 'subterfuge', is by Jalal Al-e Ahmad.

Although as a political activist Jalal Al-e Ahmad (1923–69) was a close observer of and involved in those events, and despite the fact that he was a rather outspoken social critic, he resorts to allegory as a literary subterfuge when he writes stories about this period of Iranian history. One of his first attempts in this regard is a novella entitled *Sargozasht-e Kanduha* (*The Story of the Beehives*), written just a few years after the fall of Mosaddeq's government.[3] The story is about a farmer by the name of Kamand Ali Beyg who has by chance acquired the necessary knowledge to become a beekeeper. With his new enterprise, he no longer has to work as a farmer in the fields from sunrise to sunset, in addition to the fact that beekeeping provides him with significantly more income than does farming. The bees do the hard labour and Kamand Ali Beyg exploits and profits from it. The rest of this allegorical story is about the bees that are initially at a loss as to know what happens to the honey they store in the hives for their winter food and they eventually realize that some mysterious hand regularly robs them of it and replaces it with date juice, which, as the wise elder bees tell them, is detrimental to their survival. With this realization, and under the guidance and leadership of the elder bees, one morning they set out on a journey back to the mountains, to where their forefathers lived, with an abundance of flowers and water, leaving Kamand Ali Beyg and his hives behind. While some critics as well as many readers interpreted this story as an allegory about the oil nationalization movement and its failure because soon after, the West and the Western oil companies succeeded in reinstating their influence over that industry, one Iranian critic observes that if the farmer-turned-beekeeper in this allegory is supposed to stand for the Western exploiters of Iranian oil and the bees represent Iranians, this is indeed a failed attempt on Al-e Ahmad's part, since the bees in the end free themselves from the exploiter, while in the mid-1950s when the story was written the Iranians, unlike the bees, were not wise or orderly enough to liberate themselves.[4]

The use of an allegory about bees as literary subterfuge by Al-e Ahmad is justifiable in some respect in the highly restricted political climate of martial law at the time. A decade later, the form of literary subterfuge changes and writers begin to use human characters instead. One of the earlier stories by a southern writer that indirectly deals with Western exploitation of Iranian oil is by Naser Taqva'i, originally a short-story writer who later became a prominent film director. Taking advantage of the cultural perception that exists in societies such as Iran regarding virgin girls, who must be protected from possible violation, Taqva'i chooses two virgin girls as the precious 'possessions' of the religious people of a small town in a short story entitled 'Aqa Julu' (Mr Giulio) to tell a story not only about the exploited, but also the exploiter.[5] The setting of the story is the small southern port town of Langeh, which is inhabited by minority Shi'ite and majority Sunni populations that live in separate sections and have traditionally been at odds with each other. The arrival of a seemingly vagrant Italian engineer, who has decided to make this small town his home, triggers changes for the inhabitants as the Italian begins to settle down and start a series of enterprises one after another, each failing. A happy-go-lucky character who gets drunk at night and wanders through the streets and alleyways singing loudly, he becomes a favourite character for the young children, but also a source of concern for their traditional parents. To remedy the situation, the townspeople decide that since he is going to stay, they should get him married to a local girl to help settle him down and end his carefree behaviour. They do so, and at this point Julio decides to start another business; he opens the first photography studio in town. Soon after, although this business also fails, the people find out that he has been taking nude photographs of his wife and selling them to sailors on ships that anchor near the port town. After his wife leaves him and he marries the daughter of a prominent local man, he continues with the same practice, selling nude pictures of his second wife. The story ends with gendarmes coming to town and looking to arrest Julio. They also tell the people that he has been doing similar things in various nearby towns.

Naser Taqva'i was born in 1941 in Abadan, where he spent his formative years during the oil nationalization movement. In this short story, however, rather than choosing Abadan, a city with which he is more familiar, as the location for 'Mr Julio', he not only shifts the locale but also, similar to Al-e Ahmad, chooses a symbolic plot and characters in his fictional exploration of the Western exploitation of Iranian oil, and the manner in which Iranians react to and try to cope with it.

The symbolic representation of Western exploitation of Iranian oil can also be found in a lengthy short story by Gholamhoseyn Sa'edi (1935–1985), one of the most prominent playwrights and fiction writers of the past century. 'Dandil' is the name of a poor suburban village of the city of Maragheh, which was known as the residence of pimps and prostitutes at the time.[6] Similar to Taqva'i's 'Mr Julio', this story revolves around a young beautiful virgin girl who has been brought by her duped father to this infamous village to be married off, unaware of the fact that she has ended up in the house of an old prostitute. The pimps in the village, who are trying to make a lot of money off this new find, search for a rich customer; finally, with the help of the village policeman, they find an American sergeant from the near by military base. The madam in whose house the virgin girl is staying, as well as the rest of the village, is told by the policeman that the American is very rich and will pay enough money as the girl's first customer and that the entire village will benefit and prosper. After preparing the village for the arrival of the sergeant by cleaning the street, putting up lights, and cooking a lavish meal, the customer, a fat, drunk, ugly-looking American, arrives and spends the night with the girl. The next morning, however, when the American leaves without paying, the villagers are told by the policeman that there is nothing to be done, since Americans are powerful, and if the sergeant is offended, he will destroy the entire village.

In 'Dandil', as a story of Western exploitation of seemingly the only Iranian resource of interest to Westerners, Sa'edi succeeds to a much greater degree than does Al-e Ahmad in *The Story of the Beehives*. The story works because, as a microcosm of the entire country, the village is inhabited by various characters, including the pimps, the policeman, and the father of the girl, all of whom regard the virgin as an asset for their own short-term profits. Also, the use of an American as the exploiter makes Sa'edi's story more plausible as a symbolic story about the post-Mosaddeq period of American involvement in Iran and the Iranian oil industry.

Sardonic, satirical humour is the strategy that Ebrahim Golestan employs in a parable of sorts about oil; this time, however, not in connection with the Western exploitations, but about the effects of the abundant wealth resulting from oil. Golestan's *Asrar-e Ganj-e Darreh-ye Jenni* (*The Secrets of the Treasure of the Haunted Valley*), which originally appeared as a feature film in 1971 and then as a novel in 1974, depicts the life of a poor farmer in some remote village.[7] One day, while he is ploughing his field, the plough by accident hits a rock, and when the farmer tries to move it out of the way, he discovers a large hole in the ground that, as he soon figures out, leads to an ancient burial chamber full of gold and other precious artefacts. Shrewd enough to keep his find a secret and thinking that luck has finally turned his way and he no longer needs to labour from dawn to dusk on a piece of land that hardly provides him and his family with a subsistence living, he devises what he thinks is a clever plan: to avoid suspicion he takes bits and pieces of the treasure to the city to sell. His plan works, and although the jeweller that he finds in the city is initially suspicious that the precious jewels have been stolen and tries to pry the farmer's secret from him, to no avail, eventually he befriends the farmer, happy with the profit he will be pocketing. As the days go by, the farmer continues to gradually bring more of his find to sell, and with the money, he buys all sorts of household furniture, electrical appliances, candelabras, and other trinkets that he has seen in the city and thinks are the requirements for modern living, even though the village in which he lives lacks such essential amenities as electricity and running water. Before long, his windfall wealth attracts the attention of an increasing number of greedy opportunists, who hope to get some morsel from the banquet of the farmer's riches. The wife of the jeweller, who like her husband has become interested in 'helping' the farmer to live like a 'modern' man, arranges his marriage to her maidservant, telling him that he must have a 'modern' wife; and others around him, including the village Literacy Corps teacher, who has appointed himself as the manager of the farmer's affairs, advise and assist him in the construction of a 'palace' worthy of his newly-acquired status. The rest of the story consists of a series of intrigues and quarrels among various characters, each of whom competes to endear him- or herself to the farmer. But Golestan's novel does not have a happy ending. Explosions set off by a road-building crew cause the treasures and the burial chamber to be buried and lost as easily as they had been found, and once again the farmer has to return to his previous dirt-poor life.

As some critics have pointed out, the reader can easily draw parallels between the shah of Iran and the farmer, and between the subterranean treasure and oil, among others.[8] The reader can also plausibly see the analogy between the unexpected discovery of the underground treasure by a farmer who in the midst of the twentieth century seems to be living in some mediaeval distant past, as indicated by his method of farming, and the sudden flow of petrodollars to Iran, in particular in the last decade of the Pahlavi rule when Golestan's film and novel were created. At that point in Iranian history, Golestan (as well as many other writers) were no longer concerned about Western exploitation of Iran's oil but about the way its resulting revenues were wasted on the superficial efforts made by the government of the shah to modernize the country. Golestan's outlook a few years before the onset of the Islamic Revolution seems to have been quite pessimistic, and in hindsight, realistic. The crumbling of the gaudy palace of the farmer, made of mud bricks, the façade of which is painted in glittery colours, because of the explosions at the end of the film and novel seem also analogous to the crumbling of the shah's imaginary palace, what he called the 'Great Civilization'.

Although published in the same year as Golstan's novel, Ahmad Mahmud's *Hamsayehha* (*The Neighbours*) takes the reader back to the earlier events of the 1950s.[9] Prominent among writers of southern Iran, Mahmud, the son of an oil industry labourer, was born and raised in the provincial capital city of Ahvaz, where he also worked in a variety of menial jobs during his youth. By the late 1940s and early 1950s, during the social and political upheavals of the Mosaddeq era, similar to many young people of his generation, Mahmud had already become interested and involved in socialist-inspired politics, which generally meant the expression of discontent regarding the regime of the shah and, concurrently, opposition to Western exploitation of and influence in Iran. As mentioned before, the reinstatement of the shah's government and a police state following the brief moment of hope for democracy that Mosaddeq's government had instilled in the majority of Iranians, especially the young people, was the cause of disappointment and despair for old and young alike, in particular Mahmud's generation. Hence, his first novel, *The Neighbours*, which similar to much of his work is autobiographical, is a product of and reflects the social and political events during those turbulent years.

The Neighbours is the story of Khaled, a young man from a working-class family, and his involvement in dissident political activities. The story begins during the Mosaddeq era. The locale is

Khuzestan; hence, the issue of oil nationalization is tangible to the characters in the story. Mahmud recreates in detail the general social and political climate of the time in this novel. Anti-British sentiments are prevalent in society and political discussions and demonstrations are common in the streets. The British are called 'bloodthirsty colonialists' and Britain, the 'beast who only drinks blood and whose appetite is never satisfied'.[10] Khaled is still too young to easily comprehend the meaning of these phrases that he hears on the streets or reads with difficulty in political hand-outs. In time, gradually, he is able to figure out that blood represents oil, for which the British have an insatiable appetite. He learns that the people want the British to leave, but he is at a loss when he hears the contradictory statements about them. In an argument between two factory workers, Khaled hears one of them, who has a ribbon pinned to his chest with the phrase 'the oil industry must be nationalized', say something about a 'lion'. The second worker comments sarcastically, 'So you are also wearing one of these ribbons on your chest?' He then adds, 'The lion's tail can't be yanked with what is written on the ribbon'. The other worker retorts, 'My dear friend, the lion has gotten to be too old and mangy; he has lost his hair'. Then continuing his argument, he says: 'That time has passed, the time of plundering, I mean. The lion must now put its tail between its legs and get lost. Now everything has an owner; everything must be accounted for.'[11]

Finally figuring out that by the 'lion' they mean the British, Khaled ponders, 'What are the British doing in our country anyway?' and, 'What does our oil have to do with the British?'[12] But he becomes even more confused when he hears the prime minister on the radio warning the people against throwing the British out:

> We will be destroyed if we nationalize the oil industry. It is a big mistake to drive the British out [...]. We don't have any petroleum engineers, and at the same time, the only thing we have is oil; our country is sitting on it. If they get to be stubborn and boycott buying our oil, we will be bankrupt.[13]

The people, however, accuse the prime minister of being a 'British functionary', a man about whom they say, 'As long as he is in power, the British have nothing to fear'.[14]

Khaled receives his early education in politics in the midst of this confusion. Some years later, when he has become involved in anti-government politics and an activist in dissident leftist groups, which subsequently results in his being arrested by security police and his incarceration and torture, he comes to the conclusion that his and his comrades' fight against the shah's regime and against his Western supporters are basically one and the same, perhaps reflecting the novelist's own thinking and that of his generation. Hence, Mahmud seeks symbolic revenge for the overthrowing of the Mosaddeq government, which had made an attempt at nationalizing the oil and ridding the country of foreign powers. His revenge is through the recreation of a scene in the story in which an effigy of an Englishman is set ablaze by the populace in celebration of the oil nationalization:

> In the city square, people made an effigy of an Englishman with cloth, rags, and sticks and wanted to set it on fire. They had put a pair of short trousers on the effigy and had soiled its crotch with black oil. They had placed a wide-rimmed hat on its head. From the butcher's shop, they had taken the penis of a bull and stuffed it between the lips of the effigy in place of a cigar. And the effigy had a little dog, which was dragged after him on a chain. It was made of cloth and rags. It had large floppy ears and was coloured with black oil. People were crowding around the effigy of the Englishman and cheering.[15]

Among the writers of Persian fiction prior to the Islamic Revolution in Iran, Ahmad Mahmud is rather unique in his realistic depiction of the social upheavals in the mid-twentieth century that led to the nationalization of the Iranian oil industry and ensuing tensions between the Iranian government and the West. As I have tried to demonstrate, for the reasons stated at the beginning of this discussion, most writers prior to the Islamic Revolution did not directly approach either the mid-century oil crisis or topics related to its revenues and what the government did with them. The implicit and explicit censorship restrictions specifically related to these topics were no longer in effect once the regime changed and the Islamic government came to power. But either the writers of the 1950s generation had mostly died or the more recent events, namely the revolution and the Iran–Iraq war, seem to have become more of a preoccupation for them than those of several decades earlier. This has also been true of the post-revolution generation of writers. One notable exception is Moniru Ravanipur, who, perhaps for a different purpose and in a different context, once again visits the topic of oil in her magic-realist novel, *Ahl-e Gharq* (*The Drowned*), published more than a decade after the revolution.[16]

The Drowned is the chronicle of the people of a small fishing village called Jofreh on the Persian Gulf. The story begins a few years after World War II and continues up to the Islamic Revolution in Iran and the Iran–Iraq war. The village (which was actually the birthplace of the author) was established only a generation earlier by a small number of families whose former village, some distance from their present location, had been destroyed in a storm. The novel begins with over 100 pages of detailed descriptions of the traditional life and folklore of the village population, which consists merely of a few families. As if in a different age or on a different planet, the inhabitants of Jofreh, who do not have any contact with the world outside their community, live contentedly, neither concerned for or aware of the international conflicts of the early and mid-twentieth century. As their main source of sustenance, the sea is a mysterious place to them about which they have formulated and hold certain superstitious beliefs. One, for instance, is about 'the Ugly Ruler of the Seas', Busalameh, whose wrath inflicts all natural and unnatural calamities and disasters that befall the land dwellers. At times when Busalameh becomes angry and takes away someone from the village, the inhabitants of the village know that they must avoid doing or saying anything that might enrage him. The victims of Busalameh's wrath, or fishermen who fall in love with mermaids (or as they call them, the 'blue inhabitants of the sea'), are taken away to the bottom of the sea and eventually permanently become sea-dwellers.

The village and the traditional life of its people are guarded by the sea from the outside; but eventually the sea also becomes the pathway to the village for outside intrusion and hence imminent change. Change begins to happen when one day the villagers find several boxes containing bottles full of some strange liquid they have never seen or tasted before. The content of the bottles, which according to their custom, is distributed among the inhabitants, causes unusual behaviour after they drink it. Shortly after the appearance of the boxes, a small boat with 'three tall, blond men with blue eyes' lands nearby. Upon seeing the intruders, the villagers think that perhaps it is the work of Busalameh wreaking some havoc by sending these human-looking strangers, who might be some sea creatures. The tall blond strangers have brought more bottles of the liquid the villagers have named 'magic drink'; but Zayer, the headman of the village, who does not trust the intruders and what they might be planning to gain with their gift, asks the people to destroy the bottles. Even though the villagers intend to prevent the tall blond men from returning to the village, the strangers have already found some allies among those inhabitants who have become fond of their gift of the magic drink. The intruders return several more times, and on each visit they bring other gifts of no use to the inhabitants, including a radio, which the villagers name a 'magic box' and from which they hear human voices in a strange language, and some colourful plastic objects. Nevertheless, the villagers are fascinated by these gifts, especially the radio, which, until the batteries run out, keeps them from their daily tasks of fishing and other chores. Even though the visits of the tall blond men eventually end, the lives of the inhabitants have changed. The village has now been discovered, not only by other strangers but also by the government, which opens a gendarmerie station and then decides to build a road to the village. All of this is a prelude to the discovery of oil in Jofreh. More strangers become frequent visitors to the village and tell the villagers about blond men and women with blue eyes and about oil wells that have suddenly appeared in the vicinity of village. Before long, Jofreh is devoured by industries and businesses and disappears from the map. Inevitably, the villagers also find their way to other villages and cities, and among them, Zayer, whose efforts to protect Jofreh's traditional way of life have been in vain, wanders like a lost ghost among 'the blond people in the city' and 'the oil wells that have opened their mouths in nearby and far away villages'.[17]

Oil in *The Drowned* represents the modernization and industrial progress that seem to be detrimental to indigenous traditional life. By looking back at the history of the village of her birth, Ravanipur is also casting a nostalgic glance at the traditional culture of the entire country prior to the industrialization and oil excavation, which was transformed and even erased, as was her village, from the country's map.

The last work of another prominent twentieth-century writer, Hushang Golshiri (1938–2000), is a complex autobiographical novel called *Jennameh* (*The Book of Jinns*), the first part of which presents a picture of the lives of oil industry workers.[18] Although he was born in Isfahan and spent much of his adult life in that city and in Tehran, Golshiri's formative childhood years were in Abadan, where his father worked as a bricklayer for the oil company. Similar to other southern writers, such as Ahmad Mahmud, who write about the lives and the plight of poor migrant workers, ship dock porters, or unskilled labourers working for the oil company, in *The Book of Jinns*, Golshiri begins his novel with the fictional childhood narrative of its protagonist, Hoseyn, in a working-class neighbourhood in Abadan of humble cement houses built by the oil company. The opening chapter of the novel is a childhood narrative of the protagonist that details the life of Hoseyn and his family in the modern industrial jungle of Abadan, the most important features of which are the oil refinery smokestacks, in contrast to the rest of the novel, which takes place in Isfahan, Hoseyn's ancestral city, with its centuries-old mud-brick houses, medieval palaces and covered bazaars, a labyrinth of narrow winding alleys with arched roofs, and old mosques with domes and minarets that are the landmarks of a city the inhabitants of which are the descendants of families who have resided there for many centuries. The focus of the novel, of course, is Isfahan and its ancient history and people with traditional beliefs and way of life that Hoseyn, the reader soon learns, would like to preserve. As a novelist, Golshiri's strategy requires him to choose the modern industrial oil city as the locale of the beginning of his novel to show the angst of his protagonist regarding the loss of traditions rooted in history. *The Book of Jinns* is the tale of a culture and a people that are experiencing a period of sudden change, a period of transition imposed on them by the onrush of the modern world, by the lack of social and cultural stability in a world in which science and technology, along with revolutionary and social upheavals seem to expedite unwanted change. Golshiri's protagonist is in awe of as well as horrified by this modern world, which he regards as unstable, and this seems to be, in different ways and from different perspectives, the concern of Golshiri and other writers we have discussed.

In his allegorical tale, *The Story of the Beehives*, Jalal Al-e Ahmad's solution to the dilemma of the bees and their exploitation by the farmer seems his advocating of a return to ancestral life, and Gholamhoseyn Sa'edi's cynical story of a red-light village's (representing the country's) dream of future prosperity based on its virgin resource ends in the nightmare of being robbed of it and a return to the previous abject life for the inhabitants of Dandil. In his carefully crafted and symbolically-disguised story of intrusion and exploitation of two 'virgins' in a small port town by an Italian entrepreneur, Naser Taqva'i's cynicism is no less than that of Sa'edi. Within the staunchly religious Shi'ite and Sunni communities of Langeh, the Italian engineer's behaviour and his 'immoral' acts seem even more despicable to the townspeople than the way in which the American sergeant exploits the social outcasts, pimps, and prostitutes of village of Dandil in Sa'edi's story. But while Sa'edi's use of bitter satire conveys a sense of disdain to the reader, Taqva'i's story is seasoned with humour in such a way that the reader, like the children in Langeh, even develops some liking for the Western exploiter. Similar to Golshiri's tale of a young boy growing up in the heart of rapid changes due to industrial progress in an early twentieth century 'concrete jungle', a duplicate copy of many such cities in other parts of the world, Ahmad Mahmud's *Bildungsroman* is an exploration of the question of how a young boy, *The Neighbours*' protagonist Khaled, struggles to form a new type of identity in a new alien social environment in contrast to his father's generation, for which such a question was not even relevant. How to cope with the same dilemma and the loss of identity in such a world is perhaps a question faced by the younger inhabitants of the now-extinct village of Jofreh in Moniru Ravanipur's *The Drowned*, while for the village elder, Zayer, who is now lost in the crowd among 'blond aliens with blue eyes' and the open mouths of oil wells, coping is not possible.

Oil has been the engine of modernization and change for Iran and many so-called oil-rich countries since it has provided the money with which they have attempted to join the modern caravan of change and progress. In Ebrahim Golestan's novel, the story of a farmer who finds buried treasure and spends it all on building the façade of a palace of prosperity filled with objects of no use to him, the author's view is sardonic and cynical, reminding his readers that the money from the sale of gold (or black gold) has resulted merely in artificial change and sham modernization.

Notes

1. Naser Hariri, *Honar va Adabiyyat-e Emruz* (Babol: Ketabsara-ye Babol, 1987), p. 33.
2. Regarding censorship in those decades, see: M.R. Ghanoonparvar, 'The Game of Coercion and Subterfuge', in M.R. Ghanoonparvar and Mehdi Khorrami (eds.),

Critical Encounters: Essays on Persian Literature and Culture in Honor of Peter J. Chelkowski (Costa Mesa: Mazda Publishers, 2007), pp. 73–84; Ahmad Karimi-Hakkak, 'Censorship in Persia', in *Encyclopedia Iranica, 1990*; and Naser Mo'azzen (ed.), *Dah Shab: Shabha-ye Sha'eran va Nevisandegan dar Anjoman-e Farhangi-ye Iran va Alman* (Tehran: Amir Kabir, 1978).
3. Jalal Al-e Ahmad, *Sargozasht-e Kanduha*, 5th ed. (Tehran: Entesharat-e Javidan, 1976).
4. Hasan Abedini, *Sad Sal Dastannevisi dar Iran*, vol. 1, 2nd ed. (Tehran: Nashr-e Tandar, 1989), p. 208.
5. Naser Taqva'i, 'Aqa Julu', *Arash* 2, no. 1 (Summer 1964), pp. 84–94. An English translation of this story available in Minoo Southgate (ed. and trans.), *Modern Persian Short Stories* (Washington, DC: Three Continents Press, 1980), pp. 89–103.
6. Gholamhoseyn Sa'edi, *Dandil,* 3rd ed. (Tehran: Entesharat-e Amir Kabir, 1976). An English translation of this story by Robert Campbell is found in *Dandil: Stories from Iranian Life*, trans. Robert Campbell, Hasan Javadi, and Julie Meisami (New York: Random House, 1981).
7. Ebrahim Golestan, *Asrar-e Ganj-e Darreh-ye Jenni* (Tehran: Entesharat-e Agah, 1974).
8. An example is an insightful article by Paul Sprachman, 'Ebrahim Golestan's *The Treasure*: A Parable of Cliché and Consumption', *Iranian Studies* xv/1–4 (1982), p. 156.
9. Ahmad Mahmud, *Hamsayehha*, 4th ed. (Tehran: Entesharat-e Amir Kabir, 1978).
10. Ibid., p. 80.
11. Ibid., p. 88.
12. Ibid., p. 90.
13. Ibid., p. 134.
14. Ibid., p. 135.
15. Ibid., p. 212.
16. Moniru Ravanipur, *Ahl-e Gharq* (Tehran: Khaneh-ye Aftab, 1989).
17. Ibid., p. 48.
18. Hushang Golshiri, *Jennameh* (Spånga: Nashr-e Baran, 1998).

CHAPTER 10

THE CULTURAL POLITICS OF PUBLIC SPACE IN TEHRAN'S BOOK FAIR

Kaveh Ehsani

Shortly after the end of the Iran–Iraq war in 1988, Tehran began to hold an annual International Book and Media Fair, which has become one of the largest book exhibitions in the world. The Book Fair, as I shall call it, lasts for ten days in May and, until 2006, was held in two dozen hangar-like buildings at the capital's vast and verdant International Exhibition Centre. Following the election of the mayor of Tehran Mahmoud Ahmadinejad as president in 2005, the event was relocated, despite the objection of all participants, to the equally enormous Grand Mosalla, Tehran's still unfinished monumental and government-built religious complex. The Mosalla is intended to become the symbolic centre of the capital; a sacred space designed by the state as a national place of worship, as well as for renewing ideological bonds and reinforcing public loyalty with the ruling Islamic regime. In this chapter we will analyse the dynamics of the Book Fair as a cultural event as well as a public space, and explore the extent to which the ideological intentions behind the architectural design of urban space are successful in producing different publics and shaping collective attitudes.

The 'Public' of the 'Public Space'

The 'public' is the core of the polity in the modern nation state, which claims to represent the welfare and interests of ordinary citizens and the nation. However, the public is not a given but a produced collective, and public culture in heterogeneous contemporary nation states is likewise shaped through various mechanisms. These range from the discursive public spheres of the media, patriotic propaganda, and political debates; to the disciplinary institutions of universal education; or the planned construction of public spaces. Consequently, the public spaces of grand boulevards, parks, streets, squares, and national monuments where the heterogeneous and diverse population encounter each other and internalize their shared differences as collective members of an 'imagined community' are integral to the functioning of social relations of power in contemporary societies.[1]

States often rely on designated official public spaces for the pageants and rituals that reinforce a sense of loyalty and belonging to the polity. But this reliance is based on a fragile calculation, since what makes space genuinely 'public' is its openness to all, and the generally accepted conviction that it is 'owned' by neither the state nor private interests, but by the 'public' itself, who may not always react as expected. As a result, governmental authorities often remain apprehensive about the possibility of the public rebelling against the ruling order during moments of crises of legitimacy by using available public spaces to forge a subversive sense of unity and collective power.[2]

The Iranian revolution was one of the major political events of the last decades of the twentieth century, a distinguishing feature of which was its unfolding as a sustained mass movement in public space – primarily in the streets, but also in universities, mosques, schools, and workplaces – rather than in closed rooms among conspirators hidden from the public eye.[3] In fact, the movement turned all sorts of official, semi-private, sacred, and even private spaces in cities and provincial towns, into public spaces of political debate, organization, resistance, and participation. After the collapse of the monarchy the same public spaces became the site of contention and rivalry among rival political forces that no longer agreed over the nature of the post-revolution political order.[4]

Following the civil wars of 1980–2 and the consolidation of a new regime that defined itself as an exclusively 'Islamic' Republic, the control of public space has become the cornerstone of politics in Iran. Economic, geostrategic, doctrinal, and redistributive policies have ebbed and flowed over the past 30 years, but what have remained constant in Iran are the unrelenting struggles over the boundaries and the control of public space. Thus, in a very tangible sense, many political contentions in Iran tend to be framed as some form of a politics of culture, which is often played out in and over public space. The ongoing contentions over the spatial dynamics of Tehran's annual Book Fair have been a recurring example of this politics of public space, and their analysis can shed light on the paradoxes of the relations of power in everyday urban life in the Islamic Republic.

The Book Fair as Public Space

Gradually, since its inception in 1988 after the end of the Iran-Iraq war, the Tehran Book Fair has become Iran's largest public event, regularly attracting more than 2 million visitors a year – as many as the believers who make the annual Hajj pilgrimage. At its height in 2004, some 2,200 domestic and 1,200 international publishers from 39 countries displayed some 250,000 titles.[5] The subjects of the publications on display cover virtually every field, from natural sciences to the occult, from divinities to body-building manuals. More recently the consistent bestsellers have been classics of Persian literature, specialized university entrance examination texts, technical and computer science manuals, religious studies texts, history, and a popular literature category which includes cookbooks, pop psychology, self-improvement manuals (including Islamic ones), and popular novels. In 2004, Fahimeh Rahimi's romance novel *What Happened that Night* was all the rage. Many thrillers and steamy pre-revolution serial pulp fictions were also reprinted that year, to great acclaim.

The Book Fair is the main venue where publishers get a chance to meet and interact with each other, as well as the public. The exhibition if of critical importance for the smaller provincial publishers and authors who probably would not otherwise have access to the networks and general public that this huge forum makes available. The same is true for participants from the provinces whose dominant language is not Persian. Like other provincial writers the Kurdish-, Turkish-, Baluch-, Armenian- and Arabic-speaking authors gain access to an audience well beyond what their small local markets and distribution networks provide.

Foreign publishers also enjoy success. In 2004, aside from European language publications, there was a strong presence by publishers from Lebanon, Egypt, Turkey, and Bangladesh. In particular, several publishers from Tajikistan and Afghanistan enjoyed great success at their relatively small booths.

The demand for politically- and socially-orientated books fluctuates with the state of national politics. The decline and marginalization of the reformist movement in 2005 has had a dampening effect, especially after the cancellation of all the important lectures and organized debates that used to be held on the margins of the Fair. These vibrant meetings covered all sorts of topics, from current politics to social psychology, film and literary criticism, and other topics of general interest. The demise of the reformist movement saw a shift in the attitude of the Ministry of Culture and Islamic Guidance (MCIG) toward these types of open forum that were considered seditious. After the disputed elections of 2009, a distinct air of censorship has led to the effective closure of these public meetings.

In 2005, with the presidential elections looming in the shadow of rising domestic and international political tensions, the Book Fair turned into a campaign ground for all the major presidential candidates. Many of the participating candidates used the Book Fair as a forum to present their views and to engage the public's questions in public fora, as well as in the booths of the publications sympathetic to their political platforms. The debates were vibrant and none of the presidential candidates from anywhere across the political spectrum escaped the barb of highly critical public questioning and criticism. For political leaders, especially conservative candidates like ex-police commanders and military generals, who had rarely faced direct and competitive public elections, or had any significant interactions with a critical general public, this was a new experience. Unsurprisingly, this type of openly political forum has not been repeated since 2005, even among the handful of political candidates officially sanctioned by the regime.

Aside from putting an end to political fora of this kind, a distinct chill has descended over the subsequent Book Fairs as the MCIG has refused to renew the licenses of many previously allowed titles, announcing in 2006 that all publications were now subject to re-evaluation according to new censorship guidelines. More significantly, all the cultural side events, the public meetings and debates that had proliferated during the reformist era, have been curtailed or prohibited. As a result, under the conservatives the Book Fair has increasingly turned into a shopping experience, rather than a public forum organized as a cultural event, which also involved the buying and selling of cultural products. Let us explore the implications and consequences of these shifts in public space for contemporary public culture in Iran.

The Cultural Politics of Public Space

The control of public behaviour and of public space is at the core of political life in the austere Islamic Republic. However, this obsession is by no means exclusive to the Iranian regime. In fact, power over shaping and managing public life, common social space, and the individual's body in public have been the centrepiece of modernist projects, whether of liberal capitalism, state socialism, or post-colonial nation state building. In the 1930s Iran and Turkey, the two most aggressively modernizing independent states in the Middle East, simultaneously inaugurated authoritarian secularizing projects intended to create not only the modern nation state out of the ashes of the old Qajar and Ottoman dynasties, but also the modern individuals to populate this new national society. Reza Shah, the founder of the Pahlavi dynasty, not only founded a new modern army and bureaucracy, but he decreed a whole new set of rules for presence in public life which banned all visual displays of religious or traditional garb. Women were forbidden to don the *hejab*; men had to wear Western suits and had to give up their turbans and head gear for a uniform hat modelled on the French gendarmes' kepi.[6] Reza Shah also imposed vast projects of urban renewal designed to demolish and to replace old commercial and residential neighbourhoods and create modern urban and public spaces, aimed at altering public culture and creating a modern public.[7]

Since that period, the penchant for authoritarian social engineering of public life has been at the core of the political strategies of successive political orders in Iran.[8] In a very real sense, the Islamic Republic represents continuity in that tradition. The imposition of the *hejab* on women, and of specific Islamic codes of public behaviour, as well as the obsessive attempts to police and control public space are a reversal of the Pahlavi era policies. However, this reversal is not a simple return to a putative 'traditional' Islamic past, which in all probability never existed as that ideal portrays.[9] Rather, it is an explicit attempt to create the modern, Islamist individual and public as committed and self-confident alternatives to an equally imagined secular, and Westernized other. It is little surprise that in a heterogeneous society neither attempts at the enforced secularization of public life during the monarchy, nor of authoritarian Islamization of the post revolution period were uncontested, or ultimately successful.

The consolidation of the Islamic Republic was coupled with the vigorous ideological colonization of public space, and the imposition of the Khomeinist interpretation of appropriate public behaviour.[10] Dress codes regulate the physical appearance of individual bodies in public. Streets were named after martyrs, murals and slogans covered city walls, loudspeakers imposed the call to prayer at all hours, and only public ceremonies of a religious nature were allowed. Above all, any form of public collective dissent was repressed ruthlessly in a society that had reinvented its politics through street protests and public demonstrations.

More than three decades later, there is an almost surreal oddity to the colonization of public space in the Islamic Republic as existing public places are constantly subverted out of their expected and designed functions. Thus University of Tehran, the locus of secular professional accreditation, academic autonomy, and intellectual and political activism, is still used for official public Friday prayers; while the enormous government-built Mosalla, the complex designed for Friday prayers, is used instead for commercial fairs, including fashion shows. Local mosques, in an attempt to undermine black market video rentals, were used as video and DVD clubs, or as wholesome and morally-chaperoned meeting places for young dating couples. In recent years, against public protest and resigned outrage, the Basij militia began to exhume the bodies of dead soldiers from the Iran–Iraq war and re-bury them in city squares and on university campuses, in order to claim these public and potentially dissenting spaces as shrines to the martyrs of the Islamic Republic.

In this bizarre setting the Book Fair offers a semblance of normality. For one thing it is a major annual social and public event that has a clear purpose. Of course there are plenty of religious publishers and seminary presses, military and strategic analyses from various military and revolutionary think tanks, and so on. However, these are cultural products like any other, and are on offer to the public on demand. As always, the producers of these books and studies are present at their booths to engage with questions and criticism, but they do so on an equal basis with other publishers, writers, and intellectuals.

It goes without saying that the participating public cannot act as they please, and codes of dress and behaviour are enforced perhaps more stringently than in the streets and other public spaces. There are always occasions when security personnel harass individuals, most often for transgressions of dress code, or perceived flirtation and improper contact between men and women. The severity of these incidences of moral policing have ebbed and flowed over the years, partly due to the sheer scale of the event, or in reaction to the increasing defiance of the public in recent years, or ultimately because of the sheer lassitude of enforcers over the futility of the effort.

As a public space the Tehran Book Fair is a fascinating reflection of the socio-political paradoxes of the Iranian society. The old location at the International Exhibition Centre was situated at the cross-section of two major highways in the north of the capital. The vast fair ground has the air of a spectacular carnival in the shadow of the Alborz Mountains. This leisurely atmosphere persistently annoyed the more elitist members of the cultural establishment, who grumbled about the frivolity of all the fast food stands, the flirtatious young people, and the throngs of the window shoppers. As a liberal newspaper editor, Behruz Gharibpur, wrote in a bad tempered editorial: 'I feel sick when I see so many repulsive scenes at the book fair: everywhere there is waste paper and garbage, useless young people lying on the grass, girls and boys obsessed with everything but books. It is unclear why this human wave goes through so much trouble every year to reach the book fair.'[11]

In fact, what is unique about the Tehran Book Fair is that it is a major occasion where people of all backgrounds freely mingle together and tangibly experience the diversity of the heterogeneous society they live in. The Book Fair is Iran's version of a relatively autonomous public space: turbaned and robed religious seminary students carrying huge bundles of books tied with strings rub shoulders with fashionably dressed, middle-class teenagers. Families from working-class southern neighbourhoods of Tehran come with their motorcycles and picnic

Figure 10.1 Crowds at the old Book Fair in 2003. (Credit: Kaveh Ehsani)

blankets and lunchboxes. Students and intellectuals from the provinces and even neighbouring countries, primarily Afghanistan, Azerbaijan, and now Iraq, travel long distances to buy the books they need at discounted or subsidized prices. People of all social classes, age, regional and ethnic backgrounds, men and women, of often conflicting ideological and political inclination, secularists and fundamentalists, all intermingle, argue, eat, shop, flirt, and browse for ten days in a lively atmosphere.

The Media Fair

Until recently the Book Fair also hosted an adjoining Media Fair, where journalists, newspapers, film and documentary makers also held a public forum and marketed their archives and publications. In 2006 the Culture Minister of Ahmadinejad divorced the two events and forced the Guild of Journalists to organize a separate event. Without the throngs of participants and the curious public flocking to the Book Fair, the relegated Media Fair lost its lustre and has become a far less relevant public event. The strategy was a political calculation to reduce the social and cultural impact of the highly popular independent press in a public setting of this scale.

The independent media, especially newspapers and print journals, played a major role in the political opening of the postwar period.

THE CULTURAL POLITICS OF PUBLIC SPACE   221

With television and radio under a government monopoly, international commercial satellite television broadcasts heavily filtered and of low quality, and at a time before the digital media and internet were as widely used as at present, the print media along with independent cinema played a major role in creating a public sphere of discussion and debate over the nature of politics and society in the post-Khomeini era. The proliferation of independent newspapers and journals was a conscious strategy of the Khatami administration as a substitute for the more politically contentious strategy of allowing independent political parties and trade unions to operate freely.[12]

The significance of this policy shift can be seen in the growing scale of publications after Mohammad Khatami's election. Prior to 1997, the daily printed media readership was around 1.2 million copies per day, a relatively small number for a country of more than 60 million, mostly literate, people at the time. After 1997, the readership nearly tripled to 3.2 million copies per day. However, in 2000, when newly-elected reformist parliamentarians tried to annul a set of anti-free press laws from the repressive 1960s that had been resurrected by the outgoing conservative Majles, they were harshly countermanded by the Leader Ayatollah Khamenei and forced to back down. These draconian laws arbitrarily criminalized any publication, authors, and publishers deemed as subversive of the moral order. The potential criminalization of the free press had a significant dampening effect. The conservative judiciary banned more than 150 journals and newspapers, and many journalists and publishers were hauled in front of a kangaroo court. Many were banned from working, heavily fined, and imprisoned. The rising insecurity among intellectuals, writers, journalists, and publishers, affected the former vibrancy of the media sphere and the readership deflated to 2 million copies per day by 2005.

In its heyday the Media Fair had become an important public sphere of open debates, critical discussions, and leisurely and curious loitering. Its participants were diverse and hailed from across the political and cultural spectra. In 2005, the participants included 400 conventional media outfits, some 2,500 student periodicals from around the country, and 500 publications put out by various state institutions. Many of these publications were not easily accessible in the market or to the general public. For example, military studies of the Iran–Iraq war produced by the Revolutionary Guards (IRGC), social analyses by the Intelligence

Ministry, data and analysis of welfare programmes against poverty published by the Foundation of the Oppressed, or rare documents made available by the National Archives, urban statistics from various municipalities, or opinion surveys by public polling agencies. The availability of these documents, as well as the possibility of engaging their authors and representatives, played an undeniable role in slowly increasing the transparency that has been possibly the most significant accomplishment of the reformist era.

Some snapshots from an ordinary day at the Media Fair can reveal the dynamics that characterized it before it was shut down. In 2004, for the third year in a row, our journal *Goft-o-Gu* (*Dialogue*) had the dubious honour of being assigned a space adjacent to the much larger booth of the monthly magazine *Ya-Letharat al-Hoseyn*, the mouthpiece of the radical Islamist vigilantes. In the last years of the Media Fair the controversial *Ya Letharat* had the most highly attended booth, together with several periodicals covering football, bodybuilding, and aerobics for women. But this 'popularity' was always accompanied by friction and heated arguments for a group well known for harassing student meetings, political gatherings, or women and men in public whom they considered improperly dressed or behaving inappropriately. As a result, the crowds regularly surrounding their booth at the Fair often tended to be contentious. In 2004, in a typical scene that lasted for more than an hour, a huge crowd had surrounded the booth, watching and participating in an aggressive debate between four *Ya Letharat* journalists and two young and fashionably dressed women, one of whom had bandages on her nose from a recent plastic surgery. The debate, or rather polemic, was over religious decrees and rulings and the notion of tolerance in Islam regarding public dress codes and vigilante harassment. The women were aggressive and unintimidated, the crowds were vocal and mostly supportive of the women, and the *Ya Letharat* debaters eventually looked tired and resigned, since this was a typical scene that kept being repeated every year, when they faced the public in a setting like that.

Whose Public Space?

The questions of access and control over place and behaviour, and of claims of ownership over public resources, are integral to the politics of public space.[13] The charter of public space is common ownership and open access for everyone, to be active or inactive as they choose. The notion of 'the public' itself congeals around autonomy from the domains of the public authority (of the state) and the private interests (of the family, enclosed community, the market, and labour contracts). Hannah Arendt argues that citizenship is the enactment of autonomy in public, rather than a legal right bestowed by the state on isolated individuals, as the conventional liberal discourse maintains.[14] Public space is the common arena where the plural diversity of heterogeneous societies with all of their frictions are expressed and negotiated. At the same time, public spaces are potentially subject to the inequalities and various forms of violence that plague modern societies. Racism, sexual, age, and ethnic discrimination, ideological oppression, and social inequalities of class and wealth can plague public spaces as they do institutions and social relations.[15] Public spaces can be transformed into soulless places of transition for traffic; they can be privatized for the exclusive benefit of monopoly owners. They can become unsafe and subject to physical violence and neglect. In the neoliberal era private spaces, such as shopping malls and gated communities, have staked claims as a substitute for open public spaces.[16] While states need open arenas, streets, parks, and monuments, to facilitate social life and to forge common bonds of patriotism and fidelity to the political order by staging rituals and ceremonies, nevertheless the participating public can always use these spaces to forge common bonds of solidarity in order to challenge with demonstrations and occasional rebellion against the existing relations of power.[17] Consequently, while public spaces are not inherently emancipatory, nevertheless the enactment of citizenship takes shape in the public sphere of discourse and in the public spaces of collective urban life.[18]

The struggle over claiming the right over the common spaces of social life has been at the core of post-revolution politics in Iran.[19] Given the deadlock of factional politics, and the unmistakable pressure of public opinion for fundamental political change in Iran, controlling a public event of the significance of the Book Fair has become the locus of intensified political rivalry. Nominally, the debate has been over the practical adequacy of the location of the exhibition ground for such a popular event. In fact, this encapsulates the condition of urban politics, as it is, reflecting the strengths and weaknesses of civil and political forces and urban coalitions who compete to define what form public life should take.

The 2002 elections for local city councils were a political turning point in Iran. The Islamist reformists who had swept every election after 1997 lost their seats in the governing councils of major cities. Conservatives won all 15 seats of the Tehran City Council, not because they had a popular mandate, but because only 12 per cent of the disillusioned electorate voted in the capital. The same was the case in the other major cities. Local councils are a fledgling and relatively new institutions in Iran. They were inaugurated by Khatami, as part of his reformist project of social empowerment by creating intermediate institutions of local governance which would be more responsive to the public constituents. However, these institutions are only half formed and thought-through. Their legal boundaries and range of responsibilities are still a matter of contention and as a result they have become an added layer of unresponsive bureaucracy in a sclerotic state-dominated system.

In 2005 the Tehran Council decreed that the Book Fair should be moved elsewhere to alleviate traffic congestion. The municipality, controlled by then mayor Ahmadinejad, tried in vain to shut down the event but did not succeed. Various critiques of the municipality's action pointed out that numerous other major institutions were located in the same area and cause traffic jams, and it is the municipality's responsibility to better manage traffic flows, rather than to shut down public events.[20]

In 2006, following Ahmadinejad's election, the Publishers Union was stripped of any position of responsibility over the management of the Book Fair, the Media Fair was separated from the Book Exhibition, and the Book Fair itself was relocated to the Grand Mosalla. The splitting-away of the Media Fair meant that journalists, who had been at the centre of political dissidence, were finally isolated and deprived of the sustained public audience they enjoyed in the much larger Book Fair. The removal of the Publisher's Union from the management of the Book Fair stripped the independent representatives of professional publishers of any input in the conduct of the main event related to their profession, nor could they represent or defend the rights of participating publishers against potential abuse.

Most significantly, the relocation of the Book Fair from an adequate, familiar, and professionally-designed space to a half-completed mosque was a clear signal that the state would no longer tolerate such an

Figure 10.2   The Mosalla Complex in 2006 during the Book Fair. (Credit: Kaveh Ehsani)

important public event taking on the role of an agora and an open platform for spontaneous public dissent against officially sanctioned norms and rules of conduct. Publishers, writers, and their public would be controlled in the spatial confines of a mosque that is the symbolic centre of the Islamic Republic.

However, the new location of the now-reduced Book Fair has only exposed the paradox of a state clearly at odds with its people. In the early constitutional debates of the 1980s, the political elite of the Islamic Republic strongly disagreed over what should be the spatial symbolic centre of the capital city.[21] The so-called traditionalists supported the renovation of the old city centre around the bazaar and the parliament should be renovated; the technocrats pushed for building the highest communication tower on a hill, and the most ideologically conservative advocated the building of the Grand Mosalla, a mosque and prayer centre to rival the Grand Mosque of Mecca, as a competing locus of not just a national but a global, radical Islam. Friday prayer sermons are still the main venue where key official pronouncements are made to the public, but the number of attendees has dwindled in recent years. In the early years of the revolution, the University of Tehran overflowed with the praying faithful every Friday, whose presence on the university ground signalled their domination over the secular Left forces that had historically held sway over the campus. By the end of 1990s, when an opinion survey revealed that a shocking 70 per cent of the general public confessed that they did not pray,[22] continuing to hold the Friday prayers on the university campus had become a face-saving strategy. The fact is that no official event associated with the Iranian state can fill a compound designed to display the enthusiastic mass support of 100s of 1000s of the faithful. The Grand Mosalla lies still incomplete after three decades, but it is leased out for cold cash, to be used for odd events, such as Islamic fashion shows and, since 2006, the International Book Fair.

So how do the cultural politics of an Islamist state operate in a public space of its own design? The Mosalla is a grand compound of vast, open, concrete squares and covered halls. Its heart is a domed mosque and two minarets, all of which were incomplete and surrounded with inactive cranes in 2006. It is not a space in which to linger and converse, lacking all of the spatial intimacy one finds in an ordinary mosque. Its vastness would be overawing if filled with a unified multitude. Its emptiness signals just as strongly the absence of such crowds. Upon entering this space one is immediately diminished by its scale, and assaulted by unexpected sounds echoing from giant speakers situated on every corner, broadcasting not religious hymns, but synthetic techno music.

With more than half of Iran's population aged below 35, the 'youth' are seen as a potential threat, as well as the subject of social engineering by the state.[23] Capturing the favour and good will of this youth through wholesome and ideologically-sanctioned entertainment, aimed at diverting them from the corrupting influences of commercial, secular, and Western alternative forms of entertainment, is taken very seriously in the Islamic Republic. That is why, upon entering the enormous vistas of the Grand Mosalla for the Book Fair, visitors are hit by waves of synthetic music aimed at presenting the Mosalla not as an austere religious space, but as a hip place where the young can feel right at home. Attempting to offer entertainment on a par with the old Book Fair, in 2006 the conservative-controlled MCIG had organized a series of folkloric 'coordinated movements' presentations (since dancing, especially in public, and by women, is officially forbidden), see Figure 10.4. At noon, the techno muzak was turned off and replaced by calls for prayer. 'Brothers, line up more loosely so you fill the space and appear more numerous' shouts the unwitting master of ceremonies for the prayer line-up (see Figure 10.3). But in the enormous compound it is

THE CULTURAL POLITICS OF PUBLIC SPACE 227

Figure 10.3 Prayer time at the Mosalla during the 2006 Book Fair. (Credit: Kaveh Ehsani)

impossible to figure out where the faithful have gathered to meditate. What is strikingly noticeable is that the vast crowds are impervious to their religious obligation, and seem far more interested in finding a spot amidst the stretches of un-shaded concrete to grab a bite to eat.

The ornate interior halls, which upon closer inspection are made of cheap cement blocks and prefabricated mosaics, overflow with a

Figure 10.4 Folk dancing at the Mosalla during the 2006 Book Fair. (Credit: Kaveh Ehsani)

Figure 10.5 Sacred space as shopping mall: the 2006 Book Fair at the Grand Mosalla. (Credit: Kaveh Ehsani)

shopping public who no longer linger around for debates and argument (see Figure 10.5). The exclusion of the Media Fair, and the functional compact layout of the booths, not to mention the new prohibitions imposed by the MCIG have succeeded, for now at least, in extinguishing or at least significantly diminishing the public, cultural, political debates and interactions which made the old Book Fair the public space that it was. As a result of the changing political habitus in recent years, the Book Fair is no longer as energetic an agora, a public space of free debate, dissent, contestation, and diversity as it was until 2006.

Here lies the ultimate paradox of the Islamic Republic, embodied in its cultural politics of public space: on the one hand, forcing the Book Fair to relocate to an ideologically-designed space that is organically associated with the ruling political order has succeeded in appropriating and neutralizing the subversive aspects of a vibrant and culturally pluralist public event. On the other hand, the same re-allocation of a highly popular and inherently secular public event to a sacred space, heavily laden with ideological symbolism, and inherently associated with the Khomeinist state project, has only managed to highlight the abject failure of the entire scheme. The Book Fair may have been reduced from an arena of active citizenship to a tame shopping experience, but in the process the Mosalla can no longer either act as a sacred place, nor as a public arena of political rituals to reinforce state legitimacy.

Colonizing the spontaneous public space of the Book Fair through censorship, police action, and the coerced relocation to the Grand Mosalla, the religious space of the populist radical religious community, has effectively transformed the latter into nothing but a cheaply-made and unfinished convention centre.

Notes

1. David Harvey, *Paris, Capital of Modernity* (New York: Routledge, 2003); Ju"rgen Habermas, *The Structural Transformation of the Public Sphere: An Inquiry into a Category of Bourgeois Society* (Cambridge, MA: MIT Press, 1989); Marcel He'naff and Tracy B Strong (eds.), *Public Space and Democracy* (Minneapolis: University of Minnesota Press, 2001).
2. Tahrir Square in Egypt, Gezi Park in Istanbul, the Pearl Roundabout in Manama, the Revolution Avenue in Tehran, or Zuccotti Park in New York City are only the latest examples of the politicization of public spaces by radical democratic claims made by the public. See Kaveh Ehsani, 'Radical Democracy and Public Space', *International Journal of Middle East Studies* xlvi/1 (2014), pp. 159–62.
3. For a comparative look at the political movements and the patterns of state transformations in the Middle East during the second half of the twentieth century, see Roger Owen, *State, Power and Politics in the Making of the Modern Middle East*, 3rd ed. (New York: Routledge, 2004); James L. Gelvin, *The Modern Middle East: A History*, 3rd ed. (New York: Oxford University Press, 2011), pp. 223–90; Nikki Keddie, 'Iranian Revolutions in Comparative Perspective', *The American Historical Review* lxviii/3 (1983), pp. 579–98; Said Amir Arjomand. *The Turban for the Crown* (New York: Oxford University Press, 1988), pp. 189–210.
4. On the debates over the constitution of the new regime see Asghar Schirazi, *The Constitution of Iran: Politics and the State in the Islamic Republic* (London: I.B.Tauris, 1997); Shaul Bakhash, *The Reign of Ayatollahs* (New York: Basic Books, 1984).
5. The research for this paper was carried out in 1989–90, 1992, and in 1998–2007. During the first two periods I was a regular visitor to the Book Fair. In the 1998–2007 period I was also a participant observer, as an editorial board member of the journal *Goftogu*, a consultant to the first elected Tehran City Council, and conducting research on the political economy of urban change in Iran. For an earlier discussion of the Book Fair see Kaveh Ehsani, 'Aya shahr kamakan beh forush miresad? Dastan-e donbalehdar-e Namayeshgah-e Ketab [Is the city still for sale? The continuing saga of the Book Fair]', *Goftogu* no. 40 (2004), pp. 130–38.

6. On Turkey see Sibel Bozdogan, *Modernism and Nation-Building* (Seattle: University of Washington Press, 2001). On Iran see Camron Michael Amin, *The Making of the Modern Iranian Woman: Gender, State Policy, and Popular Culture, 1865–1946* (Gainesville: University Press of Florida, 2002); Houchang E. Chehabi, 'Staging the Emperor's New Clothes: Dress Codes and Nation Building under Reza Shah', *Iranian Studies* xxvi/3–4 (1993), pp. 209–34.
7. Mina Marefat, 'Building to Power?: Architecture of Tehran 1921–1941' (PhD Dissertation, Massachusetts Institute of Technology, 1988).
8. Kaveh Ehsani, 'Tabar shenasi-ye tarhha-ye bozorg-e towse'eh dar Iran-e mo'aser [Genealogy of large scale development projects in contemporary Iran]', *Goftogu* 54 (2009), pp. 113–32.
9. See Leila Ahmed, *Women and Gender in Islam: Historical Roots of a Modern Debate* (New Haven: Yale University Press, 1993). On the construction and invention of tradition, see Partha Chatterjee, *The Nation and Its Fragments: Colonial and Postcolonial Histories* (Princeton: Princeton University Press, 1993); Eric Hobsbawm and Terence Ranger (eds.), *The Invention of Tradition*, Reissue (Cambridge: Cambridge University Press, 2012).
10. Ervand Abrahamian, *Khomeinism: Essays on the Islamic Republic* (Berkeley: University of California Press, 1993) and Farhad Khosrokhavar, *L'utopie Sacrifiée: Sociologie de La Revolution Iraniénne* (Presses de la Fondation Nationale des Sciences Politiques, 1993).
11. References to this quote and other specific instances cited in this paper can be found in Kaveh Ehsani, 'Yek Shahr Beh Forush Miresad [A City Is up for Sale]', *Goftogu* no. 33 (2001), pp. 100–05.
12. See the special issue of *Middle East Report* (Merip), No. 221, Autumn 1999 for interviews and analysis of the media and press strategies of the Khatami administration.
13. Spiro Kostof, *The City Assembled: The Elements of Urban Form through History* (Boston: Bulfinch, 1992), Chapter Three; Richard Sennett, *The Fall of Public Man* (New York: W.W. Norton, 1996); Don Mitchell, *The Right to the City* (New York: Guilford Press, 2003); Margaret Kohn, *Brave New Neighborhoods: The Privatization of Public Space* (New York: Routledge, 2004); Setha Low and Neil Smith (eds.), *The Politics of Public Space* (New York: Routledge, 2006).
14. Hannah Arendt, *The Human Condition* (Chicago: The University of Chicago Press, 1958).
15. Doreen Massey, 'Thinking Radical Democracy Spatially', *Environment & Planning D: Society & Space* xiii/3 (1995), pp. 283–88; Philip Howell, 'Public Space and the Public Sphere: Political Theory and The Historical Geography of Modernity', *Environment and Planning D: Society and Space* xi/3 (1993), pp. 303–22.
16. Mike Davis, *City of Quartz: Excavating the Future in Los Angeles* (London: Verso, 1992), pp. 221–64; Margaret Crawford, 'The world in a shopping mall', in Michael Sorkin (ed.), *Variations on a Theme Park* (New York: Noonday Press, 1992), pp. 3–30.

17. Lawrence Vale, *Architecture, Power and National Identity* (New Haven: Yale University Press, 1992).
18. David Harvey, *Rebel Cities: From the Right to the City to the Urban Revolution* (New York: Verso, 2012).
19. Kaveh Ehsani, 'The Politics of Property in Post-Revolution Iran', in Said Amir Arjomand and Nathan Brown (eds.), *The Rule of Law, Islam, and Constitutional Politics in Egypt and Iran* (Albany: State University of New York Press, 2013), pp. 153–78.
20. Ehsani, 'Yek Shahr beh Forush Miresad [A City Is up for Sale]'.
21. As far as I am aware these debates have not been analysed or published separately. This information comes from a series of interviews and discussions with a number of prominent urbanists, city planners, and officials in the Tehran municipality (*c.*1999–2005). Generally, urban matters and spatial concerns, such as property relations, and the moralization of urban space according to revolutionary/Islamic codes had a prominent role in the constitutional debates and legislative concerns during the first decade following the revolution. See Kaveh Ehsani, 'The Politics of Property in Post-Revolution Iran'; Bayat, *Street Politics*; Bernard Hourcade and Farhad Khosrokhavar, 'L'habitat révolutionnaire' à Téhéran: 1977–1981', *Hérodote* no. 31 (1983), pp. 61–83; Schirazi, *The Constitution of Iran: Politics and the State in the Islamic Republic*; Asghar Schirazi, *The Problem of the Land Reform in the Islamic Republic of Iran* (Berlin: Verlag Das Arabische Buch, 1987); Shaul Bakhash, 'The Politics of Land, Law, and Social Justice in Iran', *Middle East Journal* xliii/2 (1989), pp. 186–201.
22. Kaveh Ehsani, 'Municipal Matters: The Urbanization of Consciousness and Political Change in Tehran', *Middle East Report* (Merip) no. 212 (1999), pp. 22–7.
23. On the politicization of demographic categories and the targeting of 'youth' as a focus of social and political concern across the Middle East, see Asef Bayat and Linda Herrera, (eds.), *Being Young and Muslim: New Cultural Politics in the Global South and North* (New York: Oxford University Press, 2010).

PART IV

HISTORIOGRAPHICAL REFLECTIONS

CHAPTER 11

THE OPENING-UP OF THE PAST AND THE POSSIBILITIES OF GLOBAL HISTORY FOR IRANIAN HISTORIOGRAPHY

Maral Jefroudi

Michael Löwy, in his analysis of Walter Benjamin's thesis on history, writes: 'The future may reopen "closed" historical cases, may "rehabilitate" misrepresented victims, revive defeated hopes and aspirations, rediscover forgotten battles or battles regarded as "utopian," "anachronistic" or "running against the grain of progress"'. In this case, the opening-up of the past and the opening-up of the future are intimately linked.[1] By opening-up, Löwy points to studying 'a dizzying field of possibilities' that the path of historical process could have leaned to, without dismissing the 'objective conditions' with which the possibilities are conditioned.[2]

History writing, with its positivist claim to revive what has actually happened and find causal explanations for the current state of affairs, has been a realm of contestation, falsification, claims, and restatements not only at the popular front of readers, but also at the disciplinary debates in the literature. The dialectic relationship between the transformative changes in Iran's political history and their impact on the country's intellectual history has rendered historiography a lively terrain of inquiry in Iran.

Touraj Atabaki participated in these debates with his inaugural lecture at the University of Amsterdam in 2002, 'Beyond Essentialism', which was a critique of the historiography of modernization and modern nation-state building in Middle-Eastern and Central-Asian historiography.[3] He organized a conference at the University of Oxford in 2004 with the title 'Historiography and Political Culture in Twentieth-Century Iran', covering a vast array of subjects pertaining to nineteenth- and twentieth-century Iran. This conference led to an edited volume on historiography of Iran, titled *Iran in the 20th Century: Historiography and Political Culture* in 2009, covering a wide range of subjects including nationalist, Marxist, and Islamist historiography; the historiography of the Constitutional Revolution, the Qajar Period, and the Pahlavi era; and subjects that have found less presence in the debates of Iranian historiography such as gender, conspiracy theories, architecture, and poetry.[4] His curiosity concerning the question of agency in historiography and his interest in the history of subalterns in Iran culminated in several books, articles, and book chapters, two of the recent ones being 'Iranian History in Transition: Recasting the Symbolic Identity of Babak Khorramdin', in 2012 and 'Missing Labour in the Metanarratives of Practicing Modernity in Iran: Labour Agency in Refashioning the Discourse of Social Development' in 2013.[5]

This chapter contributes to the debate on the historiography of Iran by providing an overview of leading concerns raised in the literature, defining the main trends and introducing the possibilities that the theoretical opening of global history can offer to this debate. Global history, taken as a conceptual and methodological approach, can enrich the debates that are currently ongoing in Iranian historiography and help solve various problems that have been mentioned in the debates. It is argued that developing a pluralistic vision of history and 'not looking like the state' are not possible by merely changing the subject material of our studies and by employing different sources and archives, but necessitate a paradigm change in the way we conceptualize history.

Every Ten Years a Great Man/Who Paid the Bill?/So Many Reports/So Many Questions[6]

A general review of articles on Iranian historiography shows that interest in evaluating the state of the art appears at long intervals. The first scholarly article published in a peer-reviewed international journal on the state of Iranian historiography was published in 1974. 'Observations on Sources for the Study of Nineteenth and Twentieth Century Iranian History' was written by Hafez F. Farmayan.[7] After 15 years, and a revolution, it was followed by Abbas Amanat's 'The Study of History in Post-Revolutionary Iran: Nostalgia, Illusion, or Historical Awareness?' in 1989.[8] Stephanie Cronin's 'Writing the History of Modern Iran: A Comment on Approaches and Sources'[9] followed Amanat's article in 1998, and the last critical piece on the state of Iranian historiography '"Seeing Like a State": An essay on the Historiography of Modern Iran' by Cyrus Schayegh was published in 2010.[10] Read together, these four articles portray the state of Iranian historiography of the past 40 years in a complementing way. In addition, they present the trends in the critique of Iranian historiography.

Farmayan argued that understanding the way the Iranian state's administrative machinery worked in the twentieth century necessitated the study of the former century. Giving examples of the written chronicles of the late-nineteenth century and presenting the patronage system of the Qajar throne for supporting traditional chroniclers and translating Western historical works, he outlines the development of Iranian historiography since the nineteenth century. Parallel to dominant trends in historiography in the nineteenth century beyond Iranian borders, the discipline evolved from chronicles of princes and viziers to deal with larger segments of society after the Constitutional Revolution. The post-Constitutional Revolution regime marked a new era in the writing of Persian history for Farmayan.[11] The establishment of the Pahlavi dynasty after 1925 is said to have created a pause in historical research. The works written in the first period of the Pahlavi dynasty did not deal with the preceding Qajar period. For Farmayan this period, which ended with the Allied invasion of Iran in 1941, was one of 'strengthening and training' historians, who mostly produced translations or adaptations of Western literature and did not author critical, if any, histories.[12]

Correlating the productivity of historians with the change in the political climate, Farmayan presents the war years of the 1940s as opening new possibilities for historians to produce more diverse histories. His main concern is the lack of quality in disciplinary terms in the works produced. This involved inefficient employment of available sources and lack of commentary or analysis.[13] The article presents the scattered but useful sources on the Qajar period and underscores the lack of academic journals in the discipline of history and the lack of organized state archives in Iran at the time of its publication. The sources that are introduced by Farmayan are sources produced by elites and the state, such as statistical books, telegrams, letters, memoirs and travel accounts, personal correspondence, royal and other official proclamations.[14]

When Abbas Amanat wrote on the state of the art in 1989, ten years after the revolution and the founding of the Islamic Republic, the academic scene in Iranian historiography had already gone through a significant change. As explored in later works written by Janet Afary,[15] Assef Bayat,[16] Afshin Matin-Asghari[17] and Houchang E. Chehabi,[18] among others, this interval between Farmayan's article and that of Amanat had seen the rise and fall of Marxist historiography. The eight-year war with Iraq had not only devastated the economy but also the cultural climate in Iran, the political opposition had long been supressed, and the Pahlavi-era historiography's 'selective amnesia'[19] was replaced with the new regime's 'selective amnesia.'

Amanat criticized the histories written during the Pahlavi era for being works produced so as to create legitimacy for state-sponsored nationalism and for dismissing not only the Qajar period, as Farmayan had already stated, but also the Islamic past of Iran for the purpose of creating that official nationalist narrative. His critique is aimed not only at of the lack of scholarship on some subjects like the Constitutional Revolution and the Qajar era, but also at the 'ideological attitude' of the writers dealing with the contemporary history of Iran. Amanat argued that the revolution 'unbounded hidden cultural potentials' and brought to the surface new historical trends and preoccupations.[20] It was the social and political changes that the country went through that increased the interest in historical works that might help to make sense of those changes. So, once again, history is presented as a source of *ebrat* (lesson) for its readers in the present.[21] Revolution, with its own selective mode of persecution, set some works that were banned during the Pahlavi era free, while others had to find refuge in the storage rooms of bookstores, only to come to light when an interested reader asked for them.

The interest in the publication of primary sources is presented by Amanat as an outcome of the distrust of readers who were tired of ideological polemics before and after the revolution.[22] In this period we see foreign-sourced documents such as memoirs and the accounts of foreign diplomats. Anglo–Iranian relations, the relation of the Pahlavi state with foreign powers, 'foreign plots' in general, and the coup of 1953 in particular, were popular subjects of historical writing. Obviously, this 'opening-up' to the world beyond Iran did not bring about a challenge to the nationalist, top-down, elitist historiography; it actually strengthened it. The non-national element was used to 'reveal' the 'sinister designs' of foreign powers rather than to incorporate interconnectedness into the narration of Iranian contemporary history.[23] In 'The Paranoid Style in Iranian Historiography', Houchang E. Chehabi gives a thorough account of the multiple uses of conspiracy theories in works of historians from various ideological backgrounds to explain social, political, and economic change in Iran. Foreigners and ethno-religious minority groups were ascribed agency in these histories based on conspiracy theories.[24]

Given the political context of the era, histories of fallen aristocracies and national heroes were popular. Amanat shows how historians critical of the regime adopted a selective approach to the agents of the histories they write. Depriving the clergy of their agency in the Iranian Tobacco Protests of 1891–2 in order to refute the emphasis on the anti-imperialist stance of the clergy prevalent in the discourse of the Islamic regime, is a revealing example of such historiographical strategies.[25]

Following the trajectory, Stephanie Cronin wrote another commentary on sources and approaches in modern Iranian historiography in 1998. Cronin's critique focuses on her own subject of study, the role of the army in the years 1921–41.[26] Nine years after Amanat's piece, she follows up his point on the selection of subjects and sources that are studied in Iranian historiography. Her study presents a useful guide of available sources for different historical periods of Iranian history. Given the monopoly of the state on the production, control, and circulation of the archival sources she mentions, the direct link between changes in the political dynamics or levels of 'political stability' and the quality and availability of sources is predictable.[27] Interestingly, her example of the Allied invasion of Iran and the possibilities of this invasion in generating archival sources available for the use of contemporary historians sheds light on the underlying power mechanisms in the archives' production process. In his struggle against Rankean historicism in favour of historical materialism, Benjamin underscores the study of the process that makes the history, rather than reviving the history 'as it is' recorded and transmitted by the victors. For him, 'without exception the cultural treasures he [the historical materialist] surveys have an origin which he cannot contemplate without horror [...]. There is no document of civilisation which is not at the same time a document of barbarism. And just as such a document is never free of barbarism, so barbarism taints the manner in which it was transmitted from one hand to another.'[28]

Cronin mentions the comparative liberalization of the regime after the death of Khomeini and the end of the Iran–Iraq war as enabling a dynamic setting for historiography. It is in this period that historians living abroad and working on Iran could find access to sources in Iran. The archives of the former Soviet Union were introduced to Iranian historiography by Touraj Atabaki and Solmaz Rustamova-Towhidi in this period as well.[29]

Apart from the issue of subject and source choice, Cronin points to another foundational pillar of historiography, which is periodization. She highlights the problem of taking the conjunctures of political history as marking the cornerstones of periods under study for social history. Cronin writes that the 'rigid periodisation of twentieth-century Iranian history almost universally followed until recently: the Constitutional Revolution, a neglected hiatus between 1911 and 1921, then the sudden and largely unexplained eruption of Riza Pahlavi, obscures as much as it illuminates'.[30] By pointing to the necessity of rethinking periodization and locating Iranian history in its regional context, Stephanie Cronin takes the critique of Iranian historiography to a further level.

Written 12 years after Cronin's article, Cyrus Schayegh builds his critique on what he calls the 'methodological statism' that he claims to be dominant in Iranian historiography.[31] Inspired by James Scott's famous title *Seeing Like a State*, Schayegh argues that historians writing on Iran have appropriated the state's approach in dealing with their subjects of study, giving the main agency to the state and the elites of a top-down modernization project. His critique is addressed more particularly at the historians who emphasize a divide and a continuous zero-sum game between the Iranian state and society, the most prominent follower of this trend being Homa Katouzian.[32] Schayegh argues that historians and historically-oriented social scientists working on Iran 'have followed changes in historiography, including the social turn of the 1960s and 1970s, and the following decade's cultural turn, but subordinated them to state-centered analyses'.[33] His criticism is both to locate politics in the centre of any analysis on Iran, and to reify the state by constructing a detached image of it.[34] Apart from this particular criticism, Schayegh provides an update on the available sources for a history that 'does not see like a state'. In addition, he joins the previous critics of Iranian historiography in suggesting alternative topics of study. His analysis of the Pahlavi era goes beyond the borders, taking into account interactions with the socio-political climate of Turkey, Germany, and Italy in the making of Iranian authoritarian modernization. Moreover, he presents Iranian political activists abroad in late 1960s as agents shaping public opinion in the West.[35] Schayegh argues that methodological statism is mostly a problem related to sources of history writing. The sources that became available in the Iranian National Archives, the archives of court and police, foreign state archives, and Iranian press; use of interviews, private and non-state archives, and unpublished texts are presented as a way of overcoming this problem.[36]

These four articles that have appeared in prominent journals between 1974 and 2010 share the concern of political determinism in the historiography of Iran. They all point to the changes in the conditions of the availability of sources being parallel with changes in the political structure. They show that not only sources but also subjects of study vary according to both what is possible to write while living under a specific political regime, and the interests and necessities of readers trying to make sense of the world they live in. The points on the employment of alternative sources to the state-patronised ones, and studying the subjects and groups that do not occupy a focal point in power relations, are crucial steps to opening up history everywhere, and in Iran. However, it is necessary to take this critique further and consider the theoretical tools of historiography.

The objective conditions of history writing are more immanent to historiography than being an obstacle hindering the craft. Critics, without saying so openly, underscore the dynamic relationship between past and present in the process of history writing and the circulation of the written works. In fact, it is this dynamic relation that makes it possible to understand the meaning of a past event. From the discussion on sources, and preferred topics of study to the critical attitude to periodization and its being overwhelmed with pillars of political history, these articles aspire to build up to a discussion on the time and space axes of historiography, but in the end do not reach that point.

To rethink the problems stated in these reviews of Iranian historiography and to open up the past to talk about the missed opportunities, coexisting histories, and other possibilities that have left traces behind and that bestow meaning on our present and future, it is important to approach these alternative sources and subjects that were presented in the articles I discussed with an alternative theoretical approach. The recent debates on global history offer valuable insights for the contemplation of the time–space axes that historiography builds on.

The Time–Space Axes and the Promises of Global History

The debate on global history follows various terrains. Bruce Mazlish, in his 'Comparing Global History to World History' argues that *global* points in the direction of space. He defines global history as the history of globalization, which is the study of 'factors of globalization' and the study of processes that 'are best studied on a global, rather than a local, a national, or a regional level'.[37] While the first part of this definition points to its 'novelty' or contemporariness, the second part infers that it is an extension of 'world history', shaped by the conditions of the former. What is meant by 'factors of globalization' is explained by David Held as '(1) the extensiveness of networks of relations and connections; (2) the intensity of flows and levels of activity within these networks; and (3) the impact of these phenomena on particular bounded communities'. This approach argues that we are living in a new era not because 'global enmeshment' is a new phenomenon, but because an understanding of the intensity and extensiveness of this enmeshment is crucial for writing history.[38]

In dialogue with Mazlish, Marcel van der Linden argues that the novel part of global history is not an essential part of it. In other words, every era is a historically new era and comes with its own relations of production, power, and technology, among others. Therefore, 'all history is contemporary history' as the perspective employed in writing is rooted in the present.[39] Furthermore, Van der Linden argues that employing the global approach to history writing brings forth a new understanding of the society that we are working on. The society under study, and the social relations within the group that makes it a society, cannot be confined to local or national borders with this approach. This is an important contribution not only because of the extensity of 'global enmeshment' in the global era, but also due to its drawing attention to the interactions between multiple actors in history in the study of a social phenomenon. Acknowledging transnational and transcontinental processes such as war and migration as influential to understanding the developments within a territorial nation state breaks the monopoly of national borders in shaping the conceptual framework of history writing and changes the meaning of a society. This concept of 'society without (national) borders' introduces the necessity of the opening-up of each group under historical study and taking into account the web of social and economic relations that agents of the history we write are living in. This is very much connected to new labour history's extending the study of workers to the level of household and community beyond the borders of the factory.[40]

So far, I have emphasized global history's focus on the spatial interconnectivities and self-reflexivity on the conditions of the production of history. The possibilities this new approach promises for opening up history go further than territorial boundaries. Osterhammels' book on global history of the nineteenth century revisits the critique of linearity and emptiness of time. He writes: 'A century is a slice of time. Its meaning is given only by posterity. Memory structures time, arranging it deep down into echelons, sometimes bringing it close to the present, stretching, shrinking, or occasionally dissolving it.'[41] This questioning of linear empty time in global history is built upon the literature on the conceptualization of time in historiography starting from the critics of modernization theory. Benjamin's writings on historical understanding being an 'afterlife' of the original moment is an antecedent to this argument. This is an approach that does not aim to relive the experience empathetically (empathy with whom?) while writing its history, but to weave or unweave the historical process (hence the task of brushing history against the grain) and grasp it by unpacking the process rather than making a causal explanation.[42] It adds temporal connectivity to spatial connectivity in history writing. Here *global* comes to mean encompassing vertical and horizontal connections together and locating the historical phenomenon under study in the web of these interconnectivities.

At any given point of history that is narrated, the narrated event does not happen in a vacuum. First, there is the cultural contract that gives meaning to the act and to the way it is perceived and narrated. Second, other events are in the making at the very same time and place when the narrated event appropriates the monopoly on attention and occupies the focal point of articulation. Third, there is an interval between the event that happens and the time in which it is narrated, which is a process that is shaped by memory and the web of power relations that contribute to its making. And fourth, this list is far from being exhaustive.

Ernesto Laclau and Chantal Mouffe illustrate the first point vividly in their explanation of discourse:

> If I kick a spherical object in the street, or if I kick a ball in the football match the psychical fact is the same, but its meaning is different. The object is a football only to the extent that it establishes a system of relations, and these relations are not given by the mere referential materiality of the objects, but are rather socially constructed.[43]

The second point is very much related to periodization. Alessandro Portelli, in his book on form and meaning in oral history, draws attention to the process of making a periodization and what it excludes. He states that dating an event means breaking down continuous time into sequences. As all sorts of events are happening simultaneously at any given time, building a chronology points to a selection,[44] and hence to a production, or a fabrication. Therefore unpacking the production process of periodization in order to suggest new ones will tell us more than the clarity of taken-for-granted pillars of periodization. The third point draws attention to the previously-mentioned 'afterlife' of the original event, the perception of the original state of which goes through a process involving the mechanisms at work in the first two points.

While critical approaches to the linear understanding of time and periodization have a prominent place in historiographical debates from Benjamin to subaltern studies, post-modernism, and its critics; space has received less attention from history writers. Either taken as a bounded entity or an interconnected terrain, it is taken as frozen and open to change only with time and/or encounter with the 'other'. Even the debates on spatial interconnectivity, which acknowledge relations beyond borders, do not necessarily take space as a process in living, but as an empty and closed entity that is prone to change only by action or reaction. However, space is a process, a social product that embodies social relationships.[45] Interestingly, Lefebvre points to the globality of the making of space with reference to time, to a continuous move back and forth. He argues that the historical and its consequences get inscribed to the space, 'the past leaves its traces'.[46]

Contemplating the relation of time and space axes in the making of historical narration, and getting inspired by the approach of global history to go beyond the national borders and temporal limits of a past event, is more an acknowledgement of the social and historical web that the narrated event is located in, than an attempt to cover all aspects of it. Osterhammel gives the hint of the craft 'to have a feel for proportions, contradictions and connections, as well as a sense of what may be typical and representative; and second, to maintain a humble attitude of deference toward professional research'.[47]

Engaging theoretically with global history opens possibilities for the historiography of Iran beyond the selection of subjects and archives in favour of the unused, hidden, forgotten archives, and marginalized subjects, which is indeed crucial to writing an alternative history to the ones that are infected by the structural ignorance and erasure in the official sources. First, such an effort brings an approach that is built upon the imagination of a society without (national) borders, as stated by Marcel van der Linden previously. This does not only mean taking the 'external factors' into account while writing the history of an event or a process, but acknowledging the dialogue and interaction of agencies and ideas moving beyond borders in the making of the internal factors as well. Therefore the relationship with the 'other' is taken beyond an action/reaction paradigm, or a confrontation between two insulated entities as the nationalist historiography does, but as an interaction of permeable actors and historical phenomena with various power dynamics. This is to acknowledge the embeddedness of 'external factors' and local agencies. Touraj Atabaki's recent studies on the Indian workers in the Iranian oil industry[48] and previously-mentioned Schayegh's reference to studying the development of Iranian authoritarian modernization with the interaction it had with the socio-political climate of Turkey, Germany, and Italy can be taken as examples of such an engagement.

Second, this theoretical approach would be useful in thinking about the time axis of the narrated history. To be more specific, this involves both a critical look at periodization, and incorporating the 'afterlife' of the event/process into the history writing. Contemplating various continuities and ruptures between the politically-determined benchmarks of conventional periodization, which is skilfully done by Erik Jan Zürcher in the case of modern Turkish history, is one of the ways rethinking of time 'compartments' can help our understanding of the past (and present).[49] Studying the 'afterlife' of the historical phenomenon breaks the linear determination of the historiography and brings forth the possibility of analysing the meaning of the historical phenomenon, the way it was experienced and took part in the social memory. Ervand Abrahamian's recent book *Coup* can be read as an example of rethinking time in this line.[50] In the last chapter of the book where he discusses the legacy of the 1953 coup, Abrahamian weaves the history of the 1953 coup with the CIA operations in Guatemala, Indonesia, and Chile that come after.[51] Moreover, he points to the effect of the coup on the collective memory that gave a leading role to conspiracy theories and 'foreign strings' in the pre-revolutionary political culture.[52] While the memory of 1953 was present in the making of the 1979 revolution, the 1979 revolution rendered a new reading of the 1953 coup possible, too.

As the criticism of methodological nationalism opened up historiography to extend beyond borders, the acknowledgement of the dialectical relationship between the past event and the present, the coexistence of various histories at any time, and the time's being embedded in any social space will complicate the task of the historian but will lead to the demystification of history writing by unpacking the process of its making.

I would like to thank colleagues at the Weatherhead Initiative on Global History at Harvard University for the inspiring discussions we had on Global History in the Autumn of 2013, which planted the seeds for this chapter.

Notes

1. Michael Löwy, *Fire Alarm: Reading Walter Benjamin's On the Concept of History* (London: Verso, 2005), p. 115.
2. Ibid., p. 107.
3. Touraj Atabaki, *Beyond Essentialism: Who Writes Whose Past in the Middle East and Central Asia?* (Amsterdam: Aksant Academic Publishers, 2003)

4. Touraj Atabaki, *Iran in the 20th Century: Historiography and Political Culture* (London: I.B.Tauris, 2009), p. 336.
5. Touraj Atabaki, 'Missing Labour in the Metanarratives of Practicing Modernity in Iran: Labour Agency in Refashioning the Discourse of Social Development', in David Mayer and Jürgen Mittag (eds.), *Interventions: The Impact of Labour Movements on Social and Cultural Development* (Leipzig: Akademische Verlagsanstalt, 2013), pp. 171–95.
6. Bertold Brecht, 'Questions from a Worker who Reads', in *Poems 1913–1956* (London: Methuen, 1976).
7. Hafez F. Farmayan, 'On Sources for the Study of Nineteenth and Twentieth Century Iranian History', *International Journal of Middle East Studies* v/1 (1974), pp. 32–49.
8. Abbas Amanat, 'The Study of History in Post-Revolutionary Iran: Nostalgia, Illusion, or Historical Awareness?' *Iranian Studies* xxii/4 (1989), pp. 3–18.
9. Stephanie Cronin, 'Writing the History of Modern Iran: A Comment on Approaches and Sources', *Iran* xxxvi (1998), pp. 175–84.
10. Cyrus Schayegh, '"Seeing Like a State": An Essay on the Historiography of Modern Iran', *International Journal of Middle East Studies* xlii/1 (2010), pp. 37–61.
11. Farmayan: 'Observations on Sources', p. 35.
12. Ibid., p. 26. p. 36.
13. Ibid., p. 41.
14. Ibid., p. 38.
15. Janet Afary, 'The Contentious Historiography of the Gilan Republic in Iran: A Critical Exploration', *Iranian Studies* xxviii/1-2 (1995), pp. 3–24.
16. Assef Bayat, 'Historiography, Class, and Iranian Workers', in Zachary Lockman (ed.), *Workers and Working Classes in the Middle East* (New York: State University of New York Press, 1994), pp. 165–210.
17. Matin-Asghari, 'Marxism, Historiography and Historical Consciousness in Modern Iran: A Preliminary Study', in Touraj Atabaki (ed), *Iran in the 20th Century: Historiography and Political Culture* (London: I.B.Tauris, 2009), pp. 199–231.
18. Houchang E. Chehabi, 'The Paranoid Style in Iranian Historiography', in Touraj Atabaki (ed.), *Iran in the 20th Century: Historiography and Political Culture* (London: I.B.Tauris, 2009), pp. 155–76.
19. Atabaki, *Beyond Essentialism*, p. 5.
20. Amanat, 'The Study of History in Post-Revolutionary Iran', p. 6.
21. Ibid,. p. 3.
22. Ibid., p. 8.
23. Ibid., p. 9.
24. Chehabi, 'The Paranoid Style in Iranian Historiography'.
25. For more information on the tobacco protests of 1891–2, see Nikki R. Keddie, *Religion and Rebellion in Iran: The Iranian Tobacco Protest of 1891–1892* (Abingdon: Routledge, 2012).

26. Cronin, 'Writing the History of Modern Iran: A Comment on Approaches and Sources'.
27. Ibid., p. 180.
28. Walter Benjamin, *Illuminations* (New York: Schocken Books, 1969), p. 256.
29. Cronin, 'Writing the History of Modern Iran', p. 183.
30. Ibid.
31. Schayegh: '"Seeing Like a State": An Essay on the Historiography of Modern Iran', p. 38.
32. Ibid., p. 46. See Homa Katouzian, *The Political Economy of Modern Iran* (New York: New York University Press, 1981).
33. Schayegh: "Seeing Like a State", p. 38.
34. Ibid.
35. Ibid., p. 43.
36. Ibid., p. 49.
37. Bruce Mazlish, 'Comparing Global History to World History', *The Journal of Interdisciplinary History* xxviii/3 (1998), p. 389.
38. David Held, 'The Transformation of Political Community: Rethinking Democracy in the Context of Globalization', in Ian Shapiro and Casiano Hacker-Cordon (eds.), *Democracy's Edges* (Cambridge: Cambridge University Press, 1999), p. 92.
39. Mazlish quoted in Van Der Linden, Marcel, 'The "Globalization" of Labor and Working-Class History and Its Consequences', *International Labor and Working Class History* lxv (2004), p. 141.
40. See Marcel van der Linden and Jan Lucassen, *Prolegomena for a Global Labour History* (Amsterdam: International Institute of Social History, 1999).
41. Jürgen Osterhammel, *The Transformation of the World: A Global History of the Nineteenth Century* (Princeton: Princeton University Press, 2014), p. 46.
42. Benjamin, *Illuminations*, p. 257.
43. Chantal Mouffe and Ernesto Laclau, 'Post-Marxism without Apologies', in James Martin (ed.), *Chantal Mouffe: Hegemony, Radical Democracy, and the Political* (Abingdon: Routledge, 2013), p. 61.
44. Alessandro Portelli, *The Death of Luigi Trastulli and Other Stories: Form and Meaning in Oral History* (Albany: State University of New York Press, 1991), p. 21.
45. Henry Lefebvre, *The Production of Space* (Oxford: Basil Blackwell, 1991), p. 27.
46. Ibid., 37.
47. 'Introduction to the First German Edition' (2009), in Osterhammel, *The Transformation of the World*.
48. Atabaki, 'Far from Home, but at Home: Indian Migrant Workers in the Iranian Oil Industry', *Studies in History* Forthcoming (2015).
49. Erik Jan Zürcher, *Turkey: a Modern History* (London: I.B.Tauris, 1993).
50. Ervand Abrahamian, *The Coup: 1953, the CIA, and the Roots of Modern U.S. – Iranian Relations* (New York: The New Press, 2013).
51. Ibid., p. 205.
52. Ibid., pp. 219–20.

CHAPTER 12

VILLAGE AND EMPIRE: RECENT TRENDS IN THE HISTORIOGRAPHY OF THE LATE OTTOMAN EMPIRE AND MODERN TURKEY

Erik-Jan Zürcher

The historiography of the late Ottoman Empire and the Republic of Turkey has witnessed important changes, which will be critically evaluated in this chapter. In doing so, I am revisiting a subject I have treated before. Almost 17 years ago I was appointed to the chair of Turkish Studies at Leiden University. As was, and is, required of every new professor, I held an inaugural address. This took place early in 1998. The subject was Bernard Lewis's famous book *The Emergence of Modern Turkey* and my aim was to see how well this work had stood the test of time and to what extent our field had progressed since it was first published in 1961.[1]

Although I recognized Lewis's great achievement in writing such an elegant and erudite one-volume overview of late Ottoman and Turkish history, my review on the whole was quite critical. My critique of Lewis centred around four issues. First of all, I noted that his work clearly bore the traces of primordialist nationalism. I pointed out that already on page two of the book, Lewis says 'So completely had the Turks identified themselves with Islam that the very concept of a Turkish nationality was submerged' and, five pages later: 'the Turkish language, which, despite long subjection to alien influences, survives triumphantly'. Second, I characterized the kind of history Lewis had intended to write as rather limited: a history of the literate elite, its ideas and its instrument, the Ottoman – and later Turkish – state. Lewis clearly comes out as an idealist historian, who believes that the ideas of the elite have the power to change the world. Third, I had issues with Lewis's periodization. While he clearly belongs to the generation of scholars (like Niyazi Berkes, Stanford Shaw, and Tarık Zafer Tunaya) who see continuities between the late Empire and the Republic, Lewis, like them, tends to see the Republic of Turkey as the inevitable outcome of the historical process and hence to define the late Empire as a kind of prehistory of the Republic. His emphasis on the history of ideas also led him to disregard what was – and is – in my view the most important phase in the emergence of the Turkish nation state, i.e., World War I. As I pointed out in 1998, Lewis's treatment of the war in his historical overview is confined to two sentences: 'It was while they [the Young Turk intellectuals] were still discussing this question that, in October 1914, the Turks stumbled into a major European war, as allies of one group of European great powers against another. By 1918 it was clear that their time had run out.'

Finally, the most fundamental objection to Lewis's work and the main reason why it could be considered outdated 40 years later, had to do with the underlying paradigm. *Emergence* clearly is an expression of the ideas of the modernization school that dominated the 1950s, 1960s and 1970s in our field. It appeared only three years after Daniel Lerner's seminal *The Passing of Traditional Society: Modernizing the Middle East*.[2] *Emergence* reflects all the basic tenets of the modernization school: societies are at different stages of a trajectory that has a single destination: industrial, individual, and secular modernity. The state elites of the Tanzimat era, the Young Turk period, and the Kemalist republic are in tune with this historical process, and those who are not (in Lewis's words 'who were not able to view the march of events with the same historical realism') are automatically classified as reactionaries.

My message back in 1998 was that our field had changed fundamentally, and changed for the better, since the appearance of *Emergence* almost 40 years earlier. The premises of primordialist nationalism were much less in evidence and under the influence of the modernist school of people like Kedourie, Hobsbawm, Gellner,

Anderson, and Hroch; it was now generally accepted that the nation was a product of nationalism, rather than its creator. Historiography was no longer centred on the state and the elite. Social and economic history had flowered since the 1980s, although much more for the late Empire than for the Republic. In this development, the leading role had been taken by historians who, in one way or another, had been influenced by the dependency school and Immanuel Wallerstein's world-systems theory. Economic incorporation into the world capitalist system dominated by Europe, rather than modernization/westernization had become the dominant theme, with economic historians like Şevket Pamuk, Jacques Thobie, Christopher Clay, Edhem Eldem and Reşat Kasaba focusing on trade, banking, and investment and Donald Quataert and his pupils opening up the field of social history and labour history of the late Empire, looking at the impact of incorporation and popular reactions to it. The gradual opening up of the archives since the end of the 1980s had allowed the study of these in much greater detail and the interesting result was that the empirical studies often showed that the process of incorporation was a reality, at least for parts of the Empire, but that its results were varied and far less linear than Wallerstein and his followers would have predicted. The development of historical demography by people like Justin McCarthy, Kemal Karpat and Cem Behar was an important corollary of this development of socioeconomic history.

Other major trends that I mentioned in 1998 were the way traditional cultural history had been transformed into a history of mentalities, emphasizing practices of daily life and sociabilities, primarily under the influence of French and Francophone historians like François Georgeon, Paul Dumont, Thierry Zarcone, and Meropi Anastassiadou.

Where the periodization was concerned, I pointed out that there were now studies available that showed to what extent the developments of World War I had laid the basis for the nation state; that demonstrated that the 'National Struggle' was in the first place a continuation of World War I and that the Republic was essentially a Young Turk creation. I claimed some of the credit for this development, along with colleagues like Zafer Toprak and Mete Tunçay.

Finally I drew attention to the way in which authors like Şerif Mardin, Andrew Davison, Nilüfer Göle, and Ayşe Ayata had shown that the development of modern Islamic movements could not be characterized as a reaction against modernization, but as part of the modernization process. This was very much part of the late 1990s intellectual climate. The deconstruction of the concept of modernity would culminate in Shmuel Eisenstadt's famous article 'Multiple modernities' published in *Daedalus* in 2000.[3]

Having revisited 1998 and my analysis of the major changes in the field since the appearance of *Emergence* 40 years earlier, I would now like to look back in similar fashion on the period of the past 16 years and see what kind of innovations they have brought us. In this context we shall come across Touraj Atabaki's work more than once. At the end I should like to mention those areas where I feel much progress can yet be achieved. In my survey I shall mention some authors by name, but I want to make it absolutely clear that I mention these names by way of illustration of trends. I do not in any way claim to give a complete overview of those scholars who have contributed to these trends.

First of all, it has to be noted that the major developments of the 1980s and early 1990s (studies based on the concept of incorporation, history of mentalities, interest in the transitory period of World War I, and National Struggle), have lost none of their importance today. On the contrary, World War I, which was still a neglected subject where the Middle East was concerned when I wrote the first articles on the war experience of the Ottoman soldier in the 1990s, has become a focus of interest, with studies like those by Erol Köroğlu, Ed Erickson, and Mehmet Beşikçi. Touraj Atabaki's contribution to this field has been a seminal collection of conference proceedings on Iran in World War I in which he treats the Ottoman involvement and attempts to arouse the Azeri-speaking population in support of the Ottoman war effort, partly on the basis of the archives of the Turkish General Staff.[4]

In a less rigid and predictive form than was the case in the 1980s, the notion of incorporation still seems to be hegemonic, at least where the explanations of developments in the coastal areas of the Empire are concerned. Interest in everyday life, particularly of the urban middle class, is a strong as ever and the basic idea that it is useful to look at the second constitutional period and the Kemalist Republic before 1950 as parts of a single Young Turk period in modern Turkish history also seems to have widespread support nowadays, a degree of support that was unimaginable 30 years ago when these ideas were first launched.

There are significant new trends as well, however. The first is a paradigmatic one, which has been described clearly by Cem Emrence in his recent and thought-provoking *Remapping the Ottoman Middle East* as the 'third wave of historiography on the late empire', characterized by the focus on the mechanisms of political bargaining, particularly between the imperial centre and local elites.[5] In this approach, the West as the all-powerful agent of change, either economically through incorporation or politically and culturally through modernization, recedes into the background and indigenous Ottoman dynamics gain in importance, with the central state being just one among many actors.

The emergence of this bargaining paradigm is closely linked to the importance of case studies on local developments, which has been one of the most productive sub-fields over the past decade and a half. Examples abound. Michael E. Meeker's *A Nation of Empire* is a courageous and innovative attempt to combine history and ethnography to describe the way state-building and nation-building projects were adopted, and adapted, by local elites in the Eastern Black Sea region, particularly in the small provincial town of Of.[6] Ryan Gingeras' *Sorrowful Shores* looked at the Circassian settler population of the Southern Marmara region and the way it negotiated its way through the upheavals and violence of the period of war between 1912 and 1922.[7] Uğur Ümit Üngör's important study of Diyarbakır province from Hamidian times to the Republic, disguised by his publishers as *The Making of Modern Turkey*, is another excellent example of looking at developments through the prism, not of the central state, but of local society.[8] Students of Ottoman Syria have been pioneers of the bargaining perspective since Bruce Master's work on Syria in the 1990s, but it has also informed the study of the European provinces of the Empire (Rumeli) as in the work of George Gawrych, Isa Blumi, and Nathalie Clayer on the Albanians, and the recent outstanding studies of the Macedonian problem by Mehmet Hacisalihoğlu and İpek Yosmaoğlu.[9] Many recent and current PhD studies show the same characteristics – I could mention, from among my own students alone, Doğan Çetinkaya on the boycott movements of 1908–14, Alex Lamprou on the People's Houses, Sinan Dinçer on the anti-Armenian pogroms of 1895–6, Emre Erol on Foça between 1912 and 1922, and Sevgi Adak on the anti-veiling campaign of the mid-1930s.

What all of these studies share is that they no longer see political processes as the result of policies devised at the centre and imposed on the population but as the product of situations in which those policies find 'willing executioners' for a variety of reasons and in which state policies are very often domesticated and transformed by local actors. This is the 'bargaining perspective' at work. The major influences on the macro level – modernization, incorporation, war, state- and nation-building – are still there, but the emphasis is on what people do with them. They are given agency and cease to be the passive objects of state policies, Ottoman or foreign.

One field in which the study of the local has helped us get a better view of the bigger picture, is that of the deportation and killing of the Anatolian Armenians during World War I. We now have a much better picture of what happened on the ground in different localities than, say, 15 years ago, thanks in large part to the conferences organized by the Workshop on Armenian Turkish Scholarship, which culminated in the publication of *A Question of Genocide* but also to the meticulous scholarship of Raymond Kévorkian that resulted in his monumental *Le Genocide des Armeniens* (2006).[10] It is this focus on local realities rather than the debate on the question whether it was or was not a genocide that has furthered our understanding of what happened. The consensus view that seems to be emerging here is that at least since the Balkan War, if not earlier, ideas about ethnic homogenization (but not fully elaborated blueprints) started to circulate among the Young Turk leadership, but that the way the genocide actually evolved from early 1915 onwards was largely event-driven and incremental. This way the findings of authors like Fuat Dündar and Donald Bloxham can be reconciled.[11]

The other major trend that has helped our field forward in recent years is the exact opposite of the development of local micro-studies. It is that of comparative macro-studies. Conscious efforts have been made to create a better understanding of developments in the Empire by comparing it to the other great continental empires of Europe (Russia and Austria-Hungary). Of course, there have been comparative studies before, like *Imperial Legacy*, edited by L. Carl Brown, and even earlier the pioneering *Political Modernization in Japan and Turkey*, edited by Robert E. Ward and Dankwart A. Rustow back in 1964, but these by and large consisted of collections of case studies juxtaposed, rather than real efforts at comparison.[12] The collection that Touraj Atabaki and I published, *Men of Order*, and the sequel that Atabaki did on his own, *The State and the Subaltern*, also fall into this category, but the initiative to systematically compare the experiences of Kemalist Turkey and

Pahlavi Iran (top-down in the first volume and bottom-up in the second) was important.[13]

The recent spate of comparative studies goes beyond collecting case studies and they explicitly focus on the variables to be compared. This includes works like Karen Barkey's very interesting and ambitious *Empire of Difference: The Ottomans in Comparative Perspective*, and Michael Reynolds's brilliant *Shattering Empires: The Clash and Collapse of the Ottoman and Russian Empires 1908–1918*, which focuses not only on the comparative aspects, but also on the interaction of the two great states.[14] Aviel Roshwald's work is another good example. His *Ethnic Nationalism and the Fall of Empires* focuses on the nationalists and their nation-building programmes that took over as Reynolds's empires collapsed.[15] A subject that has proved itself very fruitful for comparative research (albeit again mostly in an implicit sense by juxtaposing case studies) is that of the modernizing city, with volumes edited by Laila Tarazi Fawaz and C.A. Bayly, and Meltem Toksöz and Biray Kolluoğlu.[16]

This growing interest in the comparative method has not been limited to Ottomanists. Increasingly, students of empire in Europe have included the Ottoman Empire in their projects. Dominic Lieven incorporated an explicitly comparative perspective when he published his *Empire – The Russian Empire and its Rivals*.[17] The work of Jörn Leonhard and Ulrike von Hirschhausen at the Freiburg Institute for Advanced Studies (FRIAS) deserves a special mention. FRIAS organized the workshops and programmes that led to the publication of their *Comparing Empires* in 2011 but it was also in the context of the FRIAS programme that Stefan Plaggenborg published his *Ordnung und Gewalt* (*Order and Violence*), which extended the comparison to the dictatorships of the interbellum period in Italy, Turkey, and the Soviet Union.[18] Cem Emrence's work, mentioned before, is of course also a broad comparative study, albeit one making comparisons within the Empire rather than between empires.

The comparative approach is serving to further 'normalize' Ottoman and Turkish history by drawing out the underlying dynamics that govern the behaviour of imperial systems and nation states. Establishing these commonalities is a precondition if we are to gain insights into what is really exceptional about the Ottoman and Turkish case.

So, in my view it is these two trends – the local micro-study with its subaltern view and the comparative macro-study – that complement each other and are invigorating the historiography of this period. But let us not forget that much excellent work is also still being done in the classic fields of political history and history of ideas. The late Stanford Shaw's massive documentary history of the independence struggle comes to mind, as do Cemil Koçak's detailed histories of Turkey in the single-party period.[19] There are many examples, but Princeton's Near East department under the guidance of Şükrü Hanioğlu has become a particular stronghold of this, in a sense, traditional part of the field, with a raft of meticulously researched studies like Mustafa Aksakal's *Ottoman Road to War in 1914* and Amit Bein's *Ottoman Ulema, Turkish republic*.[20] Hanioğlu himself has built on his detailed research on the Young Turks to produce an intellectual history of the late Empire that carries the work of Niyazi Berkes and Tarik Zafer Tunaya further. Zafer Toprak's recent history of Turkish anthropology (*Cumhuriyet ve Antropoloji* [2013]) and Emmanuel Szurek's as yet unpublished but standard-setting analysis of the Turkish language reform (both of them important parts of the nation-building programme of the Kemalist Republic) are other excellent examples of history of ideas embedded in political and social history.[21]

The reader is bound to ask: And what about gender? The answer has to be that the impact of gender studies on the historiography of Turkey and the late Empire has been at once great and very limited. With new generations of scholars building on the work of people like Necla Arat, Şirin Tekeli, Çiğdem Kağıtçıbaşı, and Zafer Toprak, there have been several monographic studies, some of them very good, about the changing perception of women and their role in Turkish society. Topics that have come in for particular attention are the new women's periodicals of the late Empire, women's (or rather ladies') organizations, legislation and legal issues and the 'model' women of the early Republic. Increasingly authors have shown an awareness of the ambiguous nature of Kemalist feminism with its idealization of professional women and at the same its focus on the role of the republican wife and mother. Meanwhile, the impact of gender studies beyond the realm of the study of the history of Ottoman/Turkish women has been more limited than perhaps it should have been. When one looks at the most important studies published in the past decade *outside* the field of women's studies (many of which have been mentioned in this essay), one does not find much evidence of a gendered gaze, or to put it less fashionably of an approach informed by concepts developed in gender studies. Touraj Atabaki's work reflects this situation: while he himself has been notably aware of gender issues and sensitive to the importance of a gendered approach for a long time, this is reflected in the fact that his edited collections (*Men of Order, The State and the Subaltern*, but also his 2009 *Iran in the Twentieth Century*) all include chapters on women's issues but they are included as a separate, in essence isolated, subject.

All in all, historiography of the late Ottoman Empire and modern Turkey is a flowering field and this is undoubtedly due in no small part to the relative abundance and accessibility of the primary sources. Many archives have opened up, creating a situation that is completely different from that of the 1970s, or even of the 1990s. Many archival inventories are now available online and large-scale digitization projects, like that of the Hakkı Tarik Us periodicals collection undertaken jointly by the Beyazit State Library and the TUFS library in Tokyo, have made rare Ottoman and Turkish periodicals available to any scholar with an internet hook-up and the necessary language skills.

Not only are the resources at our disposal growing at a staggering pace, the younger generation of scholars, now in their 20s and 30s, also bring new skills to the profession. Reared on the Internet (which had only just started when I held that 1998 speech), they are extremely adept at tracing and finding sources. The exposure from an early age to visual media means that they are also far more effective than older generations in the use of visual materials (photographs, films, posters) both as a documentary source and as a means of presentation. Increasingly historians of the late Empire also realize that this is a multicultural, multi-ethnic history. Both Sabancı University and Boğaziçi University have interesting programmes of co-operation going with the neighbours in the Balkans. Researchers increasingly realize that it pays to have more than one of the Empire's languages. We see young Greek researchers learn Turkish and Turkish ones learn Greek or Armenian. İpek Yosmaoğlu's study of Macedonia, mentioned earlier, is an example of the opportunities this opens up for multi-track reading.

Where linguistic skills are concerned, not all is rosy, however. When I was a student, learning Arabic or Persian was a precondition for achieving a Masters in Turkish Studies. Having French or German was not, but that was because 30 years ago it was unthinkable that one would want to study Turkish or Ottoman history *without* knowing French and

German. Now the number of, especially younger, colleagues able to directly access German- and French-language sources and literature is dwindling fast, in Turkey as well as in the Anglo-Saxon world. This is unfortunate not only because of the importance of French and German archival resources for Ottoman and Turkish history, but also because even now some of the best work on the late Empire and Turkey is being published in French and German and not translated into English. When one visits the bookshop l'Harmattan in Paris, one is confronted with the unique sight of 7 m or 8 m of shelf exclusively devoted to the Ottoman Empire and Turkey, almost all of it in French, most of it unknown to the international academic community. It is easy to berate French and German academia for 'not publishing internationally' but it is a reality and students of Turkish history who deprive themselves of access to this wealth of excellent research do so at their own peril.

This, however, is a small shadow in a sunny landscape. The historiography of the late Ottoman Empire and the early Republic is an exciting place to be right now, with at least a handful of really interesting innovative studies appearing each year and a vast body of as yet unpublished PhD work as well. Are there any underdeveloped areas in the landscape that would deserve to get more attention?

In my view, three areas stand out: one is that of labour history in the broadest sense (not just focusing on organized industrial labour, but including the casual workers and the agricultural sector). Gavin Brockett and others have been calling for the writing of a fuller social history of Turkey involving elements of subaltern history and modern labour history, building on Donald Quataert's work on the late Empire. The first results are there in the form of an edited volume by Gavin Brockett and Touraj Atabaki, but much more remains to be done here, especially in giving the village, where until halfway through the twentieth century three-quarters of the Turkish population lived, its rightful place in history.[22] This kind of study is, of course, hampered by lack of source materials because of the very high rates of illiteracy that plagued Turkey for so long, but scholars, taking a leaf from the book of colonial and post-colonial historiography, have become increasingly more and more adept at reading material produced by the representatives of the state 'against the grain' in order to get at the voice of society.

The second area is really a period: the 1940s and 1950s in Turkish history are still understudied, yet it is in the 1940s that many of the

Kemalist policies of the 1920s and 1930s began to bear fruit (for better or for worse). Some issues from these years have received attention, for example the *Varlık Vergisi* (Wealth Tax) of 1942 in Ayhan Aktar's books, but much remains to be done, and the same is true for the years in which the Democrat Party ruled.[23] The transition to democracy and the integration of Turkey into the Western alliance created a lot of excitement in the 1950s, with Kemal Karpat laying the groundwork in his *Turkey's Politics: The Transition to a Multi-Party System*, but again, apart from specific issues like the Cyprus question or the pogroms of 6–7 September 1955, relatively little has been published on the Menderes years in the last two decades.[24] The story of continuity and change between the one-party state of the 1940s and the democratic Turkey of the 1950s would constitute a fascinating subject.

The third area that is strikingly underdeveloped is that of the scholarly biography. While many Turks and late Ottomans of note have left memoirs and popular biographies are quite numerous, the number of serious critical biographies of important representatives of the late Empire and the Republic can still be counted on the fingers of one hand. Yet good biographies, built on the critical use of primary sources, are indispensable building blocks for future historiography. This definitely is a field that needs to be cultivated, but as a comparatively traditional genre the writing of academic biographies suffers from a double handicap: it may seem less appealing and exciting to younger scholars engaged in PhD or postdoctoral research, and in the extremely competitive world of research funding applications the bias towards innovation and valorization may work against it. Perhaps it is therefore the ideal pastime for experienced and still very productive academics enjoying retirement, of whom Touraj Atabaki now is one.

Notes

1. Bernard Lewis, *The Emergence of Modern Turkey* (New York and Oxford: Oxford University Press, 2002 [1961]).
2. Daniel Lerner, *The Passing of Traditional Society. Modernizing the Middle East* (Glencoe: Ill: The Free Press, 1958).
3. Shmuel Eisenstadt, 'Multiple Modernities', *Daedalus* 129/1 (2000), pp. 1–29.
4. Touraj Atabaki, *Iran in the First World War: Battleground of the Great Powers* (London: I.B.Tauris, 2006).
5. Cem Emrence, *Remapping the Ottoman Middle East* (London: I.B.Tauris, 2011).

6. Michael E. Meeker, *A Nation of Empire: The Ottoman Legacy of Turkish Modernity* (Berkeley, Los Angeles and London: University of California Press, 2002).
7. Ryan Gingeras, *Sorrowful Shores: Violence, Ethnicity and the End of the Ottoman Empire, 1912–1923* (Oxford: Oxford University Press, 2009).
8. Uğur Ümit Üngör, *The Making of Modern Turkey: Nation and State in Eastern Anatolia 1913–1950* (Oxford: Oxford University Press, 2011).
9. Mehmet Hacisalihoğlu, *Die Jungtürken und die Makedonische Frage, 1890–1918* [*The Young Turks and the Macedonian Problem*] (München: R. Oldenbourg Verlag, 2003); İpek Yosmaoğlu, *Blood Ties. Religion, Violence and the Politics of Nationhood in Ottoman Macedonia, 1878–1908* (Ithaca and London: Cornell University Press, 2013).
10. Ronald Grigor Suny, Fatma Müge Göçek and Norman M. Naimark (eds.), *A Question of Genocide. Armenians and Turks at the End of the Ottoman Empire* (Oxford: Oxford University Press, 2011); Raymond Kévorkian, *Le Genocide des Armeniens* (Paris: Odile Jacob, 2006).
11. Fuat Dündar, *Modern Türkiye'nin Şifresi. İttihat Ve Terakki'nin Etnisite Mühendisliği (1913–1918)* [*The Code of Modern Turkey. The Ethnic Engineering of the Committee of Union and Progress*] (Istanbul: İletişim Yayıncılık, 2008); Donald Bloxham, *The Great Game of Genocide. Imperialism, Nationalism and the Destruction of the Ottoman Armenians* (Oxford: Oxford University Press, 2005).
12. L. Carl Brown, *Imperial Legacy. The Ottoman Imprint on the Balkans and the Middle East* (New York: Columbia University Press, 1996); Robert E. Ward and Dankwart A. Rustow (eds.), *Political Modernization in Japan and Turkey* (Princeton: Princeton University Press, 1964).
13. Touraj Atabaki and Erik-Jan Zürcher (eds.), *Men of Order. Authoritarian Modernization under Atatürk and Reza Shah* (London: I.B.Tauris, 2004); Touraj Atabaki (ed.), *The State and the Subaltern. Modernization, Society and the State in Turkey and Iran* (London: I.B.Tauris, 2007).
14. Karen Barkey, *Empire of Difference: The Ottomans in Comparative Perspective* (Cambridge and New York: Cambridge University Press, 2008); Michael Reynoald, *Shattering Empires: The Clash and Collapse of the Ottoman and Russian Empires, 1908–1918* (Cambridge and New York: Cambridge University Press, 2011).
15. Aviel Roshwald, *Ethnic Nationalism and the Fall of Empires. Central Europe, Russia and the Middle East, 1914–1923* (London and New York: Routledge, 2001).
16. Laila Tarazy Fawaz and C.A. Bayly (eds), *Modernity and Culture form the Mediterranean to the Indian Ocean* (New York: Columbia University Press, 2002); Biray Kolluoğlu and Meltem Toksöz (eds), *Cities of the Mediterranean. From the Ottomans to the Present Day* (2010).
17. Dominic Lieven, *Empire: The Russian Empire and its Rivals* (London: John Murray, 2000).
18. Jörn Leonhard and Ulrike von Hirschhausen (eds), *Comparing Empires. Encounters and Transfers in the Long Nineteenth Century* (Göttingen: Vandenhoeck & Ruprecht, 2011). Stefan Plaggenborg, *Ordnung und Gewalt: Kemalismus-*

Faschismus-Sozialismus [*Order and Violence: Kemalism-Fascism-Socialism*] (München: Oldenbourg Wissenschaftsverlag, 2012).
19. Stanford Shaw, *From Empire to Republic. The Turkish War of National Liberation 1818–1923* (N.P.: Turk Tarih Kurumu, 2000).
20. Mustafa Aksakal, *Ottoman Road to War in 1914. The Ottoman Empire and the First World War* (Cambridge: Cambridge University Press, 2008); Amit Bein, *Ottoman Ulema, Turkish republic: Agents of Change and Guardians of Tradition* (Stanford: Stanford University Press, 2011).
21. Zafer Toprak, *Darwin'den Dersim'e Cumhuriyet ve Antropoloji* [*Republic and Anthropology from Darwin to Dersim*] (Istanbul: Doğan Kitap, 2012).
22. Touraj Atabaki and Gavin Brockett (eds), *Ottoman and Republican Turkish Labour History* (Cambridge: Cambridge University Press, 2010).
23. Ayhan Aktar, *Varlik vergisi ve "Turklestirme" politikalari* [*The Wealth tax and Politics of Turkification*] (Istanbul: İletişim Yayıncılık, 2012); *Türk Milliyetçiliği, Gayrimüslimler ve Ekonomik Dönüşüm* [*Turkish Nationalism, the Non-Muslims and Economic Transition*] (Istanbul: İletişim Yayıncılık, 2006).
24. Kemal H. Karpat, *Turkey's Politics: The Transition to a Multi-Party System* (Princeton: Princeton University Press, 1959).

CONTRIBUTORS

Serhan Afacan is an assistant professor of History at Istanbul Medeniyet University in Turkey. His research interests are Iranian history (particularly twentieth century); Ottoman and Turkish history; European and Middle Eastern labour history; labour historiography; and comparative historiography. His publications include 'Devletle yazismak: Turkiye ve Iran sosyal tarihciliginde dilekceler' (Corresponding with the state: petitions in Turkish and Iranian social history), *Turkiyat Mecmuasi* XXI (Spring 2011); 'Shenakhtan va shenasandan-e hamsayeh' (Discovering the next Door neighbour: a critical review of the books published in Turkey about Iran in the 20th century), *Goftogu* LIX (Spring 2012); and 'Revisiting labour activism in Iran: some notes on the Vatan factory strike in 1931,' *International Labor and Working-Class History* (forthcoming).

Janet Afary is a historian of modern Iran. She holds the Mellichamp Chair in Global Religion and Modernity at the University of California, Santa Barbara, where she is a Professor of Religious Studies. She received her PhD from the University of Michigan, Ann Arbor in History and Near East Studies. Her research interests include constitutional politics, Islam and politics, and gender and sexuality in Iran and the Middle East. She is the author of *Sexual Politics in Modern Iran* (2009) and co-editor, with John R. Perry, of *Ali Akbar Dehkhodā: Charand-o Parand, 1907 – 1909: Revolutionary Satire from Iran* (2016).

Ali M. Ansari is a professor of Iranian History at the University of St. Andrews and founding director of the University's Institute of

Iranian Studies. His most recent publication is *The Politics of Nationalism in Modern Iran* (2012). His research interests include nationalism and intellectual history in Iran, with a particular interest in the impact of the Enlightenment. He was President of the British Institute of Persian Studies from 2013-17, and was elected a Fellow of the Royal Society of Edinburgh in 2016.

Mansour Bonakdarian (PhD in History, University of Iowa) is an independent scholar specializing in British, imperial, Middle Eastern, and comparative history. He is the author of *Britain and the Iranian Constitutional Revolution of 1906–1911: Foreign Policy, Imperialism, and Dissent* (2006) and is currently completing monographs respectively titled *Éirinn & Iran go Brách: Iran in Irish-nationalist Historical, Literary, Cultural, and Political Imaginations from the late 18th Century to 1914* and *Confluences of Nationalism, Internationalism, and Transnationalism in Early 20th-Century Anti-Imperialist Struggles: India, Iran, and Ireland 1905–1921*. He is also co-editing a volume of essays with Ian Christopher Fletcher and Yaël Simpson Fletcher entitled *The First Universal Races Congress of 1911: Empires, Civilizations, Encounters*.

Houchang E. Chehabi is a professor of International Relations and History at the Frederick S. Pardee School of Global Studies, Boston University. He has also taught at Harvard University, UCLA, and the University of St. Andrews. For the last few years his main research interest has been Iranian cultural history. He has authored, edited, or co-edited over ten books, most recently (with Grace Neville) *Erin and Iran: Cultural Encounters Between the Irish and the Iranians* (2015), and (with Farhad Khosrokhavar and Clément Therme) *Iran and the Challenges of the Twenty-First Century*.

Kaveh Ehsani is assistant professor of International Studies at DePaul University in Chicago. Some of his recent publications include 'Disappearing the Workers: How Labor in Oil has been Made Invisible', in Touraj Atabaki, Elisabetta Bini & Kaveh Ehsani (eds.), *Working for Oil: Social Histories of Labor in the Global Oil Industry* (2017); 'Pipeline Politics in Iran: Relations of Power and Property, Dispossession and Distribution', *South Atlantic Quarterly* CXVI/2 (2017); 'War and Resentment: Critical Reflections on the Legacies of the Iran-Iraq War',

Middle East Critique XXVI/1 (2017); 'Oil, state, and society in Iran in the aftermath of WWI', in Thomas Fraser (ed.), *The First World War and its Aftermath: The Shaping of the Middle East* (2015); 'Radical democratic politics and public space', *IJMES* XLVI/1 (2014); 'Oil and beyond: expanding British imperial aspirations, emerging oil capitalism, and the challenge of social questions in WWI' (with Touraj Atabaki), in Helmut Bley and Anorthe Kremers (eds.), *The World During the First World War* (2014); 'Politics of property in the Islamic Republic of Iran', in Said Amir-Arjomand and Nathan Brown (eds.), *The Rule of Law, Islam, and Constitutional Politics in Egypt and Iran* (2013); 'The urban provincial periphery in Iran: revolution and war in Ramhormoz' in Ali Gheissari (ed.), *Contemporary Iran* (2009); 'Tehran, June 2009' (with Arang Keshavarzian and Norma Claire Moruzzi), in *Middle East Report Online*, 28 June 2009; 'Rural society and agricultural development in post-revolution Iran', *Critique: Critical Middle Eastern Studies* XV/1 (2006); 'Social engineering and the contradictions of modernization in Khuzestan's company towns', *International Review of Social History*, XLVIII (2003).

Manoutchehr M. Eskandari-Qajar is a professor of Political Science and director of the Middle East Studies Program at Santa Barbara City College. He received his PhD in Political Science from the University of California, Santa Barbara in 1984. His academic interests include monarchism, political theory and philosophy, Middle Eastern history and politics. Dr. Eskandari-Qajar has published yearly on the history of the Qajars in *Qajar Studies* (volumes I–VIII and X–XI), and in *Iranian Studies* No. 4, September 2007 and No. 2, March 2011 as guest editor and author. In 2009, Dr. Eskandari joined a team of scholars at Harvard University under the direction of Professor Afsaneh Najmabadi working on the NEH-funded Women's Worlds in Qajar Iran Harvard Project. The project's aim is to safeguard digitally and make available documents, photographs and oral history of women in the Qajar era. In Dr. Eskandari-Qajar was named California Professor of the Year by Council for Advancement and Support of Education and the Carnegie Foundation for the Advancement of Teaching. His articles on Sir John Malcolm and Soltan Ahmad Mirza 'Azodi are forthcoming in the *Encyclopeadia Iranica* (2017) and his translation of the *Tarikh-e 'Azodi* was published as *Life at the Court of the Early Qajars* in 2014.

CONTRIBUTORS 265

M.R. Ghanoonparvar is Professor Emeritus of Persian and Comparative Literature at The University of Texas at Austin. Professor Ghanoonparvar has also taught at the University of Isfahan, the University of Virginia, and the University of Arizona, and was a Rockefeller Fellow at the University of Michigan. He has published widely on Persian literature and culture in both English and Persian and is the author of *Prophets of Doom: Literature as a Socio-Political Phenomenon in Modern Iran* (1984), *In a Persian Mirror: Images of the West and Westerners in Iranian Fiction* (1993), *Translating the Garden* (2001), *Reading Chubak* (2005), and *Persian Cuisine: Traditional, Regional and Modern Foods* (2006). His translations include Jalal Al-e Ahmad's *By the Pen* (1988), Sadeq Chubak's *The Patient Stone* (1989), Simin Daneshvar's *Savushun* (1991), Ahmad Kasravi's *On Islam and Shi'ism* (1990), Sadeq Hedayat's *The Myth of Creation* (1998), Davud Ghaffarzadegan's *Fortune Told in Blood* (2008), Mohammad Reza Bayrami's *The Tales of Sabalan* (2008) and *Eagles of Hill 60* (2008), and Bahram Beyza'i's *Memoirs of the Actor in a Supporting Role* (2010). His edited volumes include *Iranian Drama: An Anthology* (1989), *In Transition: Essays on Culture and Identity in Middle Eastern Societies* (1994), Gholamhoseyn Sa'edi's *Othello in Wonderland and Mirror-Polishing Storytellers* (1996), Moniru Ravanipur's *Satan Stones* (1996) and *Kanizu* (2004), and *The Neighbor Says: Letters of Nima Yushij and the Philosophy of Modern Persian Poetry* (2009). He was the recipient of the 2008 Lois Roth Prize for Literary Translation. His most recent books are *Iranian Film and Persian Fiction* (2016) and *Dining at the Safavid Court* (2017). His forthcoming book is *Literary Diseases in Persian Literature*, and his forthcoming translations include Shahrokh Meskub's *In the Alley of the Friend: On the Poetry of Hafez* and Hushang Golshiri's *Book of Jinn*.

Peyman Jafari is a lecturer at the History Department of the University of Amsterdam, and Fellow at the International Institute of Social History. His research interests are labour history, social movements, political economy of authoritarianism, and international relations. His publications include *Oil, Labour and Revolution: A Social History of Labour in the Iranian Oil Industry, 1973-83* (forthcoming); 'Linkages of oil and politics: oil strikes and dual power in the Iranian Revolution', *Labor History* (forthcoming); 'Fluid history: oil workers and the Iranian Revolution', in Touraj Atabaki, Elisabetta Bini & Kaveh Ehsani (eds.), *Working for Oil: Social Histories of Labor in the Global Oil Industry* (2017);

Der andere Iran: Geschichte und Kultur von 1900 bis zur Gegenwart (2010); 'Reasons to Revolt: Iranian Oil Workers in the 1970's', *International Labor and Working-Class History* lxxxiv (2013); 'Rupture and revolt in Iran', *International Socialism Journal* cxxiv (2009).

Maral Jefroudi is a historian working on modern Iran and Turkey. She is co-director of the International Institute of Research and Education in Amsterdam. She has taught at Boğaziçi University and University of Amsterdam. She received her PhD from Leiden University in 2017. Her dissertation *'If I deserve it, it should be paid to me'* is a study of social history of labour in the Iranian Oil Industry between 1951 and 1973. Her publications include 'Revisiting "the Long Night" of Iranian Workers: Labour Activism in the Iranian Oil Industry in the 1960s', *International Labour and Working-Class History* IXXXIV (2013), and 'Asylum and migration across the Turkey-Iran border', in Baklacıoğlu and Özer (eds.), *Migration, Asylum, and Refugees in Turkey: Studies in the Control of Population at the Southeastern Borders of the EU* (2014). She has also translated a number of books and articles from English and Persian into Turkish.

Valentine M. Moghadam is a professor of Sociology and International Affairs at Northeastern University, Boston, director of its Middle East and Mediterranean Studies Program, and former director of the International Affairs Program. Prior to her appointment at Northeastern, she was a professor of Sociology and Director of Women's Studies at Purdue University and Illinois State University, and a section chief within the Social and Human Sciences Sector of UNESCO in Paris. She received her higher education in Canada and the United States, after which she spent six years as coordinator of the research programme on women and development at the United Nations University's WIDER Institute, in Helsinki. Her areas of research include globalization, transnational social movements and feminist networks, economic citizenship, and gender and development in the Middle East and North Africa. Among her many publications are *Modernizing Women: Gender and Social Change in the Middle East* (1993, 2003, and 2013); the award-winning *Globalizing Women: Transnational Feminist Networks* (2005), and *Globalization and Social Movements: Islamism, Feminism, and the Global Justice Movement* (2009, 2013). She has edited seven books, among which is *Social Policy in the Middle East: Economic, Political, and Gender Dynamics* (with Massoud Karshenas, 2006). Forthcoming publications include a comparative study of women's economic and political participation in Iran and Tunisia, and a book chapter that focuses on the evolution of patterns of women's employment in the Islamic Republic.

Peyman Vahabzadeh is a professor of Sociology at University of Victoria, Canada. He is the author of *Articulated Experiences: Toward a Radical Phenomenology of Contemporary Social Movements* (2003), *A Guerrilla Odyssey: Modernization, Secularism, Democracy and the Fadai Discourse of National Liberation in Iran, 1971-1979* (2010), *Exilic Meditations: Essays on A Displaced Life* (2012), *Parviz Sadri: A Political Biography* (2015), and *Violence and Nonviolence: Conceptual Excursion into Phantom Opposites* (2018), as well as the editor of *Iran's Struggles for Social Justice: Economics, Agency, Justice, Activism* (2017).

Erik-Jan Zürcher was awarded his PhD at Leiden University in 1984. He has taught at Nijmegen and Amsterdam Universities and been attached to the International Institute of Social History twice (1990 – 99 as Senior Research Fellow and 2008 – 12 as General Director). He has been Full Professor of Turkish Studies at Leiden University since 1997. He has been a Member of the Royal Netherlands Academy of Arts and Sciences since 2008 and Affiliate Professor at Stockholm University from 2013 to 2016. Zürcher has written or edited 12 books, mostly on Turkey in the twentieth century. His *Turkey: A Modern History* has been translated into ten languages.

APPENDIX

LIFE AND WORK OF TOURAJ ATABAKI

Touraj Atabaki was born on 23 February 1950 in Tehran, during one of the most turbulent periods in Iran's modern history, when an impressive movement was demanding democratic reforms and the nationalization of oil. Like many members of the modern middle class, Atabaki's parents strongly sympathized with this movement and its leading organization, the National Front, but they were also intensely concerned about issues of social justice. Although they leaned to the left, they were put off by the Stalinist orientation of the Tudeh Party, and drew their inspiration from independent thinkers and the leftist leaders of the National Front. Inevitably, his parents' commitment to political and social change shaped Atabaki's intellectual and political development which started at high school, but they also contributed to his growing interest in the study of global and historical topics, such as the history of the Indian subcontinent and the Indian independence movement.

By the time he enrolled in the Physics Department of the National University of Iran (renamed Shahid Beheshti after the Revolution) in 1970, the political and intellectual pessimism that followed the 1953 coup d'état had given way to a new rebellious mood among the youth. Students were reading and exchanging books and pamphlets by various revolutionary intellectuals, ranging from Frantz Fanon to Régis Debray. As a young student, Atabaki spent much of his time devouring illegal literature and discussing politics and history in one of the small informal circles that were in contact with the left wing of the National Front.

Partly inspired by his parents' views, he was looking for a brand of socialism that was critical of the Soviet Union and was thus attracted to the writings of Leon Trotsky and other anti-Stalinist intellectuals. Like most leftist-oriented students at that time, however, he soon became attracted to the Fada'iyan guerrillas, for whom Che Guevera's heroism and the Cuban revolution served as an inspiration, rather than the Soviet Union's opportunism. It did not take too long before his political activities drew the attention of SAVAK, the Shah's secret service, and he was briefly arrested in 1973. After acquiring his BSc a year later, and intimidated by SAVAK's omnipresent gaze, he decided to move to London for further education.

From 1976 to 1978, Atabaki was a Master's student in theoretical physics in the Department of Crystallography at Birkbeck College, where he also audited courses in history. Here, the lectures and writings of the Marxian historian Eric Hobsbawm had a great influence on his later development as a young historian. Feeling already uncomfortable with the crude materialism of the Marxian historiography of Iran, his encounter with the writings of E.P. Thompson further increased his attentiveness to cultural issues and social history.

At that time, London had become one of the centres of Iranian student activism against the Shah's autocratic regime. Atabaki contributed to oppositional activities by organizing meetings and writing reports to inform the European public about the repression of workers and leftist organizations in Iran. By the time he acquired his MSc degree in theoretical physics from Birkbeck College and embarked on a PhD project in quantum physics in 1978, a mass revolutionary movement had erupted in Iran. Like many oppositionists, Atabaki returned to his home country to assist the revolutionary movement and he became an active member of the Fada'iyan, contributing to the theoretical education of the rapidly growing membership. After the fall of the monarchy in February 1979, he became a member of Pishgam, the Fada'iyan's student organization, and an editorial member of its journal. Anxiety about the increasing authoritarian streaks of the new regime rapidly replaced his enthusiasm, however, and he was soon forced to go into hiding as the Islamist forces around Ayatollah Khomeini intensified their crackdown on the Left in early 1982. These were very dramatic times, in which the new regime had started arresting, torturing and executing oppositionists.

To escape the new wave of repression, Atabaki fled Iran in 1982, and acquired political refugee status in the Netherlands, where he settled to pursue his academic career as a historian. Starting a new life in exile wasn't easy, however, as the disturbing news of arrested or executed comrades and friends was unceasingly coming out of Iran. Atabaki continued his political engagement by publicizing the human rights violations in Iran and contributing to critical journals of the Left, such as *Nazm-e Novin* and *Alefba*. Despite the new hardships, he acquired his MA in history at Utrecht University in 1987, and he was invited to continue as a PhD candidate and an assistant professor. On 21 December 1990, Touraj married Sharareh Nosratifard, with whom he has a daughter (Atossa, 1991) and a son (Armin, 1996). In 1991, he finished his PhD on ethnicity and regional autonomy in the twentieth century in Iran under the supervision of Ervand Abrahamian (Baruch College). His dissertation, which was published in 1993 and reprinted in 2000, has provided significant insights into the formation of the ethnic identity among Iranian Azerbaijanis and the formation of the autonomous government of Azerbaijan in 1945–6.

From 1991 to 2006, Atabaki taught as an associate professor in the History Department at Utrecht University. It was during this time that he extended his interest and expertise beyond Iranian borders, travelling extensively to Russia and the former Soviet republics of the Caucasus and Central Asia. His work received recognition when, in 2001, he was appointed to an endowed chair in social history of the Middle East and Central Asia in the Department of History at the University of Amsterdam, where he taught until 2006. Since then, Atabaki has been the chair of social history of the Middle East and Central Asia at Leiden University where he has taught and supervised numerous PhD candidates. The International Institute of Social History (IISH) in Amsterdam is the other institution with which he has developed a long-time association. Becoming an honorary fellow of the IISH in 1995, and then a senior researcher and head of its Central Asia and Middle East Desk in 2010, Atabaki has significantly advanced the research projects and archival acquisitions of this unique institute.

Since its establishment in 1935, the IISH has developed into a leading repository of archives of social movements, labour organizations, political parties, and activists. In its early years, the institute focused on acquisition of the archives of the European social-democratic, communist, and anarchist movements, which were being threatened by the rise of Nazism and Stalinist purges in the Soviet Union. The institute spent the 1950s on recovering the losses and damages incurred in World War II, but its activities expanded in the following two decades as interest in the history of social movements and ideas increased. By saving the archives and libraries of persecuted people and organizations in this period, the IISH broadened its scope far beyond Europe, gathering materials from Latin America, the Middle East, East and Central Asia, and Africa. Researchers from all over the world consult the Institute's archives. Parallel to archival acquisition, the IISH has intensified its research activities, which have focused on social and economic history. Since the late 1990s, the Institute has played a leading role in promoting labour history and developing new perspectives by expanding its temporal, geographic, and thematic scopes. A third activity of the IISH is the construction of historical datasets and the facilitation of international collaborations to help researchers arrive at common definition of concepts, methods, annotation, and documentation in the gathering of data.

In 2010, Atabaki embarked on a new project that addresses anessential issue in Iranian historiography – the social history of labour in the Iranian oil industry. In the historical studies of Iran, labour has received little attention, and studies that deal with the issue, often focus on its political and economic, rather than its social dimensions. Moreover, the theoretical and methodological developments of the last three decades in labour history haven't been sufficiently integrated in the studies of labour in Iran. These developments include the critique of structuralist understandings of class and the incorporation of the Thompsonian notion of culture as a constitutive element in class formation. From this perspective, labour becomes a subject of study not only in the workplace, but also in the community, and through the lens of everyday life practices, gender, ethnicity, and language. New directions in labour history have also moved beyond Eurocentric notions that were once very dominant.

Taking these new inroads, Atabaki initiated and supervised a research project on the social history of labour in the Iranian oil industry covering the 20th century. This study fills a serious gap in Iranian historiography, contributing to our understanding of labour, and the social, cultural and political role of the oil industry in Iran's modern history.

Finally, Atabaki has committed himself throughout his academic career to a critical engagement with public debates, especially those on democracy and social justice in Iran, by contributing to publications, TV and radio programmes. Colleagues, friends, comrades, students and journalists have always been able to count on him for insightful analyses of current and historic events. This is particularly true for those living in Iran, as Atabaki has always enthusiastically accepted their requests for articles or interviews in his relentless effort to play his part in the intellectual and political debates in Iran.

BIBLIOGRAPHY OF TOURAJ ATABAKI

Books

Azarbayjan dar Iran-e Moʿaser (Tehran: Tus, 1997). Persian translation of *Azerbaijan: Ethnicity and Autonomy in Twentieth-Century Iran* (London: British Academic Press, 1993).

Azerbaijan: Ethnicity and Autonomy in the Twentieth-Century Iran (London: I.B.Tauris, 1993).

Azerbaijan: Ethnicity and the Struggle for Power in Iran (London: I.B.Tauris, 2000). Revised edition of *Azerbaijan: Ethnicity and Autonomy in Twentieth-Century Iran*.

Beyond Essentialism: Who Writes Whose Past in the Middle East and Central Asia? (Amsterdam: Aksant, 2003).

With Joris Versteeg. *Centraal Azië* (Amsterdam: Koninklijk Instituut voor de Tropen-Novib-NCOS, 1994).

With Svetlana Ravandi-Fadai and Solmaz Rustamova-Towhidi. *Fallen for Their Faith: From Comrades to Enemies of the People. The Iranian Revolutionaries in the Land of the Soviets* (Forthcoming).

Social History of Labour in the Iranian Oil Industry 1908–1941 (Forthcoming).

Victims of their fate: Everyday Life of Iranian Communists and Revolutionaries in the Stalinist Soviet Union (Forthcoming).

Edited Books

Ayat-e ʿeshq: sheʿr-e moʿaser-e tajiki (Frankfurt: Horizonte Verlag, 1992). Selected and edited work of the Tajik poet Golrukhksar.

Devlet ve Maduniyet: Türkiye ve İran'da Modernleşme, Toplum ve Devlet, Derleyen (Istanbul: Bilgi Üniversitesi Yayınları, 2010).

Dowlat va forudastan: faraz va forud-e tajaddod-e ameraneh dar Torkiyeh va Iran (Tehran: Qoqnus, 2011).

Entry on Avestan and Persian in P.A.F. van Veen and N. van der Sijs (eds), *Etymologisch Woordenboek* (Amsterdam: Van Dale, 1989).
Iran and the First World War: A Battleground of the Great Powers (London: I.B.Tauris, 2006).
Iran in the 20th Century: Historiography and Political Culture (London: I.B.Tauris, 2009).
Iran va jang-e jahani-ye avval: meydan-e nabard-e qodratha-ye bozorg (Tehran: Qoqnus, 2008). Persian translation of *Iran and the First World War*.
İran ve 1. Dünya Savaşı. Büyük Güçlerin Savaş Alanı, Derleyen (Istanbul: Tarih Vakfı Yurt Yayınları, 2010).
With Margreet Dorlijn. *Kurdistan in Search of Ethnic Identity* (Utrecht: Houtsma Foundation Publication, 1990).
With Erik Jan Zürcher. *Men of Order: Authoritarian Modernization under Atatürk and Reza Shah* (London: I.B.Tauris, 2004).
Modernity and its Agencies: The Young Movements in the History of the South (New Delhi: Manohar, 2010).
With Gavin D. Brockett. *Ottoman and Republican Turkish Labour History, Supplement of the International Review of Social History 17* (London: Cambridge University Press, 2009).
With John O'Kane. *Post-Soviet Central Asia* (London: I.B.Tauris, 1998).
Tajaddod-e ameraneh: jame'eh va dowlat dar asr-e Reza Shah (Tehran: Qoqnus, 2007). Partial Persian translation of *Men of Order: Authoritarian Modernization under Atatürk and Reza Shah*.
The State and the Subaltern: Society and Politics in Turkey and Iran (London, I.B.Tauris, 2007).
With Erik J. Zürcher. *Türkiye ve İran'da Otoriter Modernleşme: Atatürk ve Rıza Şah Dönemleri.* (Istanbul: İstanbul Bilgi Üniversitesi Yayınları, 2012).
With Sanjyot Mehendale. *Central Asia and the Caucasus: Transnationalism and Diaspora* (London: Routledge, 2005).

Bibliographies

With Solmaz Rustamova-Towhidi. *The Baku Documents: Union Catalogue of Persian, Azebaijani, Ottoman Turkish, and Arabic Serials and Newspapers in the Libraries of the Republic of Azerbaijan* (London: I.B.Tauris, 1995).
———, Grigol Beradze, and Georg Sanikidze. *The Caucasus Directories. Union Catalogue of Persian, Azebaijani, Ottoman Turkish, and Arabic Serials and Newspapers in the Libraries of the Republic of Azerbaijan and the Republic of Georgia* (Tehran: Resanehha, 2006).

Book Chapters

'Agency and Subjectivity in Iranian National Historiography,' in Touraj Atabaki (ed.), *Historiography and Political Culture in 20th Century Iran* (London: I.B.Tauris, 2009), pp. 69–92.
'Başkasını Reddederek kendini Yenilemek: Pan-Türkçülük ve İran Milliyetçiliği,' in Willem van Schendel and Erik Jan Zürcher (eds.), *Orta Asya ve İslam Dünyasında Kilimlik Politikaları* (Istanbul: İletişim, 2004), pp. 89–111.

'The Caliphate, the Clerics and Republicanism in Turkey and Iran', in Touraj Atabaki and Erik J. Zürcher (eds.), *Men of Order: Authoritarian Modernization under Atatürk and Reza Shah* (London: I.B.Tauris, 2004), pp. 44–64.

'The Comintern, the Soviet Union and Working Class Militancy in Interwar Iran', in Stephanie Cronin (ed.), *Iranian–Russian Encounters: Empire and Revolution since 1800* (London: Routledge, 2012), pp. 298–323.

'Constitutionalists *Sans Frontières*: Iranian Constitutionalism and its Asian Connections,' in H.E. Chehabi and Vanessa Martin (eds), *Iran's Constitutional Revolution: Popular Politics, Cultural Transformations and Transnational Connections* (London: I.B.Tauris, 2010), pp. 341–56, 481–4.

'Dialogue, a Literary Form in Persian Nineteenth/Twentieth-Centuries Political Discourse', in Bert G. Fragner et al. (eds.), *Proceedings of the Second European Conference of Iranian Studies* (Rome: Istituto Italiano per il Medio ed Estremo Oriente, 1995), pp. 39–46.

'Disgruntled Guests: Iranian Subalterns on the Margin of the Tsarist Empire,' in Touraj Atabaki, (ed.), *The State and the Subaltern: Society and Politics in Turkey and Iran* (London, I.B.Tauris, 2007), pp. 31–52, 203–6.

'The Early Labour Movement in Khorasan,' in M. van Damme and H. Boeschoten (eds.), *Utrecht Papers on Central Asia* (Utrecht: Utrecht University, Turkological Series, 1987).

'Enlightening the People: The Practice of Modernity in Central Asia and its Trans-Caspian Dependencies,' in Gabriele Rasuly-Paleczek and Julia Katschnig (eds.), *Central Asia on Display: Proceedings of the VII. Conference of the European Society for Central Asian Studies*, volume 2 (Vienna: Lit Verlag, 2004), pp. 171–82.

'Ethnic Minorities, Regionalism and the Construction of New Histories,' in Markus Ritter, Ralph Kauz and Brigitt Hoffman (eds.), *Iran und iranisch geprägte Kulturen: Studien zum 65. Geburtstag von Bert G. Fragner* (Wiesbaden: Dr. Ludwig Reichert Verlag, 2008), pp. 131–43.

'The First World War, Great Power Rivalries and the Emergence of a Political Community in Iran,' in Touraj Atabaki (ed.), *Iran and the First World War: A Battleground of the Great Powers* (London: I.B.Tauris, 2006), pp. 1–7.

'From Multilingual Empire to Contested Modern State,' in Homa Katouzian and Hossein Shaidi (eds.), *Iran in the 21st Century: Politics, Economics and Conflicts* (London and New York, NY: Routledge, 2008), pp. 41–62.

'Going East: The Ottomans' Secret Service Activities in Iran,' in Touraj Atabaki (ed.), *Iran and the First World War: Battleground of the Great Powers* (London: I.B.Tauris, 2006), pp. 29–41.

'Historiography of Twentieth-Century Iran: Memory, Amnesia and Invention,' in Touraj Atabaki (ed.), *Historiography and Political Culture in 20th Century Iran* (London: I.B.Tauris, 2009), pp. 1–4.

'The Impediments to the Development of Civil Societies in Central Asia', in Touraj Atabaki and John O'Kane (eds.), *Post-Soviet Central Asia* (London: I.B.Tauris, 1998), pp. 35–43.

'Incommodious Hosts, Invidious Guests: The Life and Time of Iranian Revolutionaries in the Soviet Union (1921-1939),' in Stephanie Cronin (ed.), *Reformers and Revolutionaries in Modern Iran: New Perspectives on the Iranian Left* (London: Routledge-Curzon, 2004), pp. 147–64.

'Iran and the Netherlands in the Interbellum,' in Martine Gosselink (ed.), *Iran and the Netherlands: Interwoven through the Ages* (Gronsveld and Rotterdam: Barjesteh L.A. van Waalwijk van Doorn, 2009), pp. 261–6.

'Iranian History in Transition: Recasting the Symbolic Identity of Babak Khorramdin', in Abbas Amanat and Farzin Vejdani (eds), *Iran Facing Others: Identity Boundaries in a Historical Perspective* (New York: Palgrave Macmillan, 2012), pp. 63–76.

'Iranian Oil Nationalised; Mosaddeq Goes to The Hague,' in Martine Gosselink (ed.), *Iran and the Netherlands: Interwoven through the Ages* (Gosselink & Rotterdam: Barjesteh L.A. van Waalwijk van Doorn, 2009), pp. 289–97.

'Kendini Yeniden Kurmak, Ötekini Reddetmek: Pantürkism ve İran Milliyetçiliği,' in Erik-Jan Zürcher (ed.), *Türkiye'de Etnik Çatışma* (Istanbul: İletişim, 2005), pp. 27–50.

'Khelafat, rowhaniyat va jomhuriyat dar Torkiyeh va Iran: barkhi molahezat-e tatbiqi,' in Touraj Tabaki (ed.), *Tajaddod-e ameraneh: jame'eh va dowlat dar asr-e Reza Shah* (Tehran: Qoqnus, 2007), pp. 65–91.

'Mashruteh khahan-e bimarz: mashruteh khahi va peyvandha-ye asya'i-ye an,' in Hushang Shehabi and Vanesa Martin (eds), *Enqelab-e mashruteh-ye Iran* (Tehran: Parseh, 2013), pp. 553–73.

'Missing Labour in the Metanarratives of Practicing Modernity in Iran: Labour Agency in Refashioning the Discourse of Social Development', in David Mayer and Jürgen Mittag (eds), *Interventions: The Impact of Labour Movements on Social and Cultural Development* (Leipzig: Akademische Verlagsanstalt, 2013), pp. 171–95.

'Pan-Turkism and Iranian Nationalism', in Touraj Atabaki (ed.), *Iran and the First World War: Battleground of the Great Powers* (London: I.B.Tauris, 2006), pp. 121–35.

'Recasting Oneself, Rejecting the Others: Pan-Turkism and Iranian Nationalism,' in Erik-Jan Z?rcher and Willem van Schendel (eds), *Identity Politics in Central Asia and Muslim Word: Nationalism, Ethnicity and Labour in the Twentieth Century* (London: I.B.Tauris, 2001), pp. 65–83.

'A Study in the History of Bukharan Modernism. The Journey of Ahmad Dānish to St. Petersburg,' in Ingeborg Baldauf and Michael Friederich (eds), *Bamberger Zentralasienstudien* (Berlin: Klaus Schwarz Verlag, 1994) pp. 263–9.

'Time, Labour-Dicipline and Modernization in Turkey and Iran: Some comparative Remarks,' in Touraj Atabaki (ed.), *The State and the Subaltern: Modernization, Society and the State in Turkey and Iran* (London, I.B.Tauris, 2007), pp. 1–16.

'Transnationalism and diaspora in Central Asia and the Caucasus,' in Touraj Atabaki and Sanjyot Mehendale (eds.), *Central Asia and the Caucasus: Transnationalism and Diaspora* (London: Routledge, 2005), pp. 1–9.

'Türkiye ve İran'da Hilafet, Ulema ve Cumhuriyetçilik: Karşılaştırmalı Bazı Tesbitler,' in Touraj Atabaki and Erik J. Zürcher (eds), *Türkiye ve İran'da Otoriter Modernleşme: Atatürk ve Rıza Şah Dönemleri* (Istanbul: İstanbul Bilgi Üniversitesi Yayınları, 2012), pp. 41–59.

Guest-Edited Journal Issues

With Marcel van der Linden. A special theme on the Social History of Iran, *International Review of Social History* xlviii/3 (2003), pp. 351–455.

A special issue on Iran and the Challenges of the 21st Century, *Iran Nameh* xxiv/2-3 (2008).
—— the Iranian Constitutional Revolution, *Goftogu* li (2008).
—— the Iranian Left Movement, *Goftogu* xxxi (2001).

Articles

'Afsaneh-ye yek oltimatom.' *Goftogu* x (1995), pp. 115–27.
'Az rafiq-e sorkh ta doshman-e khalq: karnameh va zamaneh-ye Ehsanollah Khan Dustdar dar sarzamin-e shuraha', *Goftogu* xxxi (2001), pp. 143–65.
'Azarbayjan va nasionalism-e irani', *Goftogu* xxxiii (2001), pp. 17–35.
'Constitutionalism in Iran and its Asian Interdependencies'. *Comparative Studies of South Asia, Africa and the Middle East* xxviii/1 (2008), pp. 142–53.
'Disgruntled Guests: Iranian Subaltern on the Margins of the Tsarist Empire', *International Review of Social History* xlviii/3 (2003), pp. 401–26.
'Doğu'ya Doğru: Teşkilat-ı Mahsusa'nın İran, Kafkasya ve Orta Asya Faaliyetleri', *Kebikeç* xxiv (2007), pp. 29–46.
'Ethnic Diversity and Territorial Integrity of Iran: Domestic Harmony and Regional Challenges', *Iranian Studies* xxxviii/1 (2005), pp. 23–44.
'From 'Amaleh (Labor) to Kargar (Worker): Recruitment, Work Discipline and Making of the Working Class in the Persian/Iranian Oil Industry', *International Labor and Working-Class History* lxxxiv (2013), pp. 159–75.
With Gavin D. Brockett. 'Ottoman and Republican Turkish Labour History', *International Review of Social History, Supplement Ottoman and Republican Turkish Labour History* liv/S17 (2009), pp. 1–17.
'Goftogu: vajh-e adabi-ye now dar goftar-e siyasi-ye asr-e mashruteh', *Goftogu* xxiii (1999), pp. 106–13.
'L'Organisation Syndicale Ouvrière en Iran', *Sou'al* viii (1987), pp. 36–7.
With Marcel van der Linden. 'Introduction.' *International Review of Social History* xlviii/3 (2003), pp. 353–359.
'Mashruteh-khahan-e bedun-e marz: ta'sir-e moteqabel-e jonbesh-e mashruteh-khahi dar Iran, Qafqaz, va Asia-ye Miyaneh', *Goftogu* vi (2008), pp. 33–45.
'Melliyat, qowmiyat va khod-mokhtari dar Iran-e mo'aser.' *Goftogu* iii (1994), pp. 68–83.
'Mosahebeh-ye iraniyeh', *Iranshenasi* iv/4 (1993), pp. 770–802.
'Narrating the Nation: A Study on Reshaping Identity in Azerbaijan', *Journal of Azerbaijani Studies* ii/2 (1999), pp. 79–100.
'Recasting and Recording Identities in the Caucasus', *Iran and the Caucasus* vi/1-2 (2002), pp. 219–35.
'Revisiting Social Historiography of Qajar Persia', *Qajar Studies* viii (2008), pp. 9–15.
'Ruspigari dar Iran', *Iranshenasi* iv/2 (1992), pp. 327–31.
'San'at-e naft, bar amadan-e "kargar" dar Iran'. *Goftogu* lx (2012), pp. 107–25.
'Tanavvo'-e qowmi dar Iran va hoviyat-e melli-ye Iran', *Iran Nameh* xxiv/2-3 (2009).
'Tarikh-e ejtema'i: negah az pa'in', *Ketab-e Mah - Tarikh va Joghrafia* lxxi-lxxii (2004), pp. 3–6.
'Writing the Social History of Labor in the Iranian Oil Industry', *International Labor and Working-Class History* lxxxiv (2013), 154–8.

'Yek bam va do hava: Az karnameh va zamaneh-ye komunistha-ye khorasani', *Goftogu* xi (1996), pp. 126–138.

Encyclopedia Entries

'Azerbaijan', *Encyclopedia of Islam* (supplement). Forthcoming.
'Khanate of Khiva', *Encyclopedia of Islam and the Muslim World* (New York, NY: Macmillan Reference, 2003), pp. 391–2.
'Mirza Shafi' Wadih Tabrizi', *Encyclopedia of Islam* (supplement) (Leiden: Brill, 2004).
——— Mazandarani', *Encyclopaedia of Islam* (supplement) (Leiden: Brill, 2004).
'Pan-Turanism', *Encyclopedia of Islam and the Muslim World* (New York, NY: Macmillan Reference, 2003), pp. 520–1.
'Russification and Sovietization of Central Asia', *Encyclopedia of Modern Asia* (New York, NY: Charles Scribner's Sons, 2003), pp. 108–11.
'Tudeh Party of Iran', *Encyclopaedia Iranica*. Forthcoming.

Book Reviews

Alaolmolki, Nozar, *'Life After the Soviet Union: The Newly Independent Republics of the Transcaucasus and Central Asia* (Albany: State University of New York Press, 2001)', *Journal of Islamic Studies* xiv/2 (2003), pp. 248–9.
Chaqueri, Cosroe, *'The Soviet Socialist Republic of Iran, 1920-1921: Birth of the Trauma* (Pittsburgh: University of Pittsburgh Press, 1995)', *International Review of Social History* xliv/1 (April 1999), pp. 110–13.
Dekmejian, R. Hrair and Simonian, Hovann H., *Troubled Waters: The Geopolitics of the Caspian Region* (London: I.B.Tauris, 2001)', *Journal of Islamic Studies* xvii/1 (2005), pp. 83–5.
Derakhshani, Ali Akbar, *'Khaterat-e Sartip* (Bethesda: Iranbooks, 1994)', *Iranian Studies* xxxi/2 (Spring 1998), pp. 286–8.
Derluguian, Georgi M., *'Bourdieu's Secret Admirer in the Caucasus: A World-System Biography* (Chicago: University of Chicago Press, 2005)', *International Review of Social History* liii/1 (2005), pp. 140–3.
Foran, John (ed.), *'A Century of Revolution: Social Movements in Iran* (Minneapolis: University of Minnesota Press, 1994)', *International Review of Social History* xliii/2 (August 1998), pp. 305–9.
Jones Luong, Pauline, *'Institutional Change and Political Continuity in Post-Soviet Central Asia: Power, Perception, and Pacts* (New York, NY: Cambridge University Press, 2002)', *Comparative Sociology* iv/1-2 (2005), pp. 245–7.
Roy, Olivier, *'Central Asia: The Creation of Nations* (London: I.B.Tauris, 2000)', *Journal of Islamic Studies* xiii/2 (May 2002), pp. 219–23.
Rustamova-Towhidi, Solmaz, *'Comintern Eastern Policy and Iran (1919-1943)* (Baku: Khazar University Press, 2002)', *International Institute for Asian Studies Newsletter* xxx (2003), p. 38.
Shaffer, Brenda, *'Borders and Brethren, Iran and the Challenge of Azerbaijan Identity* (Cambridge, MA: MIT Press, 2002)', *Irannameh. A Persian Journal of Iranian Studies* xxi/1-2 (2003), pp. 181–4.
——— *'Borders and Brethren, Iran and the Challenge of Azerbaijan Identity* (Cambridge, MA: MIT Press, 2002)', *Slavic Review* lxiii/1 (2004), pp. 178–9.

Smith, Jeremy, *'The Bolsheviks and the National Question, 1917-23* (New York: St. Martin's Press, 1999)', *International Review of Social History* xlvii/1 (April 2002), pp. 119-22.

Swietochwski, Tadeusz, *'Russia and Azerbaijan: A Borderland in Transition* (New York: Columbia University Press, 1995)', *International History Review* xix (November 1997), pp. 918–20.

Vassiliev, Alexei (ed.), *'Central Asia: Political and Economic Challenges in the Post-Soviet Era* (London: Saqi Books, 2001)', *The Middle East Studies Association Bulletin* xxxvii/1 (2003), pp. 158–9.

INDEX

Abbas Mirza, 36, 140
Abbot, K. E., 140
Abdülhamid II, Sultan, 61, 72 n32
Abrahamian, Ervand, 33–5, 43–4, 161, 246, 269
Afghani (Asadabadi), Jamal al-Din, 14–15, 24 n14, 34, 36, 86
Afshar, Iraj, 12
Ahmadzadeh, Mas'ud, 185–6
Al-e Ahmad, Jalal, 201–3, 210, 265
Alam al-Saltaneh, *see* Daneshvar, Taqi
Alavi, Bozorg, 43
All-India Muslim League, 85, 107 n24
Amanat, Abbas, 237–9
Amba, Sufi, 92, 94, 111 n46, 113 n52
Amin al-Dowleh, Mohsen Khan, 29, 46 n20, 48 n54
Amin al-Zarb, Hajj Hasan, 38, 139–40
Amir Kabir, Mirza Taqi Khan, 46 n39, 140
Anglo-Iranian Agreement (of 1919), 101
anjoman-e okhovvat, 29
Armenians, 65–6, 72 n20, 74 n44, 80, 84, 87–8, 99, 119 n73, 158 n14, 165–6, 215, 253–4, 257
Asadabadi, *see* Afghani

Ashraf, Hamid, 185–6
Atabaki, Touraj, 2–6, 39, 236, 240, 245, 252, 254, 257–9, 264, 267–71
Azod al-Molk, Ali Reza Khan, 28, 48 p59

Babi's, 36, 63, 69
Baha'is, 63, 69, 127, 129
Bakhtiar, Shapur (Chapour), 128–9
Bakhtiari, Sardar As'ad, 88
Baskerville, Howard, 87
Benjamin, Walter, 235, 239, 243–4
Berelian, Siazgar, 3

Cama, Madame Bhikhaji Rustom, 80, 81, 84, 104 n10, 116 n64
Caucasus, 2, 4, 7 n4, 65, 79, 83, 86–7, 92, 99, 104 n8, 116 n63, 120, 269
Central Asia, 2, 6, 7 n4, 79, 104 n8, 138, 236, 269–70
Christians (in Iran), 63, 64, 65, 69, 73 n36, 74 n44
Constitutional Revolution (Iran), 2–3, 12–13, 27–8, 35, 41, 44, 49–53, 57, 62, 69, 72 n23, 78–80, 85–9, 97, 100, 105 n17, 108 n31, 113 n52, 117 n69, 124, 145, 166–9, 200, 236–8, 240

Corm, Charles, 126, 133 n32
cosmopolitanism, 15, 77, 82, 86–7, 107 n29, 121, 128–30
Curzon, Lord George, 138, 140, 159 n37, 167

Daneshvar, Taqi (Alam al-Saltaneh), 156
Dar al-Fonun, 36–7, 46 n39
Davar, Ali Akbar, 12
Dehkhoda, Mirza Ali Akbar Khan, 32–3, 36–7, 262
Democrat Party of Iran, 67–8, 94, 118 n71
Democrat Party of Turkey, 259
Dowlatabadi, Yahya, 3, 118 n70 and n73

Enlightenment, 13–15, 22, 24 n9, 263
Eskandari, Iraj, 39, 43–4
Eskandari, Mohammad Ali Mirza, 37–8, 43, 48 n61
Eskandari, Mohammad Taher Mirza, 37, 47 n44
Eskandari, Soleyman Mirza, 37–40, 44
Eskandari, Yahya Mirza, 32–5, 37–44

Fada'i-ye Khalq, 6, 183–4, 186–8, 192–6, 268
Fakhr al-Dowleh, Princess, 29, 46 n15; 20
Farhangestan, 11, 16–17
Farsiu, Zia, 186, 190, 194
Fath Ali Shah Qajar, 36, 140
Firuz, Firuz (Nosrat al-Dowleh), 127–9
Foroughi, Mohammad Ali (Zoka' al-Molk), 3, 12–26
Freemasonry, 12, 14–15, 22, 23 n3, 24 n11, 36

Gemayel, Michel, 126–7
Ghani, Qasem, 124–5, 130
Ghorban, Zabih, 125, 129
Golshiri, Hushang, 209–11
Grand Mosalla, 213, 218, 224–9
Green Movement, 3

Habl al-Matin, 85, 88, 92, 99, 169
Hedayat, Mehdi-Qoli (Mokhber al-Saltaneh), 31, 123
Hesabi, Mahmud, 125, 129
historiography, 1–2, 4–6, 12, 14, 78, 89, 161, 178, 235–43, 245–9, 251, 253, 256–9, 270
Hôtel des Sociétés Savantes (Paris), 80–2, 89
Hoveyda, Amir Abbas, 127–9

Indian National Congress (INC), 94, 99, 101, 112 n50
International Institute of Social History (IISH), 1–3, 39, 269–70
Iran–Iraq war, 207, 208, 213, 215, 218, 221, 240

Jalal al-Dowleh, 29
Javaherkalam, Ali, 128
Jazani, Bizhan, 185–6, 192–4
Jews (in Iran), 63–5, 69, 72 n20, 73, 138

Kasma'i, Hoseyn, 88
Kasravi, Ahmad, 28–9, 33, 35, 39, 41, 43, 48 n62, 72 n23
Kazemzadeh (Iranshahr), Hoseyn, 81, 113 n52
Kermani, Mirza Aqa Khan, 36
Khamenei, Ayatollah Ali, 221
Khatami, Mohammad, 221, 224
Khomeini, Ayatollah Ruhollah, 57, 71 n19, 130, 177, 221, 240, 268
Khorasani, Soltan al-Olama, 33–4

Lewis, Bernard, 249–50

Mafi, Reza-Qoli (Nezam al-Saltaneh), 98
Mahmud, Ahmad, 205, 207, 210–11
Malek al-Motekallemin (Hajji Mirza Nasrollah), 29, 33, 35–6, 48 n58Malkum Khan, 36, 86, 90, 107 n31

Malkum Khan, 36, 86, 90, 107 n31
Manchu dynasty, 82
Mazlish, Bruce, 242
Meftahi, Abbas, 185
Mirza Jahangir Khan, 29, 31, 32, 33, 36–7, 46 n21, 48 n58
Mo'azed al-Saltaneh, 32–3
Modarres, Hasan, 70 n8
Mohtashami, Ali Akbar, 130
Mokhber al-Saltaneh, see Hedayat, Mehdi-Qoli
al-Molk, Loqman, 41–2
Moore, Arthur, 87
Mosaddeq, Mohammad, 125, 185, 199–201, 203, 205, 207

Nafisi, Sa'id, 123, 128
Nationalism, 1, 3, 4, 7 n4, 11–13, 22, 50, 77–9, 82, 84–6, 89, 90, 92, 98, 101, 102 n1, 103 n3, 110 n44, 112 n49, 118 n71, 131 n3, 167, 238, 246, 249–51
Nezam al-Saltaneh, see Mafi, Reza-Qoli
Nosrat al-Dowleh, see Firuz, Firuz
Nuri, Sheykh Fazlollah, 54, 56–8, 60, 64–5, 67, 68, 70 n9, 71 n10

Ottoman Empire, 4, 55, 71 n17, 79, 83, 86, 92, 97–101, 109 n44, 112 n48, 120, 122, 124, 126, 147, 162, 249, 255, 257–8

Pahlavi, Mohammad Reza Shah, 6, 11, 48 n64, 129, 164
Pahlavi, Reza Shah/Khan, 3, 6, 11, 12, 17, 102, 127, 146, 164, 170
Permanent Court of Arbitration, 79
Pirzadeh, Mohammad Ali, 121–3
Pourdavoud, Ebrahim, 81, 105 n13 and n14
press, 4, 31, 33–4, 52, 61–3, 69, 80, 85–6, 88–9, 91, 99, 107 n31, 221, 241
Puyan, Amir Parviz, 185–6, 194

Qajar, Ahmad Shah, see Mirza, Soltan Ahmad
Qajar dynasty (Qajars), 3, 6, 20, 48 n59, 63, 102 n2, 128, 164–7, 217, 236–8
Qajar, Mohammad Ali Shah, 27–8, 31, 33, 39–40, 50, 54, 68, 82, 85, 168
Qajar, Mozaffar al-Din Shah, 26 n35, 29, 50, 64
Qajar, Naser al-Din Shah, 29, 36–7, 46 n15 n39, 64, 140, 144, 167, 168
Qazvini, Mohammad, 81

Rahimi, Fahimeh, 215
Ramez, Mahmud M., 151–2
Ravanipur, Moniru, 208–9, 211
Renan, Ernest, 15
Revolutionary Guards (IRGC), 221
Roshdiyeh, Mirza Hasan Tabrizi, 124, 129
Russia, 7, 49, 56, 63, 68, 87, 95–6, 99–101, 137–8, 142, 147–8, 156, 254, 269

Sabet, Habib, 125
Sa'edi, Gholamhoseyn, 203, 210
Safa'i Farahani, Ali Akbar, 189
Salim, Sheykh, 66
SAVAK, 185, 189–91, 268
Shahnameh, 11, 17–18
Shahriyarinezhad (Shahriyari), Abbas Ali, 189
Sheybani, Abd al-Hoseyn (Vahid al-Molk), 94, 114 n55, 117 n70, 118 n71 n73, 119 n74
Shirazi, Mirza Hasan, 54
Siahkal, 6, 185–7, 189, 191–4, 196
Singh, Ajit, 92–93, 111 n46, 112 n50
Skocpol, Theda, 44 n3
slavery, 61, 73 n34

Smith, Eli, 121
Soltan Ahmad Mirza, 28, 48 n59
Sorel, Georges, 6, 183–4, 188, 191–2, 194–7
Soviet Union 1, 2, 4, 7 n4, 240, 255, 268, 270
Supplementary Fundamental Law, 4, 20, 52–3, 56–8, 60, 63–4, 66–9, 71 n14

Tahvildar, Mirza Hoseyn, 141
Talebof, Abd al-Rahim, 65, 74 n43 (Abdulrahim Talebof), 143
Taqizadeh, Hasan, 14, 20, 32–3, 36–8, 51, 59, 60, 62–4, 71 n14, 93, 112 n49, 117 n70, 118 n71, 128, 145, 160 n69
Taqva'i, Naser, 202–3, 211
Teymourtash, Abd al-Hoseyn, 12
Tudeh Party, 2, 39, 44, 48 n64, 185, 267
Turkey, 2, 4–5, 7 n5, 49, 71 n11, 106 n20, 117 n70, 119 n74, 175, 216–7, 241, 245, 249–50, 254–9

Universal Races Congress, 84, 118 n73
University of Tehran, 13, 125, 185, 218, 225

Va'ez, Jamal al-Din, 32, 143
Vahid al-Molk, *see* Sheybani, Abd al-Hoseyn
Vakil al-Ro'aya, Hajj Mohammad Taqi, 150–51

women, 5–6, 40, 50, 52, 57, 58, 61–2, 69, 85, 87, 96–8, 106 n17, 115 n62 n63, 116 n64 n66 n67 n69, 125, 131, 142, 146, 161–79, 185, 195, 209, 217, 219–20, 222, 226, 256–7
World War I, 250–2, 254
World War II, 127, 208, 270

Xinhai Revolution (China), 80–2, 115 n62

Yeprim Khan, 88
Young Turks 84, 86–7, 116 n66, 250–2, 254, 256

Zell al-Soltan, Mas'ud Mirza, 29
Zia' al-Soltan, 41
Zoka' al-Molk, *see* Foroughi, Mohammad Ali
Zoroastrians, 64–6, 69, 72 n20, 73 n36, 74 n44, 85, 113 n52, 129
Zürcher, Erik-Jan, 2, 5–6, 246, 249